"Raquel Cepeda has finally done justice to the mother-wit, social power, and visceral passion of hip-hop journalism. Here's an indispensable collection of pioneering, bold, visionary, and cautionary writing, a must-have for anyone who loves this culture." —**Jeff Chang, author of** *Can't Stop, Won't Stop:* *A History of the Hip-Hop Generation*

"Once in a while a book comes along that commands attention. *And It Don't Stop* is hip-hop defined by its generation's best writers and observers—definite satisfaction." —**Ahmir "?uestlove" Thompson, The Roots**

"An irresistible compilation of the most stylish prose and revelatory interviews of the last twenty-five years on hip-hop, *And It Don't Stop* is required reading for any serious devotee of contemporary urban culture. Raquel Cepeda places hip-hop journalism in a historical framework: we not only discover how writing styles have changed over the years, but we also learn how the stakes in writing about hip-hop have transformed alongside the music and culture. It's a glorious reminder of how influential journalists have been, and continue to be, in helping to shape and create this thing we call hip-hop." —**Jason King, associate chair of the Clive Davis Department of Recorded Music, New York University**

"Hip-hop is the voice of the community, and its child, hip-hop journalism, adds a new element to the mix in another medium that goes way beyond the music industry to become a true organ of news. *And It Don't Stop* is essential reading. It captures the extraordinary eruptions of word, image, and sound that hip-hop inspired, and, in itself, continues the process of self-definition and community empowerment that has characterized the movement from the earliest days to the present. Raquel Cepeda knew how to pick them. The articles she has chosen are a distillation of the significant events, personalities, conflicts, and philosophies that together shape the revolutionary impact of hip-hop on the world." —**Henry Chalfant, coauthor of** *Spraycan Art*

"AND IT DON'T STOP"

EDITED BY RAQUEL CEPEDA / FOREWORD BY NELSON GEORGE

"AND IT DON'T STOP"

BEST AMERICAN HIP-HOP JOURNALISM OF THE LAST 25 YEARS

FABER AND FABER, INC.
AN AFFILIATE OF FARRAR, STRAUS AND GIROUX
NEW YORK

Faber and Faber, Inc.
An affiliate of Farrar, Straus and Giroux
18 West 18th Street, New York 10011

Printed in the United States of America
First edition, 2004

Owing to limitations of space, all acknowledgments for permission to reprint previously
published material can be found on pages 359–61.

Library of Congress Cataloging-in-Publication Data
And it don't stop : the best American hip-hop journalism of the last 25 years /
[edited by] Raquel Cepeda.— 1st ed.
    p. cm.
   Includes bibliographical references and index.
   ISBN-13: 978-0-571-21159-3
   ISBN-10: 0-571-21159-3 (pb : alk. paper)
   1. Rap (Music)—History and criticism. I. Cepeda, Raquel.
ML3531.A53 2004
782.421649—dc22   2004004920

Designed by Dean Nicastro

www.fsgbooks.com

because of djali . . .

Contents

1980s: Looking for the Perfect Beat

2000s: Get Rich or Die Tryin'

Foreword

I was about twenty-one years old and anxious to get my career as a music critic off the ground. I wanted to write a profile about an uptown icon known as Kurtis Blow for a black publication. A Harlemite, he had become the first solo rap artist to land a record deal with a major label, the first to enjoy commercial success, and the first to embark on a national *and* international concert tour. Well, it seemed like a no-brainer to me. But the editor of the magazine, a heavyset, rather self-important product of the black middle class, looked at me with disdain. "We're not gonna cover rap," he said. "It doesn't deserve the ink."

Back in the early days, it wasn't just the black media who didn't care. Somewhere in my files I still have a copy of an article I penned in 1982 titled "A Consumer Guide to Rap," an introductory piece about the 12-inch singles of Blow, Eddie Cheeba, and the Treacherous Three. I submitted it optimistically to *The New York Times*, who rejected the piece with a note: "too specialized for the *Times* audience."

I remember receiving hostile reactions from many editors when I tried to write about it, as if hip-hop were an infection that could be cured by simply ignoring it. Others were polite in their disdain, however equally disinterested.

But an editor here and there would show me love when I pitched a rap piece, particularly those in the world of alternative weeklies like *The Village Voice* and *New York Rocker*. By the early 1980s you could (just barely) feed yourself writing about rapping DJs, break dancing, and 12-inch singles.

When I began writing about hip-hop, there were no publications like *Vibe*, *The Source*, or *XXL*. No *106 & Park* existed to broadcast images of rappers in action. No national ad campaigns featured rap music, hip-hop slang or style. In fact the culture now known internationally as hip-hop didn't even have a name. It was just a series of seemingly miscellaneous expressions that involved rhyming, dancing, spray painting, and music.

The first few times I wrote about hip-hop it seemed like, at best, a fad. Some viewed it as just some weird thing coming out of the neglected hoods of outer-borough New York at a time when the city was beat down and broke. The thing that kept me coming back to it didn't live in its expressions alone. Sure, the break dancing was amazing and the dance beats, as we used to say, were "da joint." But the spirit of invention that emanated from the scene was what was so captivating. With limited resources, no institutional support, and little interest from most adults, hip-hop was driven by a will to create and a desire to party that would, ultimately, prove unstoppable.

My contribution to this collection comes from a time when much of my energy was being spent chronicling the massive crossover success of Michael Jackson, Prince, Whitney Houston, and other pop stars of the day. However, my obsession revolved around the evolution of hip-hop, which was happening right in front of my eyes, to the delight of my ears. I befriended Russell Simmons through my roommate, who coproduced Kurtis Blow's first hits, and was amazed at how his development from club promoter to record producer/manager unfolded. I later did a profile of Simmons for *Essence* magazine, but only *after The Village Voice* and other progressive mainstream publications had validated him.

So it is with great pride that I can—along with a small group of others who are also featured in this anthology—now call myself a pioneering hip-hop writer. Now a whole generation of aspiring scribes can cut its teeth writing about MCs, multimillion-dollar stars, and the monumental range of issues that hip-hop has raised about America, capitalism, violence, misogyny, sex, and poverty. The pieces in this book reflect both the growth of the music and the spectrum of reactions to that growth. So this is a document not merely of artists and their records, but also a window into the popular dialogue that hip-hop has made possible. Whether you love hip-hop culture or are struggling to understand it, these collected texts are a road map to a journey that, despite the "haters," continues on and on to the break of dawn.

Nelson George / Brooklyn / October 2003

Introduction

My torrid love affair with hip-hop began when I was a young girl growing up in the Inwood section of Upper Manhattan. I was transfixed by the graffiti art of Fab 5 Freddy, Lee Quinones MARE, and the Manhattan Subway Kings, who were native to my neighborhood. I was overwhelmed by Red Alert's raspy voice on 98.7 Kiss FM, spinning the freshest joints at the time, and by the dancing's acrobatics and fierceness. While my neighborhood was fairly popular, or rather *infamous*, due to the graffiti, gang violence, break dancing that was ever present in the park adjoining the Dyckman projects, and the occasional film crew, we were clueless that hip-hop would one day leave the ghetto to go live with the Jeffersons. Not even when the larger-than-life TV star Lorenzo Lamas bum-rushed my babysitter's block to shoot a scene using real gang members—the Ball Busters—as extras for the saccharine *Body Rock* flick did I think that hip-hop would survive this cheesy marauding by Hollywood. While I did notice the occasional tourist snapping photos of the graffiti art that enveloped Inwood Park's baseball fields in the early eighties, neither my peers nor I imagined that our love of the genre, this pedagogy of the oppressed, would morph into a billion-dollar industry. I was wrong.

My foray into writing came in front of the mic as a spoken-word artist—a hair over a decade ago—when New York City was burgeoning with a raw underground rendering of what would become a Def Poetry jam. Spoken-word artists were, like the journalists of the decade, using rap music and hip-hop culture as a societal reflector because the genre was, in turn, defining our generation. The contradictions that existed in rap music and its participants (including yours truly), the misogyny, sex, love, hate, the schisms, were among the topics we used to move the crowd. Poets often shared the stage with rappers like The Fugees, Mos Def and Talib Kweli, Freestyle Fellowship, The Roots, and some of their forefathers like Gil Scott-Heron and The Last Poets. Some of us parlayed our thoughts into long-form, some of us became authors, and others, HBO fixtures.

This was the beginning of hip-hop journalism—a genre unto itself that would afford many of us poets-cum-journalists a way to marry our love of words and the music into potentially lucrative careers. Twenty-five years after the release of Sugarhill Gang's "Rapper's Delight," the first *Billboard*-charted rap single—but certainly not the first rap record—there is even an argument to be made for hip-hop writing's adoption as a sixth element of the culture— behind deejaying, emceeing, dancing, graffiti, and fashion—due to its critical role in archiving and reporting the history, present, and undoubtedly the future of hip-hop. It would also be fair to say hip-hop journalism is, in fact, an extension of rap music. As a verbal art form, the writings are illustrations of vivid landscapes—some sensational, some introspective, some fantastical, some of which are slices of inner-city blues, and many of which are recanted with lyrical mastery—that are narratives all the same.

This medley of literary biscuits, collected in *And It Don't Stop*, is more than just a reader, or an accessory of must-have articles for your library. It's a critical journey, exploring an unprecedented relationship between artist and journalist—church and state—and includes some of the very first hip-hop features, along with controversial articles that created rifts between hip-hop artists and the journalists who covered them, as well as those indelible writings that recorded our modern tragedies—loss of icons and loss of focus as senseless violence and the horror of AIDS infiltrated the music and culture. This is the first book to chronicle hip-hop journalism, and it does so by showcasing and celebrating the writing from the various periods of what is now known as hip-hop, rather than simply reflecting back on the movement with the ease of twenty-twenty hindsight. These articles are not removed from the context of the times they report on; these articles are the context. But most importantly, for many hip-hop aficionados, including yours truly, who feel hip-hop's most popular element, rap music, has run away from its creative and critical beginnings, *And It Don't Stop* is a reminder of hip-hop's remarkable staying power and still untapped potential.

So, we begin with the all-but-forgotten humble beginnings of hip-hop. The graffiti artist, the breaker, the deejay, and the emcee. Graffiti artists became the first *djalis*, or storytellers, of this New World of hip-hop by using New York subway cars as a means of sounding the alarm that heralded the arrival of an infectious new force. That force, later christened hip-hop, was spawned from New York City's concrete jungles in the 1970s to become the ultimate expression of black youth resistance to poverty and oppression. First in the South Bronx and then throughout each of New York's five boroughs and beyond, hip-hop was further embodied in the breaker's psychedelic dance movements, the deejay's rhythmic party beats, and the emcee's poignant and stirring lyrics.

From the outset it was clear that this hip-hop was no fad. It was instead the rumblings of a movement—strong enough and necessary enough to evade all efforts to quiet its call, including not only Mayor Edward I. Koch's declared war on our beloved *djalis*, but also President Reagan's failed Reagan Revolution, which, while intending to bring to the inner cities "the great confident roar of American progress and growth and optimism," in fact did little to give our crack-infested urban centers the necessary face-lift. Hip-hop would survive these early attacks and grow like an errant vine to overtake America's sound garden and at once become the needed didactic response, if you will, to the schisms plaguing the direct descendants of the Civil Rights generation.

Hip-hop, like rock music in the 1960s, morphed into *the* dominant rebel yell of youth culture in New York City. Chuck D, front man for Public Enemy, one of the most influential and dynamic groups of our history-in-the-making, said it best in a controversial statement after the release of their classic album

It Takes a Nation of Millions to Hold Us Back, in which he dubbed hip-hop the "black CNN." He believed that rap music related what was happening in the inner city in a way that mainstream media could not project or even understand. Hip-hop journalism built on the tradition of hip-hop as a societal reflector. The hip-hop journalists not only understood, but were themselves participants also aching to be understood. This collection is then a slice of the rousing perspective of journalists who sent dispatches from hip-hop's epicenter, who took their roles as historians, chronicling the culture, defining the tenets that made this genre become such a powerful voice, and pointing out its contradictions and its potency at once, quite seriously.

By the time "Rapper's Delight" was released, hip-hop, which was initially being covered as just listings and blurbs in the black press, had surprised us all and gone pop, sprouting up and out of every crevice of the planet where youth culture expresses itself through art, music, dance, and fashion. And as with most things that go "POP!" in American culture, what started out primarily as a black and Latino subculture has been uprooted and co-opted by mainstream marketers who neatly package everything from soft drinks to game shows and fast food. The mainstreaming of hip-hop has made it almost impossible to distinguish it from a commercial jingle. Still hip-hop has done more for our generation—whose core demographic is now in its thirties and forties—than what even basketball has done for kids in the inner city. For better or for worse, the wild success of rap music has created not only a handful of coveted positions for the lucky few who have managed to flex their lyrical mastery in front of the mic, it has also created positions in recording, publishing, fashion, film, and journalism.

Today, would-be hip-hop journalists are faced with a challenge to explore the substance beneath the surface. While the writings about hip-hop in the alternative press legitimized the music because it helped identify it to the masses in the eighties, and helped our generation define *itself* within its social and political paradigms in the nineties, we are now being faced with the task of covering more interesting aspects than what the mainstream predicates. And while we're ushering in the new millennium, writing about hip-hop still has the potential to be used as a conduit for change. Journalists should take a cue from what has been written in the previous decades and add to the discussions cemented by the writers featured in this collection, as well as that of their peers, to use hip-hop as a powerful tool for a new age of thinkers.

The articles featured here are also a matter of passion versus, if you will, access. Now that hip-hop has been repackaged to be made accessible to every young, white mall rat in Middle America who is buying into the negative, in-flated stereotypes affirmed by the artists themselves, mainstream media have adopted widespread coverage of the feral child ignored at birth. The articles featured in the following pages are a humble attempt to capture moments that have contributed to shaping the culture and propelling the various subcultures it's influenced, like new jack swing, hip-house, and hip-hop soul, for instance, into the mainstream. It's important to capture these lyrical portraits, these mo-ments that helped shape the new pop culture—hip-hop—because not doing so is to ignore a significant volume of American history.

This collection is also an ode to the writers who inspired me, and count-less other would-be journalists, to fuse their love of words with a commitment to the art form unconditionally, regardless of how it oftentimes did not love us back. I honor every single contributor who participated in the creation of this joint for the vivid telling of how it really is *and* was.

It's been long overdue.

Raquel Cepeda

1980s:

Looking for the Perfect Beat

In the 1970s, hip-hop culture arose in and out of the Bronx—where Kurtis Blow claimed the people were fresh, by way of its innovative B-boys, rappers, DJs, and graffiti maestros cultivating their art. Its proud adoptive father Afrika Bambaataa eventually christened the culture *hip-hop*, a term that first appeared in print in an article written by Steven Hager, "Afrika Bambaataa's Hip-Hop," etching Bambaataa's place in the testament of the movement.

By the time the multiplatinum classic record "Rapper's Delight" by the Sugarhill Gang proved commercially viable in 1979, a rainbow coalition of journalists, photographers, filmmakers, producers, fashionistas, and promoters was conspiring in documenting and defining the art form. When the general public got a whiff of just how funky the B-boy (and B-girl) was, he became the media darling and an essential prop to any fresh party. The graffiti documentary *Style Wars*, and films like *Wild Style*, the Hollywood co-opted *Flashdance*, *Beat Street*, *Breakin'*, *Breakin' 2: Electric Boogaloo*, and later, the Russell Simmons–produced *Krush Groove*, propelled break-dancers, graffiti artists, and rappers to celebrity status not just in the States, but all over the world.

Their global popularity soon led to a demand for a showcasing of the culture on foreign ground, which was met when the first international "rap tour," plucking a group of talented young blacks and Latinos from the streets of New York City, journeyed to Europe's hot spots. Attempting to re-create in writing the booming club scene abroad, writer and editor David Hershkovits accompanied the tour only to end up documenting the cultural divide that gaped between the entertainers and their global audience, and at the same time the universality of the music and the dancer, in his article "London Rocks, Paris Burns, and the B-Boys Break a Leg," for the now defunct *Sunday News Magazine* insert for the New York *Daily News*.

Hershkovits, a fixture in the psychedelic melting pot of the downtown New York scene in the 1980s where the art world and B-boys would collide harmoniously on the dance floor, was also an editor who encouraged other writers, like Steven Hager, to pursue their curiosity about the burgeoning hip-hop scene. Along with Hager, Bill Adler, dance critic Sally Banes, Nelson George, and other early journalistic pioneers, Hershkovits made the first attempts to truly define what hip-hop culture was and its potential as an international force with which to be reckoned. What particularly defined this nascent hip-hop culture in the 1980s was the club and party scene. One of the most popular attractions in the Bronx, other than the zoo, was Sal Abbatiello's Disco Fever. Some fifteen subway stops north of Studio 54, Disco Fever, as Bill Adler wrote in 1983 in his article "The South Bronx Was Getting a Bad Rap Until a Club Called Disco Fever Came Along," had "emerged as the headquarters of rap music." So important were the DJs at the Fever that if they didn't spin your record, felt Russell Simmons, your joint was just wack. And who would know better than Simmons, who was already being touted a mogul by *The Wall Street Journal* at twenty-seven, as reported by Nelson George in his article "Rappin' with Russell."

Simmons would eventually be responsible for making rap music equal big business, and the bigger the business the more dire the need for competent and accurate coverage. This need for coverage soon cemented an unprecedented closeness between the artists and those who wrote about them. Hip-hop personalities weren't as accessible or on the World Wide Web, and the genre wasn't synonymous with pop culture at this time, so journalists covering this insular scene had to parlay in the cut with the artists they wanted to write about.

Signaling the possibilities of this new relationship between hip-hop artists, their handlers, and the writers who covered them, Bill Adler went from writing about the art form and participants like Russell Simmons to becoming someone to be covered himself. Nelson George was soon writing about his journalistic peer, and his lifelong contribution to hip-hop, as Adler morphed from hip-hop writer to director of publicity for Rush Artist Management and Def Jam Recordings in 1984, becoming Simmons's second full-time employee. Adler also has the distinction of being the only writer of this period to still be almost exclusively immersed in hip-hop culture, penning an authorized Run-D.M.C. biography, and founding a New York City–based gallery devoted to showcasing hip-hop photography.

By the mid-eighties, rap was becoming bigger business, giving those who wrote about it much more to do. Graffiti art and breaking gave way to rapping with the crossover success of artists like Run-D.M.C., whose collaboration with Aerosmith on "Walk This Way" in 1986 marked rap's arrival on Music Television, better known as MTV, exposed rap to an audience of rock enthusiasts, and led to the debut of *YO! MTV Raps* in 1988. L.L. Cool J, the Beastie Boys, Slick Rick, EPMD, and 3rd Bass then muscled aside the pioneers with their mainstream appeal and corporate sponsorship.

By the mid-eighties seminal groups like KRS-One's Boogie Down Productions and the controversial Public Enemy, like no other collectives before (or since), also began using rap music not only as a method to entertain, but to educate the masses—"edutainment," as described by KRS-One, ironically paving the way for both the innate anger in the rap expression of South Central, Los Angeles, and the pan-Afrocentric Native Tongues Movement. Public Enemy's Chuck D became a media obsession because of his brutally honest depictions of life in the inner cities at the mercy of policemen and other social ills, and the contradictions that plagued his group. John Leland, who began writing about hip-hop in 1982, had a special relationship, if you will, with Chuck D. Giving us a hint about what would become a running theme of tension between artists and the writers who critiqued their music, Leland managed to tick Chuck D off with a record review he had penned for *The Village Voice*, which resulted in threats. The article featured in this section represented the first time the two had met since the one-sided war of words had begun.

While the dance and graffiti art of hip-hop became less popular as the hybrid sound of A Tribe Called Quest, De La Soul, Jungle Brothers, Black Sheep, Brand Nubian, Queen Latifah, and others was embraced, rap music's colorful, sometimes erratic creators were by the late eighties proving to be the stuff great stories were made of, both in print and in the films of young directors like

Spike Lee, and later John Singleton and Albert and Allen Hughes. By the end of the decade, journalists, and those aspiring to be, had found the perfect beat to cover in hip-hop.

However, there would not have been a platform to set it off had it not been for the trailblazing efforts of the journalists with the vision, who announced to the world that this wild child had been born. And because of their efforts, featured in the following pages, everybody knew its name was hip-hop.

Physical Graffiti

Breaking Is Hard to Do

SALLY BANES

Chico and Tee and their friends from 175th Street in the High Times crew were breaking in the subway and the cops busted them for fighting.

"We're not fighting. We're dancing!" they claimed. At the precinct station, one kid demonstrated certain moves: a head spin, ass spin, swipe, chin freeze, "the Helicopter," "the Baby."

An officer called in the other members of the crew, one by one. "Do a head spin," he would command as he consulted a clipboard full of notes. "Do 'the Baby.'" As each kid complied, performing on cue as unhesitatingly as a ballet dancer might toss off an enchainement, the cops scratched their heads in bewildered defeat.

Or so the story goes. But then, like ballet and like great battles (it shares elements of both), breaking is wreathed in legends. "This guy in Queens does a whole bunch of head spins in a row, more than ten; he spins, stops real quick, spins . . ."

"Yeah, but he stops. Left just goes right into seven spins, he never stops."

"There's a ten-year-old kid on my block learned to break in three days."

"The best is Spy, Ronnie Don, Drago, me [Crazy Legs], Freeze, Mongo, Mr. Freeze, Lace, Track Two, Weevil . . ."

"Spy, he's called the man with the thousand moves, he had a girl and he taught her how to break. She did it good. She looked like a guy."

"Spy, man, in '78—he was breaking at Mom and Pop's on Katonah Avenue in the Bronx, he did his footwork so fast you could hardly see his feet."

"I saw Spy doing something wild in a garage where all the old-timers used to break. They had a priest judging a contest, and Spy was doing some kind of Indian dance. All of a sudden, he threw himself in the air, his hat flew up, he spun on his back, and the hat landed right on his chest. And everyone said, 'That was luck.' So he did it once more for the priest, and the hat landed right on his chest. If I didn't see it, I would never have believed it."

The heroes of these legends are the Break Kids, the B Boys, the Puerto Rican and black teenagers who invent and endlessly elaborate this exquisite, heady blend of dancing, acrobatics, and martial spectacle. Like other forms of ghetto street culture—graffiti, verbal dueling, rapping—breaking is a public arena for the flamboyant triumph of virility, wit, and skill. In short, of style. Breaking is a way of using your body to inscribe your identity on streets and trains, in parks and high school gyms. It is a physical version of two favorite modes of street rhetoric, the taunt and the boast. It is a celebration of the flexibility and budding sexuality of the gangly male adolescent body. It is a subjunctive expression of bodily states, testing things that might be or are not, contrasting masculine vitality with its range of opposites: women, babies, animals; and death. It is a way of claiming territory and status, for yourself and for your group, your crew. But most of all, breaking is a competitive display of physical and imaginative virtuosity, a codified dance-form-cum-warfare that cracks open to flaunt personal inventiveness.

For the current generation of B Boys, it doesn't really matter that the Breakdown is an old name in Afro-American dance for both rapid, complex footwork and a competitive format. Or that a break in jazz means a soloist's improvised bridge between melodies. For the B Boys, the history of breaking started six or seven years ago, maybe in the Bronx, maybe in Harlem. It started with the Zulus. Or with Charlie Rock. Or with Joe, from the Casanovas, from the

Bronx, who taught Charlie Rock. "Breaking means going crazy on the floor. It means making a style for yourself." In Manhattan, kids call it rocking. A dancer in the center of a ring of onlookers drops to the floor, circles around his own axis with a flurry of slashing steps, then spins, flips, gesticulates, and poses in a flood of rhythmic motion and fleeting imagery that prompts the next guy to top him. To burn him, as the B Boys put it.

Fab 5 Freddy Love, a graffiti-based artist and rapper from Bedford-Stuyvesant, remembers that breaking began around the same time as rapping, as a physical analogue for a musical impulse. "Everybody would be at a party in the park in the summer, jamming. Guys would get together and dance with each other, sort of a macho thing where they would show each other who could do the best moves. They started going wild when the music got real funky"—music by groups like Super Sperm and Apache. As the beat of the drummer came to the fore, the music let you know it was time to break down, to free style. The cadenced, rhyming, fast-talking epic mode of rapping, with its smooth surface of sexual braggadocio, provides a perfect base for a dance style that is cool, swift, and intricate.

But breaking isn't just an urgent response to pulsating music. It is also a ritual combat that transmutes aggression into art. "In the summer of '78," Tee remembers, "when you got mad at someone, instead of saying, 'Hey, man, you want to fight?' you'd say, 'Hey, man, you want to rock?'" Inside the ritual frame, burgeoning adolescent anxieties, hostilities, and powers are symbolically manipulated and controlled.

Each segment in breaking is short, from ten to thirty seconds—but packed with action and meaning. The dancing always follows a specific format: the *entry*, a stylized walk into the ring for four or five beats to the music; the *footwork*, a rapid, circular scan of the floor by sneakered feet while the hands support the body's weight and the head and torso revolve slowly—a kind of syncopated pirouette; the *freeze*, or stylized signature pose, usually preceded by a spin; the *exit*, a return to verticality and to the outside of the circle. The length of the "combination" can be extended by adding on more footwork-spin-freeze sequences. The entry, the footwork, and the exit are pretty much the same from dancer to dancer—although some do variations, like Freeze from the Breakmasters crew, who stuffs a Charleston into his entry, and then exits on pointe. But it is largely in the freeze that each dancer's originality shines forth, in configurations that are as intricate, witty, obscene, or insulting as possible. A dancer will twist himself into a pretzel. Or he will quote the poses of a pinup girl. He might graphically hump the floor, or arch up grabbing his crotch. Someone else might mime rowing a boat or swimming or emphasize acrobatic stunts like backflips and fish dives. Sometimes two breakers team up for a stunt: imitating a dog on a leash, or a dead person brought back to life by a healthy thump on the chest. According to Rammelzee, a DJ who's gotten too tall to break, the set of sequences adds up to a continuing pantomimic narrative. It is each dancer's responsibility to create a new chapter in the story. "Like if you see a guy acting like he's dead, the brother who went before him probably shot him."

When you choose your moves, you not only try to look good; you try to make your successor look bad by upping the ante. That's one way to win points from the crowd, which collectively judges. Going first is a way to score a point, but so is coming up with a cool response, chilling out. Through the freeze, you insult, challenge, and humiliate the next person. You stick your ass in his direction. You hold your nose to your spine, signaling a move so good it hurts. But the elegant abstract dancing that couches these messages counts, too. B Boys from the Bronx and Manhattan look down on the "up rock" prevalent in Brooklyn, a mere string of scatological and sexual affronts without the aesthetic glue of spinning and getting down on the floor.

Naming and performing the freezes you invent are ways of laying claim to them, though some poses are in the public domain. A lot of breakers are also graffiti artists, and one way to announce a new freeze is to write it as graffiti. Speed and smoothness are essential to the entire dance, but in the freeze humor and difficulty are prized above all. "You try to put your head on your arm and your toenails on your ears," says Ken of the Breakmasters. "Hard stuff, like when I made up my elbow walk," says Kip Dee of Rock Steady. "When you spin on your head. When you take your legs and put them in back of your head out of the spin."

During the summers the B Boys gravitate to the parks, where DJs and rappers hang out. Younger kids learn to break by imitating the older kids, who tend to outgrow it when they're about sixteen. Concrete provides the best surface for the feet and hands to grip, but the jamming is thickest in the parks, where the DJs can bring their mikes and amplifiers. During the winters, breakers devise new moves. Crazy Legs, of Rock Steady, claims the "W," in which he sits on doubled-back legs, was an accident.

"Once I was laying on the floor and I kicked my leg and I started spinning," says Mr. Freeze, of Breakmasters. But inventing freezes also demands the hard daily work of conscious experiment. "You got to sweat it out." You don't stop, even when you sleep. "I have breaking dreams," several B Boys have told me. "I wake up and try to do it like I saw it." Kip Dee dreamed he spun on his chin, "but I woke up and tried it and almost broke my face."

Part of the macho quality of breaking comes from the physical risk involved. It's not only the bruises, scratches, cuts, and scrapes. As the rivalry between the crews heats up, ritual combat sometimes erupts into fighting for real. And part of it is impressing the girls. "They go crazy over it," says Ken. "When you're in front of a girl, you like to show off. You want to burn the public eye, because then she might like you."

Some people claim that breaking is played out. Freddy Love disagrees. "The younger kids keep developing it, doing more wild things and more new stuff. We never used to spin or do acrobatics. The people who started it just laid down the foundations. Just like in graffiti—you make a new style. That's what life in the street is all about, just being you, being who you are around your friends. What's at stake is a guy's honor and his position in the street. Which is all you have. That's what makes it feel so important, that's what makes it feel so good— that pressure on you to be the best. Or to try to be the best. To develop a new style nobody can deal with. If it's true that this stuff reflects life, it's a fast life."

The Village Voice / April 22, 1981

Afrika Bambaataa's Hip-Hop

STEVEN HAGER

Never one to let Black History Month slip by without commemoration, Afrika Bambaataa held his third annual party celebrating the occasion on February 25, 1982. As usual, the festivities were staged at the Bronx River Community Center, a squat, fortresslike structure located in the heart of the southeast Bronx. An impressive list of prominent rappers, DJs, and MC groups, including Kool Herc, Grandmaster Flash, the Treacherous Three, Grand Wizard Theodor, and the Cold Crush 4, had promised to drop by and perform. The concert was free, and like most rap music extravaganzas, it was expected to be a loose, informal, and unpredictable affair. For this reason, few audience members would have been shocked if many of the advertised performers failed to appear—which, in fact, is exactly what happened. Around noon, a sound system was installed in the center's gymnasium, and a few hours later dance music began blasting out of a pair of five-foot speaker columns. Almost immediately, a smattering of young black males began drifting into the gym, most of whom lounged against a back wall and stared at the stage.

It would be difficult to designate a precise moment when the concert officially "began." It's fairly easy, however, to pinpoint the moment the concert first stopped. That happened at 7:15, shortly after a gun fight broke out just outside the center's main entrance. The shots sounded surprisingly innocuous—"like a string of firecrackers," said one observer—and most of the audience never heard them because they were dancing to "I Want You Back" by the Jackson Five. It didn't take long, however, for news of the fight to reach every corner of the gym, causing the crowd to grow restless and uneasy. The mere sight of a revolver at an event like this is usually enough to send everyone stampeding for the exits, in which case the show would be over.

No one knew exactly what had happened but a lot of wild rumors were spreading. Everyone's worst fears seemed to be confirmed when a housing cop, the sole representative of adult authority, reached behind a stack of records, retrieved an automatic rifle, and ran out the back door. The music stopped and the overhead lights came on. Squinting from the sudden brightness, the audience drifted aimlessly around the room. "Yo, man, what's goin' on outside?" someone asked.

The barrel-chested Bambaataa stood stoically behind the turntables, a set of earphones turned askew on his head, the expression on his face vacillating between concern, anger, and disappointment. He noticed a group edging aggressively toward the main entrance and picked up the microphone. "Where you goin'?" he asked, his authoritative voice booming over the sound system. "There ain't nothin' goin' on out there."

Bambaataa paused and then addressed the whole audience. "No violence . . . no violence . . . no violence," he said evenly, calmly, his voice having a pronounced effect on the more skittish ones in the group. He set the needle on a James Brown record and let it play a few seconds before abruptly lifting it. A few members of the audience—the hard-core dancers—moaned. "You like that?" taunted Bambaataa. "Music. That's what I'm talkin' about." He put the needle back on the record and let it play. The lights went out and the crowd began to dance. Apparently no one there was hurt and the dispute was moved out of the area.

An hour later, the collective moment of panic was forgotten and the gym was filled with several hundred happy, sweating, undulating bodies. The stage, already jammed with equipment, had also become crammed with people, some of whom were waiting to perform, most of whom were just trying to get as close to the action as possible. Periodically, Bambaataa ordered the stage cleared, in which case his security forces would halfheartedly usher a few off the stage. "You can come back later, but you have to get off now," said Smitty, head of security, while ejecting them.

Finally, the rapping segment of the show began when Bizzy Bee Starski, the rap equivalent of a leadoff batter, grabbed the microphone and cut a wide swath through the crowd as he pranced across the stage. The dancers, many of whom were dressed in hooded sweatshirts, leather bomber jackets, basketball shoes, and jeans, pressed closer to the stage.

"Everybody who likes sex throw your hands in the air!" screamed Starski. The audience threw up its hands and roared in approval. With his double-knit slacks and clunky black shoes, Starski looked a little out of place, but he was obviously a favorite here. "What's the name of this nation?" he shouted, his wiry body quivering with energy. "Zulu! Zulu!" chanted the audience. "And who's gonna get on down?" asked Starski with a smile.

"Bambaataa! Bambaataa!"

Lil' Vietnam

Afrika Bambaataa, founder and number one DJ of the mighty Zulu Nation, grew up at the Bronx River Project, which is situated near the intersection of the Cross Bronx and Bronx River expressways and looks like every other low-income housing project in the city: a cluster of unadorned, fifteen-story brick buildings circling two small playgrounds. Unlike the nearby South Bronx, the neighborhood survived the sixties relatively intact with few buildings abandoned. The surrounding community is filled with row after row of identical, two-story brick houses, most of which have tiny concrete yards framed by cast-iron fences. It looks quiet here but this neighborhood once had a reputation for violence that was unequaled in New York.

It all started in 1968 at the nearby Bronxdale Project when seven incorrigible teenagers, who were terrorizing playgrounds, robbing bus drivers, and wreaking havoc throughout the southeast Bronx, began calling themselves the

Savage Seven. In imitation of the Hell's Angels, they began wearing Levi jackets with a ganglike insignia emblazoned on the back. Before long, others wanted to join and the name had to be changed to the Black Spades. The group was then an official street gang, one of the first to appear since the late fifties, when the widespread use of heroin demolished what was left of the original gangs.

Almost immediately, gangs modeled after the Black Spades appeared at every project in the Bronx, all wearing the same uniform: jeans, Levi jackets, garrison belts, black engineer boots. At first, teenagers joined because they liked the style and because it was fun to drift around the city like a pack of wild wolves. Later on, it became necessary to join in order to survive. Without a gang affiliation, a young boy was vulnerable to beatings, robbery, and general day-to-day harassment. However, as soon as he started flying colors, everyone knew he couldn't be bullied without arousing the wrath of several hundred well-armed compatriots. A division of the Black Spades was founded at Bronx River Project in 1969, and Bambaataa, then a junior high school student, immediately became a member. But he was far from being a typical one; while other gang members were playing basketball or hanging out on street corners, he was scouring record bins for obscure R & B recordings.

"Bam was never interested in sports. As long as I've known him, he's always been the music man," says Jay McGluery, who grew up at Bronx River with Bambaataa. "His mother is a nurse and she was constantly on the go, so we always went to his house to party. He had every record you could want to hear, including a lot of rock albums. James Brown and Sly and the Family Stone was his favorites."

Bambaataa was also more attuned to politics than most of his fellow gang members, many of whom reportedly understood only three basic concepts: "crush, kill, and destroy." When he was twelve, Bambaataa had already begun hanging out at the Black Panther Information Center on Burton Road. His political leanings were encouraged by the appearance of songs like "Say It Loud, I'm Black and I'm Proud" by James Brown and "Stand" by Sly and the Family Stone.

However, like many gang members, Bambaataa had a reckless, unpredictable streak. McGluery recalls the time they were playing war games and he took refuge in one of the project's apartment buildings. Bambaataa poured gasoline on the sidewalk in front of the building, lit it, and announced he was holding everyone hostage. That same summer he convinced his friends to buy target bows and arrows so they could hunt rabbits on the banks of the Bronx River. "Bam was always a leader," says McGluery. "He was always full of crazy ideas."

It wasn't long before the war games ended, however, and the real wars began. It seemed natural for the street gangs to turn against the local heroin dealers. After all, drugs had destroyed the original gangs and were certainly capable of having a similar effect on them. "Getting rid of the pushers caused great problems for us because we grew up knowing most of them," says McGluery. "Yet they was causin' great harm in the community, so we came to the conclusion that gang members from other projects would do the work. We just had to point them out and that night they might get a good beating." Many dealers quickly relocated to different parts of the city. The more difficult cases were often found thrown off a roof or shot to death. The Royal Charmers went so far as to erect a paint-splattered sheet across 173rd Street that read, "No junkies allowed after 10 o'clock."

The number of gangs in the Bronx kept growing through the summer in 1971, but this development went unnoticed until Stevenson High School opened its doors in September. Located in the North Bronx, Stevenson had been a predominantly white school that was now receiving busloads of blacks and Hispanics from the South Bronx. The first day was quiet. The second day a few gang members decided to wear their colors to school. The third day it was apparent that almost the entire male population belonged to one gang or another. Finding themselves outnumbered, a variety of white gangs merged into a single gang called the Ministers. Fights between the Black Spades and the Ministers became a daily event and continued for the next two years.

Fortunately, a conclusive battle between the two groups was never fought. A few major rumbles were arranged by the warlords on each side, but whenever the Black Spades boarded a bus headed uptown, it would be surrounded by squad cars before it could reach the Ministers' turf. Typically, the windows of the bus would fly open and a shower of chains, knives, bats, and zip guns would hit the pavement. On June 27, 1973, a brief battle was broken up by police in front of P.S. 127 on Castle Hill Avenue, resulting in the arrest of eighteen Black Spades. The police, almost entirely white at the time, were constantly accused of racism, a charge that might have some foundation considering newspaper stories from this time indicate that white gang members were seldom arrested.

As the gangs of the south and southeast Bronx grew progressively violent and uncontrollable, they eventually began to turn on each other, a development that produced the bloodiest confrontations. One feud between the Black Spades and the Seven Crowns lasted for ninety-two days, during which time the Bronx River Project was constantly peppered with gunfire from passing cars. Shoot-outs became so common that the residents started calling it Lil' Vietnam. "I was into street gang violence," admits Bambaataa. "That was all part of growing up in the southeast Bronx." However, that's about all he'll say on the subject. "I don't really be speaking on that stuff because it's negative," he explains. "The Black Spades was also helping out in the community, raising money for sickle-cell anemia and gettin' people to register to vote." "He was not what I would call gung ho," adds McGluery, who became warlord of the Bronx River division before quitting to join the marines. "Bam was more like a supervisor. There was so many different gangs and he knew at least five members in every one. Anytime there was a conflict, he would try and straighten it out. He was into communications."

Gang activity probably peaked in 1973, when there were an estimated 315 gangs in the city with 19,503 claimed members. The Black Spades was by far the largest and most feared, with divisions in almost every precinct. However, by 1974, the Black Spades began to disintegrate. "Girls got tired of the gangs first," says Bambaataa. "They wanted to raise families and they'd seen too many people dyin'. Some gangs got into drugs. Others got wiped out—by the police or by other gangs."

After many of the original Black Spades were killed, jailed, or dropped out of the gang, Bambaataa took on an increasingly influential role. His affiliation continued until January 10, 1975, when his best friend, Soulski, was shot and killed by two policemen on Pelham Parkway. Bambaataa insists the shooting was nothing short of an assassination carried out during a police crackdown on gang activity. He keeps a Xerox of his friend's death certificate in his bedroom. "He got shot in about nine different places," says Bambaataa. "The back, the stomach, the face. At first I wanted to go to war with the police, but we couldn't really win. The *Amsterdam News* calmed everybody down and told us to fight through the system. It went to trial but the cops never got convicted."

For over five years the Bronx had lived in constant terror of street gangs. Suddenly, in 1975, they disappeared almost as quickly as they had arrived. This happened because something better came along to replace the gangs. That something was eventually called hip-hop.

The Zulu Nation

An independent entrepreneur armed with a portable sound system and extensive record collection, the DJ emerged as a new cultural hero in the Bronx in 1975. In Bambaataa's neighborhood, the first DJ with two turntables, a mixer, and a cult following was Kool Dee, whose repertoire consisted primarily of the same disco hits aired on black-oriented radio stations.

"We began to hear about a DJ in the West Bronx who was playing a new sound," says Bambaataa. "His name was Kool Herc and at first I didn't like him because I sided with Kool Dee. But Herc's music was more funky than Kool Dee's, so I switched."

Kool Herc had moved to New York from Kingston in 1967 and his DJ style was patterned after the great Jamaican DJs, who had developed a technique for talking over instrumental records known as toasting. In the early sixties, reggae singles were already being pressed with a dub side, a musical track without a vocal, so these DJs could provide their own impromptu lyrics.

When Herc came out as a DJ in 1973, he had plenty of dub records but he couldn't play them because the audience wouldn't accept reggae. So he played funky disco records with a Latin flaunt. No record better epitomizes his favorite style than "Apache." The song was originally recorded by the Ventures in the early sixties. In 1973 the Incredible Bongo Band removed the Indian drumbeat and replaced it with conga drums, but failed to make a hit with it. Two years later, Herc resurrected "Apache" and turned it into the Bronx national anthem.

Herc was the first DJ to buy records just for a fifteen-second instrumental solo, which he would often play over and over, while at the same time talking over a microphone connected to an echo chamber. Not exactly toasting, it was a kind of primitive rapping, consisting mainly of new slang words and an occasional joke that might be making the rounds at the local high schools. "Rock on my mellow," Herc would say. "This is the joint." Talking on the microphone during a party became a favorite pastime and everyone wanted to get in on the act. Herc later turned most of the rapping over to Coke-la-Rock and Clark Kent, who became the first MC group.

Held at the Heavalo, the Twilight Zone, or the Executive Playhouse, Herc's parties became immensely popular and began to draw a particular type of dancer known as the B-boy, or "break-dancer." "If you was at one of Kool Herc's parties, it was something big, something you'd go home and brag about," says Grand Mixer D.ST., who was one of the original B-boys and has since become a popular DJ. "Herc would play disco with a bebop. When 'Apache' came on, everybody would form a circle and the B-boys would go into the center. At first, the dance was simple: touch your toes, hop, kick out your leg. Then some guy went down, spun around on all fours. Everybody said wow and went home to try to come up with something better. At first, you'd be in the center for a half minute, then one minute, then two minutes. People started puttin' perfection into the dance."

Within a few months, "breaking" evolved into a highly acrobatic, ritualized contest that replaced fighting as a major outlet for aggression. The Levi jackets disappeared, replaced by the new B-boy style, which consisted of sweatshirts with individual names, bell-bottom jeans, which were always rolled up on the outside instead of being hemmed, Pro Keds tennis shoes, and white sailor's caps with the brims ironed to stick straight out.

Meanwhile, at Stevenson High School, Bambaataa formed a small social group called the Zulus, inspired by the recent release of a feature film on the tribe. (The original Bambaataa was a Zulu chief at the turn of the century.

Translated into English, the word means "affectionate leader.") In many ways, the Zulus were an extension of the B-boy style. They were a more sophisticated version of the Black Spades, a gang into music and dance instead of violence. When Bambaataa graduated in December 1975, his mother bought him a sound system. His first official performance as a DJ was at the Bronx River Community Center on November 12, 1976. By this time, dancing was taking over the Bronx. While the intense competition between DJs was considerably less dangerous than the gang scene, it could capture the excitement of a rumble. Two DJs, each representing a different musical style, would meet at a junior high school or community center and engage in a bloodless "battle," which usually consisted of playing at the same time with both systems cranked to maximum volume. "There was a lot of confusion going on at the time," laughs Bambaataa. "If you outblasted the other DJ, he'd get mad, cut off his system, and leave."

There were also less honorable methods of competing, methods Kool Herc remembers well: "If Bam and I had a battle, we knew it was just a gimmick to attract people," he says, "but the Zulus would take it to heart and start pulling plugs. Bam is not to be blamed for that," Herc adds quickly. "He ain't that type of person. Anybody who picks up the wax is a friend in my heart, but Bam is the only DJ I really respect because he always plays music I never heard before."

During one legendary battle against Disco King Mario, Bambaataa opened his show with the theme song from *The Andy Griffith Show*, taped off his television set. He mixed the ditty with a rocking drumbeat, followed it with the Monsters' theme song, and quickly changed gears with "I Got the Feeling" by James Brown. His knack for coming up with unexpected cuts and "bugging out" the audience earned him the title Master of Records.

There is much more to Bambaataa's mystique than a few novelty records, however. For many kids he provides a hip yet strongly moral role model. "Bam tells them not to drink, smoke, or take drugs, and to stay in school until they get a diploma," says McGluery. "He's a Black Muslim, and when he talks to the kids, you can feel the vibrations from the Muslims coming through." When asked what the Zulu Nation is all about, Bambaataa simply replies, "It's about survival, economics, and keeping our people moving on."

D.ST. remembers the first time he discovered the Zulus. "My friends and I were checking out all the dance parties," he says. "We heard about this guy Bambaataa and went to P.S. 123 to see him. I remember seeing all those B-boys and thinking, 'Yeah, they got them over here, too.' I started going to more of Bam's parties and was invited to join up. It wasn't like being in the Black Spades. The Spades were heartless lunatics. The Zulu Nation was about bringing peace. Force was used only if necessary. Bam had a good idea. He brought people together from all parts of the Bronx. It was one of the main factors to end the warfare."

In 1977 the ranks of the Zulu Nation were spreading into other boroughs as well. Becoming a Zulu wasn't difficult, all you had to do was to show up at the right parties and express an interest in joining. What was remarkable, however, was the number of kids seeking application, a number Bambaataa says he can no longer estimate but one that undoubtedly runs into the thousands. "Bam has some kind of gift with kids," says McGluery. "I don't think even he knows how the Zulus got so big." "A lot of people liked our style," says Bambaataa with his usual understatement.

Not only do they like his style, the Zulus exhibit a fierce loyalty to their leader. "He is the music," says Cholly Rock, an original Zulu B-boy who is often credited with spreading break dancing into Manhattan. When Cholly Rock tries to explain Bambaataa's role, he hesitates as if what he wants to say is too complicated to put into words. "He makes it all come together," he says finally.

In 1977, a young DJ in the South Bronx named Grandmaster Flash began revolutionizing rap music. Flash had started his career by bringing his sound system to the local parks, hot-wiring it to a streetlight, and providing free concerts. By playing short, rapid-fire cuts from a wide variety of records, while at the same time maintaining a steady dance beat, Flash created the art of the musical collage. He also began experimenting with an electronic percussion machine called the beat box. Around the same time, another South Bronx DJ, named Theodor, invented a turntable-manipulation technique called scratching, which enabled a DJ to obtain percussive effects by rapidly shifting a record backwards and forwards while keeping the needle in its groove. Depending on what type of record he used, Flash discovered he could produce a variety of weird effects using the scratching technique.

Just as important, however, was the contribution of Melle Mel and the other four rappers who made up the Furious Five, Flash's MC group. Mel created an angry, aggressive, percussive style of rapping that put a much greater emphasis on rhythm and rhyme.

**To the hip hop, hip hop, don't stop,
don't stop that body rock.**

Relying on an inventive use of slang, the staccato effect of short words, and unexpected internal rhymes, the Furious Five began composing elaborate rap routines, intricately weaving their voices through a musical track mixed by Flash. They would trade solos, chant, and sing harmony. The result was dazzling. It was a vocal style immediately imitated by every other MC group in the Bronx and one that shifted the attention away from the DJs and onto the rappers. At the same time, Bambaataa was working with a number of MC groups, including the Soul Sonic Force, the Cosmic Force, and the Jazzy Five. However, he freely admits the most "treacherous" battles were taking place between Flash and the Furious Five versus Breakout and the Funky Four (later known as the Funky Four Plus 1). "Flash was on top," says Bambaataa, "but they was battling for that number one spot. Both groups was doin' flips on stages and settin' off smoke bombs."

"Planet Rock"

For five years the B-boys, rappers, DJs, and graffiti writers of New York continued to expand and develop their unique artistic vision in almost complete isolation from the rest of the world. Until 1979, little attempt was made to spread the subculture, now collectively known as hip-hop, beyond the boundaries of New York. When the Fatback Band released the first rap record, titled "King Tim III," a few of the original MC groups were inspired to put out a record of their own. (Until this time, rap had been transmitted primarily through live cassette recordings, which were noisily displayed via the ghetto blasters, a portable tape machine carried by every self-respecting hip-hopper.) The first rap solo record to come out of the Bronx was "Rapper's Delight" by the Sugarhill Gang, which unexpectedly sold 2 million copies, launched a new independent label, created a vast audience for rap around the country, and unleashed a mad scramble of MC groups looking for record contracts. The song's success was partially due to the musical track, which was lifted from "Good Times" by Chic, already a national disco hit. The major record labels warily kept their distance, and a number of small independent companies began producing rap records. Bambaataa visited several, dropped off tapes, and received only minor encouragement. Finally, in 1980, he succeeded in obtaining a deal with Paul Winley's struggling label. In November, he recorded two 12-inch versions of "Zulu Nation Throwdown," one with the Cosmic Force and the other with the Soul Sonic Force. When the first single was released, however, Bambaataa discovered Winley had added instruments without even consulting him. "It was crazy," says Bambaataa. "I recorded the songs to just drums. When the record came out, Winley added a bass and some crazy guitar music. Then, when it came time to get paid, he started jivin' us. A lot of groups at the time wasn't business wise and didn't know about contracts or royalties. We just wanted to get a record out."

Instead of moving forward, Bambaataa felt he was losing ground. He hated his own record and knew he wasn't getting the recognition he deserved. The precariousness of the situation was all the more evident by what had happened to Kool Herc, who was now working for a record store in the South Bronx. Herc's slide from power had started one night at the Executive Playhouse, when he stepped in to break up a fight. "I knew one of the guys," says Herc, "but one of his friends thought I was messin' with him. He stabbed me three times. After that the door was open. How do you think people feel about comin' to a party when the host gets stabbed? Then, my place burned down. Papa couldn't find no good ranch so his herd scattered." In 1981, Bambaataa had just established a relationship with a fledgling label called Tommy Boy Records when he received a phone call from graffiti artist Fred Braithwaite, who was about to co-curate a graffiti exhibit at the newly opened Mudd Club Gallery. Braithwaite asked Bambaataa to perform at the opening and he readily accepted the invitation. It was his first contact with the downtown music scene and Bambaataa was greatly impressed, not only by the enthusiasm and energy of the crowd, but by their appreciative response to "Zulu Nation Throwdown." "They thought it was a classic," says Bambaataa incredulously. "After that, I started to like it, too." "Bambaataa is a smart guy," says Braithwaite, who was one of the first graffiti artists to mingle with the East Village art scene, hanging out at Club 57 and exhibiting at alternative spaces like P.S. 1. "After the Mudd Club, he knew just what to do. The rest is history."

What Bambaataa did was to go into the studio and immediately begin work on a new record, one that would appeal to the new wave crowd as well as the hip-hoppers. He raided musical fragments from sources he felt were appreciated by both groups: Kraftwerk, the film *The Good, the Bad, and the Ugly*, and Captain Sky. With the help of producers Tom Silverman and Arthur Baker, keyboardist John Robie, and a Roland TR 808 drum computer, Bambaataa created an eerie yet throbbingly funky musical track. He encouraged Soul Sonic to come up with a new style of rapping to augment the music. The result, invented primarily by G.L.O.B.E., discarded the staccato delivery of most rap songs and replaced it with one that extended notes into a chant before abruptly cutting them off. It had none of Melle Mel's impact, but it was a peculiar vocal technique that well suited the song.

The final result, titled "Planet Rock," was released in May 1982, and according to *Billboard*, the record was "an instant club and retail hit of formidable size, shipping near gold upon release." Bambaataa suddenly found himself catapulted into national recognition. "One thing we like to stress," says Bambaataa, who has just returned from a whirlwind tour of Florida and South Carolina. "Success will not make us big-headed. Some people say, 'How does it feel to be a star?' We don't look at ourselves as stars. 'Cause stars fall. We want to be like the moon and stay put. We still go to the same places we always went and we still talk to everybody, whether they're young or old. We wish everybody the best. We paid our dues and we'll reach down and pull others up with us. We want to keep our money in the community." In his many snapshots from the sixties, Bambaataa looks young, lean, and angry, his eyebrows fused in a permanent scowl of disapproval. Today, however, the angry young man has put on weight and mellowed considerably. He projects a guarded, reserved aura that is sometimes shattered by a smile so friendly it disarms and infects everyone around him. As soon as "Planet Rock" took off, he went out and celebrated by getting a Mohawk haircut. "In the future, I just hope all my groups keep piping," he explains. "See, George Clinton took the music of James Brown and Sly and the Family Stone and made a whole funk empire out of it. That's what I'm trying to do with rap."

Who knows? In another five years, hip-hop could be considered the most significant artistic achievement of the decade. There are certainly signs that its influence is on the rise. For example, in a recent issue of *Flash Art* magazine, Diego Cortez, an influential freelance curator, said, "The rap and breaking phenomenon is just starting to have an effect on the official culture in New York and elsewhere, and I think that this will be clear in the next couple years, this influence as the New York image, music, and gesture. I think the work should be looked at as a highly sophisticated art form which is the image of New York. It's definitely the soul of the underground scene at the moment."

Even more recent was Malcolm McLaren's keynote address at the 1982 New Music Seminar in New York. The creator of the Sex Pistols surprised his audience by devoting most of the speech to rap music. "'Planet Rock' is the most rootsy folk music around," said McLaren, "the only music that's coming out of New York City which has tapped and directly related to that guy in the streets with his ghetto blaster. The record is like an adventure story; it's like that guy walking down the street. And, if Elvis Presley was that in the fifties, then Afrika Bambaataa is that for the eighties . . . This music has a magical air about it because it's not trapped by the preconditioning and evaluation of what a pop record has to be."

Few New York subcultures in the past decade have been so relentlessly creative as the one that has given us rap music, graffiti writing, and break dancing, perhaps the first youth culture to put its highest premium on individual imagination. It isn't enough for a DJ to merely spin records, he has to amaze his audience with a display of turntable pyrotechnics. It isn't enough for a graffiti writer to scribble his name, he has to devote hours to create a mural that will cover an entire subway car. It isn't enough for a break-dancer to do a flip, he has to learn to spin like a top while doing a headstand.

If subcultures are the experimental laboratory where society tests new cultural concepts, then hip-hop represents the most imaginative leap forward since the sixties. And like the counterculture of the sixties, hip-hop has the capacity to infiltrate and subvert the mass media culture, energizing it with a fresh supply of symbols, myths, and values. Certainly the potential is there and the outcome now depends largely on whether artists like Bambaataa, who are finally enjoying a measure of success, can rise to the occasion, hold on to their principles, and spread the hip-hop sensibility across the globe.

The Village Voice / September 21, 1982

London Rocks, Paris Burns, and the B-Boys Break a Leg

DAVID HERSHKOVITS

The New York City Rap Tour lands at Orly Airport on a gray
and cloudy 6:00 a.m. in late November. Jet-lagged from the six-and-a-half-
hour flight, they step toward the minibus awaiting their arrival, wiping sleep
from their eyes. Their primary mode of transport for the two-week tour to
Paris, London, Lyon, Metz, Belfort, Strasbourg, and Milhouse, the bus is fresh
and clean, tanked up and emblazoned with the "Europe 1" logo of the radio
station/music conglomerate that is cosponsoring the tour.

Never one to pass up such an inviting opportunity, Fab 5 Freddy uncaps
the black marker he keeps handy and leaves his "tag" on the side of the bus.
Futura 2000 and Dondi White, two artists who made their reputations "bombing" subways with spray paint, follow suit. Others in the group line up to have
a go at it when out pops the bus driver, outraged by the desecration of the vehicle in his charge. Chasing everyone away from the side of the bus, he gesticulates wildly and shouts choice French phrases that fall on uncomprehending
ears. Anyway, it is too late. The damage has been done and the message is out.
Like the nouveau Beaujolais, the New York City Rap Tour est arrivé.

The specialty of the twenty-five-member troupe is throwing parties and
making you feel good enough to "put your hands in the air / and wave them like

you just don't care." They are the black and Hispanic stars of rapping, breaking, double Dutch, and spray-can painting, a quartet of folk-art forms known collectively as hip-hop. Having journeyed from the streets of New York to the chic clubs of Manhattan, they've come to rock the citadels of European culture with their juice. (That's slanguage for the positive force released when urban aggression is plugged into a creative outlet.)

It began on the asphalt of "Boogie Down" Bronx. A power source hot-wired to a utility pole, two turntables, a microphone, a DJ with an extensive record collection, and suddenly the neighborhood ain't so bad after all. DJs develop followings, and pretty soon they start throwing parties, charging a little cash. Competition being what it is, rival DJs throw rival parties. Word gets out, records appear on independent record labels, and overnight "Money Making" Manhattan gets a whiff.

With a fresh graffiti paint job and a spacious dance floor, a roller disco called the Roxy becomes a mecca for rap every Friday night. It attracts a racially mixed crowd that includes a solid following of art-music-and-fashion folk who once championed punk but are now in love with rap.

Playing records, however, is only a part of the DJ's chores. Top dogs like Bambaataa and Grand Mixer D.ST. (after Delancey Street on the Lower East Side, but pronounced "D.S.T.") are turntable technologists, playing the "wheels of steel" like instruments, intentionally "scratching" records to the beat, pulling out segments from favored cuts and back-spinning for repetition. With the DJs at the controls, m.c. (microphone control) duties are given over to rappers like Fab 5 Freddy, Phase II, Rammelzee, and the Infinity Rappers, fast-talking rhymers who speaksing to the beat, either extemporaneously or as performers doing their own songs. They've got the juice and their job is to give it to the people in the house whose job is to dance, dance, dance. When the music's hot, the B-boys can't restrain themselves. "Breaking" from a standing position, B-boys from Crazy Legs' Rock Steady Crew throw themselves to the ground like acrobats, bounding, twisting, and spinning on their heads like tops. Breaking, the story goes, had its roots in gang warfare before throwing parties became a better way to meet girls and get famous. The only way the girls can get in on the hip-hop action in this macho-dominated scene is through the competitive sport of double-Dutch jump roping. Between two turning ropes—one going clockwise, the other counterclockwise—the World Champion Fantastic Four Double Dutch Girls go through a series of compulsory jumps and tricks while chanting street rhymes for timing. "The whole idea is to get everyone dancin ," says Kool Lady Blue, the originator of rap nights at the Roxy and producer of the European tour, which is cosponsored by Europe 1 and FNAC department stores. "It's not a band we're bringing over. We don't want people to stand and watch. We want people to participate. It's a party thing, not a gig."

Still, one wonders how hip-hop will play on the Continent. With the music, the dancing, and the art (surprisingly, rap is known and popular in France) comes something more difficult to embrace: the dress, language, manner, and style of the New York ghetto. For the great majority, it's the first time they've been so far away from home, and a degree of culture shock is expected. Ditto for the thousands of Europeans who will get electrified by their juice. Warning: Exposure to the New York City Rap Tour may be dangerous to your health.

After a quick check-in at the hotel, the troupe is back on the bus, heading for a rehearsal at Europe 1 in the center of Paris. Donna Lee, a teacher brought along to tutor the girls and the B-boys still in high school, recommends a visit to the Louvre, but other topics tend to dominate the conversation. Mr. Freeze, the Electric Boogie dancing man, is a native of France who was brought up in the Bronx. "Police here," he says advisedly, "they can shoot at you if you don't stop when they call."

"Where's the hunchback?" D.ST. calls out laughingly from the back of the bus as it passes Notre Dame Cathedral along the banks of the Seine. "I'd like to shake his hand."

Appetites whetted with the prospect of lunch, they disembark at Europe 1 and march through the maze of halls to the basement cafeteria like a squadron of combat troops impervious to their new surroundings. In the cafeteria, the grumble of disappointment spreads like a chain reaction. Greeting them is an array of unfamiliar appetizers, as well as the unwelcome news that they are expected to pay for this exotic repast. "Let's get some real food," someone calls out. "Let's go to McDonald's!" Shouting epithets behind them, they break out en masse toward the Champs-Élysées and the world's largest Burger King.

With the departing group is Bernard Zekri, a French journalist based in New York. As the only bilingual known and trusted by the performers, he has the unwelcome task of serving as mediator between the visiting, impatient New Yorkers and the frequently perplexed and shocked Europeans. By the end of the tour, Zekri is sure of one thing: "Americans don't know how to travel."

The following night, rested and ready to party, they arrive at Bataclan, once an old theater and now a concert hall. Amid the tumult of sound checks, jumping double-Dutch girls warming up, and B-boys breaking down, Phase II steps up to the microphone and sings a few lines from his record, "The Roxy." That's all the rehearsal he needs. A thirty-one-year-old veteran breaker, DJ, rapper, and graffiti writer, he leaps off the stage in search of someone to accompany him to buy a camera. Not finding any cameras in the nearby department store, he stops to admire some sweaters instead. "Things are so bugged in the Bronx," he says, examining one carefully, "that I don't ever wear good clothes."

Dressed in an array of leathers, sneakers, jumpsuits, down coats, caps, and hooded sweatshirts, they are a sight for the fashion-conscious French to behold. So much so that even when the show is in high gear, the people at Bataclan prefer standing and analyzing, making polite conversation, and dancing only sporadically. In other words, it's not exactly Friday night at the Roxy.

"They're trying to understand it the best way they can," says Crazy Legs, the sixteen-year-old president of the Rock Steady Crew. "This dude comes up to me and says he wants to go to New York to learn to do breaking in school. And I tell him we make it up and he don't believe me." Back on the bus after a postconcert dinner at a fancy French restaurant serving the kind of food that gets some people longing for McDonald's, the mood is ebullient. Destined to drive all night to catch the 6:00 a.m. Calais ferry to Dover on their way to London, they have no thought of sleep, only music from Bambaataa's box.

"It takes a while to get them going, to get them loose," says Bambaataa, evaluating the French reaction to the rap and electronic-funk records he played. Along with the title Master of Records, conferred on him for his extensive record collection and the uncanny knack he has for coming up with unexpected cuts and "bugging out" his audience, he is also known as the King of the Zulu Nation—a loosely knit group said to number in the thousands and held together by Bambaataa, who explains, "It's about survival, economics, and keeping our people moving on." A former gang leader, Bambaataa seems able to instill a sense of pride in his followers without appearing to be trying. A self-described Muslim who doesn't eat "swine," he wants to follow in the footsteps of James Brown, Sly and the Family Stone, and George Clinton and make a funk empire out of rap. He seems well on his way. His first record, "Planet Rock," went gold, and his second, "Looking for the Perfect Beat," seems destined for the same fate.

By 4:00 a.m., the bus is still alive with the chatter of people too wound up to sleep.

Dondi White is talking about Europe 1. "They called us animals because we were cursing in the restaurant," he says. "They wanted the New York scene and now they have it."

Futura is feeling good. "I'm a very lucky boy right now," he says. "I wish my mama was around to check this out." At twenty-seven, he's one of the tour's senior citizens. "The crowd was into it," he says, "but not into it as fun."

"I've been thinking of the whole thing as a military maneuver," says Fab 5 Freddy, better known as Fred Braithwaite when his graffiti-inspired artworks hang in established galleries. He comes from a family rooted in jazz and politics—his father was a follower of Malcolm X and his godfather is drummer Max Roach. "Jazz is an original art form, and this is an extension of that art form," he says.

Night turns into day. London, Lyon, Metz, new faces, new hotels, more long bus rides in and out of towns for one-night stands and shopping sprees for "fresh" Nikes, sheepskins, and sweaters. With $50-a-day expenses and a $100 per show payoff, there's plenty of crazy money, especially since the dollar is worth more abroad.

In London, a B-boy quarrel turns sour and fighting gets out of hand. At showtime, however, it's as though peace reigned supreme in the land of rap. Like family, they are quick to anger, quick to forget.

In Lyon, it's 3:00 a.m. and snowing. Futura, Fab 5 Freddy, and Rammelzee are waiting for a cab because they can't gain admittance to a restaurant. "I'll give them a hundred francs [about $15] if they let us in," says Futura.

Meanwhile, back at the hotel, there's a blackout and the halls are alive with the sound of screaming girls and playful boys making scary noises. The hotel manager wakes up Kool Lady Blue and threatens to kick them out in the middle of the night if she doesn't restore order.

Early morning and it's back on the bus to Paris again, where the New York City Rap Tour is the number one media story. On TV, they demonstrate their talents. In the press, they explain themselves. On the radio, they DJ. In posh clubs like Le Palace, they party and pose for photographs. The French are fascinated by the New Yorkers who've got the juice. The New Yorkers seem blasé.

In Belfort, there's a party after the show at a club where a beer costs $7. Staying just long enough to down a few complimentary drinks and a couple of helpings of pâté, they break for the bus, but not before Dondi, who sold a painting in London, springs for a $65 bottle of champagne. Not to be outdone by his co-artist, and always anxious to add to the party, Futura buys a bottle of his own. B-boy Take 1 wants to follow their lead but is a minor and can't.

For the first time since the tour began ten days ago, there's no show the night they arrive in Strasbourg. A genteel and sophisticated city set among the rolling hills of Alsace-Lorraine, it's been the site of tension between France and Germany for generations and still has a strong German presence. Graced with Gothic cathedrals, as well as all-night burger stands and video games, Strasbourg is the second-richest city in France.

For the troupe, the layoff is welcome and the time is used for—what else?—shopping and partying. The prospect of going home soon makes everybody's fatigue easier to deal with. Futura has an opening at FNAC. And records by the rappers, released on a subsidiary of Europe 1, are selling well.

In the dressing room prior to the first night's show, Phase II is miming a jump shot and talking about how he wishes he were back home so he could get into a game.

"Cool out, my girl's trying to do homework," says D.ST.

Being in the middle of backstage madness doesn't seem to bother double-Dutch girl Deshaun's concentration. Hygiene, economics, English, now it's American history.

"It doesn't make a difference where I do it as long as I get my work done," says Deshaun, who has seen the Eiffel Tower, visited "old churches," and read act 3 of *Hamlet* while on the road. What bothers her most is "the way people look at me—they think I'm from Mars or something. I still want to travel around more, but right now I want to go home."

By nine-thirty, one hour behind schedule, Bambaataa and D.ST. are at the wheels of steel and the party is off and cooking just as it has been throughout the critically successful tour. Then, for no reason that anyone can immediately discern, a couple of beer bottles are thrown on the stage by people in the audience. Abruptly, the music stops.

"This ain't no ----- ------- punk rock!" Fab 5 Freddy says into the microphone. "We don't go for that—here. Whoever did that ain't got no mother!"

With no security in the house to protect them, the New York City Rap Tour has to take matters into its own hands.

"We're not taking no ---- from nobody because I'll ---- fifteen of you up," says Futura, whipping off his belt and waving its huge buckle at the crowd. "I don't care if you understand me or not. We don't take that ---- in New York City!"

D.ST. jumps down on the floor, breaks a beer bottle on the edge of the stage, and waves it at the crowd menacingly, cutting himself in the process. Flanked by Futura, backed up by Rock Steady armed with cans of spray paint and other implements of destruction, supported by Phase II poised with a chair over his head ready for action, Shahiem, Dondi, and others ready to brawl, D.ST. stares at the crowd, holding his ground. Punches are thrown, and in a few minutes it's all over, just eight stitches for D.ST. and a couple of unfortunate local bad boys who messed with the wrong people on their way to the hospital.

The problem dispensed with, the audience demands more party sounds. Bambaataa, quickly back at the controls, gets on his beat box, sets the wheels in motion, and peace is restored.

"The fight was in the air," said one eyewitness, a Frenchman in the music business. "There were many racist people there. And I heard many racist comments about Negroes."

The last bus ride to Paris for the grand finale at Le Palace is touched with a sense of completion. Reflection seems like a natural thing to do.

"What went down with the tour will affect the people because they ain't never seen anything like it," says Fab 5 Freddy, whose French-English rap record, "Une Sale Histoire" ("A Dirty Story"), tops the Paris club charts that week.

"Unfortunately, we had to get rough in Strasbourg," says Futura. "This is what people expect. They have an impression that the boys from New York, they're ignorant and all they can do is fight."

"Hey, Bambaataa, hey, Bambaataa," comes the backstage rallying cry, as the New York City Rap Tour members get ready for their Le Palace finale. From the corners of the cavernous club they come together to rock the house one more time. Fab 5 Freddy, Rammelzee, Phase II, Dondi, K.C., Shahiem, Futura, Rock Steady, the Double Dutch Girls—they've all got the juice. Grand Mixer D.ST. sets the wheels of steel spinning and the music takes over. The capacity audience starts to dance and in a few minutes borders melt in the heat of the soul-sonic blast.

Sunday News Magazine / April 3, 1983

The South Bronx Was Getting a Bad Rap Until a Club Called Disco Fever Came Along

BILL ADLER

It's 4:00 a.m Friday, and up in the deejay's booth at Disco Fever—the rap capital of the Solar System, not to mention the South Bronx—DJ Starski revs five hundred dancers into action with Michael Jackson's "Billie Jean." He does it using only the first eight bars of the song, cutting back and forth between two copies of the record. When he's got the whole house rocking to the rhythm, Starski opens the mike:

"What's that word when you're bustin' loose?" he shouts.

"Juice! Juice!" five hundred voices chant.

"And how do you feel when you got that juice?"

"Loose! Loose!" comes the reply.

Right on the beat, too.

The beat goes on, night after night, at Disco Fever, the home of the rappers and the hottest hot spot in New York today. Located some fifteen subway stops north of Studio 54 and the rest of the pleasure palaces of midtown Manhattan, Fever is the tom-tom heart of the South Bronx, one of the few places its disenfranchised citizens can go to forget the harsh reality of their lives.

The South Bronx, of course, has been *the* national emblem of urban decay since Ronald Reagan toured its rubble-strewn landscape as a presidential candidate in 1980 and proclaimed, "I haven't seen anything as bad as this since London after the blitz!" Things have improved some since then, but there's still as much accuracy as self-interest in club owner Sal Abbatiello's assertion that "the only things happening in the South Bronx today are Yankee Stadium and Disco Fever."

Disco Fever has emerged as the headquarters of rap music, which is usually heard on city streets. Rappers transpose street slang into chanted couplets. The words are spoken (or "rapped"), not sung, over a stark, rhythmic base and deal with topics as diverse as unemployment and birth control. The first international rap hit was 1979's "Rapper's Delight," and the music has so matured since then that an apocalyptic rap anthem called "The Message," by Grandmaster Flash and the Furious Five, was selected by *The New York Times* as the most powerful pop single of 1982.

Disco Fever is mentioned in "The Message," and on almost any night of the week, whether they've just finished performing at some chic underground boîte downtown or returned from a tour abroad, Flash and the Five can be found "chilling out" at the Fever in the company of other rap stars such as Kurtis Blow, Afrika Bambaataa and the Soul Sonic Force, the Sugarhill Gang, and the Fearless Four. Blow (born Kurt Walker), twenty-three, had one of his earliest club gigs there as house emcee in 1979 and still insists, "The Fever's where I go to get ideas for my albums. You get to see what the street likes." Russell Simmons, Blow's twenty-five-year-old manager, is even more emphatic about the club's role in the business: "If a rap record doesn't go around in the Fever, it's fake."

But rap alone cannot account for the fact that the Fever has become, in Abbatiello's words, "the YMCA of the Bronx." Last fall the community-minded club raised $8,000 for the United Negro College Fund with its own twenty-seven-hour "telethon." The Fever also organizes bus rides to local prisons so that families and inmates from the neighborhood can visit. And last month the club opened its doors to some 250 youngsters for an Easter party with free admission, refreshments, and gifts.

The Fever draws its clientele from a community where nearly 55 percent of the total population has been officially unemployed for so long that they are no longer considered part of the workforce. With admission rarely more than $5 per person, the club is packed six nights a week (closed Mondays) from 10:00 p.m. until 4:00 a.m.

Self-described Fever Believers include people like Dino Gary, twenty-five, who works as a cook and cashier at a local McDonald's. When Dino gets off work at three-thirty in the afternoon, he goes home and sleeps until midnight or so, then hits the Fever and dances till dawn. "The Fever's like a center," says Dino. "The music is good, and everybody here is family."

Cecily Garner, a twenty-seven-year-old mother of four and part-time cashier at a department store, tries to participate in all of the Fever's various Thursday-night entertainments, like *Name That Tune*, *The Dating Game*, and a *Gong Show*, each one fueled by local talent. Garner entered the Fever's bathing suit competition last year, "but," she reports, "I turned out to be pregnant so I had to drop out of the finals a few weeks later." Cecily considers her thrice-weekly pilgrimages to the Fever her vacation. "I don't get to go away in the summertime," she says, "so this is my summertime."

The unlikely head counselor at this year-round summer camp is Abbatiello, thirty, a hip and energetic Italian-American. He is not surprised to find himself running a club where the clientele is almost totally black and Hispanic. "The nightlife is in my blood," he says, black nightlife in particular. Sal's father, Albert, runs two black nightclubs in the Bronx, and it was he who started Disco Fever in March 1978. The club failed to catch on right away, so Sal convinced his father to let him take a crack at running it the following September. His first move was to bring in rappers to perform on a steady basis. "No one else would hire them," he recalls, "because they drew such a dangerous crowd." Abbatiello's life revolves around Disco Fever. He spends twelve to fourteen hours a day on the Fever's business. "I separated from my wife over this club," confesses Sal. "The club is my wife now."

Abbatiello is aware of the uniqueness of his position. "Some of my customers," he says, "had never even spoken to a white person before me. Once a girl came up to me and asked, 'Can I touch your hair?' My white friends asked me how I get away with it. I tell 'em I don't get away with nothing. Just show my customers a little kindness, and they act all right."

Even so it comes as no surprise that the Fever's staff includes people like Michael Lewis, better known as Mandingo, who at six feet four inches and 260 pounds is head of security. Lewis, thirty-five, says that he's spent almost fifteen years of his life in various federal and state jails. But "ever since Sal picked me out of the crowd to work here, I've learned how to deal better with other people and I've learned how to respect myself more," he says. "This is the first time I've been on the street for four years straight since I was twelve." Lewis feels that the Fever succeeds in some cases where places like Attica and Sing Sing (both of which he is familiar with) fail. "Big as I am," he says, "I've only had a couple fights here in all that time. I feel that we rehabilitate people." This sentiment echoes an observation by Russell Simmons: "People rap to stay out of trouble, like people who play basketball."

The Fever's most enduring feature is the optimism it generates, an optimism that is often expressed in rap. One such passage occurs in "Yes, We Can-Can," a single released by a group of Fever regulars, the Treacherous Three. They sing:

**That we're not out 'cause
wherever there's a will there's a way**

People / May 16, 1983

Rappin' with Russell

Eddie Murphying the Flak-Catchers

NELSON GEORGE

The offices of Rush Productions are two cramped little rooms on Broadway in the Twenties, which on any given afternoon are filled by the loud voices of black men and women. They are mostly young, real street, and real anxious. On this day in January a graffiti artist sits in one corner of the outer room with hopes of painting an album cover. Over on a beat-up couch is a girl in striped pants and a Run-D.M.C. T-shirt waiting for her old man, one of the twenty-two street-oriented acts managed by Russell Simmons's Rush Productions, to find out when his next gig is. Three young dudes dressed in the B-boy-style—untied Adidas sneakers, jeans, sheepskin coats, and Cazals—are leaning against a wall joking and eyeing the girl waiting on the rapper. The token white is Bill Adler, a former *Daily News* reporter who is the company's full-time PR man. Behind him, shifting through papers and cradling a phone on her shoulder, is Heidi Smith, once Russell's lone overworked office staffer and now one of several overworked office employees.

I stick my head in the other room, seeking Russell. Instead, sitting behind Russell's desk in front of the bright orange-and-red mural that says "RUSH" in letters the size of subway car graffiti, I find the king of rap himself, Kurtis Blow. I congratulate him on his recent marriage and the birth of his son, known affectionately around Rush as "Joe Blow." I also praise his production of the Fat Boys' album, which will soon go gold. I tell him that I'm writing a piece on Russell, he tells me that's all right but I really should be doing his life story. I say I'll think about it and ask where Russell is. I'm supposed to be accompanying Russell and Kurtis Blow's producer, Robert "Rocky" Ford, to a meeting with Cannon Films about a rap movie. After urging me again to consider writing his life story, Kurtis tells me they are over at this putrid Chinese restaurant that Russell loves because they make screwdrivers strong, the way he likes them. I run into them in the street. "Yo, home piss," says Russell, "you ready to serve the Israelis or what?" Rocky and I laugh and just look at him. This is the man *The Wall Street Journal* calls "the mogul of rap"?

At twenty-seven, an age when most of his black business contemporaries have designer suit tags branded into their breastbones, Russell promotes street music and makes no apologies. The staccato, crashing drums, the gritty, uncompromised words about life in Kochtown, and the downplaying of melody that marks the music of Blow, Whodini, Run-D.M.C., L.L. Cool J, and the other acts he manages are his lifeblood. He loves all this loud, obnoxious aural graffiti. As far as I can tell—and I've known Russell about six years' worth of headaches, triumphs, and late-night phone calls—he never intends to do anything else but make street records, chain-smoke, talk fast, and uninhibit the inhibited.

Russell is hyped for the meeting. He's puffing on a Kool, bouncing around in shiny black penny loafers, and rubbing his bald spot comically for me. Russell's about five foot ten and 165 pounds, with the complexion of a ripe squash and a generally sunny disposition. He's the kind you can tell your worst joke to and get a laugh. I wish I could do justice to the rapid-fire monologue he delivered in the cab up to Cannon's East Side offices, but without a tape recorder it's hopeless. The gist of it was that we were about to see Russell act like Eddie Murphy in *Beverly Hills Cop*. That's why he asked us along. We're gonna be the reasonable Negroes and he's gonna be the bad nigger, sort of a mercenary eighties version of mau-mauing the flak-catchers. Russell wants to make a point: he's not some dancer shuffling for a (pardon the expression) break. He wants respect and Cannon has already showed a lack of it. Cannon sent a writer uptown to hang out and get a feel for the scene. The writer listened to Russell's ruminations on rap and shook his head affirmatively when Russell emphasized that he wanted no part of another *Beat Street*—all fake dialogue, gospel singers at the Roxy, and other disagreeable Hollywoodisms. The writer, a white Californian who told Russell he sees a black about once every three months in his neighborhood, said, "Yeah," "Uh-huh," and "I understand your concern." And still wrote a jive treatment as much about a white girl trying to break into the music business as the uptown scene. In addition, Cannon, in a full-page *Variety* ad, announced that their rap movie would be shot in, of all places, Pittsburgh! Thickening the plot, a black production company from Los Angeles had approached Russell, guaranteeing him considerable creative input and serious profit participation. "All the VCR money. You hear me, Nelson," he shouted in the cab. Unfortunately, the brothers had a shaky reputation and short bread. We knew Cannon wasn't the classiest studio in the world—the bulk of its films were substandard Forty-second Street fodder (one upcoming project is called *Godzilla vs. Cleveland*). Cannon had, however, committed several million to the project and would undoubtedly make a profitable, chintzy flick.

But Cannon's minions had already lost Russell's goodwill, and in the meeting he truly Eddie Murphyed them. He talked loud and fast and was contemptuous of the film's portly producer, a man who bragged, "I dined with Hepburn last night," and then called Kurtis Blow Curtis Brown. Russell responded by emphasizing how important his acts were in the music business, and basically, with just slightly more subtlety, that he really didn't need them. "I've been working for ten years to make this music mean something," Russell said at one point. "You can come in with one film and ruin everything I'm trying to build." To say the least, ye olde film producer was surprised at Russell's impertinence. So was I. From my pragmatic post as "reasonable Negro" Russell was alienating folk who'd definitely make a rap film, if not the one he wanted made, in exchange for a maybe situation. Russell calmed down after a while— even listened to them a little bit. However, the spirit of Murphy had seized Russell's soul, and with a gleeful smile, he chortled later with Andre Harrell, aka Dr. Jeckyll, about serving them at the meeting, then complained that Rocky and

I had been too good at our assignment. We almost stopped him from having fun. The next day Russell signed a deal with the black production company and was rewarded with the wooing of Michael Schultz, the black director who handled *Cooley High*, one of Russell's favorite films, to supervise the project. In turn he delivered Run-D.M.C., Blow, Whodini, and the Fat Boys, whom he doesn't manage. By denying all that top rap talent to Cannon he would certainly hurt their project and, as blaxploitation films used to advertise, "stick it to the man."

Russell is a product of that generation of blacks who spent early-seventies Saturdays enthralled by the white-bashing activities of Shaft, Super Fly, Trouble Man, Coffey, etc. At times he seems to fantasize about being as cold-blooded promoting raps as they were kicking ass. And if you think about it, Eddie Murphy, another product of the blaxploitation generation (remember Murphy's film critic Abdul Rahiem championing the virtues of Isaac Hayes's Truck Turner?), is nothing but an intentionally funny version of those badass heroes in *48 HRS.* and *Beverly Hills Cop*.

Unfortunately, for Russell being badass isn't enough anymore. Since that meeting rap has exploded yet again. Run-D.M.C., the Fat Boys, and Whodini have all sold over five hundred thousand albums and Blow's *Ego Trip* is in the ballpark. Their videos are on MTV. Russell's acts are being swamped with endorsement and film offers. And, perhaps most profitably, the record industry itself is finally giving up the only kind of respect it can understand—money offers.

But therein lies the rub. You could call Russell a mogul. It is to some degree an apt description, since he certainly has a deep economic stake in rap's present and future. But *mogul* also suggests someone who dominates an industry, and Russell, for all his influence, is at the mercy of many elements he does not control. Unlike the big tickets of pop culture—your George Lucas, Michael Jackson, Grant Tinker–level mogul—Russell doesn't have the financial clout or emotional distance to manipulate. You see, Russell really is his audience. He lives the B-boy life, and the values are found in his records. Unlike Afrika Bambaataa or Russell's brother Joey, aka Run of Run-D.M.C., who are part of a vanguard of rap innovators, Russell is one of the few products of the rap generation to become an important businessman. He doesn't battle other rappers or spinners for record sales. Instead he engages wily, older business-men in treacherous battles for survival. Russell's not going bald 'cause it's been easy.

At least the business side hasn't. Life for Russell has never been that rough. His background belies the stereotype that rap music is the pure prod-uct of ghetto life. Both he and his brother grew up in the middle-class Queens neighborhood of Hollis, an area of home-owning, upwardly mobile dreams that has flourished since the fifties on the premise that life in two-story dwell-ings with furnished basements is superior to that in the tenements and proj-ects of Brooklyn and Harlem. The parents of Hollis (and St. Albans and Ozone Park and Jamaica) were beneficiaries of the post–World War II striving for in-tegration and the opening of civil service jobs to minorities. Russell's father, Daniel, supervises a Queens school district and teaches black history at night. His mother, Evelyn, works for the Parks Department. Back in 1976, when Rus-sell enrolled at City College's Harlem campus, where he'd earn 112 credits toward a sociology degree, he seemed headed in the same direction. What was always surprising—at least to me when I attended St. John's University in the late seventies—was how fascinated with street culture the children of Hollis were. I came from Brownsville, an area that could easily have been Melle Mel's model for "The Message"; I knew "the ghetto" was nothing to romanticize. Yet here were kids like Russell, who grew up in their own houses, with access to cars, furnished basements, both parents, and more cash than my friends ever knew, acting (or trying to act) as cool as any street kid. Russell's embrace of street life, and, ultimately, his movement into it as a businessman, occurred in the CCNY lounge. There he fell in with a group of aspiring party promoters, in-cluding a brash Music & Arts senior named Kurtis Walker, who used to sneak over to CCNY when he should have been in school. Calling themselves The Force, throughout 1976–77 they gave parties in Harlem at Smalls' Paradise and the now defunct Charles Gallery. Walker, assuming the streetwise persona of Kurtis Blow, began rapping over records, influenced by the work of an older man, Pete "DJ" Jones, whose style was similar to that of boasting radio jocks like Frankie Crocker, and by DJ Hollywood, a young rapper who gigged regularly at a Bronx club called 371 and encouraged call-and-response interaction with partygoers. It is Hollywood who originated the "hip hop de hippy hop the body rock" that led to the rap-breaking-graffiti scene being labeled hip-hop.

In New York in the mid-seventies, rappers and their deejays were the nightclub equivalent of synthesizers in the recording studios. While synthesizers began replacing musicians in the studio, effectively cutting production costs, black discos with teen and young-adult audiences used rap acts to replace bands. "They were a lot cheaper and they drew the same kinds of crowds," says Russell. "Lots of times, we'd give shows with rappers and get bigger crowds than if we had a guy with just records. The more exposure you got, it seemed like the bigger your name got. The more flyers and stickers and posters that you could get your name on, the more popular you'd become as a rapper." "There was so much competition by then [1977] in rapping and deejaying uptown, Russell and I went to Queens, the boondocks, and started promoting there," remembers Kurtis Blow. Moving to Queens broadened rap's base in the city, reaching teens like Russell who were removed from ghetto life but not immune to the invention and flamboyance of its style.

Still, rap and Russell didn't hit their stride until he started promoting rap shows at the Hotel Diplomat on West Forty-third Street in 1977. The Times Square location meant that the shows could attract black teens from the outer boroughs as well as Harlem. Coinciding with this move was the brief mating of Blow and Grandmaster Flash, with Kurtis on the mike and Flash on the turntables. To promote this superstar hip-hop duo, fifteen thousand flyers were distributed and another couple of thousand stickers plastered in subways by Russell. "We had two thousand kids come see them that first night at the Diplomat," Russell recalls. "You know, people were standing outside Xenon's waiting to be picked to go in like Studio 54. And down the block you had B-boys coming down the street to go to the Diplomat two doors away." The Diplomat's shows truly helped widen rap's audience (people like Hollywood, Eddie Cheeba, and the Furious Five all eventually appeared there). Yet there was danger surrounding these shows. "We went through a lot of security companies," Russell says. "They worked one show and then the next security company would come. They'd work one show and that was it. It was like that rough.

The Diplomat had bulletproof box offices. We stayed back there for most of the night. And Kurtis"—Russell starts to laugh—"would always come in the box office and stand around. When it was time to go onstage, he'd run up there and perform and come right back in."

The insular, occasionally violent world of rap was changed forever in the summer of 1979 when first the Fatback Band's "King Tim III" and, most profoundly, the Sugarhill Gang's "Rapper's Delight" hit the streets. The success of "Rapper's Delight," by three kids with only a tenuous connection to the original rap scene, shocked the established rappers. "There was a show in October or November in the Armory in Queens," Blow remembers. "We had, like, four thousand kids. All the original rappers were there and 'Rapper's Delight' was a big hit. Starski said on the mike, 'Yeah, y'all know we're still gonna be on the moon.' We all resented it. Everybody hated it. Now I see that they opened the doors for us and I'm grateful now. But at that time I was so furious."

I first met Russell and Kurtis in the offices of *Billboard* in the summer of 1979. *Billboard* staffer Rocky Ford and J. B. Moore had brought them up to the office to talk about making a rap record. Rocky had written the first piece in the established media about rap, a funny little story in *Billboard* prior to "Rapper's Delight," and, with help from me, then a St. John's University student working part-time at the *Amsterdam News* and freelancing for *Billboard*, had been researching the rap scene. He and Moore had decided to work with Kurtis, because compared to Grandmaster Flash, Starski, and the other original rappers, he was the most clean-cut and articulate. And he had Russell, someone who knew the rap scene and was itching to learn the record business. Looking back on it now, I know that Russell's presence was as important as Kurtis's talent in getting them to invest their then meager resources in a record about Santa Claus in Harlem. "Christmas Rappin'" would eventually sell nearly a million copies. Six years ago Russell was even more frantic than he is now, partly because he was doing a lot of drugs (he says solemnly that those days are over) and partly because he was just one overactive, anxious young man. Every meeting with him was like being injected with a thousand cc's of adrenaline. His energy fascinated me, though our friendship had its rough spots. One night he left me stranded in Long Island following a Kurtis Blow gig at some Hempstead dump. Another time he took me to the Disco Fever in the days before it became a musical tourist trap and left me in a room full of coked-up stickup kids and rappers.

What redeemed our friendship was that despite his occasional lapses, Russell was the only guy on the rap scene who seemed to have any long-term goals. He was serious where his contemporaries just wanted to party. Everybody wanted to make records. But did everybody realize what promotion and marketing to the nonrap audience would entail? Did they realize that if rap was successful, they'd be approached by record industry pros, people who didn't give a fuck about anything except their ability to make a quick buck? Russell did. In fact, it used to drive him crazy. He'd call me or Rocky at any time of the day or night to complain about how someone was trying to serve him or his artist. In his early twenties Russell was trying to woo finicky reporters, get his money from small-time concert promoters, and make the major labels pay attention to him. His paperwork was sloppy. He slept in the recording studios. He told his skeptical parents he'd made the right decision in leaving school. He was happiest when he talked about the music he wanted to make. Not the "pop-rap" Ford and Moore were making for Kurtis, but "beat" records that captured the feel of clubs like the Fever.

It wasn't until Russell teamed with ex–jazz bassist Larry Smith, creator of the bass line of "The Breaks" and Ford's childhood chum, that he had someone who could translate his beat fanaticism into music. Together they made two recordings that would change New York street music: Jimmy Spicer's humorous, Jimmy Castor–influenced rap "The Bubble Bunch" and Orange Krush's "Action," which featured Alyson Williams's sensual shouting. The key to both was the "bubba bubba tap" rhythms of drummer Trevor Gale, a chucky bass drum stop that has become standard for rap music (e.g., "It's Like That").

Another child of "Action" and "Bubble Bunch" is L.L. Cool J's "I Need a Beat," the first record on Def Jam Recordings, an indie label started by the record producer Rick Rubin that Russell is now a partner in. The drum machine is slow and, as Russell says, "sleazy," the cymbal is hot, and the other instruments serve to intensify the rhythm. It's a record for dancers who know that the spaces between the beats aren't really spaces, but sounds of pleasure where your body—suspended in action, chilly in motion—awaits its guidance to slide over a few soul-satisfying inches. It is a statement of principle that says Russell and Rubin are going right for the core B-boy audience.

Def Jam is also very much a product of Russell's economic frustrations. Executives at the major companies have refused to believe in rap or the long-term creativity of its makers. When Blow signed with Mercury in 1979, I assumed every label would have at least one rap act within two years. Instead, rap acts have come and gone from the roster of the corporate music machines because these organizations, very often advised by their black executives, have shown no interest in or outright contempt for the music.

Epic's rap history is illustrative. Back in 1980 the company released a 7-inch (7-inch!) single by DJ Hollywood featuring a cooing girl chorus, then didn't promote it. Hollywood is a legend in this city, yet rap's pioneer was quickly forgotten at Black Rock, headquarters on West Fifty-second Street. When Epic briefly distributed Aaron Fuch's Tuff City rap label in 1983, they had Davy DMX's "One for the Treble," a beat-box record by an ex–Kurtis Blow spinner and prolific hip-hop songwriter-musician. It was an instant B-boy classic, as fresh as Run-D.M.C.'s "It's Like That." Yet "One for the Treble" sold about 80,000 copies for Tuff City while "It's Like That" did approximately 250,000 for Profile. The difference? Epic didn't see the potential in the music and couldn't be bothered with what it saw as an experiment. Subsequently Run-D.M.C.'s debut album sold over 500,000, a genuine RIAA gold record, because president Cory Robbins and Russell worked the 12-inches "It's Like That"/"Sucker M.C.'s," "Hard Times"/"Jam Master Jay," "Rock Box," and "30 Days" with the zeal of a major label; promoted Run-D.M.C.'s black hats and leather to give them an iconic image (cf. Jackson's glove and Cyndi Lauper's hair); and reached out to the substantial hip white audience that—very much like reggae's white aficionados—identify with its raw, outlaw attitude. Arista did (eventually) get behind the English label Jive and its efforts to win a U.S. audience for the rap duo Whodini. As a result, Whodini's Larry Smith–produced *Escape* went gold. Representative of Jive's commitment is that Whodini has had four videos in support of two albums while Blow, with five albums at Poly-Gram and a steady seller of 100,000 to 300,000 units, just got his first for his current single "Basketball."

Russell's dream has been for all his acts to be signed to one label that he controlled. Under the aegis of PolyGram's late black-music vice president, Bill Haywood, it almost happened. But after Haywood's death in 1983, the remaining executives, white and black, didn't understand the music or deal. Jimmy Spicer's "Bubble Bunch" and Orange Krush's "Action" were released on Mercury. The failure of both commercially outside the New York area definitely hastened Russell's hair loss. After those records, the arrangement died of corporate malnutrition. As a result, Rush's acts are now strung across the roster of several, mostly independent, labels: Profile, Jive, Mercury, Disco Fever, Nia, and now Def Jam. As a result, most of the acts live from record to record. When Russell brags, "None of our records have ever lost money," he doesn't mention just how essential that situation has been to his economic well-being.

Ex-indie Sugarhill Records, now distributed by MCA, once dominated the rap market with an enviable in-house setup: a two-story building in Englewood, New Jersey, contacts to record distributors going back over a decade (Sugarhill owners Joe and Sylvia Robinson once owned All-Platinum and control the Chess catalog), a brilliant house band that will one day be regarded as the Booker T. & the MG's of the early eighties. While Russell was still building his roster of rappers, Sugarhill Records, with the Sugarhill Gang, Grandmaster Flash and the Furious Five, Spoonie Gee, and Sequence defined the music's cutting edge. The grooves were varied and, except for streaks of unabashed sexism, the raps were always clever. But the across-the-board acceptance of Grandmaster Flash and the Furious Five's "The Message" in 1983 ended up hurting the label. In its wake Grandmaster Flash exited to Elektra records after a lawsuit over money and creative control. So did many musicians, such as "Message" cowriter Duke Bootee, who signed with PolyGram, and Reggie Griffin, who signed with Qwest Records and arranged Chaka Khan's "I Feel for You." Only the brilliant Melle Mel, with his caustic, biblical attack on racism and corruption, and commanding delivery, remains a vital sales and creative force for Sugarhill.

Sugarhill's loss was Russell's gain as young rappers who might have gravitated to the Jersey label instead turned to Rush Productions. For a time it looked as if Afrika Bambaataa's space-rap sound, through his liaison with Tom Silverman's aggressive Tommy Boy label, would succeed Sugarhill's. But after "Planet Rock" and "Looking for the Perfect Beat," innovative recordings coproduced by Arthur Baker and John Robie and heavily influenced by Kraftwerk, Bambaataa's been a commercial bust. His collaborations with Material, Johnny Rotten, and other "new music" types have given him a high media profile, but his terrible misuse of James Brown on "Unity" illustrated why Bambaataa hasn't tapped the hip-hop soul in almost two years. As a result, the most significant rap hits of the past two years have been in some way connected to Rush Productions. He and Smith coproduced both Run-D.M.C. albums; Smith produced Whodini and Blow produced the Fat Boys. The hottest rap 12-inch of 1985, UTFO's "Roxanne, Roxanne" was produced by the Brooklyn band Full Force, who've written for and played on the last two Kurtis Blow albums and whose manager, Steven Salem, once shared office space with Rush.

It's an incestuous little world that Russell works in, one he feels has values and attitudes that aren't understood by outsiders. To him that's the reason rap and New York street music in general haven't yet been embraced by the music industry mainstream. Significantly, Russell doesn't call his music "rap" or "street" but "black teenage music." He sees his records not as part of a genre but a statement from a new generation—a generation, coincidentally, that puts great stock in machismo.

To Russell, for example, the reason there are so few female rappers "is that the most progressive forms of music are too hard-edged for women. What do heavy metal and wrestling say about women? I ask that because rap has the same kind of audience and feeling to it. But you'll never hear any of our artists rapping about getting over on a woman in a vulgar way. You can listen to all the records I've been involved in and not hear that stuff about busting out young girls in them. We already have this bad image with black program directors about the country, so I'm very careful about what I say. I'd do a record like 'No Sell Out' [a rap record on Tommy Boy using excerpts from Malcolm X speeches] if I could make it work. A good track could support any idea. But I'm not gonna lecture the audience. I'm not a teacher. I make music based on the ideas my artist gives me. If Run wants to do 'Hard Times' or 'It's Like That,' I'm gonna help them make it work. The only thing I ask is that it have an edge. Teenage music is rebellious."

To his taste, most mainstream black pop is "too polished, too slick." "I like real-sounding music, real-sounding instruments—even our drum machines sound hard, and I like loud music. Music feels good loud," he says, explaining why on "Rock Box" and most of the *King of Rock* he employed black rock guitarist Eddie Martinez to such crunching effect. "I can't help it if it's called rock 'n' roll. It's still B-boy music. It still has breaks, it still has def beats. The difference between white teenage music like Quiet Riot or AC/DC and black teenage music right now isn't that big."

Russell has been very open-minded about building bridges between the uptown scene and the more progressive white rock clubs. Before it was fashionable, he was hanging out at Disco Fever and Danceteria, rapping with Melle Mel at 1:00 a.m. and Malcolm McLaren at 4:00 a.m. So when he looks you in the eye and says excitedly, "I want to produce Devo," you don't bust out laughing, but ask, quite respectfully, why? "I believe I could make Devo def. Hear me, I'd make Devo def. I love all those sounds they make. Don't like the songs. But I could fix them and make them def."

Looking ahead five years, Russell hopes he'll "be able to pay for this loft I want and have four or five major stars. I'll be involved in black teenage music if I still understand it. I might not be able to still make it. I at least hope I'll understand what's good about it enough to hire someone who does." Russell stops, pauses a minute, then adds, "I want to make successful black heroes, like what I've tried to do with Run-D.M.C. and Kurtis. I didn't say 'positive' because that's a trap. It's got to be real."

"Russell Simmons is a bloodsucker," a prominent record producer tells me in late February. "That's the feedback I'm getting on him, man. They say he's unorganized and that his artists would be better off somewhere else." Then the producer laughs. "You know what that means, man, it's character assassination. They are after him. He has a thing going. When it was that street level, selling 12-inches on indie labels, they left him alone. But now rap is selling LPs. Run-

D.M.C. and Whodini have broken in the rock and black markets. The Fat Boys are a novelty act that works. So now the industry is coming after him just like they did to George Clinton, Gamble and Huff, and every black music entrepreneur. If his shit isn't together, they'll take everything that isn't nailed down."

By March my friend has proved prophetic. Larry Smith, another Queens native who has explored the darkest corners of the South Bronx with Russell, has signed his publishing to Jive's Zomba Music for a large advance. Unfortunately, Russell has promised that publishing to another company as part of another deal, putting Russell in an embarrassing, potentially litigable position. Aggravating the tension is that Larry agreed to produce the sound track for Cannon's rap film. The two are still friends, and outside the Beacon Theatre where Run-D.M.C. recently headlined, they could be seen embracing. For Larry they were good business moves, which didn't prevent them from taking the smile off Russell's face. They were a signal to him that his rap kingdom was hardly secure.

There were more lessons to come. While negotiating with a major record label for a production deal, he made the tactical error of including a group in his proposal he has a business relationship with but no papers on. The company does some checking and the next thing Russell knows that group is cutting its own deal. In the world of rap 'n' roll neither the record label nor the group was wrong. They were trying to do the best they could for themselves. Russell left a loophole, the kind he can't afford anymore.

Russell is taking all this with surprising calm. He understands his mistakes and is trying to tighten his operation. In the last six months he's added a number of administrative staffers, and he's seeking larger offices. Andre Harrell has quit his day job as a time salesman at WINS to become vice president of Rush with an eye toward nailing down some of the endorsements the company is being offered. Russell may be a bit shaken by the wheeling and dealing swirling around him, but that only brings out the Eddie Murphy in him. I mention one of the people in the industry who questions Russell's business acumen.

"That guy can only suck my dick when he sees me," he tells me with a conspiratorial chuckle. "I'm invaluable to the success of his company. He never says that to my face. I'd serve him." We laugh, and I tell him to save that crap for the next Run-D.M.C. album.

As *Billboard*'s black-music editor, I interact daily with sleaze, stars, starfuckers, and a few honest businessmen and musicians. All of them are out to make money. So is Russell. But in Russell there is a love of music, at least his particular brand of it, that is real. Like another middle-class hustler with good ears, Berry Gordy, Russell Simmons is trying to build something that will last. I'm not totally convinced it will happen. So much rests on the durability and continued evolution of a decidedly radical musical style. One of Russell's favorite sayings comes from Dr. Jeckyll: "Inside of every suppressed black man is an angry nigger." I suspect that as long as Russell believes that and promotes music that sounds like it, homeboy will be all right. Even if he is from Queens.

The Village Voice / April 30, 1985

Teddy Riley's New Jack Swing

BARRY MICHAEL COOPER

This is the story of a new Harlem Renaissance—on floppy disk.

My mother told me that when I was about eight months old,
I climbed on top of this old record player, turned it on
somehow, and stood on the turntable, going around and
around. She said I was trying to find out where the sound
was coming from.
                                                    —Teddy Riley

'Round and 'round I go . . .

The bass kicking from the Kenwood in the golden Acura Legend shook
126th Street like an earthquake traveling on Pirelli tires. The line of special
guests, amateur-night contestants, and groupies grew longer and longer,
stretching like a dancing, human inchworm from the Apollo backstage doors to
Eighth Avenue. Every time a Euro/Asian big-money sedan passed the anxious
crowd—music sweeping over and beyond darkened power windows—they began to dance, hunching their shoulders and jerking their bodies in short, ab-

breviated versions of the James Brown. It was like the best block party diced up into five-second segments.

"Groove me/(Ah yeah)/Baby/Tonight . . ."

A triple-white Milano zoomed down 126th Street, then slowed to a stylish cruise, and the crowd started to shimmy to its music. The driver—who looked young enough to be in junior high school—wore a tan leather baseball cap with the insignia MCM (Germany's Modern Creations of Munchen, the emblem that has replaced Gucci as the inner city youth's status advertisement) and a *My Uzi Is My Best Friend* sweatshirt. He stared straight ahead, hunching his shoulders and rocking in his lumbar-contoured seat.

"Gina, ain't that Gee-Money from One Hundred and Twenty-second Street?" a slim if wide-hipped girl in a white Le Coq Sportif sweatsuit and monstrous gold shrimp earrings asked. "Nah, that ain't Gee-Money," answered Gina, a tall, attractive girl wearing a green Nike warm-up suit and around her neck a gold cable thick enough to tow cars or beat elephants. "Gee-Money got a thin beard and whatnot. That's just a baby driving that Milano. Plus, this boy got that low-budget Milano; Gee-Money got that Platinum Level Milano." "Word," Gina's friend verified. After freaking the crowd for the mandatory five seconds, the young kid and his weak Milano—*only* the $20,000 Gold Level, not the $26,000 Platinum—sped west toward St. Nicholas Avenue.

Tonight, September 15, was the taping for the late-night TV extravaganza *It's Showtime at the Apollo* (NBC). Since it was a freebie, the theater got very crowded, very fast; everybody wanted to sit up front or in the balconies that framed the stage. It promised to be a high-powered show, with Guy, Al B. Sure!, Pebbles, and Kool and the Gang on the bill. The crowd was getting fidgety, because the once balmy weather had turned chilly, and the person who had the guest list was already thirty minutes late.

"Where's that stunt with the guest?" Gina's friend spat. "It's gettin' cold out here." "Word," Gina chuckled. "But why you gotta break on the girl like that? She just doin' her job, and whatnot." Gina's friend feigned anger, her voice growing shrill. "Wha's up, you her lawyer now?! The bitch is late. We tryin' to get in and see the show and I got a little something to do with Al B. Sure! before he goes onstage, to help that pretty boy sing better." We all laughed, while she mockingly rolled her eyes. Our appreciation must have been some sort of cue, because Gina and her friend broke into an impromptu routine.

"Oh," Gina said, "I guess you gonna *help* him out like you *helped* Biz Markie out that time backstage." Gina's friend displayed no embarrassment at this disclosure. She wore her sexual aggressiveness like a police badge. "Yo," Gina's friend answered matter-of-factly. "I just whispered a *little something* in his ear." We broke into giggles until a hush came over the line of star-worshipers-screwers-wannabes.

A cliché black stretch limo pulled up. The door opened, and out popped a diminutive, handsome young man wearing enough gold to throw England's bullion market out of whack. He was impeccably dressed in a rust-colored de-signer shirt and pants outfit, sleek brown lizard penny loafers with solid gold buckles across the vamp. There was the obligatory gold cable hula-hooping his neck. For young gangsters and their facsimiles, here's the new jack talisman, warding off the evils of poverty, failure, and longevity—eternity is only a bul-let's breath or crack-toke away. So this is about living now, *money*, and living large. But there was something different about this young man, something el-egant, something graceful. He exuded a gangster's confidence, but he also had a scholarly self-absorption about him, like Kant mesmerized by the church's steeple. The crowd got hyped.

"Oooh, Teddy Riley! He's so cute I wanna take him home!"

Gina's friend, licking her lips, took on the look of a python.

"Oooh, *I want him*, yup-yup . . ."

Teddy Riley, leader of Guy, simultaneously bathed himself in the adoration and ignored it all. He grinned, shook my hand. "Yo man, why you waitin' in line?" He grabbed my elbow and led me away from the starstruck captives. "We outta here, man."

Gina's friend tapped me on the shoulder before I walked away. "I'll do anything for an autograph, word."

* * * * * *

Teddy Riley finds sanctuary in the recording studio, at home with his family, and behind the wheel of his red BMW. He writes songs in his BMW; he previews new tunes for his friends in his BMW. The BMW as solace seems strange, but only if you are aware of the environment that Teddy comes from.

The half-mile stretch of Eighth Avenue between 125th and 135th streets, right around the corner from the Thirty-second Precinct, is one of drugs, poverty, and contract murders (often executed on dopeboys sitting in the driver's seats of luxury cars). The stretch tends to fool people because of the urban renewal of the Lionel and Gladys Hampton Houses beautifying the area, but those that live here realize this place can be little Beirut. This was a place where things always *happened*.

It's a little quieter now, but during the late seventies–early eighties, it was one of the city's major heroin/cocaine bazaars. I remember watching one junkie using a Louisville Slugger to open up the back of another one's head like a brown egg, right on 125th Street, and a crew of young, white undercover cops shut down all of 129th Street between Eighth and St. Nicholas, as if they were filming *Starsky and Hutch*. Small, glassine bags of white powder, stamped "Wizard," "Snowball," and "Blue Magic," littered the sidewalk and street. I often heard about bodies turning up in the courtyard and stairwells of the St. Nicholas projects, or the St. Nick.

Teddy Riley heard about them, too, because he lived in the St. Nick. As a matter of fact, he knew a few of the corpses. Some were buddies; the dopeboys, the lullaby specialists—hit men paid to put heads into eternal sleep—the young guys who wore the Damon knits and Caron-Champagne cologne from A. J. Lester's on 125th Street, and drove Mercedes-Benzes and BMWs before they left high school. Gangsters taught Riley how to play basketball on the courts on the Seventh Avenue side of the St. Nick, or up on "the Terrace"—Hamilton Terrace, setting for the action in Kool Moe Dee's "Wild Wild West" and Spoonie Gee's "Hit Man." (Riley had a major hand in both songs.)

Gangsters, a few years older than he, took up the fourteen-year-old in fights, sheltering him from the street, from *them*. Instead, they ordered him to stay in school, and to *come off like the Feds* with his music.

"I never saw any violence," Teddy said. "Violence around me had either started or ended by the time I got to the scene. I had a lot of people looking out for me. Guys like Big Al, Stanley, Dwight, and Little Shaun, until he got shot. We all rolled together. And even if they were into the street, they kept me out of it." So, with the loving and steady hand of his mother, Mildred, his stepfather, Edward, his godfather, Gene Griffin (now his manager and consigliere), and friends, Riley stayed out of trouble and into his music.

Guy's dressing room was on the Apollo's third floor. Painted pink, with big windows, it was cramped but comfortable. Kevin Mathis, Guy's choreographer and lead dancer known as Shake, was dressing for the evening's performance. His brother, Chris, a rapper and a dancer known as K-Loose, was putting mousse on his hair in the bathroom. Shake has to be one of the best street choreographers in the business. With freaky dope maneuvers learned on the street corner and in the rap clubs, he's the one who turns the house and block parties out. He's responsible for a lot of the latest dances: the Shaka-Zulu, the Gucci, and the coolest dance on the set today, the James Brown (the funky chicken, the jerk, and the namesake's sliding shuffle). Shake also choreographed the frenzy in the club sequence of Johnny Kemp's video "Just Got Paid," a Teddy Riley track.

Nearly a half hour before showtime, and the dressing room was crowded. Guy is a sizable band—two dancers, two background singers, a drummer, four keyboard players (including Riley, who also sings backup), and two lead vocalists—and it seems like a cast of thousands. While waiting for Guy's stage call, lead singer Aaron Hall III passed time by cutting cameos—a mod, cubist Afro derived not only from the heads of Grace Jones and Cameo's Larry Blackmon, but from the ancient busts and funerary masks of the African Benin and Ibo peoples—and was doing better than a lot of professional barbers. With his mahogany good looks, muscular physique, and sinewy melismata—that gospel yodel-warble, the stamp of a powerful soul singer when not overdone—this young man might go down in the record books with Sam, Otis, and Jackie. Not only a masterful singer and formidable keyboardist, he cowrote Bobby Brown's "My Prerogative" with Gene Griffin. He also wrote the potentially classic ballad "Goodbye Love," on *Guy* (MCA), the group's recent debut LP.

If Hall can handle the fame, a rich career seems certain. But so many gospel singers who cross the line into secular wickedness—R & B and pop—go on to mutilate themselves, as an act of repentance for turning their backs on God the Father Almighty in Heaven. (Every member in Guy comes right out of the church, and the oldest of them is twenty-four.) Aaron shares the singing spotlight in Guy with his brother Damion, and they're the sons of the popular Brooklyn minister Aaron Hall, Jr. A protégé of the Winans and James L. Cleveland, Aaron III doesn't show signs of unraveling, and the church still has a powerful tug.

"I'm going to do a gospel album," Hall said. "Gospel and the church are my roots, my foundation, and I'm definitely going back."

Teddy Riley came back in the dressing room and said, "Yo, you cutting hair? I could have saved twenty dollars, man."

Hall said, "I should stop singing and just cut hair."

The control room backstage was jam-packed. Performers for the amateur-night segment paced back and forth, puffed Kools, talked at 78 rpm. Friends, family, and observers of the headliners glued their eyes to the TV monitor. Kool and the Gang were winding up their *Showtime at the Apollo* lip-synch performance of "Rags to Riches," which sounded like a throwaway from Earth, Wind & Fire. With the departure of lead singer James "J.T." Taylor, and their reluctance to couple the raw funk of "Hollywood Swinging" or "Funky Stuff" with the pop success of "Celebration," Kool and the Gang looked like they were going through the motions. The crowd's applause was courteous.

Next was current king of the charts, Mr. Al B. Sure! I'm not certain about his voice—he sounded a bit off-key at times—but B. Sure! had undeniable presence and the light-skinned, mulatto looks that many women go crazy for. "High yalla" tones and a "good grade" of hair are things that black people don't want to speak on, but as Spike Lee's *School Daze* depicts, that racially twisted itch still scratches my people the wrong way.

Al B. Sure! was up there, though, to get famous, get paid, wet some panties, and kick bass, not genetics. In his toe-up jeans, he wiggled, squiggled, and screeched through the irresistibly dark synth-orchestrations of "Rescue Me," making the girls at the Apollo *bug*. When four of them jumped onstage and began humping on his thighs, butt, and hips, B. Sure! cooperated with the eros of the moment and *skeezed* them. Then he turned vicious.

With all of his might, he humped each one of them away, the last girl so hard that she toppled off the stage, which drew a shocked "Oh shit!" reaction from the audience, and in the control room. It was a move that jumped up out of nowhere, the epitome of surprise. An exciting show has a way of dulling rationality without narcotics, bringing out the masochist in a crowd, especially if a pretty boy is inflicting the pain. So when B. Sure! — in his best jimmy-grabbing, Michael Jackson grimace — told the girls, "All the ladies in the house, say Al," you know what the young ladies did.

When Guy was performing, the members of Kool and the Gang, as well as everyone else in the control room, were up on their feet dancing. In this lip-synched performance, the music was razor sharp and tight-computerized, digital hokeypokey. His recordings have a "live concert" feel. As Riley, Damion, Shake, and K-Loose stepped with the precision of an avant-garde militia, Aaron Hall belted out "'Round and 'Round (Merry Go 'Round of Love)," the second single from *Guy*.

An older stagehand, who had seen everyone from Dinah Washington to Luther Vandross become legends, shouted, "Hey, the *funk* is back, baby!" Bassist Robert "Kool" Bell nodded in agreement as he shuffled and watched the TV monitor Etch A Sketch a figure of his group's past and future.

Teddy Riley was born on October 8, 1967. His whirl around the turntable as an infant must have been one of God's metaphors. At four, he was playing complex piano pieces by ear. At six, he had his first manager. "Teddy was in a group called Total Climax," says Gene Griffin, who was then a talent agent. "He was only six years old at the time, but I knew he was a genius. I became his manager." To this day, when Griffin makes suggestions, Riley listens carefully. Not many in or out of the industry bestow the same courtesy on the bald and nattily dressed Griffin. Whispers follow him like a shadow: murderer, drug czar, crime-boss-cum-record-magnate who don't take no shorts. The forty-five-year-old Griffin—a powerful, barrel-chested man—is not a murderer, but he did sell drugs.

Griffin, who grew up in Harlem's Sugar Hill and majored in music at Howard University, ran his own record label, the Sound of New York, which had the hit "Last Night a DJ Saved My Life" by Indeep. He admits he erred: "I did sell drugs at one time, and it was the biggest mistake of my life. Two years ago I went to jail for alleged possession of drugs—there were never any drugs found on my person—and served two years of a six-to-ten sentence. Now I have completely turned my life around. I don't smoke, drink, or do drugs. I can stand the frisk, because my life is as clean as the president's."

Even when Griffin wasn't around, he made sure Riley was looked after. At nine, Riley was the organist at the Little Flowers Baptist Church on Eighth Avenue near 133rd Street. He left Little Flowers because "everybody was too busy talking about each other, instead of getting into the *word*," and joined the Universal Temple of Spiritual Truths on 136th Street. There, Riley added, he had some of his happiest childhood memories. "We used to go a lot of places," he said, "and play a lot of churches out of town. We also used to go on a lot of trips, like Disney World, and other places. I felt very protected there."

By the time Teddy Riley was ten years old, he was a solid musician. With other boys, he played keyboards on 121st between First and Second avenues for nickels and dimes, drawing huge crowds. By then Riley had six instruments down cold: guitar, bass, several horns. In the daytime, he went to P.S. 195, where he learned the three Rs and ran wild during the lunch hour with his buddy, Doug E. Fresh. At night, he would play the smoky Harlem nightclubs with Total Climax—the Red Rooster, Lickety Split, Smalls', even the upscale Cellar Restaurant on 95th Street. It was on the club circuit that he met Bahamian transplant Johnny Kemp, who was with the group Kinky Fox, and Keith

Sweat, who was with the bar-band Jamilah. In the clubs Riley learned how to please the crowd and how to improvise, turning bits of keyboard vamps into compositions.

"At first, the crowd would do a double take," Griffin said, "at this little kid on a stack of telephone books—he was so small then—playing the piano like an adult. The club owners turned their heads the other way, because Teddy was bringing in business."

As a freshman at Martin Luther King High School, Riley played with the senior band. After having some "static" with another student—"One of my boys from St. Nick was getting jumped by this crew," Riley told me without going into the details, "and I just wasn't going to stand there and let them beat my man down"—he left MLK and finished high school at Park West, where he became very interested in rap music. He was a good student, but "was bored in class. I couldn't stop thinking about the music."

After high school, Griffin enrolled his godson in a summer composition and theory course at Columbia, and a few electronic-music classes at the Manhattan School of Music. Following class, Riley would go up to the Bronx River Project with his drum machine and Casio keyboard and jam with the MCs and DJs in the courtyard. Admittedly, he was nervous about going to the spawning ground of hip-hop music—"Yo, some of the knuckleheads was always trying to *house* my beat box and Casio." Confrontations notwithstanding, it was in Bronx River that the young man mixed rap, gospel, jazz, funk, go-go, and gothic-romanticism by way of synthesizers. After worshiping and playing in several churches, playing and learning in several playgrounds and music classes, he found the elements to put together a totally new form of R & B. I call it the New Jack Swing.

Standing on the patio of Teddy Riley's rooftop condo-on-the-Hudson, I could hear the music of a new era. If Hendrix, Brown, Stone, and Gaye are the starting point, and Prince the bridge, Teddy Riley is the other side. Many stars are biting the New Jack Swing, including producers Jimmy Jam and Terry Lewis—there's a story that when they presented New Edition's latest album to an MCA honcho, he wouldn't accept it until they had the "Teddy Riley sound on some of the tracks," a sound you can now hear on the group's hit "If It Isn't Love."

Everybody wants to get paid. Deborah Harry's getting the New Jack Swing treatment on a rerelease of "Rapture," Boy George is slated for a Teddy Riley–Gene Griffin production, and there's a Riley tune on the Jacksons' next album called "She."

Riley's music is full of historical references. If you ask him whom he listens to, he'll tell you Herbie Hancock, Chick Corea, P-Funk—his faves—and Big Daddy Kane, but the orchestras of Ellington, Oliver, and Basie play in his head, and he doesn't even know it. In ten years, God willing, I'll listen to the Classical Two's "New Generation," or Kool Moe Dee's "Go See the Doctor," or Keith Sweat's "I Want Her," all Riley works, and think about the sexual terrorist-trauma of the AIDS epidemic, or fifteen-year-old students toting Uzis and cellular phones in their bookbags. As Fitzgerald's Nick Carraway watched the flappers, gangsters, and social climbers shout "Yowsah!" while spinning around and down the gin-filled toilet and pegged it as the "hour of profound human change," so does the updated Teddy Riley, who paints this decade as "Monster Crack." A time of minor chords, dark clouds, and a beat so hard and relentless, it makes me wonder—does Riley have the heart of a killer under his friendly smiling face? Can you really be sheltered from the savagery of the street? Or do you just try to internalize, to cage the rage?

In Riley's case, I think the latter is true. The synthesized orchestral punches of Sweat's "I Want Her" are not used to soothe; they scream, they shake, they frighten you. Then when I heard the nagging bass line of "Groove Me," I knew I was listening to pure gangster music. Riley used the verbal animus of rap to enter his beastmaster subconscious, and when he found himself inside, he slammed the door and swallowed the key.

The first time I tried to dance to "Groove Me," I got more than hot and sweaty, I tired. Riley has so many things happening at once—bass lines, strings, multileveled percussion tracks, computerized samples from James Brown and Stax records. Then there are Riley's own street mantras: *yup-yup* and *that's it, that's it.* This is a polyrhythmic community turned vigilante. There is no space to breathe in Riley's music. The orchestration slams you, the drums tear out your heart. Riley's music is *RoboCop* funk, in full effect; go-go music gunned down by rap and electronics, then rebuilt with more vicious beats, an in-charge, *large* attitude. I hear that hubris on Moe Dee's "How Ya Like Me Now," the ultimate yuppie-buppie-million-dollar-lottery-winner-new-jack-nouveau-riche anthem, and I hear it on Doug E. Fresh's "The Show," a hip-hop landmark Riley wrote but didn't want credit for. Riley's New Jack Swing is indestructible.

And I heard it in Riley's $200,000 digital home recording studio, while he worked the last of the keyboard overdubs on Stephanie Mills's next single, "Fast Talk." Inside the plush, black and gray carpeted area—once the condo's living room—he has ceiling-high stacks of gleaming machines, their red and orange lights blipping soundlessly above the piano keyboards. Chlorine-blue VDT screens visually isolated separate instrumental tracks.

Riley sat like Huxley behind the master mixing board of his *Brave New World*, oblivious to everything except his six-month-old daughter, DeJanee, in the arms of his younger brother Tito. When she called out, "Da-Da," he ran over to kiss the pretty little doll, then hustled back and scooted into the slit between the keyboards and computers. He rifled through a silver Halliburton case, searching for one beat among the thousand-plus he keeps stored on floppy disks. Riley worked quietly and very fast—writing not just the drums and bass line or melody in step-by-step fashion, but using the computer to focus on the mass, the entire work.

Griffin said Riley "thought up 'Fast Talk' while he and I were driving home one night from a dinner downtown. We were riding through Central Park, and he stopped the BMW on Ninty-sixth Street. It took me by surprise when he opened the door and got out. I thought he was sick or something. I asked him, 'What's wrong? You okay?' He tapped on the hood of the car for a few minutes, and then he jumped back inside. 'I just thought of this new song,' he said, 'and I gotta hurry home.' By the time we got back to the house, he hummed the en-tire song, from beginning to end, in less than a half hour."

On a Friday night, September 23, there was a crowd of people at the Apollo's backstage entrance trying to get in and see Guy's live set. Rap stars peppered the crowd—Big Daddy Kane (the current heavyweight speak-ician and scientist), Heavy D, Pepa. Inside, there were more celebs, like soul crooner Glenn Jones, whom Riley is about to produce, and the stone-faced Eric B., who carried a baseball bat, presumably to discourage any new jack's ideas about trying to snatch the massive gold cable that hung around his collarbone.

Noticeably absent were Keith Sweat and Al B. Sure!, two chart-toppers who, in whole or in part, have benefited from Riley's New Jack Swing. There's a nasty feud going on between the Riley-Griffin camps and those of Sweat and Sure! and his manager, Andre Harrell. This situation is most unfortunate, because a lot of major talent is being distracted. Sweat's breakthrough last year, *Make It Last Forever*, went platinum, and Riley's contribution to it is much in dispute. Some say Riley, who received producer and writer credits on the LP jacket, was only a "rhythm and groove" man. Others say he was the auteur, period.

In the case of Mount Vernon's Al Brown—aka Al B. Sure!—there were aesthetic differences between Brown and Riley, hired as producer of *In Effect Mode*, among the year's best pop albums. The disagreements between Riley and Brown became so intense that Riley left the project. After that, accusations were made that Riley walked off with "You Can Call Me Crazy," an original tune Sure! claims to have written. The song's on side one of *Guy*. In retribution, Riley's people say, Sure!'s manager, Harrell, pocketed "If I'm Not Your Lover," which Riley claims to have written, arranged, and produced. (He's given an arranger credit on *In Effect Mode*.) Each side of the dispute denies the accusations of the opposing camp. The legalities are yet to be ironed out, but all serious fans of New York's music are wishing for a truce.

Besides, it didn't matter who was or wasn't in the Apollo audience, not this night anyway. Riley had other things to worry about. Tonight was no lip-synch to a record. This show was the real McCoy. Would the wireless mikes go dead during their performance? Would the sound people overamplify the keyboards and drown out the vocals? Would the crowd understand funk this thick? Would Aaron's dream he had earlier in the week, which he hoped to dramatize, work in reality? Could Guy take it to the stage? Riley fingered the gold Gucci link necklace, closed his eyes, and said a silent prayer. He'd find out in fifteen minutes.

After the reggae-rap tease of Shelly Thunder, a young Bronx-via-Jamaica lady who has a killer grassroots hit, "Kuff," Guy came on the Apollo stage wrapped in smoke; strains of digital violas, cellos, and violins; and silky, druidic capes. The crowd went crazy, especially the young girls. Aaron Hall, seated in the audience (following the script of his dream), finally jumped out of the crowd and joined the group. Guy broke into Zapp's "More Bounce to the Ounce." This showcased Riley's frightening keyboard ability. He tore into the keys, spinning gospel and jazz runs all over the place.

I hadn't seen a show like this since P-Funk played the Garden September 10, 1977, when Riley was a ten-year-old, jamming in the St. Nick. Backup singers Khadejia Bass and Michelle Hammond wailed in the background, Abe Fogle brought drumsticks down from the sky, Bernard Belle, Arcell Vickers, and Dinky Bingham snatched a holiness-stomp symphony from their heads and their hard-disk memory banks. Shake and K-Loose dazzled us with space-age steps. While helping out on syndrums, Damion Hall harmonized with brother Aaron like they were back in church. Riley conducted this New Jack Swing session; it was like watching P-Funk, Kraftwerk, Weather Report, the New York Philharmonic, and Blue Magic blur.

After Aaron ripped off his shirt and started to hump the floor, many young women ran up to the stage and drooled. Among them was the young woman, Gina's friend, I saw outside the backstage entrance two weeks ago. In a sprayed-on minidress stretched tight over her ample butt, she screamed, "I want the church boy!" A woman in front of me shouted, "Yo, baby, you got them condoms?" Another woman shouted, "Later for them condoms, you need a scuba outfit for that bitch!" The entire front row—even the victim of this Apollo vitriol—cracked up.

Yup-yup, Guy were devastating. They ripped. I guess they don't know that young black men from Harlem are not supposed to put on shows like this. Society says young black men from Harlem are murderers, dope sellers, losers. Any other category is an aberration. True enough, Teddy Riley is an aberration. With a loving family and friends—including the murderers and dope sellers who protected this genius—he rose above society's low opinion of the inner city. But since he's calm, cool, and collected, a smiling killer who makes us dance to death, one of the fellas, he doesn't fit contemporary definitions of a freak. Lest we forget, to be a real freak you have to play the Jheri curls and plastic surgery or pose naked with flower petals shaped like a glans penis. And if you ain't got enough to buy a dead man's bones to curl up with when you go to sleep at night, then you just as well forgit it, 'cause you ain't wid it.

The Village Voice / October 1988

Armageddon in Effect

JOHN LELAND

It was an old-style protest handbill, unsigned, dropped anonymously on every seat at the New Music Seminar's panel on racism. Across the top, handwritten in artless capital letters, it read, DON'T BELIEVE THE HATE. And for the remainder of the page, in cramped, single-spaced type, it presented its case:

The World According to Public Enemy:

"Cats naturally miaow, dogs naturally bark, and whites naturally murder and cheat ... White people's hearts are so cold they can't wait to lie, cheat, and murder. This is white people's nature ... Whites are the biggest murderers on earth."

"There's no place for gays. When God destroyed Sodom and Gomorrah, it was for that sort of behavior." (*The Face*, July–Aug. 88)

"The White Race or the Caucasian Race came from the Caucasus mountains ... It was not black people who made it with monkeys, animals, and dogs, but it was white people . . . White people are actually monkeys' uncles because that's who they made it with in the Caucasian hills."

"They say the white Jews built the pyramids. Shit. The Jews can't even build houses that stand up nowadays. How the hell did they build the pyramids?"

"If the Palestinians took up arms, went into Israel, and killed all the Jews, it'd be alright." (*Melody Maker*, May 28, 1988)

It was July 18, the opening day of the Democratic National Convention, and the emotional circus that had been building around Public Enemy all summer just kicked up a notch. By the time the night was over, and Public Enemy lead rapper Chuck D had denounced writer and supporter Greg Tate as *The Village Voice*'s "porch nigger," New York was swinging. We'd never seen anything like this before.

It was also nine business days after the release of Public Enemy's second album, *It Takes a Nation of Millions to Hold Us Back*, and the record had already unofficially gone gold, sating the very different hungers of black and white audiences. It seemed to be booming out of every car at every traffic light in the city. *The Wall Street Journal* had recently discovered car stereos that approached the decibel level required to bore a hole in a piece of wood, and this was the perfect program material—dense beats, fragments of sound and meaning, vituperative word-association: "Suckers, liars, get me a shovel / Some writers I know are damn devils / From them I say don't believe the hype / Yo Chuck, they must be on the pipe, right?"

What might have been a simple, bodaciously funky message of black self-determination, delivered by two college friends from Long Island, had turned into a liberal apologist's nightmare, a martyrdom in the making. At the center of it all, Chuck D, a virtual red diaper baby with a degree in graphic design, compared himself to Marcus Garvey and Nat Turner and let the contradictions swirl.

For the record, Chuck D didn't make the statements quoted in the handbill. They belong to Professor Griff, Public Enemy's Minister of Information, and leader of the S1Ws (Security of the First World), Public Enemy's plastic-Uzi-toting, paramilitary Muslim security force.

Like Chuck D's logo, a silhouette of a black youth inside a rifle sight, and like the S1Ws' plastic Uzis, Public Enemy merges the rhetoric of militancy with that of advertising in ways that sit uneasily for both camps. The crew is both rational and hysterical at the same time. It offers hysteria as a rational response to the times.

Chuck D: "It's definitely Armageddon. The black man or woman is at war with himself or herself, and with the situation around them. Armageddon is the war to end all wars. That's when everything hopefully will be all right, the last frontier. Of course we're in it. I'm in it. Maybe you're not in it. You can afford not to be in it, because it doesn't confront you on a daily basis. Black people in America are at war."

Chuck, what's your reaction to the handbill distributed at the New Music Seminar?
They're making a whole lot of shit about nothing. A lot of paranoia going on. People think I got the ability to fucking turn a country around.

Do you back the statements that Griff made?
I back Griff. Whatever he says, he can prove.

You mean he can prove that white people mated with monkeys? That it wouldn't be such a bad idea if the Palestinians were to kill all the Jews in Israel?
Now that was taken out of context. I was there. He said, by Western civilization's standards it wouldn't be bad for the Palestinians to come into Palestine and kill all the Jews, because that's what's been done right throughout Western civilization: invasion, conquering, and killing. That wasn't mentioned.

It's no secret that white people lived in caves while blacks had civilizations. Marcus Garvey said the same shit Farrakhan's saying today. Black people know this. White people do not.

Now, people think we're building up some kind of anti-Semitic hate. Black people's feeling around the country, 98 percent of them say Jews are just white people, there ain't no difference. That's my feeling. I don't like to make an issue out of it.

Does Griff speak for Public Enemy?
He speaks for himself. At the same time, Griff's my brother in Public Enemy. People are gonna see that Griff said this, and in the same interview, I said something else. It's up to them.

Do you consider yourselves prophets?
I guess so. We're bringing a message that's the same shit that all the other guys that I mentioned in the song have either been killed for or deported: Marcus Garvey, Nat Turner, all the way up to Farrakhan and Malcolm X.

What is a prophet? One that comes with a message from God to try to free people. My people are enslaved within their own minds.

Rap serves as the communication that they don't get for themselves to make them feel good about themselves. Rap is black America's TV station. It gives a whole perspective of what exists and what black life is about. And black life doesn't get the total spectrum of information through anything else. They don't get it through print because kids won't pick up no magazines or no books, really, unless it got pictures of rap stars. They don't see themselves on TV. Number two, black radio stations have neglected giving out information.

On what?
On anything. They give out information that white America gives out. Black radio does not challenge information coming from the structure into the black community, does not interpret what's happening around the world in the benefit of us. It interprets it the same way that Channel 7 would. Where it should be, the black station interprets that information from Channel 7 and says, "This is what Channel 7 was talking about. Now as far as we're concerned . . ." We don't have that. The only thing that gives

the straight-up facts on how the black youth feels is a rap record. It's the number one communicator, force, and source in America right now. Black kids are listening to rap records right now more than anything, and they're taking it word for word.

I look at myself as an interpreter and dispatcher. To get a message across, you have to bring up certain elements that they praise, or once did praise, 'cause I've seen a change in the last year and a half.

What do you have to bring up that they praise?
Violence. Drugs. I'll give you a good case, I'm warming up, you know. It takes me a while to warm up into an interview. Two years ago black kids used to think that saying nothing was all right; getting a gold rope, a fat dukey gold rope, was dope, was the dope shit; it's all right to sniff a little coke, get nice for the moment; get my fly ride and do anything to get it, even if it means stomping on the next man, 'cause I got to look out for number one. It's all right for a drug dealer to deal drugs, it's all right 'cause he's making money.

1988, it's a different thought. Because consciousness has been raised to the point where people are saying, "That gold rope don't mean shit now."

Are you taking credit for these changes?
Yes. When I say, "Farrakhan's a prophet and I think you ought to listen" [on "Bring the Noise"], kids don't challenge the fact that Farrakhan's a prophet or not. Few of them know what a prophet is. But they will try to find out who Farrakhan is and what a prophet is. It sounds good to them first, then at the same time they're going to say, "Well, it interests me, let me get into it." Their curiosity has been sparked. Once curiosity has been sparked, the learning process begins. You can't teach, or a kid can't learn, unless their curiosity is sparked.

Okay. ". . . That I think you oughta listen to." Kids will say, "Let me listen to the man." I think the man lays down a decent game plan that has been misinterpreted. He lays a solution and he inspires and challenges the black man to use his brain and understand what has happened be-fore. Which brings up the point of, "Listen, that was then, this is now." Far-rakhan says no. That phrase should never be used. Because you're dealing with the after-effect. When I offer that line, that's what goes off in kids' heads. Or, "Supporter of Chesimard." Twelve-year-old kids would not know about Joanne Chesimard. But their curiosity is sparked.

When I came out with my first records, I had to be shocking in order to be heard. My job was just to tune the radicalness a little bit more. And to be shocking once again sparks the curiosity.

You make a lot of assumptions about black youth. You treat them as a singular idea, and as having one attitude, one mind, one situation.
Yeah. On the whole. Because on the whole everybody's falling victim to the same obstacles. To be able to dissect and understand what's happen-ing to them or what's happening to us, it takes years, or it takes constant teaching. And these things aren't being taught in schools. They throw a bunch of facts about history, they throw you math and science, which are needed, and a bunch of things that are not needed in life. And the kids are not trained to challenge the information. For example, the kid that says, "Listen, I just don't agree with you" to the teacher, the teacher can't deal with that most of the time, because they have to move the class on. They can't go back. So a lot of black kids can't challenge information.

And that's where rap is filling a void, where before the parent used to talk to the child and say, "Listen, you watch this program, son, this is what it's about, this is what he's saying here," and the kid is not getting his information just through what he's watching or what he's listening to or what he's reading. He's getting an interpretation from the parent who un-derstands. Right now we're in a situation where the parents don't under-stand. Or if they do understand, they don't know how to break it down for their son or daughter, because they don't know how to communicate on a regular basis. Or in most cases, it's not a father around, it's a mother around, and she's young herself, she ain't got nothing in her head, or she ain't got time.

I happened to fall into a situation that allowed me to have a thorough education, because if something came across and my mother said, "This is what it's about," my father would say, "I don't think so." Even if they got into an argument, this would be interesting to me. My mother was a social activist in the sixties. I guess whatever movement went down, she would support it: Angela Davis–type shit. My mother was very strong. She always gave me that sense of radicalism from day one. And this weekend happens to be my mother and father's birthday. I'm planning a big shindig. It's probably going to be the happiest day of my life, to throw a party for my father.

What was the Afro-American Experience?

Afro-American Experience was a supplementary educational program for the black youth of Nassau County, Suffolk County, and Queens, run by Panther leaders.

Which ones?

I can't tell you who exactly. I remember Brother Lee. It wasn't any big leaders. 'Cause the Panthers had headquarters in every black community back then. The Nation of Islam had temples in most of the communities. The Black Panther Party was viewed as a positive organization for the betterment of black people and their communities, to get what they wasn't getting. And they joined together with college students to create this program.

How old were you when you were in this program?

When I went, I was eleven. Don't print my age. I was eleven in 1971. Don't print my age.

Why not? What's the big deal?

The big deal is that in order to communicate to the youth you have to be recognized as a peer. Something has to be there that they can say, "This is me." So I'd rather not have my age printed. But at the same time I was eleven years old in 1971. My parents sent me, and I was reluctant at first, 'cause I felt I shouldn't have to go to no summer school. I did well.

The program consisted of eight hours, Monday to Friday, education. I think it had maybe fifteen hundred kids. Hank Shocklee [Public Enemy's producer] was there. We dealt with classrooms. I'm not saying disciplinary actions are right, but a couple times kids got out of line, and how a lot of the brothers would discipline the kid, everybody else would have to punish this person. Not by beating him up or spanking, but everybody would talk to him at once and tell him how fucked-up he was for acting the way he did.

Were you ever punished?
No, no.

How did you like administering punishment?
I felt good, because I was convinced that it was for the betterment of all of us. Like a person broke a window on campus. Somebody was going to get yelled at, usually the brothers. First of all, they weren't wanted on the campus. The communities forced the campus to allow this program to exist. So I felt pretty good.

You said in the NME that you went to the Spin party looking for me, that you wanted to fuck me up bad.
I sure did. You appear to be a nice guy. Did you used to have long hair? I just wanted to speak to you mainly that night. I heard you was hiding out.

Everybody's entitled to their opinion, I guess. But it's bad that you keep your opinion limited. Because the whole market of rap is basically unable to judge information. I know that most of the market doesn't read the magazine, but some do.

Black kids and the black market right now, they're unable to challenge information. Or they're unable to weigh logic. My challenge is to put A and B up and say, "Damn, don't you see B is fucked-up, and that A would be a lot better for you?" They have to get this, 'cause they're not getting it in the school systems.

But do you really think they're getting it from you? The objections I raised were that a lot of your lyrics were sloganeering.

Yeah, they're getting it from me. You got to understand, the black market is schizophrenic. A lot of things are said with words or body language or things meaning something else. It's like, if you go up to somebody and he says [sputtering], "Nigger bugging," he's saying a lot of things besides "nigger bugging." It's felt.

And I could understand it. Some white person with a middle-class background or little contact with black people won't understand that shit at all. There's a lot of people in Creedmoor [psychiatric hospital] that people can't understand. You have to find people that are able to communicate to those that are unable to communicate to the rest of the world. Rap is a true reflection of the streets. It's what R & B once was: the slang that you invent through music or the slang that you can pick up on the streets and then present through music. Motown was once that. Marvin Gaye comes out with "I Heard It Through the Grapevine," based on his interpretation of what his mother told him. It became slang in the street. It was a teaching process and it was a reflection at the same time. R & B doesn't do that anymore. Rap does it. It's able to open doors to the mind. Rap deals. It's abrasive. It doesn't hide shit. R & B hides shit. It's Barry Manilow, it's Frank Sinatra.

I hate to talk about communism as Western civilization knows it, or even communism as it's known today, 'cause it's not fair, it's not people dealing with people. There's still somebody at the top, manipulating people. But I think capitalism should be a mixture. I think people should be treated fair from day one. In this situation right here, in the United States of America—I don't even want to get mad at the fact that it's so unfair.

If you get mad, what do you get mad at? Where do you direct your anger?

I try to direct the anger on trying to do something constructive for my people that are at a disadvantage.

That's what you do with it. But who do you get mad at?

Right now, it's hard for me to say, because it goes by the moment. There's a lot of people I could get mad at, but I understand people, so there's no hatred. I just try to throw a monkey wrench in the motherfucker. It all goes back to people saying, "Chuck D, what kind of government system would you have here in America in 1988?" I say, "One that says black people shouldn't have to pay taxes." It's compensation. Matter of fact, it's overcompensation that we need to be behind the eight ball from 1609 to 1865 and thereafter, 120 more bullshit years. Slaves were brought to this continent in 1609; 1865, 256 years later, the so-called black man was free, quote-unquote "free." So that's 256 years of free labor to build this country. And then the animosity and hatred that went with the package afterwards. When I say black people shouldn't have to pay taxes, it's because we haven't been compensated. I think that's fair. Do you think it's fair?

No. No, I don't.

Ha ha. That's one thing I think should happen. Black people shouldn't have to pay taxes.

That's a bullshit reform . . .

That's a bullshit reform. Also, we should be compensated $250 billion or whatever it takes to get each black family on its feet. Not saying that it will help a whole lot, because there's still no brains. The slum of black America is in the mind of black America. But it would help. I'm talking about that's a solution, A-plan. That will never happen. So we're talking fantasy. People say, "Well . . ." What do you think I am, fucking Albert Gore? If I could give you A to Z, I might as well run. But I can do it. Give me some time.

People are always looking to catch me in fucking double-talk and loopholes. They treat me like *I'm* Jesse Jackson. I'm not running. I'm just offering a little bit of a solution, or at least explaining why things are the way they are. Which are fucked-up.

Are you paranoid?

No, I'm not paranoid. I know there's other things for me to do in this music. If it has to come through other means, I could give up doing records.

Your last single, "Bring the Noise," was basically about what other people are saying about you . . .

Oh, yeah, that was about you. I was talking right about you . . .

And now your new single, "Don't Believe the Hype," is also about what people are saying about you . . .

"Don't Believe the Hype" is about telling people, "Listen, just don't believe the things that are told to you." Go out and seek, challenge information. "The follower of Farrakhan / Don't tell me that you understand." We both know what's happening, but we're treated like we're bugging. That's why I say I'm treated like Coltrane. 'Cause when Coltrane took his stance in the mid-sixties, a lot of writers came crashing down on him because of his radical stance. He started becoming more and more radical until the day he died, started speaking his mind. A lot of people thought he was losing it. Today they recognize the man as a genius. I'm not telling you I'm a Coltrane fan because I'm getting into Coltrane. You probably know more about him than I do.

You call yourselves Public Enemy, and build a strong identity on that, but then the minute you get a little piece of criticism, you fly off the handle.

Don't you think that makes it a little exciting?

It makes it exciting. It also makes it untrustworthy.

Listen. The only one I'm furious at over the past year is Greg Tate. That motherfucker sold out. I'm pissed at him, man.

I think that's because you can't take criticism.

I can't take motherfuckers calling me a motherfucker.

Aw, big deal, Chuck.

I ain't got to feel bad. At the same time, was it an album review or a character review?

I also deal on "Louder than a Bomb" with the FBI tapping my phone.

Have they really, or are you just guessing?

I'm guessing. Because it's happened to most black leaders. It's no secret. The FBI does get involved with somebody even a slight bit outspoken. So it would be ludicrous and naïve to believe that they won't do it today. So if they do it, so what? What I say comes through on records and in interviews. It's no secret at all what I say, 'cause I'm louder than a bomb. They can tap my phone. The FBI had King and X set up. "Party for Your Right to Fight" deals with COINTELPRO, FBI, CIA, assassinations and destruction of the Black Panther Party, Martin Luther King, Malcolm X, the Nation of Islam.

You don't believe that X was killed by the Nation of Islam?

No. And if he was, it was a setup, some snake that was paid.

Do you have any reason to believe this, or is it just something that's convenient for you?

It's something that's convenient for me. But also, if you look at it, it's a pattern. It's a real good guess.

You used to come out in the beginning of your concerts and say that the Klan was outside, ready to shut you down. But there was no danger of this.

No. But at the same time, I was letting people be aware that these forces exist.

And you feel justified in manipulating the facts in order to make that point?

Uh-huh.

That's the mark of a politician, to manipulate the truth to get across an agenda.

To manipulate the truth? You tell me another way to tell the truth to black people if they don't want to hear the truth straight out. I'm open to answers.

You've complained constantly, in interviews and on records, that you can't get your records on black radio, because black radio perceives you as being "too black," too aggressive, too loud. So you make louder records, and you get them on black radio. Does that mean that you're wrong about black radio, or wrong about the records?

My whole point is that black radio has a responsibility to the black community. Its responsibility, if the black community and the black youth wants to hear 50 percent rap records in that community, it's black radio's responsibility to play 50 percent rap records. Now don't get on the demographic tip of trying to reach 25 and over of demographic black females, who aren't listening to radio at night anyway. My wife don't listen to radio. She's watching TV till she falls asleep.

But you listen to the radio. I listen to the radio. Anyone in a car listens to the radio.

No. Anyone that drives in a car listens to tape decks. See, we're dealing with different sciences here. That's what's accelerated the rap album public: car tape decks. Ten years ago, you bought an album so you could take it home to your turntable to play. I know, because I was there—I went out and bought an album to play on the stereo system at home, that I couldn't play loud.

Over the last ten years, the advent of the car stereo, the tape player, and also the box, and the Walkman—now a kid says, "I can take my tape, and I boom that shit loud." Motherfuckers going out now and getting big systems, and it's music to play loud. It deals with loudness. It deals with noise. I can turn it all the way up, park myself in the car, and play the tape that I just bought. Which explains why people are buying every rap album.

This is not a music that you can go home and kick up your feet and listen to. This is music that requires activity; or if you're gonna cool out, you're gonna be in something that can be active in a minute, like a car.

Like I wrote "Bring the Noise" driving along the ocean where I live. Matter of fact, I wrote my first album in a car. I had a track in the tape deck, and I'm writing it on the Long Island Expressway, I'm writing it on the seat.

What's the function of noise in your music?

To agitate, make the jam noticeable. When I originally made it, I wanted some shit where, when a car passed my house, I know that's my song. It grew into a political thing, but I'm telling you the basis. Do you really find that much noise in our music now? It was something that we just put a label on and found that people believed the label. Now it serves as a uniform. We wear it sometimes, and sometimes we don't. We try to set trends, so we don't stay on things too long. Now you hear it everywhere.

Nobody wants to judge us on our music. Everybody wants to judge us on our character. Journalists only cover me because right now it's exciting. It beats the hell out of covering Morrissey thirty, forty, fifty times, talking about the state of rock 'n' roll, which isn't exciting at all.

Why do you take the bait every time an interviewer offers it?

Taking the bait? I'm not actually taking the bait. Sometimes the bait is thrown at you and you can't get out of the way. It's easy to attack us.

It's no problem at all. It's a matter of throwing you guys a noose and letting you put your neck in it.

Uh-huh. But at the same time, I don't look at it as putting my head in a fucking noose, because it's not really dying. The music they can't stop.

I'm just saying, being that I'm the only one that's making this shit kind of exciting for a little period of time, don't take this shit so seriously that you get hurt. 'Cause I got a job to do.

All right, Chuck, I'm straight. We can wind this up.

C'mon, you can't be straight, man. Let's keep talking . . .

Spin / September 1988

1990s:

Pop Goes
the Weasel

While hip-hop journalism of the 1980s primarily served as a documenting tool and nascent mechanism for defining the burgeoning culture, it also did much to forecast the genre's potential staying power, and early in the 1990s, it was more than evident that hip-hop was not only going to stick around, but it was also going POP! The coverage of hip-hop then took divergent paths. On the one hand, the journalism of the era moved away from just documenting the phenomenon to a mode of critique, exploring hard-hitting issues that ranged from politics, censorship, misogyny, economics, class, gender, religion and spirituality, to other sociopolitical issues. On the other hand, a cross section of the journalism sadly followed some of the artists down the Benjamin-paved road toward mainstreaming, and thus coverage shifted from a previously all-inclusive air on hip-hop culture to one whose sole focus became consumerism in rap music.

This section provides a sampling of journalism that took on tougher concerns by journalists who are credited with challenging both the hip-hop artist and the hip-hop fan. Writers like Joan Morgan, Kierna Mayo, Danyel Smith, Karen R. Good, and dream hampton, for instance, made as much noise as the artists they profiled, critiqued, and sometimes quite literally came to blows with (Danyel Smith's profile of raptress Foxy Brown, featured here, was followed by a physical assault on Smith, who was editor in chief of *Vibe* at the time, by an enraged Brown, over the cover story that was published) as they explored in their journalism the gender politics of hip-hop and the role of feminism within the culture.

Writers like Kevin Powell, who costarred on the first MTV's *The Real World* and gained acclaim as a hip-hop journalist in *Vibe*'s 1992 preview issue with his feature on the rap triumvirate Naughty by Nature, proved hip-hop journalists to have as much star power as those they covered. Writers like Cheo Hodari Coker, whose writing on the recently murdered Notorious B.I.G. profiled an introspective man reflecting on his life and intrinsically aware that his fame and platinum records didn't ensure his own immortality, and Carter Harris, who reported on Eric "Eazy-E" Wright's heartbreaking death from AIDS, showed hip-hop journalism also to be about unraveling the complexities and the demons of our artisans, and the conditions that create and sustain them and us—church and state. But as we each, artist and journalist, struggled with these complexities—journalist sometimes challenging and exposing those who wished neither to be challenged nor exposed—the unprecedented symbiotic relationship between the two became ever more contentious, fraught with assaults, threats, and physical altercations carried out by rappers and record producers toward editors and journalists. Beefs ensued and quickly became like a black plague for hip-hop journalists everywhere, attracting lavish mainstream attention and resulting in a demand for other publications and outlets dedicated to covering hip-hop music and lifestyle.

The Source, founded as a newsletter in 1988 by Harvard alumni Dave Mays and Jon Schecter, would grow by the year 2000 into the nation's number one selling music magazine and is credited with documenting some of hip-hop's most indelible moments, most notably in the first half of the decade. The magazine became a home that was, for the most part, hip-hop's monogamous partner, with a staff of colorful writers and editors like James Bernard, Rob Marriott, dream hampton, Cheo Hodari Coker, Kierna Mayo, and others who in their own right became celebrities within the culture. But while *The Source* stood alone in the beginning of the decade as the genre's premier magazine, this would not be the case for long.

Vibe, founded soon after by entertainment baron Quincy Jones, also recruited journalists and photographers from major publications to report on rap, R & B, and reggae royalty, while becoming a platform for younger writers to hone their skills in exploring the music that they were passionate about. While the magazine was never a direct competitor to *The Source*, because *Vibe*'s coverage extended well beyond rap music and hip-hop culture into surveying other forms of black music and lifestyles, it did feature some of the best writings about hip-hop in the nineties. *Vibe*'s feature well of writers like Powell, Danyel Smith, Joan Morgan, Scott Poulson-Bryant, Hilton Als, Greg Tate, Carter Harris, and others who wrote about hip-hop for other publications came together as one trenchantly focused on exploring the schisms within hip-hop culture.

The Source and *Vibe* were joined by some notable underground publications like *ego trip* and *Rap Sheet*, both boasting to be the world's first hip-hop newspaper! Soon after, Larry Flint Publications' *Rap Pages* was also launched. These underground publications, relying less on ad revenue, were able to focus on hip-hop's (nearly) forgotten elements, like graffiti art and dance, as well as artists that weren't necessarily platinum sellers or mainstream, and were at times seen as the brazen voice within hip-hop subculture, filling a gap that ironically widened due to the mainstreaming and growing appeal of the now majors like *The Source* and *Vibe*, and the ad dollars they were reaping.

And then there was *XXL*. The preview issue, released in March 1997, contained one of the most polemic inaugural editorials ever written at the time, which questioned hip-hop's "artistic confusion and moral ambiguity" and promised a platform for "a mature and intelligent look at" the culture. Initially, *XXL* was supposed to become hip-hop's self-professed intellectual answer to *The Source*, as illustrated in Robert Marriott's feature on rap's original lyrical architect Rakim Allah. However, in its current incarnation, seven years later, it has instead found a niche as a direct competitor to not be reckoned with.

By the end of the decade, when artists like Missy Elliott, Jay-Z, Foxy Brown, Method Man, Busta Rhymes, Redman, Da Brat, Ja Rule, Mase, Mos Def, Fat Joe, and Big Pun (who would die of a heart attack in 2000) were in heavy rotation, access to the rap community and its stars seemed to be just as important as the writer's innate desire to write about hip-hop. The articles in the upcoming pages are, for the most part, written by journalists whose desire to be critical and concurrently passionate about documenting the genre overruled the lure of consumerism and has made their pieces literary snapshots of hip-hop's indelible moments.

The House That Rap Built

CAROL COOPER

On Friday night at the Tunnel, Bronx, Jersey, and Brooklyn posers with high-top fades, or one patch of hair dyed psychedelic orange, bob and weave to reggae, rap, house, and imported disco. One block east on West Twenty-seventh, the membership-only Sound Factory pumps this music to a similar audience over one thousand strong. Up near Fifty-fourth and Ninth, a more eclectic mix of Hispanic, white, Asian, and black club bunnies vibrates for six hours straight at Red Zone to records that will probably never get within earshot of America's Top 40. Bratty quips and arch mannerisms cut through the darkness as straights absorb gay attitude like a second language.

Sweaty and svelte, these are the shock troops of the hip-house revolution, and the Technotronic's "Pump Up the Jam" (Belgium's long-shot leap into the pop charts) could be their anthem. Crossing barriers—musical, sexual, national, and conceptual—is all part of what hip-house is about. Anyone with a good sense of rhythm can do it: women, foreigners, whites. Yet this utopian inclusiveness is still subject to the bigoted world hip-house kids theoretically reject. Gay, straight, and multiethnic, this is the mixed demographic no record company dared to predict—and one that an international underground of DJs/producers labored years to create.

Its origins here in Gotham date back to 1987, when the last few all-rap clubs were closing because of constant eruptions of violence. While rap spaces dwindled, more and more straight kids found themselves dancing at house clubs catering to a more subdued gay aesthetic. Rap choreography already encouraged men to dance together, so there wasn't as much immediate conflict as you'd expect. Soon you started seeing B-boys in big black boots, exotic cameo haircuts, and baggies—just like their gay counterparts. And as fashion converged, so gradually did the music.

By December of '87, DJ/producer Todd Terry finally got one of his edited tape reels pressed up into a volcanic piece of vinyl called "Party People" (Idlers). Three grungy keyboard chords borrowed from Chicago's Marshall Jefferson were looped and sequenced relentlessly under the sampled vocal hook "party people" from "Planet Rock." Rap kids loved it because it payed homage to Afrika Bambaataa and retained none of the elegiac (they might say "faggoty") softness of Chicago house. Latin kids embraced it as quickly as they had "Arroz con Pollo"—a Spanglish answer record to Jefferson's "Move Your Body." And houseketeers liked the odd energy emanating from a syncopated backbeat that resembled a drunken rumba more than the traditional house 4/4. A unifying hip-house prototype was born.

So when the Chicago label D.J. International brags on the back of the 1989 *Hip House* compilation that their producers Fast Eddie and Tyree Cooper were the first (in '88) to combine house and hip-hop "in a way that created a whole new style," they are both right and wrong. Yes, Tyree and Eddie's rejection of traditional melodicism in favor of transmuting found noises into music stemmed the tide of cannibalized Philly International riffs that had previously defined house. But popular singles like "Let's Go" and "Turn Up the Bass" paid as little attention to conventional song structure as did their ancient template "Planet Rock" and thereby lost those of us who need stabilizing referents to the past. When New York's Jungle Brothers recorded the 12-inch of "I'll House You" (Warlock) in May of '88, they improved upon an emerging formula, largely by tailoring the free association raps that earmarked Tyree and Eddie's fusion.

Over riffs appropriated from Todd Terry, the J.B.s execute not only verbal hooks but complete verses, bridges, turnarounds, and choruses, all laced with a satirical edge that still makes "I'll House You" the funniest lyric of its kind. Here the rap is part of, not subordinate to, the logic of the track. Remove the lugubrious textures conveyed by lines like "jump, jump, a little higher / jump, jump until you get tired . . ." and you lose some of the record's most beguiling instrumentation.

The best hip-house vocals are integral to the charm and swing of their backing tracks. The ultimate expression of this schoolyard scat is Ya Kid K's syntactic acrobatics on the Technotronic hits "Get Up" and "Pump Up the Jam." Her weird diction flows around notes and beats like an eleven-year-old's feet dodge double-Dutch twine. And whether she or the departing Felly actually sang the melodic chorus, "Get ya booty on the floor tonight . . . make my day" on "Pump Up the Jam," that brassy taunt becomes the linchpin of the entire song.

Although Chicago's Mr. Lee is closing the gap with the poppy kineticism of singles like "Get Busy" (Jive), Ya Kid K's closest male competitor is Atlantic's Doug Lazy, a D.C.-based radio jock who collaborated with disco vet Vaughn Mason on last year's debut single "Let It Roll." Lazy's declamatory style is deceptively laconic, full of surreal images afloat in some of house's spookiest instrumentals: "On the mike and I'm sparking / Like a jumper cable." Unafraid of the music's gay associations, Lazy takes full advantage of its sleaziest sounds. His fat bass figures eel suggestively under your hips. His cowbells come off the business end of a voodoo ceremony. And his contrapuntal keyboard fills could be Lurch playing suggestive night music for Morticia and Gomez Addams.

But in the coming together of any of two established genres there is a scary period where artists worry if their fans will accept their adoption of the sound. Hostility is still flung by conservatives in both toward rappers or househeads who record a token "crossover" tune just to boost sales. Big Daddy Kane's "The House That Cee Built" from *It's a Big Daddy Thing* (Cold Chillin') and Queen Latifah's "Come Into My House" (Tommy Boy) show the ways two major rap voices approach the challenge of hybridization. To hedge against being tagged a collaborator with the gay underground, Kane undercuts his LP's house track with a "faggot" lyric in another song, "Pimpin' Ain't Easy." True to her unifying mission, Latifah feels no need to hedge. Not only is her house experiment a charting single, but voguing pioneer Willie Ninja choreographed the video with all the muscular extroversion of uptown drag balls, carefully enhanced by the Pan-African subtext Latifah is already famous for. The color and movement of "Come Into My House" make Madonna's "Vogue" video look dead. It's the difference between a mainstream artist reaching down to an underground fad in a parody of street credibility and an artist who still inhabits that underground helping to reinvent it.

Visionary hip-house performers already know that the future for this music is to use its anarcho-outlaw status to walk a fine line between entertainment and politics. That's why all the "jack your body" lyrics don't upset those of us who like a message in our music; double meanings are implicit. These songs extol the physical beauty of dance as the first level of a more general examination of the people and culture that produce it.

So when KYZE (aka Kevin Davis) raps, "What if it was all work and no play / Once a year you'd get one day," in "Stomp (Move Jump Jack Your Body)" (Warner Bros.), he offers an Orwellian vision of the blue-collar future, one that struck a responsive chord in young working stiffs all over the country. His video shows the dapper Davis as a circumspect used-car salesman who daydreams of being a Rhythm Nation lieutenant leading dance-floor troops to unity and liberation through the boogie. Dance has always been a metaphor for freedom, but it becomes more emphatically so in the synthesis of youth, libido, and self-affirmation that is hip-house.

The upcoming KYZE album sought producers who, whether their specialty was rap or house, were willing to contribute topical material as well as party jams. For extra diversity, some cuts will follow the Afro-Caribbean formula pioneered by Keith Thompson's "Can't Take It" (Capitol), which used a ragamuffin house beat to hammer home a scathing catalog of racist oppression. Pan-African permutations in hip-house are increasingly popular because its martial rhythms are only enhanced by tribal embellishments.

Rising out of this profusion of jungly tom-tom beats is "Grandpa's Party" (Cooltempo), last year's U.K. debut by Brit rapper Monie Love. This primal bit of tribal house swept through New York as an expensive import on the strength of its resounding digital conga pattern. Love's guest vocals with Queen Latifah and De La Soul already have her looming large on the hip-hop map, yet her first solo effort was a hip-house praise poem honoring Afrika Bambaataa, spiritual father of the musical Zulu Nation—the spearhead of hip-hop's global dispersion.

So is hip-house the next phase of rap or the next phase of house? To which lineage does it most rightfully belong? That answer depends on whom you ask, since Kevin Davis still has a vested interest in being considered a member of rap orthodoxy, while Doug Lazy would rather rule in clubland than serve rap apprenticeship. Right now its white practitioners are few (Michele Visage of Seduction is one proven talent), but the field is wide open to others. Will hip-house spawn another "Rapture," another "Genius of Love"?

For anyone who wants to try, there are still only two valid approaches: hip-house that uses conventional song structure (proving that it is possible to get very sophisticated with street music and still have enough balls to tear up the dance floor), and raw yawps over found noises and mathematically determined repetition (which is a voodoo bridge to the microtonal avant-garde). As it looks right now, the former is the newest mutation of American R & B. The latter, however, sounds like an open invitation for Philip Glass to join the dance.

The Village Voice / May 15, 1990

The Nigga Ya Hate to Love

JOAN MORGAN

Snatch 1

Greg Tate calls and strongly suggests I do a piece on Ice Cube's new album, *AmeriKKKa's Most Wanted* (Priority), for *The Village Voice*. I refuse, which I suspect he expects. It's no secret that I found N.W.A's *Straight Outta Compton* nothing short of demonic. "But someone needs to do this who grew up in the hood." I tell him for the umpteenth time that I'm not the one trying to reconcile my black middle-class intellectual complex with wannabe-down ghetto romanticization. What I don't tell him is I'm still weirded out from last summer when I found myself singing the chorus to "Gangsta Gangsta" in the kitchen long after I decided *Straight Outta Compton* was the most fucked-up, violent, sexist rap album I'd ever heard: "We wanna fuck you E-Z / I wanna fuck you too."

Snatch 2

The next night in Harlem, USA, me and a posse of homeboys, ages ten to fourteen, check out a familiar scene. Two white Five-Os are busy looking terribly bored on the most well-lit block on Amsterdam Avenue, seemingly unaware that there's plenty to do a half a block away in either direction. Money Grip turns to his cadre and they break into a midsummer night's ghetto serenade: "Nine one one is a joke / Ow-w-w / Nine one one is a joke." The cop on the right fingers his holster absentmindedly while the one on the left reduces them to little black gnats and waves them away. The kids are not unaware of the gesture. Gnats turn into killer bees and chant, "Fuck tha police," all the way home. Not thinking a damn about Philip C. Panell, Michael Stewart, or Edmund Perry.

Snatch 3

I'm doing the piece.

Snatch 4

I gotta hand it to Cube. Even if he weren't rap's most proficient raconteur since KRS-One, and even if *AMW* were straight-up wack, he'd still have to be congratulated on marketing strategy alone. Unmitigated black rage prepackaged for your cathartic or voyeuristic convenience. Hip-hop macabre. It's a brilliant concept. Peep this . . .

The first track, "Better Off Dead." The empty, echoing footsteps of a young black man's final walk down death row. He and a black (yes, black; turn to "Welcome to the Terrordome" if you need a refresher course: "Every brother ain't a brother 'cause a color / Just as well could be undercover") corrections officer engage in the following discourse: "You got any last words?" "Yeah, I got some last words. Fuck all y'all." "Switch." Fry. Sizzle. Dead nigger. Then he evokes the specter of the dehumanizing media by using the same emotionless newscaster's voice that matter-of-factly told us that black men in Harlem had a lower life expectancy than those in poorer-than-poor Bangladesh: "White America is willing to maintain order no matter what the cost." Execution, however, is not quite that easy. On "The Nigga Ya Love to Hate," Ice Cube reemerges as the quintessential Black Phoenix, whom even the fires and electric chairs of white racist oppression could not destroy. "I heard payback you motherfuckin' nigger / That's why / 'Cause I'm tired of being treated like a goddamn stepchild / Fuck a punk 'cause I ain't him? / You gotta deal with the nine double M / The day has come that you all hate just think / A nigger decided to retaliate . . ."

He's back, he's black, and badder than ever. How's that for a Rude Boy/ Revolutionary fantasy?

Snatch 5

I leave Yankee Stadium, full of good vibes and Mandela fever, and head for the Vineyard. Cape Cod is a sharp contrast to Africa Square, but I'm willing to play cultural chameleon for a little sea air and solitude. *AMW* peeks out from my pile of dirty laundry and I shudder. Ice Cube and South Beach seem somewhat incongruous. Reluctantly, I put it next to my bag of black-hair-care products so I don't "accidentally" forget it. We're in the car only twenty minutes before Kianga slips it in the Benzy. I don't riff too much, figuring that even that has got to be more bearable than this pseudo-reggae UB40 shit Leslie's making us listen to. It doesn't take long before Negra, Leslie's sweet, black, and respectably corporate car, is turned into a thumpin', bumpin', finger-poppin' Negro mobile. Yeah, boyee. This is work-booty music in a big way. Great. Chuck D, Hank and Keith Shocklee, and Eric Sadler gave *AMW* all the kick that was sorely missed on *Fear of a Black Planet*. This is straight-up, hard-edged warrior music. Like the beats of African prebattle ceremonies, it either makes you want to dance into oblivion or go off and bum-rush somebody. Kianga flips the tape to the B side. "Joan, you know this motherfucka must be bad if he can scream *bitch* at me ninety-nine times and make me want to sing it." Yep. This one's deffer than dope.

Snatch 6

Some say the mob ain't positive
Man fuck that shit 'cause I got to live how I live
. . . Some rappers are heaven sent
but "Self Destruction" don't pay the fuckin' rent.
So you can either sell dope or get your ass a job
I'd rather roll wit the Lench Mob
                                        —"Rollin' Wit the Lench Mob"

Things are not going as planned. How the fuck could I remember to bring Ice Cube and forget my bag of black-hair-care products? There's not a bottle of TCB anything anywhere to be found, and the most tan we got today was in the parking lot, waiting three hours to get on the ferry. By the time we get to the beach I'm a walking time bomb. Leslie, Kianga, and I get into a thing because they think I overintellectualize everything. Maybe. But what's so cute about "A Gangsta's Fairytale"? "Little boys and girls they all love me / Come sit in the lap of MC I-C-E / And let me tell you a story or two / About a punk ass nigga I knew / Named Jack / He wasn't that nimble / Wasn't that quick / Jumped over the candle stick and burned his dick / Went up the street 'cause he was piping hot / Met a bitch named Jill on the bus stop / Dropped a line or two and he had the ho / At that type of shit he's a pro / So Jack and Jill went up the hill to catch a little nap / Dumb bitch gave him the clap." Just what our community needs. Ghetto fairy tales. Andrew Dice Clay style. I ask Leslie if she would want her kids singing this? Exasperated, she asks if everything has to be political.

Snatch 6½

"Not a baby by you / The neighborhood hussy . . . / All I saw was Ice Cube in court / Paying a gang of child support / Then I thought deep about giving up the money / What I need to do is kick the bitch in the tummy / No 'cause then I'd really get faded / That's murder one 'cause it was premeditated . . ."

Leslie is appalled. "Do we have to listen to this shit?" I crank up the volume. The sense of pleasure I feel is almost perverse.

Snatch 7

The Vineyard is a romantic place. Leslie, Kianga, and I become products of the environment and spend three-quarters of our "weekend away with the girls" talking about the men we left at home. We can't figure out whether it's the combination of the beach, the fog, the gazebo, and the lighthouse or the fact that the few brothers we did see on the island were all cut from the same soft, prep-school, young black Republican cloth. Either is enough to make three street-wise, ex-prep-school sisters very homesick/horny for what they have at home. "I need the element, my sister," says Leslie. My mind races back to a scene that took place two weeks ago. I'm listening to *AMW* when my terribly significant other emerges from the shower, wet, glistening, and wrapped in a towel. My audio catches up with my visual and I hear him singing, albeit softly, "I'm thinking to myself why did I bang her / Now I'm in the closet looking for the hanger." That's great, Z. Just great. "Sorry, baby," he says, "it's crazy seductive." He reassumes gangster position and nods his head to the beat. I look up and see the beads of water dance around the slight snarl on his lip. Seductive? . . . Yes, Lord.

Snatch 8

We catch a four o'clock ferry. There's a carload of black folks behind us playing Ice Cube stupid loud. There are carloads of white folks looking over at the car, extremely uncomfortable. "Damn, Kianga," Leslie says, "maybe that's what we should have done last night when that ignorant white waitress asked you if you didn't have an easier name to pronounce than `Kianga'!" "Word, that bitch didn't even want to take the order. What the fuck, is my name supposed to be Mary or Sue?" I suggest we run back up in there with a broom and cold-blast that shit. We all laugh. Bum-rush fantasies. Kianga stops. She looks away and touches my arm. Homeboy is holding a baby girl in his arms. She's about a year old and nodding her head to the music. That's the problem with unmitigated black rage. It grabs white people by the jugular with one hand and strangles black folks with the other.

Snatch 9

**Yo, Ice Cube, man why you always kickin' the shit about the bitches
and the niggers
Why don't you kick some shit about the kids man
The fuckin' kids.**

—"A Gangsta's Fairytale"

I'm back on 125th Street. One week later folks are still buying Mandela T-shirts at almost the same rate they're buying the Black Bart T's. I stop in Sikulu, the record shop of the righteous, to find out how *AMW* is doing. Reluctantly, they tell me it's one of the top five sellers. I'm looking for a young urban male type to talk to about it. For some reason, they're few and far between today. I move and stand in front of the children's clothing store that has those black mannequins. I realize that I've stood there umpteen times and never noticed how fucked-up they are. I'm transfixed. They're all white models that were painted shit-brown. The boy mannequin has his head contorted to the side, like his neck is broken, and his hand is missing; it looks blown off. The bright red shoulder-length wig sadly parodies the weaves that keep the Korean hair store down the block in business. At least the "negative" images Cube feeds us are our own. A posse of youngbloods walks by. All of them have heard it but they're as reluctant to talk about it as the sister in Sikulu. Finally one asks me what it is I wanted to know. "I want to know what you think about it."

"What I think about it?"

He looks at me like I'm from Mars or Martha's Vineyard.

"Yeah, do you like it?"

"Yeah, I like it. I like it a lot . . . money can rap."

He reads in my silence that I'm waiting for him to say more.

"I like him."

"But why? . . . Why do you think he's good?"

It took me a while to realize that the look he was giving me was the same look Andy Kirk, the legendary swing bandleader, gave this young guy in the elevator when he asked him what made those old jazz greats so great . . . Because they could play, son. They could play.

Homeboy mouths the words again for me, slowly.

"Because . . . he . . . can . . . rap."

The Village Voice / July 17, 1990

The Rebirth of Cool

SCOTT POULSON-BRYANT

Round 1

L.L. Cool J is looking for a cue. The tour starts in four days and the eight female dancers need to dance in this section—the "Rebirth of L.L. Cool J" sequence—of the *Mama Said Knock You Out* tour. I light a cigarette (I feel like dancing) and watch L.L. check out his big ol' chorus line as "Jingling Baby" revs up again: "Uncle L, Future of the Funk / Records are recorded minus all the junk." The large studio space, where Michael Bolton rasped through faux blues just yesterday, booms with the groove of L.L.'s comeback single, a hip-hop classic of remixed, revitalized energy. "No, no. You have to start on *this* beat," L.L. says as Cut Creator halts the music. "Move on the eighth beat."

"That's hard to do," one of the dancers complains.

"No, it isn't. If I can rap it"—L.L. laughs—"then you can dance it."

He turns to me. "Scott, will you excuse us?"

I'm out of there.

Round 2

Where I come from, the *B* in *B-boy* stands for *banjy*, for the down-to-earth, streetwise pose cherished by black youth eager to stake a stylish claim on the world. And the most famous banjy boy in the world—James Todd Smith, aka L.L. Cool J—is now conducting auditions for his chorus line of around-the-way girls and jingling babies. After one woman leaves the room, pulling at her tights, giggling nervously—"It's him," her brown eyes flash—L.L. turns to the rest of the group and shakes his head. "I asked for dancers. Do I look like a dance teacher? Next . . ."

As the auditions continue, I flash back history with L.L. I knew I had to quit my postcollege job at a PR firm when a very prominent music critic dismissed *Mama Said Knock You Out*, saying the slang wasn't "current" enough. I wasn't offended because L.L. was one of the clients I represented as a publicist; I was offended by the way the scribbler had casually tossed aside one of the most breathtaking and sensuous musicians to ever represent the spectacular visibility of American black-boy life. Here was one more person who wanted L.L. to be over, kaput, one of a long line of rappers to run out of metaphors and run out of steam. If hip-hop was about *slang* to that writer, he obviously missed some of what was going on here.

Round 3

Just before we board the tour bus I'm sitting on one of the plush leather couches in the rehearsal studio. L.L. walks in and winks at me, reaching out as if to shake my hand. I take it and he yanks me up off the couch into the air. I land just in front of him toe-to-toe. I gotta play it up, so I say, "Didn't know you were so strong."

"Thought I was weak?" he demands.

I gulp. Is this how he treats all journalists? I thought we were friends.

Round 4

He's twenty-three years old. He grew up in Queens, a much maligned borough of New York, which nonetheless is the hometown of numerous hip-hop heavies. They say his early singles and first LP built Def Jam. He wrote and rapped the first hip-hop love song "I Need Love," a tune about male desire in a field usually devoted to male demands. He's been compared to a young Muhammad Ali: ambitious, sexy, confident, and ready to take all comers. He was crowned an African chief in Abidjan, Ivory Coast, way before most rappers boarded hip-hop's Afrocentric bandwagon. He stepped out of a giant ghetto-blastin' radio as headliner of the '87 Def Jam Tour.

But:

He suffered a few slings and arrows in some very public feuds with the likes of Kool Moe Dee and Ice-T. He's been criticized for some shockingly satiric boasts (ponder: "I'm so bad I can suck my own dick"). He got booed at a Harlem rally for slain black teen Yusuf Hawkins for not being down with the political causes of the moment.

But:

He's the type of guy who makes women excited and men envious. He's the type of guy who makes *men* excited and *women* envious. He's a pop culture icon for the times, a sex god and savior, bringing his positive-aggression style to bear with an enticing street-kid savoir faire. He's a star.

But he doesn't think so.

Round 5

My next encounter with L.L. is in the back of the tour bus as the front comes alive, mile by mile, filling with the sound of young black folks getting their lives. Valet Cornell Clark leads the off-key guys in an a cappella version of Luther Vandross's "A House Is Not a Home." Somebody solos, "Sayin' that you're still in love with meee . . ."

"She ain't in love with you 'cause you can't sing!" teases one of the female dancers. Soon, two women are harmonizing a Teena Marie ballad.

Between sets, L.L. and I talk.

"*Walking With a Panther* didn't do as well as expected, did it? And a lot of people dissed you for being arrogant. I thought it was some arrogant bullshit, personally, when I first heard it," I tell him.

L.L. does a TV-announcer voice: "I came up with a formula"—long, dramatic pause—"that didn't work." He chuckles. "I admit I got into myself a little deep, fell victim to a musical self-centeredness. Some could deal with it, but a lot of people didn't like the vibe. By the same token," he continues, stretching his long legs into the aisle, "if nobody had been running around degrading my image or downgrading me, people would have looked at that album as something clever and witty with balls, instead of something arrogant or in-your-face cocky.

"But things change," L.L. says with a customary lick of the lips. "I was trying to grow. I can't be mad at the public. And I thank God I got through that phase."

"Let's talk about your image—"

"I don't have an image."

"Of course you do—"

"I don't have an image. I never had one. Look at me, Scott. Think about *Radio* and what I'm wearing now." He points to his Harvard T-shirt and jeans and Chicago Bulls jacket.

"Your image is realness," I suggest.

"Then it wouldn't be an image, it would be real. Real isn't an image. An image is up-front, meant to be something, to mold someone. I never had one. If I did, *Panther* would have crushed me because there would have been something to expose. In other words, I'm not frontin'."

I propose to L.L. that hip-hop sells realness. That's the image, the pose: around-the-way boys, homeboys . . .

"Some groups perpetrate realness but they ain't real, not being themselves. They're another person when you meet them backstage. I'm the same person onstage as I am here."

I tell him about Walking for Banjy Realness, the category in black gay social balls in which contestants don B-boy apparel, striving to become as "real" as their straight counterparts.

"I'm just me, all the time. I'm not fronting," he insists.

"When we were fifteen, sixteen, Run-D.M.C. looked like us," I remind him. "Not like the Commodores or Cameo. The rappers were kids we'd go to school with—"

He starts to catch on. "They were easy to relate to. That was part of the success of rap. But having that reality and maintaining that are two different things. You have to do what you feel. Stay true to yourself. That'll make you successful."

"So do you think Madonna's real?" I ask him, hitting on a frequent touchstone of our conversations.

"Yeah, she's doing what she feels. That's why she changes so much. If she wasn't Madonna, she'd probably be a woman who came to work every day with a different hairdo."

I don't necessarily agree with him on the realness tip, but I'm starting to see where's he's coming from.

Round 6

I'm the shit. The answer. I'm good, better—actually, if you want to know the truth—the best.

Better yet, let L.L. say it: I explode, and my nine is easy to load. When I roll up, it's like hip-hop vice. I excel, they all fell. I got a gold nameplate that says I wish you would. I'm the type of guy to _____ (fill in the hyperbolic metaphor of your choice).

The young black man has to soup himself up. He has to say, at least to himself, I'm bad. Because he knows that thinking any less leaves him, more often than not, wanting for a piece of the pie that someone else is baking and distributing. And that's the basis of rap: no matter how politically sophisticated or sonically experimental it becomes, no matter how progressive the slang becomes, rap will always be about young, black self-assurance. And L.L. Cool J knows that.

From jump, L.L. made a plea for the ordinary through the extraordinary use of his vocal cords, eroticizing and celebrating symbols of urban boyhood (the radio, the police siren, the Jeep, the Kangol) and turning them into quintessential icons of authority and passion. Admitted or not, self-mythology was the aim of hip-hop, and L.L. Cool J was the artist most successful at constructing a mythic space for himself, where he could tap into the realness of his existence and turn that realness into larger-than-life, yet accessible, folk culture gone electronic.

Round 7

You have to take your shoes off at Russell Simmons's house. I sit on the beige couch and stare at my Nikes as he winds up a phone conversation.

"Todd's like a sponge," says Def Jam's owner with characteristic bluntness. "He's one of the brightest and most learned artists there is. That's because he borrows—not steals—from successful artists and reinterprets. You heard a little Run-D.M.C. on *Radio*, the spare beats and stuff. There's a little Kane on songs like 'Mr. Goodbar.' That's what makes him current—he's abreast of what's successful. He's not necessarily a groundbreaking artist, but he's a commercial artist and we need that. We need people who take pop culture and decipher and redefine it. And he's one of the greatest vocalists in the world.

"Todd is a real black urban kid, the realest act I represent. All that stuff that went down after *Panther*, he was open-minded enough to take the criticisms and do something positive with it.

"He has a good grasp of his position in the marketplace. He can cross over but he's still concerned with black people, even if he talks about the universal line. He wants around-the-way girls to buy his shit. That's what makes him accessible but he's still black. He's honest."

Round 8

L.L. is eating a fried sea bass as the tour bus rolls along. The crew is still singing, the bus driver's lost, we've been on the road two hours, trying to find Philly.

L.L. explains that his acting debut in Michael J. Fox's straight-to-cable action-comedy *The Hard Way* was intended basically to expose him to a wider audience. "I'm not an actor," he stresses.

Yeah, right. L.L. Cool J has made some of the most interesting and compelling videos ever, precisely because he is such a good actor. Pop video thrives on cliché, particularly when dealing with the shorthand and *slanguage* of hip-hop culture. L.L., though, finds a way of making the clichés resonate by bringing a presence to the screen that is at once knowing and completely in the moment. As he maneuvers himself around the party-hearty revelers in the "Jingling Baby" clip, he commands space with authority. The artiness of "Goin' Back to Cali" compels him into a black-clad study of alienation and dislocation.

And what about the *Saturday Night Live* episode where he played Sean Penn's lover in a parody of *Fatal Attraction*? Funny, risky stuff. And whereas Big Daddy Kane, that other hip-hop love man, needs Barry White to prop up his love jones on vinyl and video, L.L. Cool J pines through "I Need Love" on his own, with the lonesome look of a teen-macho man-child. L.L. Cool J knows how to manipulate hip-hop's communal excess into streamlined declarations of independence. *That's* good acting.

Round 9

"You're a superstar," I say to him.

He shakes his head.

"You're a sex symbol."

"That's just a label. I'm not concentrating on that. I could get third-degree burns tomorrow and that would be all over with. I believe in the power of God, which makes me beautiful inside as well as out."

"Sure, and I put you, Madonna, and Prince in the same category insofar as striking a balance between the sacred and the profane," I offer. "Remember we saw Madonna's show? She was fucking one minute and praying the next . . ."

"In my music and shows, I like to release the pressure, but at the same time mold the audience with God. I want my music to cultivate and stimulate some sort of spirituality. You're right, there is a fine line here."

"It's all about ecstasy, right? Orgasm . . ."

"Yeah, like orgasm, a release of energy. At the same time I'm bringing that physical pleasure—"

"Turning them on," I prod.

"—I'm bringing God to them, too. I guess it's like, 'I'll screw you for eight hours straight, if you promise me you'll give your soul to God.'"

He pauses, pondering the confessional tone of the conversation. "Actually, to be honest? If I'm feeling a little sexy and I get up and scratch my *cojónes*, I write a jam about it. No deep philosophy to it. I was just being real analytical about it. I'm not really an analytical person."

At this point, Kristen, the only white dancer on the tour, wanders to the back of the bus and listens to L.L. and me talking. "What do you think of L.L. Cool J?" I ask her.

"I respect him. He doesn't dis women. Every rap record has at least one bitch-ho song. L.L. has more substance. He uplifts women."

"How?"

"The right way, baby," L.L. says.

"Like, he has 'Jingling Baby,' which is a fun song."

"He also has 'Big Ole Butt,'" I say.

"But that's different. It's bringing out a part of her body. Celebrating it."

"It could have been 'Billy's Got Some Big Ole Nuts,'" L.L. interjects with a smile. "And a female could have made it. That would have been funny. Has there been a male group mad at Madonna yet with her men mermaids?"

"I think she thinks she was empowering gay men and playing around with issues of sexuality, poking fun at straight men. Should they have complained?"

"I guess not," allows L.L.

Round 10

As we pull into Philadelphia, we see a steel statue, a sturdy and abstract depiction of Benjamin Franklin's key, stunned by a lightning bolt. Soon we turn and we're driving down Race Street, through the middle of Chinatown. Two homeboys stand near the curb, and I wonder what they'd do if they knew L.L. Cool J was riding through their City of Brotherly Love.

"'Cheesy Rat Blues' is about anyone who gets too big for their britches. It's not autobiographical, 'cause it never happened to me. But I'm not a star. I just make music. They're my supporters, the fans. They wanna dance to the music, I wanna make it. We all wanna take each other to that natural high. I want people to say, 'He has the ability to crush the world, but he don't hurt a fly.'"

Round 11

We get to the hotel. L.L.'s personal manager goes to the front desk to dole out scheduling and room keys. L.L. gets his first and quietly walks away. I watch him go up alone in the glass elevator.

Later, I knock on his door. He opens it, invites me in. "Are we alone?" I ask him.

He nods and sits on the couch, still in his Harvard T-shirt, wrapped in sheets and a comforter.

I flash back on one day when I was a publicist. L.L. noticed the hoop earring I wear and asked, "Aren't you afraid someone's gonna think you're gay?" "No, I'm not," I told him. He just looked at me. "That's cool," he said. "That's cool."

So now I ask him about homophobia in rap.

"Look, I respect all people. As long as people get their work done, they can deal with whoever they want to."

"You deal with women in a really romantic way," I suggest. "As opposed to, say, Brand Nubian, who are quote unquote righteous and for the people and dog women out."

"Every person deals with things differently. You know that. Some car dealers deal their cars differently."

"Interesting metaphor, Todd."

He laughs. "Or some men, whatever—you have to give people respect."

I suggest that hip-hop has elements of male insecurity behind all the braggadocio.

"If someone says, 'I would never do "I Need Love,"' well, why not? You insecure about something? You definitely need love. That's fear, if not straight-out insecurity.

"A lot of these guys who dog women out in records are mad 'cause they didn't get any women before they made records. Now they got a chance to disrespect all the women who they thought dissed them. If they get themselves together, maybe they can make records complimenting women. Or maybe they can get some women."

"You excited about the tour?"

"Oh, yeah. Originally, I wanted to do a club tour, get intimate with the crowd."

"Kind of like take hip-hop back to the roots?"

He shakes his head. "I'm not into that 'It started here, let's keep it here' stuff, I just wanted to have fun. McDonald's started in one place—why can't they sell burgers everywhere, knowwhumsayin'?"

"Another interesting metaphor, Todd."

He laughs again. "This tour is the beginning of the making of a legend. Like Ali, but way bigger. Boxing is the only sport that shows true aggression. Truly a display of everyman's ego."

"Like rapping."

"But it's not the ego of hip-hop that makes it threatening. It's the groove."

"So, it's not the sight or sound of a young black man talking about himself and how bad he is?"

"It's the groove," he insists. "'I'm bad, I'm really bad' [in harmless pop crooner voice] versus 'I'm bad!!!' Two different things."

"Speaking of the groove, Max Roach called your music the most African of hip-hop."

"He said that about my music?! Interesting, maybe subconsciously I'm tapping into something from back in the day. I'm proud of being black. When I went to the Ivory Coast, I felt like I'd been there before."

Suddenly he states, "I want to be legendary. I want to reach the Golden Microphone."

"What is that?"

"The ultimate in success. Michael Jackson's there. Madonna. Prince is almost there. I'm not even halfway there in terms of sales, respect . . ."

"So what does it take to be a legend?"

"Good music and the power of God."

Round 12

He's six feet two. He's now 201 pounds, having lost fifteen pounds for the tour. He swears he doesn't work out; I guess he has one of those natural black male bodies. He finally started dancing in his act after people asked him why he didn't.

He writes and records sinewy songs of day-to-day life like "Illegal Search" and "Boomin' System," shaping the B-boy into an identifiable and influential image across the world—but he says he's not political. He commands the stage and screen with a communicative energy of movement and expression—but he says he's not an actor. He causes women to faint at his concerts and men to adopt his street-tough style—but he says he's not a star. In his resistance to the imposition of labels, while defining *himself* with the best boast raps around, he is a typical young black man negotiating the ins and outs of self-representation. Ultimately, he says, he's not at the forefront of rap. "I'm at the forefront of being me. I don't think of any of this as a competition. I just want my airtime. To show the world who I am."

"Who are you?"

"The seed of David. A person who's the rightful heir to Solomon's knowledge," he says, pointing to his hat, which, at this late, late hour, as he's snuggled up in bedsheets, is still on his head.

"Why do you wear the hat? I always thought maybe you had an ugly head or bad haircut."

"First of all, it's my trademark. Secondly, all your energy is contained in your head. You notice, in a lot of religions, holy men wear things on their heads. It's my crown." Then he starts to laugh. "Nobody worries about what my balls look like. Nobody asks me about my feet. Michael Jackson has his glove. I have my hats. Why can't we just leave it at that?"

"Because you're already a legend, Todd."

"Yeah, you're right. The world will never see such a display of power after my career is over. I'm gonna sound-blast the universe." He flashes that charming Cool J smile, but I know he means it. "I've wanted to rap since I was nine years old. Since I was a little boy, running around in my Superman pajamas with a towel hanging out the back of my shirt."

"You're still kind of doing that, right?"

"If I had some kind of wild fantasy with a female, I might, but other than that, nah." He shrugs.

"You're kind of Superman. Ordinary guy by day, bigger-than-life hero by night."

He thinks about this. "Yeah, maybe. But ain't no Kryptonite here."

Spin / July 1991

Native Sons

KEVIN POWELL

This is the only real concern of the artist, to re-create out of the disorder of life that order which is art. —James Baldwin

And now you want me to rap and give, say, something positive! Well, positive ain't where I live. —Treach

Naughty by Nature are the last act on the Apollo bill, and the throng of swaggering, foulmouthed B-boys and gum-popping B-girls is restless. It has been a typically disappointing evening of hip-hop in Harlem. But when co-rapper Vinnie steps out and demands, "Throw your hands in the air!" homeys jump from their seats in a frenzy, thrusting knuckles upward like mesmerized Holy Rollers. Vinnie intoduces DJ Kay Gee as a phalanx of boys from Naughty's East Orange, New Jersey, neighborhood lines the stage, suited in NBN hoodies, baseball caps, and T-shirts. Kay Gee cuts and scratches Treach's name on the turntables and the audience erupts again. (My own adrenaline is pumping: In the heart of Uptown I'm yellin' "Yeah, y'all, Jersey's in da motherfuckin' house!"—proud, for once, to be from *that* state.)

Treach glides across the stage like a panther: black, lean, his narrowed eyes riveted on his prey; he grips the mike tightly in one hand while the other slashes air with his ever-present machete. Draped in a baggy blue prisonlike outfit, a black Malcom X tee, and the latest B-boy headgear—a striped knit cap more appropriate for sleepin' than sportin' outdoors (though B-boy logic says otherwise)—Treach savors the moment and looks genuinely inspired by the chorus of screaming voices.

When Kay Gee launches "Guard Your Grill," Treach high-steps across the stage as rapid-fire lyrics eject from his mouth. With his impish charm, long braids, and dark brown baby face, Treach explodes the notion that hip-hop doesn't produce sex symbols. Throughout the evening women fawn over his pelvic gyrations and tongue acrobatics ("How many of y'all ladies like a nice wet tongue?" he asks seductively), and even the homeboys in the house readily give Treach his props.

Instantly my mind replays the incredible rap show of yesteryear: Doug E. Fresh and Slick Rick at the Funhouse, Public Enemy at Studio 54, Big Daddy Kane at an outdoor rally/concert in Harlem. But nothing compares to Treach's funky coup d'état. There are no gimmicks, no fancy stage design except for Kay Gee's high-rise boulder with an electronic Naughty sign, and no dancers. Treach is just a regular brother from around the way, rippin' the mike and doin' it because he loves his craft. Tonight Treach is hip-hop: in dress, in talk, in spirit.

East Orange, New Jersey, to use one resident's term, is "an extension of Newark." Many of the city's black inhabitants moved here from that larger, crime-ridden metropolis after the riot of 1967. East Orange's population is an eclectic bunch: the spacious homes of upwardly mobile black professionals butt up against the rat-infested tenements of single-parent families. Paradoxically, East Orange's hilly roads, tree-lined side streets, and beautiful row houses give the illusion of suburb. But packed tightly on many of these blocks are legions of young black men drifting somewhere between poverty and death. Each year some of these boys/men graduate from the city's two public high schools—East Orange and Clifford Scott—into a shapeless, unpredictable future. Like inner-city youth elsewhere, some will escape to the military or, if they're lucky, to college. The rest linger at home, forced either to take near-minimum-wage jobs or seek refuge in the streets.

Don't ever come to the ghetto
'Cause you wouldn't understand the ghetto

Ghetto dwelling breeds distrust and hypersensitivity. I grew up in Jersey City and later in Newark, watching B-boys walk down my block, only to be jumped because they were strangers. As far as we were concerned, the hood was all we had and we would defend it at any cost. I recalled that world, my world, as I rode the No. 21 bus through Newark—past garbage-filled lots, smoked-out buildings, and nodding junkies—into East Orange for my interview with Naughty by Nature.

"We don't let nobody come around here if we ain't never seen them before," Treach would tell me later. "We live on North 18th Street but we call it 118th Street 'cause there's a hundred *real* niggas we roll with, and we don't take no shorts. Ain't no female or no nigga from the outside gonna step up and cause any friction between us."

When I get off the bus at Williams Street and Eighteenth, I realize I don't know where I'm going, and even if I did, I'd still be simply an intruder on someone else's turf. I stop at a pay phone and call Kay Gee's house.

"They ain't here," a woman with a sweet, maternal voice says. "They went to the store. They ain't say nothin' about no interview. But I'll tell them you called."

Click.

On the PATH train back to Manhattan, Naughty's Apollo show floods my brain. Treach's world infuses his lyrics, and his aura makes it impossible for his audience—black and white, poor as shit and squeaky-clean—to ignore what he's saying. But the music itself is the music of every black male I know who's hustling on the street or rotting in jail or taking a dirt nap somewhere. After all, as has been the case with me, Treach, Vinnie, and Kay Gee have learned most of their values and guidelines for survival from the streets. There's nothing complex about B-boy culture: we fight, we drink, we bond. The hood is often all we know; it cannot thrive without us, and we cannot live without it.

On the set of *YO! MTV Raps*—a colorful, oversized playground complete with a basketball hoop and dangling *YO!* signs—Treach, Vinnie, and Kay Gee are subdued, watching Ed Lover and Dr. Dre kill time before a taping by dissin' everyone within reach.

"Hey, Dre, you know who Kenny looks like?" Ed Lover, the tall, lanky co-host shouts to his shorter, overweight partner.

Kenny Buford, *YO!*'s thin, light-complexioned production assistant, braces himself for the inevitable.

"Sade with a receding hairline!"

The camera crew and other production assistants crack up, but the trio remains mute. Bored by the delay—one camera isn't working properly—Vinnie breaks into a beat-box routine (his skills are amazing), and like any old-school rapper, Treach jumps in with a crotch-grabbing rhyme. The set quiets down momentarily, and he ends the impromptu show with a when-the-fuck-is-the-shit-gonna-start? look. I wonder if Treach realizes how large he is. How many self-proclaimed ghetto bastards have their first single go double platinum, their debut album do nearly as well, and earn an American Music Award and a Grammy nomination all in the space of ten months? Not Public Enemy, not Boogie Down Productions, not N.W.A or Ice Cube, and not even that other home bred B-boy, L.L. Cool J.

"Treach is the first authentic hip-hopper I've seen in a long time," Ed Lover tells me after "Uptown Anthem" is taped. "Yeah, he wants to get his, like everybody else, but there's a sincerity there, too. Look at him; you can see that he's had a hard life, and it comes out in his music. His hard-core ain't made-up; it's real. And he wants everybody to know that."

B-boy culture, in order to sustain itself, often exaggerates and creates un-realistic images. These hyperboles are at best coping methods and at worst lu-dicrously false senses of security. Treach is real precisely because he is not out to startle or please anyone; his life is his music and his music is his life. "Naughty by Nature has this total pop sensibility," says Benny Medina, senior vice president of A&R at Warner Bros., "yet their big concern is about staying true to the street, true to life. Most people in rap go pop at the expense of their street credentials and don't seem to care." But Treach insists you either accept him for who he is or don't accept him at all.

Midtown's Unique Recording Studios is located in a high, undistinguished building just off the corner of Seventh Avenue and Forty-seventh Street. In a dimly lit tenth-floor lounge nestled between two studios, Treach, Vinnie, and Kay Gee's cousin Gene (Naughty's road manager) are playing pool. Across the hall in Studio C, Kay Gee (born Kier Gist) is laying down tracks for NBN's second album, tentatively titled *19NaughtyII*. Hidden behind dark glasses, a gray hoodie, and black bandanna, Kay Gee gives the definite impression that he doesn't want to be bothered.

"So why do you always wear the hood and glasses?" I halfheartedly ask him.

Kay Gee looks up from his stack of 45s and, for a second, grins. A gold cap beams from the left side of his mouth.

"I'm always in the chill mood," he responds coolly, before turning back to his work permanently.

Kay Gee cues the engineer and she clicks on the anthem "Hip-Hop Hooray," a smoothed-out R & B track with chanting chorus.

I live and die for hip-hop . . .
So hip-hop hooray

Besides "Hip-Hop Hooray," Kay Gee lets me listen to a hard-core jam called "The Hood Comes First" and the funk-filled "Lyte Taste of Nature." Although *19NaughtyII* has the band's characteristic hooks and live samples, I can also hear and feel their maturation. Animated for once, Kay Gee insists this album is going to be different from the Tommy Boy debut. "Our music is like classical hip-hop, you know, it has that hard-core street sound, but we also like to use live instruments and whatnot," he says. "*19NaughtyII* is gonna let people know how serious we are. Hip-hop is all we think about."

Treach, in a better mood than he was on the set of *YO!*, greets me with a big "Whaddup?" and a bear hug, while Vinnie and Gene argue shots at the pool table. We sit down at a cafeteria-style booth at the front of the room. Bigger up close, his biceps are thick, and save a few old nicks and bruises, his skin has a smooth chocolate glow. Wearing a black T-shirt, sagging black denim jeans, and black Timberland boots, Treach looks every inch the wickedest man alive.

Born Anthony Criss twenty-one years ago in Newark, Treach moved to East Orange at age two. He has two brothers and two sisters, but only he and his younger brother lived with his mother. The product of a single-parent home, Treach only saw his father sporadically. As in the autobiographical "Ghetto Bastard," anger fills Treach's voice when he speaks of his father. "I met him, yeah, I met him," he mutters, then pauses. "I saw him a few times, but I never knew him."

I think of my father, who disowned me when I was eight, whom I didn't really know either and haven't seen since, and I remember, the first time I heard "Ghetto Bastard," how I rewound the tape over and over again to those jarring words: "Never knew my dad / Motherfuck the fag!"

"'Ghetto Bastard' is my world too," I say to Treach, and his face relaxes a bit, a serious, solitary "Word" falling from his mouth.

"It's all of us," he says, his eyes moistening. "Me and Vinnie come from broken homes. Most of our friends is like us—ghetto bastards. Kay Gee is the only one that got a pops in the house." He pauses, catching his breath. "The last time I saw my father was when I was thirteen. He was in town for a while, and I would see him every now and then. Around Christmastime I scraped up some money and bought him something—cologne or a tie or something. It was snowing, and I walked to this house, and they told me he had moved again. That was the last time I ever heard anything about him. I don't even remember walking home; that's how hurt I was. I just know I was there."

Throughout his teens, Treach became even more alienated from everything and everyone around him. With his mother struggling to feed two children and school being little more than a hangout, Treach ran the streets of East Orange, immersing himself in the rites of B-boy passage: cutting school, having sex, drinking, and smoking. Though at seventeen he worked for a few months at a Grand Union warehouse packing and unloading boxes, after he was laid off, his mother, fed up, finally threw him out.

"I wasn't comin' home and wasn't making no money to help her out either," he says, resigned, as if he'd expected it all along. "I really *wanted* to work, but I couldn't find nothin'. The streets was the only place I could turn."

Treach slept in parks, friends' homes, and anywhere else he could, selling drugs at night and sporadically attending East Orange High during the day. "A week after my mother threw me out, I got locked up for selling . . . it wasn't for too long, though, and I was right back out there doin' it again. I didn't know what else to do."

Ask most ghetto children what they want to be and their faces go blank, unsure why the question has any meaning for them. We live, as Ralph Ellison put it, literally on the run, from a world that views us as a threat to be either subdued, intimidated, or even eliminated. As a kid I knew I wanted to be a writer, but I didn't dare tell anyone because I didn't believe it could happen. Treach, too, knew he wanted to be a weaver of words—a rapper—since he was in the seventh grade. From the time he heard the Sugarhill Gang and Kurtis Blow he knew that *that* was what he wanted to do. Treach is one of those rare brothers who knew he could when everyone and everything around him told him he couldn't.

Vinnie, also twenty-one, joins Treach and me at the table. A short, stocky individual with close-cropped hair, Vinnie is the most gregarious of the three and outrageously funny. The history of Naughty by Nature, he says, dates back to an eleventh-grade health class he shared with Treach. Whenever the teacher was less than inspiring—which was often—Vinnie would do the human beat box as Treach dropped freestyle lyrics. DJ Kay Gee lived on the same block as Vinnie, and the two would team up after school to practice the beat box and turntable scratches.

A year ahead of Treach and Vinnie at East Orange High, Kay Gee decided to participate in his senior class show and asked Vinnie to join him. Since they didn't have an MC, Kay Gee invited Treach over to his house and they quickly formed the New Style (a phrase borrowed from a Beastie Boys song). "We wrecked the show," Vinnie boasts. "We kept the name and did shows all over the area. We knew from there that we wanted to be in the music business."

After Vinnie and Treach graduated from high school in 1988, the New Style signed with Sylvia Robinson's Bon Ami label and, like hundreds of aspiring rap stars before them, received a harsh lesson in the music business. They locked themselves into a production deal and wound up making an album, *Independent Leaders*, an unsuccessful effort that led them nowhere (Naughty by Nature ultimately settled with Bon Ami for an undisclosed amount in 1990.) All three turned back to selling drugs to support their musical ambitions.

"We was dirty niggas clockin'," Treach says reflectively. "We put our money somewhere that would help us in the future. We always knew we'd make another record."

In 1989, Queen Latifah, whom the trio knew from neighboring Irvington, released her first album on Tommy Boy. "Latifah was managed by the Flavor Unit, and we figured if they helped her, they could help us," Vinnie says. "Kay Gee called Latifah's producer DJ Mark the 45 King, and he camcordered us performing in his basement. That tape started all the buzz."

When the New Style gave themselves a fund-raiser at East Orange's Upsala College, Flavor Unit members Lakim Shabazz, Apache, and Queen Latifah attended. Impressed with the group's potential, Latifah and Shakim Compare immediately signed the New Style to Flavor Unit Management and then took their demo tape to Benny Medina at Warner Bros., who gave them a contract in 1990. After their album was completed, Medina approached Warner's new subsidiary, Tommy Boy—the label of De La Soul and Digital Underground—about distributing the album. "I liked Tommy Boy's marketing techniques for street audiences," Medina explains. "Sometimes an act, a really significant act, can get lost at a major label because of its stupidity or weakness. Tommy Boy started building street knowledge two months before the release of 'O.P.P.'"

"We actually turned them down in 1989 when they were still the New Style," says Tommy Boy president Monica Lynch. "We felt they hadn't clarified their style yet." But after that initial contact with Tommy Boy, the New Style became Naughty by Nature (the title of a song on that first album, which, Treach says, neatly sums up the group's persona) and polished their sound, moving away from freewheeling braggadocio to anecdotes about Illtown. Hearing Naughty by Nature the second time around, Tommy Boy jumped on "O.P.P."

"I just thought it was the coolest," says Medina. "I'd never heard anyone use a Jackson sample before, and with the grooves, the smooth bass lines, and melodic structure, it was a totally new sound. I thought we'd have a fairly successful record, but no way did I know it was going to be *the* phrase, *the* rap song of the year."

But Tommy Boy worked the single from the ground up, with a major promotion including stickers, T-shirts, and a national tour long before the single dropped. "We wanted something everybody could get wit: the kids to the older folks, the girls and the guys," says Treach. "We figured even the hardest of the hard would be like, yeah."

Treach still insists, somewhat disingenuously, that Naughty by Nature "just wanted to be a nice underground group like Brand Nubian." But B-boy culture is about being large—being known in your world as the best, be it a local drug dealer or a hip-hop artist. Indeed, Naughty by Nature has spawned a number of Treach imitators, most recently Das EFX and Kris Kross. Monica Lynch's assessment is blunt: "The effect Treach has had on hip-hop has been enormous. I call it 'Treach-isms': the way he delivers lines, his stage presence, and his charisma. Treach has that star power that is unbelievable. Guys admire him for his rhyme skills, but women want to sleep with him."

Inside the poolroom, Treach's lean body pushes against a window as he peers down on Times Square and the rush-hour crowd. Glassy-eyed and mellow after a long day in the studio, he's sipping on a forty-ounce of Olde English. Alone with him, I wonder aloud how it feels to be a star.

"Everything is still the same," Treach says, his voice low and raspy. "The only difference is that financially we ain't gotta struggle and hustle on the streets. We still live on the same block, hang with the same people. A lot of people are lookin' up to us, where it wasn't like that before."

The role-model tag will probably stick to Treach for a long time. He's employed many of his homeys already and plans to hire his friends who are in jail when they get out. In addition, Treach, Vinnie, and Kay Gee sell Naughty by Nature paraphernalia—hoods, baseball caps, pajamas, and condoms—at a profit and expect to build businesses at home in East Orange.

Judging by the number of women who have passed through the studio today, it seems the only thing missing from Treach's life right now is one steady love interest. "I don't have time for that right now," he says matter-of-factly. "Our music comes first. I have companions, but it's not like I'm home long enough to get serious with someone. And I tell them that. It's an understanding from jump."

If Treach is avoiding relationships—ones that might lead to a family of his own—it may be because he's recently been trying to repair the one with his mother. It is perfect, in a way, that Treach would rise above the resentment he must harbor for her and do what is probably the right thing. That, it seems, is where his success comes from: the ability to control the rage and cultivate the creativity, a powerful combination that will allow him to move up.

Where his mother is concerned, perhaps he's backing up, in a sort of retroactive attempt to make the past right—playing the part that his father so pitifully neglected. He's buying her a house. Sending her to school.

He says resolutely, "I'm not bitter or nothin' about what happened. She had to do what she had to do."

But someday, Treach wants to be able to do things differently: "I wanna have a family with some type of structure, you know what ah'm sayin'? That's why I haven't had any kids yet." He looks down at his large hands and ponders them for a minute. "I wanna have it so my kids will know me." He pauses again. And then lifts his head and looks straight at me. "My family would come first."

Vibe / September 1992

Caught Up in the (Gangsta) Rapture

Dr. C. Delores Tucker's Crusade Against "Gangsta Rap"

KIERNA MAYO

You got the older generation of so-called leaders want to come talk to us, want to sit down and rap to us. But it's no dialogue there. They always let the small things or small differences interfere with the bigger picture. If I use the word *bitch*, to me it's just language.
—Ice Cube, from a recent *New York Times* interview

I think she called me "baby," or something like that. Maybe "sweetheart." Whatever the case, it was clear to me as soon as she opened her mouth that this would be a difficult interview. To be a journalist is one thing, to confront and challenge a sixty-some-odd-year-old black woman is another. So, as convicted as I was about calling her anti–"gangsta rap" rhetoric to task, I dutifully reminded myself that she could have been my grandmother. And really, I had to admit that I agreed with a lot of what she says. This music *is* often painfully violent and misogynist—there is no denying that. It definitely legitimates and probably enhances violent and misogynist action—there's little denying that either. So why does her anti–"gangsta rap" mission put such a bad taste in my mouth?

Dr. C. Delores Tucker fancies herself a type of modern-day Moses—one who will lead her people to liberation, freeing them finally and for good from the hell of "gangsta rap" and the wrath of its oppressive craftsmen. She is offended and incensed and claims she would rather die before she would sit idly by and continue to let "the children's" ears meet with such "pornographic smut."

She is crusading against *it*, this horrific, monstrous thing—making public appearances, marching, picketing, getting arrested and crying. She says she won't stop until *it* stops. And ever since her concerted efforts began some year and a half ago, there has been a multifaceted assault on "gangsta rap" never before seen on any other type of artistic musical expression. No, not even Tipper Gore's (Vice President Al Gore's wife's) 1985 raid against violent heavy metal will match this all-out attack. Tipper and her organization, the Parents Music Resource Center, won partial compliance from record companies, who have agreed to voluntarily stamp their morally questionable music (anything with curses) "parental advisory: explicit lyrics." But with hard rock as its primary target, Tipper's campaign didn't speak directly to black America (with the exception of her notorious but brief bout with Luther Campbell).

Black folks are listening now.

It was a psychic friend and a famous welfare recipient that set it off.

Of all people, Dionne Warwick and Melba Moore were the "young entertainers" who first alerted Tucker to so-called gangsta rap's undeniably brutal lyrics. It was at a brunch held during the annual Congressional Black Caucus weekend. "Those young women said they were tired of being disrespected and insulted," Tucker says. The two artists now cochair the entertainment commission of Tucker's organization, The National Political Congress of Black Women.

The NPCBW is a nonprofit, nonpartisan organization for "the political and economic empowerment of African-American women and their families." It is this crew—one composed of socially stalwart, scholarly, super-well-to-do divas—that is putting a match to the kerosene of the (anti-) gangsta rap debate. Led by Dr. Tucker, these women have been successful in galvanizing not only the mainstream media but the black church, the NAACP, the U.S. Congress, and a host of other groups and individuals to take up their struggle.

And a well-publicized struggle it is. You may have seen Dr. Tucker on the Geraldo circus—the CNBC special on gangsta rap featuring Schoolly D, Ed

Lover and Dr. Dre, Freddie Foxxx, Luther Campbell, and Joseph Madison of the NAACP. Or maybe you've seen her gracing a page or two of your local newspaper. Or perhaps you've even caught a glimpse of her downtown at the precinct (she's been arrested for protesting, you know). Nowadays, Dr. Tucker is everywhere. The former Pennsylvania secretary of state is a very powerful woman. She knows struggle and she understands government. Although it will be a fight (after all, rap made an estimated $1.4 billion last year and you can bet, of that, gangsta rap represents a nice portion), she's up for it. Dr. Tucker picks up where the Reverend Calvin Butts left off. She wants to stop the gangsta rap insanity, and there's a good chance she will. *Everyone* is officially listening now; no matter how you see it, the stakes are high.

Eleven flights up, Dr. Tucker is sitting high and mighty on the latest official anti-gangsta-rap throne. It must be because the central office of the NPCBW is located at the new Kennedy Center in Washington, D.C., that oil paintings of lilies (or was it cherry blossoms?) decorate the waiting-area walls, and a huge brass eagle is permanently perched on a stand. That's also probably why opera is playing lightly. I suppose it's because of these classic things much adored by "Americans" that on first sight, I really can't tell that this office has much to do with women *or* blacks. But it does. Ah yes, a better look around reveals ten *Jet* magazines spread out neatly on a coffee table.

Back in Dr. Tucker's personal office space, though, spatterings of black womanhood are immediately evident. There's the Rosa Parks watercolor, the Sojourner Truth iron sculpture, and Dr. Tucker's many plaques and awards. There's also the photo of Dr. Martin Luther King and Dr. Tucker marching somewhere, arm in arm. "See that?" she points to the picture. "I didn't have to do that. I've been fighting for a very long time."

Although some of us will, it's a little scary that Dr. Tucker would assume that Snoop Doggy Dogg, or me for that matter, cares that she marched with King. I didn't have the heart to tell her that for a generation of black and poor, and black and not-so-poor, young people, Dr. King has become less than a hero, role model, or intrepid warrior but instead, more of an intangible icon that every February, McDonald's insists we remember. It wasn't in me to say that for too many black kids there is no historical connection to that place in time—that sadly, the political and economic "gains" of the sixties civil rights movement have backfired against our community in many injurious ways.

At this very moment, the gap between the generations in black America is as wide as the Sahara. "Kids have it better today," she tells me.

Really?

Dr. Tucker: I didn't call the Senate hearings for them [the gangsta rappers]. Let me explain what I did. I called for these hearings against racism and greed, pure and simple. They [the music industry] can stop it. They don't do it to their own. They won't let it be sold to Jews. They won't let it be sold to white kids, only to black kids.

THE SOURCE: But for us to take matters to Congress or any arm of the American government seems pointless considering, historically speaking, they have never acted in our best interest.
Because they have never been forced to. When they were forced to, they did! They did act in our best interest when Rosa Parks sat in the back of the bus; we don't have to sit there anymore. How do you think we came to where we are if they didn't ever do anything?

A lot of young black people today would rather have their own bus and not have to ask anything of anyone.
If we want to, we ought to have the right to promote the best in us. We did not just "sit with them." We promoted our greatness to our children. That little two-year-old girl who said she wanted to be a m.f. gangsta . . .

What are some things that have been done before now to correct the conditions facing young black people? This attack on music just all seems like a very late reaction to one of the many things that merely mirrors our pathology, not creates it.
Well, nobody seemed to be doing anything until I went to jail and took up this issue, had a press conference. Why now? Why wasn't it raised before? Since nobody else raised it, I did when the entertainment women came

here. So after I raise the issue, of course, there is a lot of money flowing. I could take money. People want to know what I want. I could get fifteen or so million. What do I want? I want dignity and justice and quality life for my people. That's what I've always wanted. I don't get paid. I'm not on anybody's payroll.

Do you think that the absence of a quality life for black people started with gangsta rap?
We have never had a phenomenon where kids were planning their own funerals at thirteen and twelve. We never had that. I am going after the record industry because they are the ones that are out of control. There's the Nation of Islam in the hood. They honor their mothers and don't drink or use drugs. Let them get a contract, they could sing as good or better as anyone, but they never will get a contract. Never! Lena Horne couldn't get a decent contract because they said you have to play these roles and she refused. She would not promote the racist stereotypical images that they wanted her to play. So what's new? Nothing. They [gangsta rappers] are just the new Stepin Fetchits. Someone said Amos and Andy of the 1990s. We can't say that they are just speaking of reality. The reality is that they don't hate their people; they are paid to say that. So many of them have said that it's the money. *The money.*

Conspiracy theories about the record industry weave in and out of Dr. Tucker's argument. "When these white kids see the blacks, they think, 'Oh, that's black. That's the way they live. That's the way they are.' What [record companies] are doing is programming them to say that we are not people, and when the man comes to exterminate us and put us in concentration camps, the white kids are going to be happy about it," she explains. She believes that "someone" is in the process of building concentration camps for blacks. "There's one already in New Orleans," she confirms. She is convinced that this music sends a message to the entire world that black people are subhuman.

But for such radical concerns, her response is rather weak. Dr. Tucker is a woman who actually believes that use of the vote alone will change the concentration camp reality. And it is this type of impossible reasoning that is really the telltale problem with Tucker's philosophy around gangsta rap. Not that gangsta rap isn't problematic with its repeatedly self-hating, anti-life themes. Not that the recording industry isn't making googobs of cash by exploiting those who exploit the worst of black people's conditions. Not even that a good slice of the gangsta rap pie isn't composed of minimum-talent, fake-gangsta wannabes who get over on their fans *and* The Box by flashing '64 Impalas and big-booty girls in three-minute videos. All of this, of course, is true.

Tucker's major flaw is in her fundamental belief that gangsta rap is a cause and not an effect: the cause of violence and misogyny in black communities, not the effect of these two proudly American social ills. The cause of black exploitation by the music industry, not the result of a long history of white exploitation of trusting black talent. The cause of substandard, low-grade product, not the result of a capitalist system infamously known for encouraging cheap product "get overs."

Nonetheless, the fears and concerns of Dr. Tucker are very widely shared. The conspiracies she refers to could more simply be called white supremacy (racism), as it plagues every American institution. She doesn't know that countless panels and discussions and fights have transpired for years between young people (both in and out of the music industry) trying to make a little sense out of what is too often sheer madness. Heated sessions take place between black women and girls (who listen to and love this music) as they defend themselves against the same hateful threats and images that black females have always had to fight. Nasty editorials challenging rap artists to check themselves are written.

Still, in order to be respected in the hip-hop critique arena, *at the very least* you must possess a genuine love for the artists, the audience, and *some* appreciation of the art form itself. Anything else is like a car mechanic trying to appraise a diamond.

When the congressional hearings took place two months ago, Congresswoman Maxine Waters was the only public official to openly support the rappers and their right to simply be. Her testimony gave voice to a unique position—one that saw gangsta rappers as part of the community, not immoral aliens who had dropped out of the sky.

"These are my children," she said. "I do not intend to marginalize them or demean them. Rather I take responsibility for trying to understand what they are saying. I want to embrace them and transform them . . . I don't encourage the use of obscenities. I just think we should stop pretending we are hearing them for the first time . . . Let's not lose sight of what the real problem is. It is not the words being used. It is the reality they are rapping about. For decades, many of us have talked about the lives and the hopes of our people—the pain and the hopelessness, the deprivation and destruction. Rap music is communicating that reality in a way we never have."

Waters is involving rappers in a project, called L.A. 17 to 30, that will try to help young people between seventeen and thirty years old in Los Angeles "clean up their acts and reenter the mainstream." For this project to work it will cost $17 million dollars. Much of that will come from the entertainment industry.

The major voice of reason in the Tucker camp comes from Von Alexander, the New York–based director of the entertainment commission of the NPCBW. She has been an active member of the music industry for seventeen years. She is also a community activist and really tries to keep her finger on the pulse of young people's concern. Von contends that years before taking anything to Dr. Tucker and subsequently Congress (in fact, before going public at all), her office printed up thousands of letters urging men in the industry to take a stand against what was happening in hip-hop. "It began after the Dee Barnes incident," she says. "But there was virtual silence. And know that we didn't just respond to this. When *The Color Purple* came out, we jumped up and said, 'No, Steven Spielberg, you can't talk about our men like that.' But when women are attacked, brothers sit back and let it happen."

Von is well aware that throughout the music industry Dr. Tucker does not win Most Popular, but has no fear of that thwarting their objective. "If Dr. Tucker's boisterous and righteous mouth will bring about dialogue, then I welcome her conversation. Finally brothers and sisters are having the talk that we should have been having in the first place. Dr. Tucker has brought the conversation back to the place where it should have been all the time."

Since it is Von who generally ends up communicating her organization's concerns to key players in the music industry, she is forced to listen to everyone. She knows that there are women who share her concerns but are conflicted by the conservative and unwavering politics Dr. Tucker has brought to the debate. "That's all right," she says. "We can agree to disagree and still be on the same team." No matter what, Von stands firmly by her mentor. "All these people claiming that Dr. Tucker isn't out in the streets don't know what they are talking about. Besides, they aren't out there themselves. People don't put their money where their mouth is. Dr. Tucker does. She walks the streets, she believes in rights for black women. I wouldn't have the courage to do much of what I do if it weren't for her example."

As we go back and forth, Dr. Tucker makes it clear to me that she is not about to define gangsta rap. "You know exactly what it is," she says. But honestly I don't. In fact, I'm slightly afraid that she could be working this diligently to win legislation to silence all rap with, yes, cursing. So away with everybody, even Queen Latifah. You know, the gangsta rapper.

But the truth is because no "genre" of rap music has ever been self-conscious enough to actually name itself, it's obvious the term is one that was imposed from outside the rap community. Many "gangsta rappers" themselves reject the term. Because Dr. Tucker refuses to respectfully enter into any dialogue with members of the hip-hop community (see the same Geraldo circus where she actually spent time telling Ed Lover she didn't want kids to end up like *him*), she finds herself working with definitions created more by Dan Rather and Peter Jennings than Scarface and MC Eiht. But, OK, supposing we agree there's such a thing as "gangsta rap," shouldn't we be clear about whether it is the rap performed by gang members specifically, by everyone from L.A. in general, Kool G Rap, Bushwick Bill, or what about Luke? He *did* appear on the special.

It's obvious gangsta rap, at least as far as its biggest detractors have determined, is any "negative" rap (read: not upholding the imagery of successful, refined, happy, proud-to-be-black blacks). In actuality, the only people who could possibly determine what gangsta rap is, *if* it is, are the black people who make it and the black people who listen to it. But since most of us haven't been asked what we think, it's not surprising that the term is used quite loosely, even ridiculously, by everyone—preachers and protesters alike. This is too bad. Isn't semantics, language, the crux of this entire debate?

It is an understatement to say that the words are vile. Harsh. Offensive. But even more devastating are the realities to which the words speak. Author and critic Nelson George writes, "To discuss this subset of rap outside the framework of the forces that influence it . . . is to rip this music out of context and endow its creators with a profound power that I don't believe they have."

Is it possible to recognize the pathology and potential danger of some rap music and still enjoy aspects of it? For millions of us, there is no question. Rap music, like the generation that gave birth to it, is schizophrenic and takes on the different faces and attitudes of its many players. Too much has been said about our so-called lost generation by everyone except us. That is one of the major dangers of eradicating gangsta rap—it would silence an extremely important voice. Without it, who will (accurately) report about the nuances, pathology, and most importantly, resilence of America's best-kept secret? The black ghetto.

Go ahead and lump gangsta rap in the group of things that divide black America. As the ties that bind the different socioeconomic classes of black people continue to fracture, so will the link between our sensibilities and concerns. It's been three long decades since the sixties. No longer are all of our eyes on the same prize. Author and professor Michael Eric Dyson wrote that "gangsta rap's greatest sin is that it tells the truth about practices and beliefs that rappers hold in common with the black elite. This music has embarrassed black bourgeois culture."

Gangsta rap really has no shame. The why is obvious. This music makes far too much money at a time when *56 percent*, more than half, of black America's children are born into poverty. We are going to need a whole lot more than a "just say no to gangsta rap." Legislation won't put a dent in white supremacy. Who wouldn't love for our music to reflect a better reality? For our men to love our women? For our men and women to love themselves? But right now, the reality is that "positive" means nothing to a whole lot of people.

More people than Dr. C. Delores Tucker cares to know.

The Source / June 1994

Hell-Raiser

DREAM HAMPTON

When I see wildness gone in a person, it's sad. That special lack of restraint, which is a part of human life and is best typified in certain Black males. It's in Black men despite the reasons society says they're not supposed to have it. Everybody knows who "that man" is, and they may give him bad names and call him a "street nigger"; but when you take away the vocabulary of denigration, what you have is somebody who is fearless and who is comfortable with that fearlessness. It's not about meanness. It's a kind of self-flagellant resistance to certain kinds of control, which is fascinating. Opposed to accepted notions of progress, the lockstep life, they live in the world unreconstructed, and that's it.   —Toni Morrison, Nobel Prize–winning writer

JUNETEENTH 1994
DETROIT, MICHIGAN

I have this recurring dream about Tupac. I'm riding around L.A. in the middle of the night with Tupac and his boys. Whoever's driving stops at a red light. Tupac, who is sitting in the front seat, cranes his neck in both directions of the crossroad. "Nigga, what is you *doing*?" he screams at the driver. "Ain't no cars coming. The white man got you so fucked-up that he flash a color at you and you'll stop!" The driver tries to laugh him off, but Pac is dead serious: "Nigga, drive." The rest of us look around at one another. Is he serious? "Nigga, look if you gon' sit here and be a l'il bitch, I can't fuck with you." And with that he jumps out of the car.

There's a purity to Tupac's rage. Yes, he's dangerously emotional, but righteously so. He believes something and is willing to act on it. For him conformity means the death of truth. We plead for him to return to the car but he has already pimped his way into the darkness.

JANUARY 31, 1994
BLUE PALMS RECORDING STUDIOS
BURBANK, CALIFORNIA

They got toys for guns / Jails for guns / But no jobs for guns. Tupac likes to add effects to his vocals: Chuck D–style reverbs and echoes that give his voice that godly quality. He instructs his engineer, a black man at a black-owned studio, to isolate the track so he can perfect the pitch.

In exactly twelve hours, Tupac will be required to appear in a Los Angeles municipal court for a case filed against him by Allen Hughes, one half of the directorial team that brought us *Menace II Society*.

"I been sitting on this all day." He pulls an eighth of L.A.'s now infamous chronic from his back pocket, appraising the red hairs in the Hawaiian sinsemilla. His older brother Mopreme rolls up no less than six blunts in a row. As everyone else gets more mellow, Tupac picks up steam.

"Nigga, pass that!" Tupac has been dying to get his clown on. Stretch, Tupac's producer/collaborator and constant road dawg from Queens, is holding the blunt. "Fuck you—she just passed it to me." Tupac's eyes light up, his whole face starts beaming with his smile. A challenge. He looks Stretch up and down for a total of five seconds before he gets in that ass.

"This nigga got blue carnations on his drawers."

"Fuck you, nigga." Stretch passes him the blunt but it's too late.

"Blue mothafuckin' carnations. Can you believe this, dream? Feminine-ass blue carnations. Look at me!" Tupac raises his shirt—THUG LIFE, his now infamous tattoo, sprawls across his abdomen—the small of his back reads EX-ODUS, his pants are sagging, and his boxers are navy. "I got some masculine-ass plaid mothafuckin' drawers! We go shopping together, Stretch, niggas could see you bend over and think I wear flowers on my ass!" He grabs his forty; by now Mopreme is doubled over and the engineer is in stitches.

"That did it for me, all niggas from Queens wear flowers on they drawers!"

"Aw nigga, suck my dick." Stretch is a laid-back brother but he's had enough.

Tupac throws his head back and laughs, a big, beautiful, infectious laugh, and all is forgiven. "It's all good.

"Wait! Don't ever let me say that again. Can you believe that?" All of a sudden Tupac's changed the subject to Hammer, and I'm still trying to peep Stretch's boxers while he's not looking.

"How does he do it?" he asks me.

I'm too slow, the chronic is kicking my ass.

"Timing. This nigga manages to come out while everybody else is getting arrested and shit."

"Naw, it's his crib. It's 'cause he threw his crib up in the video," I offer.

"You might be right." Then from nowhere he wheels his swivel chair in my direction. "You know what Thug Life's new code is: 'No mothafucking comment.'"

"I ain't ask you no question yet," I spit back a little defense.

"Naw, I'm talking about to them." He motions outside the back door, to the studio's parking lot, where teams of invisible cracker journalists are hiding in the bushes.

"'Why are you so angry? Why do you smoke chronic? Why cain't you stay out of trouble? Why is the earth round?' Eat a dick!" He leaps to his feet, frustrated with the pesky media. "Niggas ain't meant to be understood. *Thugging*. So back up off me!"

I remind Tupac that the latest attack on him has come not from Dan Rather, but Dionne Warwick, who objected to his attendance at the NAACP Image Awards, along with the National Political Congress of Black Women.

"These niggas ain't want me there and they gave mothafuckin' Michael Jackson a standing ovation. Ain't that a bitch! How much money you gots to sling at them sorry-ass Negroes to get them on they feet!" He rolls a little closer and confides, "I'm fucking grown-ass women. That's my crime—I'm a freak! I let a bitch suck my dick in the middle of the dance floor." He's referring to November 16th of last year. He was at Nell's, a New York nightclub, dancing with a young hottie when she dropped to her knees and did her thing. Three days later she would accuse him of rape. "Goddamn them child-molesting, fake-ass mothafuckas, damn them all to hell!

"And Dionne Warwick." I thought he'd never get to homegirl. "Fucking dream reading, psychic bitch! Don't get me started, I'll tell the real on they whole family!" He's on his feet again, throwing up Thug Life.

Stretch and Mopreme aren't even listening anymore. Pac notices his audience is diminishing and changes the rules. "The first nigga to fall asleep is getting hot-ass quarters on they forehead. You hear that, Mo? You gots to stay up and trip with the rest of us, nigga."

An assistant from the studio is going on a food run to the rib shack. "Y'all better put your order in, 'cause when my ribs come, I don't want none of you righteous vegetarian smegetarians up in my shit."

In less than twenty minutes Mo is snoozing. Pac pulls a lighter from his pocket. "Who got a quarter?" He heats the quarter with a devilish grin on his grill. "That nigga is crazy," Stretch says, shaking his head.

"Oww!!! What the fuck!" Mo comes out of dreamtime swinging. "Get yo' crazy ass away from me!"

Pac gives Stretch a pound. "I got 'em! You saw that, right? I'll teach you never to fall asleep on one of my sessions!"

The Hughes brothers arrive at court with four bow-tied hired security, presumably the Nation of Islam's. Tupac strolls in twenty minutes later with the completed tracks from last night blasting in his headphones. He sits several rows in front of his brother Mo and his manager, Watani, so that he can stare Allen and Albert down while he waits for his case to be called. When the clerk calls the case, *The People v. Shakur*, we are informed that there has been a change of venue. We are required to make our way to Division 75, located in a separate building. Two of the Hughes brothers' security post themselves outside the courtroom as the Hughes brothers' entourage prepare to make their exit. Tupac makes it outside before Allen and Albert and walks up to one of the brothas in the bow tie.

"What I wanna know is, since when did y'all start protecting niggas from other niggas?" he demands. The brother is taken off guard but he tries to answer Tupac with a blank military stare. Just then the Hughes brothers come out of the courtroom.

"Aww, you li'l bitch!" Allen Hughes throws up his fists at Tupac. "Put 'em up!"

Tupac's heart asks his ears for a sound check. Still, he's not at a loss for words. He begins stripping—he tosses me his Walkman. "Li'l bitch? Nigga, you wasn't saying that shit when I was whoopin' yo' ass all up and down the set of your video!"

"You and about twelve of your niggas," retorts Allen with newfound confidence.

By now the bodyguards are holding Allen and Albert back and creating a barricade between the two crews, making the mistake of pushing Pac. Le'chelle Wooderd, Tupac's attorney, and I try to calm Pac down but it's way past that. Before we can say "chill" Pac has both Hughes brothers, their boy, and all four of their security backed up against the wall.

"You gon' need mothafuckin' Farrakhan to calm me down! You got that? Farrakhan! You bean-pie-slinging, bow-tie-wearing bitches. You wear *bow ties*, remember that! I'll have niggas from Crenshaw with AKs and rags up here! Nigga, you don't even know who you fucking with—these roots run deep!"

Finally, the sheriff's department come storming around the corner. They throw Tupac against the wall and instruct the Hughes brothers to make their way downstairs.

"*Officers*. I'm glad you arrived. These men were trying to attack me! Can you *believe* that? They tried to attack *me* with the Nation of Islam. Those are Farrakhan's boys, you know." Tupac isn't so hyped that he doesn't know how to feed fat white boys lies. "I'm so glad you're here. I have full confidence in the law's ability to handle the situation." Watani rolls his eyes at Pac and refuses the sheriff's offer of an escort. After five minutes have passed, the officers allow us in the elevator. When we get to Division 75, we're searched and seated on separate sides of the courtroom from the Hughes brothers, who arrived five minutes earlier. Two of the bodyguards pull Pac aside. They want to assure him that although they are fans, they were hired by the Hughes brothers. They tell Pac that Allen and Albert are cowards, something he already knows, and seek Pac's reconciliation.

"This is the only one I'm really guilty of." There are more than four outstanding criminal charges against Tupac, including rape and a possible manslaughter charge. But the Hughes brothers case is the most annoying for him. There's an unspoken law in our community that two black men should never be in court for battery. They should avoid fighting when possible, and when they do it, it should be fair and not fatal. Someone loses, someone wins. There may be retaliation. In worst-case scenarios it may escalate into full-blown violence and neighborhood wars, but never should it be taken to the police.

As part of evidence, Allen Hughes submits photos taken the day he was beat down by Tupac. Allen claims that Tupac jumped him with a crew of people. Outside of the courthouse Pac denies planning to outnumber the Hughes brothers. "Them niggas [the ones who jumped in once the fight began] knew them [the Hughes brothers] just like they knew me—from around the way. That wasn't my video. That was a Spice 1 video. I got them niggas started mak-

ing videos anyway. Plus, I came ready to kick both they asses myself!" Then
with a grin: "Those other niggas didn't get down with Thug Life until *after* that
shit happened."

FEBRUARY 10, 1994
LOUISE'S PASTA
MELROSE BOULEVARD, CALIFORNIA

After a relatively boring morning in court we decide to lunch at a sunny, posh
Italian restaurant Tupac remembers enjoying. Even as we dine, a New York court
is examining evidence in the rape case that has become Tupac's personal demon.

The rape charges surfaced amongst a barrage of others. Most significantly
they came a short three weeks after the cop-shooting case earned him front-
page status. The obvious irony is that he was accused of rape as "Keep Ya
Head Up"—the most genuine peace offering to B-girls to date—flooded the radio waves and implored black men to love and respect black women. The alleged victim claims she was sodomized by Tupac and two other codefendants.
A fourth suspect disappeared from the hotel room before the police arrived
and has never been found. While admitting that he and the alleged victim did
engage in consensual sex since their first meeting at Nell's, Tupac emphatically
denies that he raped anyone. He claims that he and the alleged victim did not
even engage in sexual intercourse the night of the alleged rape. Nor did he aid
and abet in, as New York dailies reported, any "gang bang."

Earlier this week I spoke with a sister who'd been active in nationalist
struggle, as has Tupac's family, for years. I admire this sister for her political
consistency, her grassroots work ethics, and her genuine desire to understand
and support young people. She is torn with ambivalence, as are most of us, because of the charges that Tupac allegedly raped a young woman in a New York
hotel room. She's met with other sisters, her comrades in struggle, and has decided that his behavior is neither revolutionary nor New Afrikan. She and her
sisters are planning to share their position with Pac through Watani, also a
long-standing political and community activist. I've not yet found a way to talk

about the real concerns and criticism that black women in particular have around this case. I decide that these sisters and their obvious integrity is a possible way to get him to respond to these issues. What I don't realize is that in the week that passed they've not spoken with him.

"Fuck those bitches! I don't need that shit!" I'm frightened by his venom. "I'm on the front lines of this shit. Not thirty years ago. Now! Where were they when we didn't have no food or fucking electricity? When we were eating hard-boiled eggs and they pulling off million-dollar heist and shit!" He's referring to the years spent as an infant of the black power movement when his mother, a convicted and certified revolutionary, found herself struggling to support her baby. The "million-dollar heist" were those bank and Brink's robberies, some of them foiled, that placed every known member of the Black Liberation Army on the FBI's most wanted list. "Fuck them! I need support, not criticism!"

I've opened a painful space for Tupac. That of betrayal. That I should expect Tupac to regard these sisters' opinions with more weight than anyone else's has to do with my notion of Tupac's respect for legacy and the movement in general. Afeni Shakur, Tupac's mother, was numbered amongst the Panther 21, members of the New York Panthers accused of conspiracy to blow up the Brooklyn Botanical Gardens. She and her comrades stood defiantly on the principle of anti-imperialism during their hearings. They were imprisoned when she was pregnant with Tupac. In 1986 Tupac's stepfather, Mutulu Shakur (also Mopreme's biological father), was convicted of conspiracy linked to the Assata Shakur case. An extremely high-profile political prisoner, Assata was liberated from prison in New Jersey after being convicted of killing a white police officer who killed her partner, Zayd Shakur, one fateful night on the New Jersey turnpike. In Assata's autobiography she recalls reuniting with Afeni, then pregnant with Tupac, in a prison gymnasium.

To suggest, as many do, that Tupac should be "responsible to his legacy" in some ways simplifies the legacy. But to suggest that Tupac's interpretation of this legacy should fit some romantic ideal of "the movement" is to deny reality specificity. Tupac's childhood—those years underground, aboveground, the years when his disillusioned mother began smoking crack—is as much a part of his legacy as the black leather jackets and clenched fists.

Outside the restaurant a vagrant brother is arguing with himself. He's oily and tattered, but he wants no money. He may not even want an audience for the argument he is staging with his ghosts.

"That's gonna be me. Watch!" Tupac is actor now; he performs a dead-on impersonation of the schizophrenic brother. "Standing on a fucking corner talking about 'Fucking black panthers, hip-hop bitches, bitches, niggas, niggas get away from me, you mothafuckas! Back up—it's loaded.'" He laughs, then looks back as he crosses the street. "Yup, if I make it. That's gonna be me."

MARCH 9, 1994
MIDAFTERNOON
SUNSET BOULEVARD, L.A.

When you're a rap star, you never know when something's gonna jump off. It's one of the reasons you roll so thick. There's the constant threat of being "tested" by that one fan who is sure he can replace you or at least brag to his hood about how he robbed or humiliated you. Ask any number of artists, each will have at least a half dozen stories about the peculiar combination of awe and animosity particular to hip-hop and its audience.

There's a Shell gas station located on eternally upscale Sunset Boulevard, around the corner from La Montrose, the hotel Pac lives at when in town. Pac throws his rental Lexus LS 300 coupe in park and rushes into the gas station's convenience store for magazines and munchies.

While he's browsing, a group of five brothas from some Crip hood recognize him. One of them decides to fuck with Pac.

"Where you from?"

It takes Pac a second to place the thinly veiled hostility in his voice, but it's the middle of the afternoon, he's all alone, and he really just wants a little reading material. Under ordinary circumstances (at least when you're talking to a Crip in Los Angeles), the question carries enormous weight—as in "What set are you from?" i.e., what's your gang affiliation. Pac is more from Oakland than most places, but he's definitely not down with banging.

"All over."

"No, you ain't, you from Baltimore. But you don't never claim it. I know 'cause my homeboy used to take care of you."

"Well, your homeboy lied, 'cause ain't nobody take care of me while I was in Baltimore."

Teenage customers, completely unaware of the escalating confrontation, interrupt, asking Pac for his autograph. While he's hitting them off with his signature, he hears the nigga he's been beefing with tell his boys, "I'm finst to jack this nigga!"

Pac glances a pair of scissors in his peripheral and grabs them, facing homeboy. "Well, come on, nigga, let's do this!"

The Korean merchant behind the counter gets nervous and picks up the phone. The four other Crips, who look sorry that they brought their trouble-making homeboy out of the hood, back up toward the double glass doors.

The Crip with the homey in Baltimore tags Pac in the eye and runs out of the store. Pac chases him around his car before he jumps in and they speed out of the lot down Sunset.

MARCH 10, 1994
LOS ANGELES COUNTY MUNICIPAL COURT CASE #R0617,
THE PEOPLE V. SHAKUR

The press begins fighting for prime shooting positions by eight forty-five. MTV, local affiliates, and national networks send out the same gumpy white-boy cameramen they send everywhere. When Tupac steps off the elevator, the media comes alive. The bright fluorescents turn on his chiseled features, creating blinding glares and casting disfiguring shadows. "Don't touch my lawyer." Tupac places a protective arm in front of petite Le'chelle Wooderd, who is nearly toppled by the swarm.

The Honorable George H. Wu, the judge presiding over the Hughes brothers' case, will sentence Tupac after closing statements are made.

Attorney Chokwe Lumumba, national chairman of the Revolutionary New Afrikan People's Organization, is in L.A. working on the defense in the Reginald Denny case. He is Tupac's constant legal adviser and part of Tupac's ambition, his productiveness, and his desire to be useful to his community. Le'chelle Wooderd reminds the judge that although the media and the prosecutor's office have pursued the case as if it were murder, it is simply battery. She pleads that his sentence be congruent with his crime, one that for the most part Tupac never denied.

The attorney for the prosecutor's office, a perpetually disheveled-looking black woman, asks for the harshest sentencing available. She attempts to weave images of cop-shooter, gangsta rapper, rapist, and ghetto bastard into one giant menace to society. At one point she introduces a man who was the subject of a magazine article she read, one born in the perilous Cabrini Green projects of Chicago who apparently overcame white supremacy and capitalism to embody the American dream—a model Negro. Why can't Tupac overcome his anger and do the same? she almost asks. Throughout her diatribe Tupac shifts in his seat anxious to defend himself. The judge allows him an opportunity.

"Your Honor, I don't know anything about the South Side of Chicago or Cabrini Green projects. I never tried to explain my temper by telling you stories about my childhood, poverty, the plight of black people or even rappers. I work hard and I have a lot to contribute to my community. And I can best do that by being on the streets, not behind bars. I got into a fistfight with a grown man and I'm willing to accept responsibility for my actions. But I'm not the monster she wants you to believe I am."

Judge Wu sentences Pac to fifteen days in L.A. County, a sentence that is, as he points out, relatively moderate. The sentence is suspended and Pac is to report to the jail at 9:00 a.m. on May 10.

Reporters rush outside the courtroom to tape the statement Pac promised them. "Ask me the questions respectfully and I'll answer them," he regulates.

MTV asks the predictable: "What advice do you have for your fans?" Tupac turns his baseball hat backward. "Think about it. A fistfight becomes battery in the courts. Two and a half minutes just cost me fifteen days."

"Can I get the real niggas in the house to get my back!" The real niggas are slightly afraid for Tupac. They've spent $15 to see him at Clark Atlanta University's gymnasium and there's a good chance they will head back to their dorms without a full concert. The promoters, also Atlanta University students, spent nearly a half hour backstage reiterating the school's strict rules about drug use to Tupac. (Apparently neither school officials nor hired security are willing to engage in any lengthy debate about marijuana as healing herb, non-"drug.")

He holds the blunt high above his head and the crowd. "What I want to know is, if I light this, will you let them take me to jail?" The ladies, many of them prim, proper Spelman virgins, shriek at the top of their lungs in support of the most beautiful rapper alive. Nobody's fool, Pac includes the brothas. "I need to know where the thug niggas is at!" A masculine war cry echoes throughout the gym. "If they arrest me, I'ma jump in this sea of niggas and they gone haveta arrest each and every one of us." The crowd erupts into what they dream is an impenetrable wall of defiance.

It's common knowledge that Pac is completely unpredictable. And tonight he really surprises. He gives one of those rare things in hip-hop—a good show, and his tightly rolled blunt remains unlit. Until of course he jumps in his Benz and he and his boys, another two cars, head to Midtown, where he has a hotel room for the night.

Two traffic lights from the hotel, at the Piedmont and Spring streets intersection, Pac notices some kind of commotion at the car ahead of him as he slows down for the light. From the driver's seat, Pac can see two white boys reaching in the window of the car ahead of him. It's dark but Pac is certain that the single person in the car is a black man. Without a second thought Tupac jumps out of the car and asks what the fuck is going on. The Southern white boys lose their grip on the driver and the car speeds off.

The white boys, brothers Mark and Scott Whitwell, look up and find their audience is three cars full of black men. They panic. Mark Whitwell pulls out a gun and tells Pac to "Run!"

Tupac can hardly believe his ears. "I started havin' mothafuckin' flashbacks of Rodney King and Kunta Kinte," he remembers. "We been running all our mothafuckin' lives," he thinks. He reaches in his car for his heat. Mark Whitwell fires his gun. Pac, who spends free time at firing ranges, leans over the hood of his car and catches both of them nonfatally; Mark in the abdomen and Scott in the ass.

There's nothing in Tupac's personality that would have allowed him to be passive to this kind of attack. In fact, there's little in his person that would've allowed him to sit there and watch — or drive by and not look — as two white boys harassed that black driver. As so many of us would have. We would have hesitated, considered "reality," which has so little to do with truth, imagined innumerable "real" consequences, and sped by. If we hope to understand Tupac at all, we must realize this is impossible for him.

Truth is these were two white boys who'd threatened and attacked him. Reality is they're both off-duty cops, with the authority of Confederate Georgia behind them. This Tupac finds out only when he is arrested an hour later at his hotel room in the Sheraton. Because the Whitwell brothers are so shady — the gun that they possessed was stolen from the room at the precinct where confiscated weapons are held and they were both drunk — a formal indictment has yet to be filed against Tupac.

The night has mythic potential: black knight slays cracker dragons (centuries old) who emerge in the night, fangs bared. In the South no less! It's the kind of community work we all dream of doing.

Shooting another black man post-crack-era requires little courage. The genocidal repercussions of racism are clearly evidenced in our ability as a people to elevate self-hatred to an art form and staggering national homicidal counts. In this equation, white boys in particular are untouchable. We talk a good game when it comes to the white devil, but rare is the brotha (or organization) who even imagines physical confrontation with his oppressor. Let alone acts on it. It is in this way that Tupac's actions Halloween night are so utterly fearless.

"I'm staying right here in this little-ass room. Nigga gotta stay out of trouble," says Pac. The Notorious B.I.G. is visiting Pac at his hotel. The two did some Gemini bonding the instant they laid eyes on each other more than a year ago and have been road dawgs ever since. Pac practices some of his new lyrics on Big over blunts and Hennessy. I videotaped the exchange with a brand-new camera Pac purchased.

The phone rings and again Pac is required to defend himself. Two nights earlier he'd dropped by NBC studios to watch Snoop's performance on *Saturday Night Live*. I'd seen him backstage, but hadn't noticed the pasty white-girl following him around by the tails of his leather coat. I was standing there talking with Malika Shabazz, Malcom X's daughter, when Pac rushed by and gave us hugs.

"Is that Madonna?" Malika whispers as Pac walks away. I jump to his defense, "Are you buggin'? Pac wouldn't be caught dead with that bitch."

Then they emerged from Snoop's dressing room, Madonna's hair dyed jet-black, her eyes red from chronic. I just kinda stood there with my shelltops in my mouth.

It's not that they were intimate at all, even though the outing earned them a "Couple Made in Hell" insert in the *Enquirer*. It's just that we got that treasonous feeling sisters get when they see a brother with a white girl. Not to mention white-girl culture vulture.

"Look, Madonna is just another white bitch? I ain't even fucking with her," Tupac insists to the concerned caller. "She's nothing but money and that was nothing but business." With that, he ends his call and reaches into his bag from the electronics store.

"Big, did I show you what I bought today." He pulls out a complicated gadget with wires and transistors. "A bug.

"From now on, bitch wanna fuck me, I'm getting it all on tape." He puts the headset around his bald head to demonstrate.

"Whatchyou say? You wanna give me some pussy . . . repeat that." He moves closer to the imaginary hoochie, forcing his shirt collar into her face. "What's that? You want to engage in consensual sex at my hotel room . . .

"Or I could use it to hear niggas talking shit. Put this little piece right here"—he plants a microscopic bug under the hotel's lampshade—"leave the room"—he actually leaves the hotel room—"hear 'em scheming on me and come back blasting. *Blaow! Blaow! Blaow!*" He practically kicks the door in as he reenters. It's not the first time I see Bishop, the haunting character from the movie *Juice*, reemerge in Tupac.

The phone rings again. This time it's a girl Tupac has been trying to see for a while. She's afraid he just wants the pussy. "No, we can go to dinner, anything you wanna do . . . It's not like that . . . Can't a nigga just want to see you, take you out?" When he hangs up, he has a date.

He turns up his snifter and starts getting dressed. He decides to change shirts. First he drapes his perfectly toned abdomen with a plain white Hanes, then he slides into an official bulletproof vest. He hides the vest with an over-sized shirt. He leaves his gatt in the room. We walk him down to the lobby.

"Aiight, nigga"—Big gives him a pound—"good luck catching a cab."

"That's all I got is good luck."

JULY 4, 1994
DETROIT, MICHIGAN

Dear Lord, can you hear me? / It's just me / A young nigga tryin' make it on these rough streets . . .

There's a moment in "Hell Razor," a song on Tupac's forthcoming album, where Tupac submits totally to pain and vulnerability. Of all the things about Tupac, his music is the least noticed and most improved. "Hell Razor" is com-pelling testimony to that. Like most hip-hop, it's autobiographical, but it's his passionate delivery that invokes midnight tent revivals where the testifier is possessed by the Holy Ghost. The song is actually an open letter from Tupac to the Lord. It's not your typical rapper venting empty anger.

Dear Lord if you hear me / Tell me why / A little girl like Latosha [Harlan] had to die . . .

If I close my eyes, I can imagine him locked in a sound booth, the veins throbbing from his neck, voice hoarse, sweat drippin' down his face, grippin' the mic tight like a vise.

Motherfucker I lick shots . . . drop two cops . . .

The Source / September 1994

Eazy Living

CARTER HARRIS

On March 15, Eric "Eazy-E" Wright lay in the intensive care unit of Cedars-Sinai Medical Center in Los Angeles. He was thirty-one years old and fighting for his life. Heavily sedated, Eazy-E had a respirator tube running down his throat to help him breathe. In the cramped, fluorescent-lit room, a few close friends and Tomica Woods—his new wife and the mother of his youngest son—gathered around his bed.

"We told him we loved him," says Jacob T., a six-foot-three, three-hundred-pound Samoan, one of Eazy's longtime twin bodyguards. He and his brother, John T., were with Eazy through most of his last days. "But he couldn't talk. Then we said, 'If you can hear us, just squeeze our hand.' He did."

Big Man (aka Mark Rucker), who grew up with Eazy in Compton, removed a gold ring his wife had given him on their tenth anniversary. He slipped it on Eazy's index finger. "I told him, 'I want you to give this back to me when you get out of here.'" But Eazy never got out.

His immune system had become too weak to fight off the infection that was ravaging his lungs. About a week later, Eric Wright fell unconscious and remained so until he died on March 26, 1995, at 6:35 p.m., from AIDS-related pneumonia.

The announcement that Eazy had AIDS sent shock waves throughout the hip-hop nation. Fans, friends, even journalists wept openly on March 16 as his attorney, Ron Sweeney, read a statement from his client outside the old Motown building in Hollywood.

The founder of N.W.A, the man who popularized gangsta rap worldwide, was suddenly thrust into the role of AIDS educator: "I would like to turn my own problem into something good that will reach out to all my homeboys," Eazy said through Sweeney. "I want to save their asses before it's too late. I'm not looking to blame anyone except myself."

Though Eazy didn't say (and perhaps didn't know) how he contracted the virus, he implied that it was through unprotected sex with women. "I have seven children by six different mothers," said the statement. "Maybe success was too good to me."

At the Beat, L.A.'s KKBT-FM, where Eazy had hosted a show every Saturday, the phone rang. It was Snoop Doggy Dogg, who, in a call filled with long, pregnant silences, said he was praying for Eazy. The next day Ice Cube phoned in. "Me and Eric worked out our differences," said Cube. "I had just seen him in New York, and we talked for a long time. We was laughing and kickin' it about how N.W.A should get back together. I'm just waiting for a call that says he's cool enough for me to go to the hospital and check him out . . . and let him know that he's still the homey, when it comes to me."

On Friday, March 17, Dr. Dre—who's traded wicked insults with Eazy since the dissolution of N.W.A—paid a visit to Cedars-Sinai. Dre got in; he saw Eazy. Only he knows what, if anything, was communicated.

By that time, the hospital's switchboard had been blowing up for two days straight. "We've been overwhelmed with thousands of phone calls asking about Eazy-E," says Paula Correia, Cedars-Sinai's director of public relations. "Lots of young people—emotional, upset, concerned. We've had a high volume of calls for other celebrity patients—Lucille Ball, George Burns, Billy Idol—but never this many."

But not everyone was sympathetic. According to one hospital staffer, some women claiming to be Eazy's former lovers were phoning in death threats. Across the country, at a panel discussion in Virginia, Compton rapper DJ Quik was saying that Eazy-E knew he had the disease two years ago and vowed to spread it around. (Ruthless employee Keisha Anderson went on KKBT on March 16 and said that "Eazy was tested eighteen months ago, and it was negative.") Rumors were snowballing: Eazy was a closet homosexual, Eazy was a heroin addict. Eazy was on his deathbed, Eazy was getting better. On and on.

The fevered gossip said more about the anxiety running through Planet Hip-Hop than it did about the truth. Eazy-E was the first major pop music figure who was not openly gay to die from AIDS. But instead of seizing this opportunity to educate, the media downplayed Eazy's death. MTV had devoted around-the-clock coverage to Kurt Cobain's suicide, but squeezed only a few paltry minutes on Eazy into their regular *MTV News* broadcasts. *The New York Times* and *People* offered slightly expanded obituaries, and *BET* seemed asleep at the wheel. The media's laxity was especially shameful considering that Eazy's core audience—young people of color—are currently contracting the virus at such an accelerated rate.

A middle-class kid from Compton who got caught up in drug dealing and petty crime, Eazy went legit by investing his money in his own label, Ruthless Records. With his distinctive, high-pitched whine, Eazy coined the term "Boyz-N-the Hood" and ushered in the gangsta rap era. "As long as you're being talked about," said the man whose rhymes enraged the FBI—yet who, in 1991, took time out to hang with George Bush—"people still remember you." Right before he got sick, Eazy was at his busiest: shopping a screenplay, executive-producing Bone Thugs 'N' Harmony's upcoming album, and preparing to release his own oft-delayed double album—a collection culled from more than seventy tracks recorded with everyone from Bootsy Collins to Slash of Guns N' Roses.

"He was driven by the thought that when he was sleeping, he was missing something," says Jerry Heller, Eazy-E's longtime friend, personal manager, and the controversial former general manager of Ruthless Records. "He worried that people were getting ahead of him. He just never slept."

"Eazy lived the life of a straight-up G," says Rhythm D, one of Eazy's former roommates and producers. "You know. A mack." Heller puts it more gently: "Eazy loved women. He had lots of them. Lots of kids. They were a big part of his life."

"I knew he was sleeping with other people," says one of Eazy's most recent girlfriends. "But I didn't know to what extent. It was only after he went into the hospital that I found out he was living with this other woman, Tomica. But he was never anything but good to me. As far as I was concerned, we were still together."

Linda Bell, the mother of Eazy's second-oldest child, a nine-year-old girl, says she and Eazy were no longer seeing each other but that he willingly provided for their child. On the day of her own HIV test, she spoke highly, if somewhat numbly, of her former lover: "Eric was so busy it was hard for him to spend time with his daughter. Just before he got sick, he said he was gonna come pick her up and take her to some event—the Ice Capades. He never did get the chance."

Even though Eazy was living a player's lifestyle, his death seemed to come out of nowhere. "It was a shock to everybody," says Steffon, a former cohost of the syndicated video show *Pump It Up* and an MC signed to Ruthless Records. "About a week before he went into the hospital, I was at his house and he was the same ol' E. We was just chillin', bumpin' tunes, smokin' weed, talkin' about business."

According to his bodyguards, Eazy was having cold symptoms and some difficulty breathing as early as mid-January but avoided seeing a doctor. "He'd had bronchitis off and on since he was a kid," says Big Man. "So it wasn't completely new."

But Eazy's breathing became increasingly strained, and on Thursday, February 16, Jacob T. and Big Man took him to the emergency room of Norwalk Community Hospital. "He sounded worse than I'd ever heard him," says Big Man, "but he wouldn't have gone if it were up to him. We practically had to force him to go." Eazy was admitted for a breathing problem and released on February 19.

After leaving the hospital, he went home to Topanga Canyon, where he rested, trying to get over what everyone assumed was bronchitis-related asthma. "That Thursday, we slept over at his house," says Jacob. "Eazy was still wheezing and short of breath. He had an appointment with his doctor the next day." On Friday, February 24, Eazy-E was admitted to Cedars-Sinai Medical Center.

Under the alias Eric Lollis, Eazy stayed in room 5105, where he was given antibiotics for an infection in his lungs. "He was smaller because his appetite had decreased. But there were no lesions or dementia. None of the other things you associate with AIDS," says Charis Henry, Eazy's former personal assistant and longtime friend. "I know because I lost an uncle to it last year."

In the hospital, Eazy wore black Calvin Klein long underwear and sometimes a gown to cover his upper body. His mom was bringing him home-cooked food and fresh fruit. He had a radio but spent most of the time watching television.

"Me and one of his girlfriends would get him to sit up and move around," says Henry. "But he couldn't walk much because it was hard on his breathing. His spirits went up, then down, and we'd try to cheer him up. I did the running man to Montell Jordan's *This Is How We Do It*, and he laughed."

Eazy was diagnosed with AIDS March 1. "He told me it wasn't fair," says Henry, her voice tense with emotion. "That he didn't want to die. He said he wouldn't care if he didn't have a dime; he said he wouldn't care what anybody said if he could just drop the top on his car and ride up the coast one more time."

"She told you, right?" is how Eazy-E told Big Man and Jacob T. that he was dying of AIDS. The "she" was his soon-to-be wife, Tomica, who had been keeping a bedside vigil since Eazy was hospitalized.

Eazy was scheduled for surgery the next day, March 15, so that excess fluid could be drained from his lungs. Amid concern that he might not survive the surgery, he married Tomica Woods. Woods and her daughter subsequently tested negative for HIV, though they may not be out of danger, as the virus sometimes takes months to show up in tests.

Eazy recited his wedding vows at approximately 9:30 p.m. on March 14. He was unable to stand. His parents, Kathie (a grade-school administrator) and Richard Wright (a retired postal worker), were in attendance, as were his sister and brother, Patricia and Kenneth. The same night Eazy reportedly signed a will naming attorney Sweeney and Tomica Woods cotrustees of his estate.

The surgery, however, never happened. Shortly after dawn, Eazy was transferred to the hospital's intensive care unit. There he was hooked up to life support. "I was told that they couldn't drain his lungs because he was too weak," says Jacob. From that point on, Eazy remained in critical condition.

Charis Henry saw him on March 24, two days before he died. "I was talking to him but he didn't respond," she says. "It looked as if he was asleep. It was the first time he looked comfortable in a while. He looked peaceful."

Less than twenty-four hours after Eric Wright's death, war broke out over his estate. Mike Klein, Ruthless's director of business affairs, filed a $5-million lawsuit charging that Tomica Woods and Ron Sweeney, who became Eazy's attorney in January 1995, wrongfully claimed ownership of Ruthless. In a motion filed March 27 in L.A. Superior Court, Klein claimed to own 50 percent of the label, per an agreement signed with Eazy in 1992. Klein says he fired Sweeney on March 24, and then when Klein showed up to work at Ruthless on March 27, ten security guards blocked his entrance. The LAPD subsequently shut down the company's Woodland Hills offices until the legal dispute could be settled.

Klein told *Vibe* that Eazy had expressed "no interest" in getting married and that whatever will he may have signed on his deathbed, "he signed because he was not in the right state of mind." Sweeney and Woods declined to comment. More than one of Eazy's ex-girlfriends have expressed concern over whether their kids will continue to be provided for. "I'm not some groupie tryin' to jump in for money," says Tracy Jernagin, owner of a music production company and the mother of Eazy's four-year-old daughter, Erin Wright—who has since retained a lawyer to assure that her child's interests are protected. "Eric was very generous and loving toward his daughter. I know he wanted her provided for."

Regardless of who inherits his ample fortune (estimated at $35 million), Eazy-E deserves props for many things: for pioneering some of the funkiest hard-core music ever made; for opening people's eyes to how bad things have gotten in urban America; for being a successful entrepreneur; for being one of the first people to tell cops to fuck off in song.

But since his death, the fact that stands out more than any other is that his music unabashedly glorified the lifestyle that ended up killing him. "Feel a little gust of wind / And I'm jettin'," he rapped in *Straight Outta Compton*. "So what about that bitch who got shot? / Fuck her / You think I give a damn about a bitch?" Well, E got taken.

The truth is, hip-hop's attitude of invincibility is a joke in the face of the AIDS virus. "When Magic got it, people thought about it for a minute," says former N.W.A member DJ Yella. "But everybody knew Eric; he's right there in the streets. His dying from AIDS has got a lot of people thinking, 'Now that's close, it can't get no closer but me getting it.'"

Only days after Eazy passed, a young street vendor stood on the corner of Florence and Crenshaw boulevards in South-Central Los Angeles selling T-shirts. Two weeks ago they might have borne messages like FREE OJ or BITCHES AIN'T SHIT. Now the shirts say in big black letters: AIDS IS RUTHLESS. SO TAKE IT EAZY. RIP 3/26/95.

Vibe / June/July 1995

Diatribe

GREG TATE

Define what you mean by the illest,

Aaiight. The sickest, the silliest, the smartest, the most repressed, art-damaged, paranoid-conspiratorial, and ready to tell the world about it. Los Angeles takes the cake for the most psychopathic and genuinely genocidal niggas on the planet, and nowhere in the Western world will you find bloods more assimilated and dislocated than those in London. But black men in New York are true New Yorkers, i.e., brilliant and obsessively private people whose choice of residence forces them to lead fatuously public lives.

Being a New Yorker means never having to say you don't have an opinion about every little thing, and a Unified Field Theory to boot. Brothers in New York want to live large like brothers everywhere, but the intellectual current this town runs on demands they develop theories, methods, doctrines, ideologies, and agendas. In New York, a Big Willie can't just do it: he must have ideas, a master plan. Vernon Reid couldn't just be a black rocker, he had to form a coalition first.

Who are some other archetypal moving and shaking New York brothers? Chuck D, Al Sharpton, Colin Ferguson, the RZA, Colin Powell, Russell Simmons. See, brothers in New York have to explain themselves to white people, to *The New York Times* even, not so much because white people matter, but because a basic tenet of being a New York hustler is that you must have as much game as the Other man.

What does this theoretical baggage have to do with A Tribe Called Quest's new release, *Beats, Rhymes and Life*? Everything and nothing. Give me a minute and I'll figure something out because I'm a brother from Planet Rock New Yawk.

Hip-hop as defined by Bahamadia at the journal *Elementary*'s roundtable is beats, rhymes, and skills. Fair enough, my sister, but hip-hop is also about memorable songs. What is a hip-hop song? One where all the words matter, compelling us to memorize every noun, verb, preposition, and gerund. Nothing about the craft of hip-hop is more amazing than that the writing—the words themselves—is as smart and stimulating as the beats, the samples, and the attitude. The task of the writer in hip-hop is to actually be hipper than the music, to circle back in on music's power, to speak the unspeakable and say more than music could ever say by itself. Chuck D once praised Rakim for writing a song that went one step further than James Brown in lyrically rendering the philosophy of soul.

What is a hip-hop song? A thematically coherent essay in rhyme form. It doesn't have to get any deeper than Special Ed singing I'm your hero, your idol, your highest title, and that whole willie bobo; it just has to sensibly, catchily flow. Once upon a time, Q-Tip took the rhyme further than sensible, dropping great aphorisms, parables, and novellas on our heads. Once upon a time, A Tribe Called Quest, De La Soul, and Brand Nubian defined the term *progressive hip-hop*, setting the standards for thematic genius in the idiom. So what happened?

I'll tell you what happened. But only after I quickly define what I mean by progressive hip-hop: hip-hop praxis wherein lyric content and raising the art form to the next level outweighs the profit margin. So what happened was West Coast blewthafukup, New York eventually retaliated with its own gangsta rap in the circled-wagon form of Wu-Tang Clan and Biggie Smalls, all that Native Tongue progressive-hip-hop-type yang got lost in the East Coast/West Coast shuffle, and right about now Q-Tip and Posdnous must feel like strangers in a house they helped build from scratch. Or maybe more like ripped-out pages in their own anthology. In the guise of being at war with gangster rap, they're really at war with their own hip-hop irrelevance. Not hip-hop as defined by the industry-controlled masses, but hip-hop as defined by the ancestral Afrikan muses.

Hip-hop, to paraphrase Baraka, is vicious modernism, so dependent on the shock-of-the-new for its power that falling off in hip-hop can result merely from no longer being the rapper we've never heard before. There are rappers whose mediocre recordings we tolerate because they have such classic and idiosyncratic hip-hop voices, voices we would never have heard without hip-hop, voices whose torrid tones thaw our frozen blood, voices we never tire of hearing no matter how tired the material because they're so distinctly hip-hop: MC Lyte, Rakim, Guru, KRS-One, Erick Sermon, Method Man, Q-Tip.

All the same, there's nothing like hearing those voices in the service of a truly inspired hip-hop song, per our definitions above. *Beats, Rhymes and Life* sadly lacks more than a couple such songs, yo.

Don't get me wrong. Tribe has made a respectable fourth album in a field where producing a decent second album is relatively equivalent to the length and strength of Duke Ellington's and Miles Davis's entire careers. I'd love to give Tribe props for making a respectable fourth album, but who wants to see hip-hop turn respectable? If I wanted respectable, I'd throw on Marcus Roberts. When I listen to hip-hop, I want to be like Snow White, swept off her feet and ravished by Prince Charming. With echoes of People's Instinctive Travels and the Paths of Rhythm and The Low End Theory (the epitome of hip-hop perfection) dancing in my head, I've been listening to Tribe's *Beats, Rhymes and Life*, waiting to be nagged, hooked, corralled, seduced, or snared strictly on the mental. But with the exception of the opener, "Phony Rappers," the album's flyest hook, and "Get a Hold," where Tip rocks instructional verses for those drowning in industry bullshit, I am not moved. The music and production by Ali Shaheed Muhammad, alias the Ummah, upholds the Tribe tradition of upright bass seduction, but yo-yo-yo brother QT: How many ways can you say I'm sick of phony gangster rappers, this album's dominant theme? I for one am sick of hip-hop lyrics about the sorry state of hip-hop in general, and other rappers, phony or otherwise, in particular. By the third song, *Beats, Rhymes and Life* has smothered the life out of this straw man.

What happened to the Q-Tip I loved? The self-proclaimed Abstract Poetic who quixotically rhymed about leaving his wallet in El Segundo, sweet-talked Bonita Applebum into turning him on, and bemusedly introduced us to the plight of the immigrant Lucien? The man who upbraided us that what men and women need to do is stick together because progressions can't be made if we're separate forever, who promised that his job wasn't temporary because "my father well prepared me"? The bro who rhetorically posed the syllogisms "What's an MC if he doesn't have stamina" and "What's America without greed and glamour"? I'm just not hearing that level of hip-hop lyric writing on *Beats, Rhymes and Life*; Sun, and Tip probably isn't either, which is why the damn drums are mixed so loud on this muhfuh. The logic probably being that if one must be ass-out on the inspiration tip, don't show up naked to the party.

Q-Tip, we now hear, is an orthodox Muslim, a celibate-noninhaling-in-hip-hop Muslim at that. Fine, bro, so where's the epic album about that revolution of the mind? I read somewhere (like *Stress* or *The Source*, maybe) how Tip doesn't want to drop too much knowledge on the audience at once. This is an oddly patronizing notion from a rapper who once casually served definitions of terms like *ménage à trois* with his rhymes. Are we to assume that Tip thinks the hip-hop audience of today is dumber than those back in the day? But who can listen to Raekwon's syncopated and highly complicated ciphers and think some nonsense like that? I ain't no ignoramus, yet feel like I could use hell-a-more schooling whenever Raekwon catches wrek.

The hip-hop youth of today are obsessed with virtual hardness and virtual realness, and unfortunately not so concerned with hard thinking about the world beyond hip-hop, which is why I ain't trying to fuck with them much personally. But Tribe and De La possess the intellect to take hip-hop culture there with whimsy and wisdom. Actually, both groups have been there, done it, lost the groovy T-shirt. If the Native Tongues can get back to being the future again, progressive hip-hop might still have one, but if they can't, then it seems like boo-ya-ka will go on ruling the boom-bip. (A parting shot: The Fugees don't move me as hip-hop but as pop. It's that lyric thing again, yo.)

The Village Voice / September 3, 1996

Chronicle of a Death Foretold

CHEO HODARI COKER

Everything was looking good for Biggie Smalls on March 8. It was a warm and sunny L.A. Saturday, and he was chillin' like a star. The big man had spent much of the day with his agent, Phil Casey, discussing his upcoming tour with Dru Hill, Blackstreet, and Heavy D. The day before, he'd presented a Soul Train Award to Toni Braxton before spending the evening in his plush hotel suite, watching the awards show on TV, and talking with a journalist about how far he'd come in his twenty-four years.

When Biggie showed up at the Peterson Automotive Museum in L.A.'s Mid-Wilshire district Saturday night for a party cosponsored by *Vibe*, Qwest Records, and Tanqueray, he was dipped in a black suede shirt, a gold chain with a Jesus pendant, and clear-framed, wraparound shades. He looked confident and relaxed, a long black cane supporting the slight limp he'd acquired in an automobile accident six months before.

"The party was a nice scene, especially after the stress of the Soul Train Awards," said Kevin Kim, security guard for Big's ex-wife, Faith Evans. "Nothing but celebs there, people having a good time. Everybody was dancin' together; artists hugging each other, congratulating each other on the awards they won." Shortly before midnight, the DJ blew up the spot with Big's new single, "Hypnotize."

"I was sitting across from Biggie for most of the night," said Def Jam president and CEO Russell Simmons. "I was throwin' paper at him, tellin' him how much I liked his record. These girls were dancin' for him, and he was just sittin' there, not even movin' his cane. I told him I wanted to be like him. He was so cool, so funny and calm."

At around 12:35 a.m., fire marshals shut down the party, apparently because of overcrowding. People filed out into the parking structure connected to the museum and found their rides. After bumping some tracks from his then unreleased album, *Life After Death . . . 'Til Death Do Us Part*, Biggie got into the front passenger seat of a GMC Suburban. His man D-Rock was driving. Little Caesar from Junior M.A.F.I.A., Big's own lyrical cartel, was in the back. When they turned out of the lot onto Fairfax, they were traveling in a line of three cars. Directly in front of them was another Suburban containing members of Biggie's entourage; behind them, a Blazer with personal security guards.

According to police, the three cars had slowed to a stop at the first intersection, Fairfax and Wilshire, when a dark sedan pulled up along the right-hand side of Biggie's vehicle and someone fired six to ten shots from a 9mm weapon. Biggie lost consciousness immediately after being shot. He was rushed to nearby Cedars-Sinai Hospital and pronounced dead at 1:15 a.m. Bad Boy Entertainment president Puffy Combs and Faith were both at the hospital when the announcement was made.

The LAPD's Lt. Ross Moen said that the Blazer with Big's security guards chased the dark sedan for a couple of blocks but lost sight of it without getting a license plate number. At press time, the department had assigned twenty-two detectives to the case and was interviewing two hundred witnesses. According to Moen, they had some solid leads but could describe the suspect only as "male, black, early twenties."

"We're not ruling out the fact that this was possibly a hit," said Moen at a press conference the day after the murder. "We're investigating possible connections to other murders in New York, Atlanta, and L.A. We can't ignore the fact that there have been a number of murders involving rap singers recently." Moen said also that they were looking into the possibility of the killing being gang-related, but wouldn't elaborate.

"This was a hit, something preplanned," said one Compton resident a day after the murder. "And there's going to be a few more hits." According to another source, the hit was pulled off by gang members who came to the party in the entourage of a well-known rap artist and coordinated the shooting over cell phones. Another report put an individual outside the party with a cell phone saying, "He's comin' out now," as Biggie left the party.

Various industry insiders have speculated that the killing had more to do with personal beefs than with rap itself, but that it's now spilling over into the music. "Puffy thought it was all calmed down out here," says Phil Casey. "But at Soul Train there were boos, and they were throwin' up Westside from the balcony. That should have been a sign right there."

Sources close to Bad Boy and Death Row dismissed widespread speculation that Wallace's slaying was payback for Tupac's murder. "It's ludicrous for anyone out there to blame Death Row," said Norris Anderson, who took over as label head after Suge Knight was jailed. "We do not condone this activity, and Death Row certainly had nothing to do with it."

"It didn't have nothin' to do with East-West rivalry, but it does now," says one former Death Row artist. "I heard somebody say it's over now. How can it be? Now you're gonna have muthafuckas from the East who gonna just start to shoot at muthafuckas from the West. It shouldn't have to be this way . . . doesn't make no goddamn sense."

SEPTEMBER 27, 1994; NIGHTFALL
BROOKLYN, NEW YORK

"Whatup?"

The Notorious B.I.G. sits on the front stoop of a brownstone near the corner of St. James Place and Fulton Street in Do-or-Die-Bed-Stuy. His first album, *Ready to Die* (which would eventually go double platinum), has been in stores for just over a week, and already every car that passes seems to be playing a different cut. Today Brooklyn; tomorrow—who knows?

As twilight slips into darkness, Big calmly recounts his life story in the same ultrarealistic terms that made his album so damn compelling. As he talks of his own criminal days—doing everything from subway robberies to selling crack to pregnant moms—his eyes begin to fire up. Not with anger, but as if he's watching each episode unfold with the telling.

"When I say I'm *Ready to Die*, people may be, like, 'Oh, he's on some killing-himself shit,'" says Biggie. "That's not what I meant." He pulls out a lighter, flicks it, and brings the flame up toward his lips, where a tightly rolled blunt awaits his attention.

"I meant that I was willing to go all out a hundred percent as far as the music was concerned. When I was hustlin', I was doing that shit every day—waking up, putting drugs in my pocket, and not even thinking about the police, stickup men, or my competition. I was riskin' my life, so that meant I was ready to die."

Even at this early stage of his career, it was already clear that Brooklyn couldn't contain Biggie much longer. "Juicy," one of the weaker tracks on the album, was leaping the *Billboard* charts with alarming speed. The cream of his dreams was within reach: fantasy houses in the country, girls in the pool. And then what?

As he talks, Biggie's eyes suddenly widen with fear. He actually seems frightened at the thought of leaving Brooklyn.

"How real can your music be if you wake up in the morning hearing birds and crickets? I never hear birds when I wake up. Just a lot of construction work, the smell of Chinese takeout, children screaming, and everybody knocking a different track from *Ready to Die* as they pass down the street," he says. "Brooklyn is the love borough. Everywhere you go, we're already there."

I ask if it's true that he's just gotten married. Biggie turns his head from the street and looks into my eyes before telling me about Faith. "When you start hustlin', you get introduced to shit real fast," he says. "You be gettin' pussy real quick, because you be fuckin' the users sometimes. I done had every kind of bitch. Young bitch, old bitch, users, mothers, grandmothers, dumb bitches—and I never, ever met no girl like my wife. She talks to me like nobody else talked to me before. When I first saw her, she was killing me with those eyes. I rolled up to her and said, 'You're the type of girl I would marry.' She said, 'Why don't you?' So I was like, 'Fuck it, it's on.' We had only known each other eight days."

I ask him if that wasn't kind of soon.

"She ain't speaking to me right now," he says with a smile, "but it's all good."

When we met again almost three years later, Big and Faith's marriage wasn't all good. They had been involved in a messy separation that got played out in the press. Tupac's B-side "Hit 'Em Up," in which he called Big a "fat muthafucka" and claimed to have slept with Faith, couldn't have helped them work things out.

Biggie clears up the misinformation in matter-of-fact tones: "People was like, 'When she stopped fuckin' with Big, she started fuckin' with Tupac, and Big started fuckin' with Lil' Kim.' That's the summary of the Biggie Smalls/Faith shit right there. But we wasn't fuckin' with each other way before the rumors popped off.

"I married her after knowing her eight days and I was happy," he says. "That was my baby. At the same time, with us being so spontaneous, we did it backwards. Maybe she won't admit it, but I will. We should have got to know each other and then got married. The relationship kind of dissolved, but we're still going to be friends. I love her. We have a baby together, and we're always gonna love our kids. Who knows? Ten years from now we might even get back together."

I ask the baby's name. "Christopher Jordan Wallace," Big proudly replies. And what of his sarcastic comments on wax, like the line on "Brooklyn's Finest," his duet with Jay-Z? "If Fay has twins, she'll probably have two pacs. Get it? Tu . . . Pac's."

Biggie laughs deep, long, and hard. "I got to make jokes about the shit," he says, his stomach damn near jiggling. "I can't be the nigga running around all serious. The shit is so funny to me because nobody will ever know the truth. They'll always believe what they want to believe. Pac says he fucked her. I asked Faith. You fucked him? She said no. I can't get to ask him about it. So am

I gonna hate her for the rest of her life thinking she did something, or am I gonna be a man about the situation? If she did it, she can't do it more, so let's just get on with our lives. I hold grudges but I can't hate nobody, that's not my nature."

Born Christopher Wallace to Jamaican parents, the man who would one day call himself the Notorious B.I.G. had strikes against him from the moment he checked into this world on May 21, 1972.

His father left his mother when he was just one and a half. Other than pictures in a scrapbook, Biggie had no tender memories of him. "I didn't know him and I don't want to know him," he says coldly. "Moms should have just pushed him off and not even had me if he wasn't going to handle his business. I couldn't even speak to him. I don't need that cocksucker for nothing."

So little Christopher grew up with his mother in Brooklyn and spent the first twenty-two years of his life on St. James Place. Working two jobs and attending night school, Voletta Wallace remained a stable presence in her son's life. She tried her best to shield her sensitive, introspective child from the streets.

The only problem was that nobody was protecting the streets from young Wallace. Way before he hooked up with Puff Daddy, Biggie already had visions of becoming a bad boy. "I was a sneaky motherfucker, I guess," he says with a laugh. "I was real, real bad. You know what made it worse? Motherfuckers would tell my mother that I did something, and she just wouldn't believe them. 'Not my Christopher,' she would say."

One of Big's earliest interests was art; but growing up young, black, and poor, he found there was little he could do in that field that would change his everyday reality. "Back in third grade they used to say, 'Take whatever talent you have and think of something you can do with it,'" he recalls. "I liked to draw, but what could I do with it? Maybe I could be an art dealer—nah, can't see myself doing that. Maybe I could do commercial arts? But once I got introduced to the crack game—commercial arts? Please."

At thirteen, he was schooled in the game by a member of the Junior M.A.F.I.A. clique (the street gang the rap group took their name from), and things started rolling quickly. In the space of a few weeks he went from begging his mother for ice cream money to never having less than $700 in his pocket, and all the designer gear he could imagine.

"I couldn't bring any of my clothes to the house, 'cause my moms would flip," he says. "I used to hide all my shit on the roof of our building, leave for school in the busted shit my moms gave me, and change my whole outfit on the roof."

By sixteen, he had to move out of the house when his mother, who had caught on, couldn't handle his profession. He and his crew were making trips down to North Carolina, where he could sell rocks for even more cash. It was in North Carolina that, at age seventeen, he did his first long stretch. He was locked up for nine months before he finally broke down and called his mother to tell her where he was.

After Big came back, he stayed in the game for a few more years. The pressure increased once he had his first child, his daughter T'Yanna. His conscience had begun to creep up on him. Hustling was turning more violent, and he realized that if he kept going in that direction, he'd end up with hard time or worse.

And then, almost by accident, he became an MC. "I put one hundred percent of my time into hustlin'," he says, "but at the same time, when I was waiting on corners, I'd hang out with niggaz and we'd go downstairs to the basement. This DJ, 50 Gran, he'd flip the records and just rock the instrumentals," Big says. "I came in and said, 'Yo, I get busy,' and he was like, 'Yeah, right.' I picked up the mike and rhymed, and they were like, '*Damn*, he's nice.'

"I'd just flow over the beats, and he started taping everything. Kane's DJ, Mister Cee, heard one of the tapes and told me about this shit in *The Source* called Unsigned Hype. I said, 'Fuck it; send it in.' And [former *Source* editor] Matty C loved it. He played it for Puffy."

Big smiles at the memory of that meeting with the rising rap mogul. "Puff told me, 'It sounds like you could rhyme forever. I want to sign you.'" From the start, Combs warned Wallace against the dangers of the drug game and said he'd try to get him paid as quickly as possible.

But during the long wait for his deal to go through, Big moved back to

North Carolina. He and some mutual acquaintances were sharing an apartment with a new connection they didn't know too well. Then came the phone call that changed his life.

"Puffy called me on a Monday," Big recalls, "and told me that the contracts would be ready on Tuesday. He said, 'Come on up, and I'll have the check waiting for you.' I was gonna stay till Tuesday because it was near the first of the month and we were gonna get those crackheads' welfare checks." But something told him to leave right away, and thankfully he did.

"The same night I was on the train coming back to New York, the cops ran up in our spot," Biggie says. "It turns out the nigga that we didn't know had been on the run for over seven years, and the other two niggas that was with him got conspiracy charges."

I may be a big, black, ugly dude; but I got style. I kinda uplifted big black ugly dudes for real.

FEBRUARY 14, 1997; 4 P.M.
VALENTINE'S DAY, BEVERLY HILLS, CALIFORNIA

Three years, a divorce, a multiplatinum album, a baby son, and numerous beefs later, Biggie Smalls reclines in a cabana near the pool of the Four Seasons Hotel, lamping like an Iranian oil tycoon. The sounds of birds chirping and children splashing fill the air on this bright, sunny afternoon.

"Look at all of this," he says with a wide smile, a pungent blunt dangling from his lips. "It feels like a few million miles from Brooklyn."

I remind him of our long-ago conversation about his fear of falling off if he ever left the Ave. "I'm not scared of that anymore," he says. "I hear so much of what's going on from people coming to my house—they'll just tell me an ill story and I can build that into something. I was never one to say that all my rhymes were my exact life experience."

What else has changed? I ask. Why is the new record called *Life After Death*? Isn't he ready to die anymore?

"When I was writing stuff like 'Fuck the world, fuck my moms and my girl,' I was dead, man," he says, his expression suddenly serious. "There was nothing but anger coming out. Nothing but anger. But now, I can't do that no more. People know that Biggie ain't on the corner selling drugs anymore. Why would anyone want to hear about that?

"I'm really no different than anybody else," he continues. "I say grow from your mistakes and hopefully you can stand the repercussions. I caught some cases and I'll handle them accordingly." The three latest charges—the alleged assault and robbery of a concert promoter in June 1995, the run-in with an aggressive New York autograph seeker in March 1996, and the night last July when police searched Biggie's house in Teaneck, New Jersey, and found marijuana, infrared scopes, and illegal guns with scratched-off serial numbers—would later be highlighted in nearly every obituary of the slain MC.

"My temper be fuckin' me up sometimes," he admits. "I often have to tell myself, 'Watch what you doing, Big, 'cause you're not on Fulton Street anymore. If a nigga say, "Fuck you," you can't shoot at him. Okay?' Fine. I'll be the cool dude, write the raps, do the shows, I have security." He nods out through the opening of his cabana at a six-foot-seven, muscular black man with a shaved head, who nods back.

"This shit is beautiful, man," he says again, sipping some lemonade. "You got palm trees and all types of stuff right here. I wouldn't want to lose it for anything in the world."

My next question breaks the serenity. Where was he on the Friday the thirteenth that Tupac died.

"I got home and it was on the news, and I couldn't believe it," he says with genuine sadness. "I knew so many niggaz like him, so many ruff, tuff motherfuckers getting shot. I said he'll be out in the morning, smoking some weed, drinking some Hennessy, just hanging out.

"You ain't thinking it's gonna happen to him," he continues. "This is just like when Eazy died. You be thinking that when a nigga is making so much money that his lifestyle will protect him, that a drive-by shooting ain't supposed to happen. He was supposed to have flocks of security; not even supposed to be sitting by no window."

Biggie shakes his head. "Tupac, at one point, was my dog. He was funny as a motherfucker, too," he adds with a smile. "People don't know that."

So why did things fall apart?

"I can't really call that one, because I don't know what happened in that camp. But the way I looked at it, it was like an ongoing role, a character he couldn't get out of."

And how does the death of his friend make him feel?

"I'm just realizing that nothing protects you from the inevitable. If something's going to happen, it's gonna happen, no matter what you do. It's crazy for me to even think that a rapper can't get killed just because he raps. That shit can happen. Even if you clean your life up, it comes back at you. What goes around comes around, 'cause karma is a motherfucker."

So we all just have to play whatever cards fate deals us?

"Fuck that. I'm gonna deal the cards of my own fate," he says triumphantly. "I'm gonna cheat. I got to, man."

MONDAY, FEBRUARY 24, 1997; 8:35 P.M.
THE WAREHOUSE SET FOR THE "HYPNOTIZE" VIDEO

Amid the usual video-shoot pandemonium, two animal trainers wheel Crystal, aged black panther, up a cargo ramp. The animal saunters around the confines of her small cage, reacting subtly to the bouncy funk of "Hypnotize" wafting softly in the background.

"Whose idea was the shit?" says one excited Brooklyn kid, checking out the jungle predator.

"Puff's," says the Notorious B.I.G., casually lounging in his cloth-backed director's chair. "That just adds ambience, that's all."

Combs, who's copiloting the video with dreadlocked director Paul Hunter, darts over to check the latest footage. Biggie and crew, meanwhile, are amusing themselves with the panther.

"Lookit," says Biggie with exaggerated bravado. "You got to show the cat who's boss, that's all." It's high comedy, and everybody's loving the performance. "They better let that cat know who's running this video. I'm about to call my barber and have him cut my initials into his fur. I'm trying to sell five million albums this time out, nigga. If I need to, I'll ride that cat tonight."

"Real quiet," barks the assistant director as they open the animal's cage. "No sudden movements."

Biggie looks directly at Crystal and begins twitching on purpose, making nothing but sudden movements. He bugs his eyes, barks like a dog.

Hunter calls Puff and Big in from the sidelines, and the dynamic duo take their places next to each other. They're dressed identically in lavender silk suits and matching shoes. The trainer hands Biggie the chain that's connected to the panther's neck, like it's his pet, and explains that the cat is also secured to a ring in the ground. "She's stronger than you or I could even imagine," he warns.

But Biggie protests with shooting-marbles-in-the-schoolyard defiance. "I'm telling you, I can handle that," he says. "That chain is for the safety of the cat, 'cause I'm a wild nigga."

FRIDAY, MARCH 7, 1997; 8:30 P.M.
THE WESTWOOD MARQUIS HOTEL

"Maxwell is such a smooth muthafucka, boy, you know he got to be from Brooklyn." Biggie laughs while kicking back on a couch in his expansive suite. The TV is turned to a tape-delay broadcast of the eleventh annual Soul Train Music Awards, which concluded only an hour before. "I bet you he be getting all them exotic bitches, too."

Everyone's tired, but there's still work to be done. At ten o'clock they're due in the studio to finish tracks for Puffy's upcoming solo joint, *Hell up in Harlem*. Big munches on a room-service sausage pizza. He was supposed to catch a flight to London at eleven the next morning, but he's just decided to cancel those plans.

"I just ain't fucking with it," he says, exhaling heavily. "I don't want to go to Europe right now. The food is horrible. I just finished my album; it's about to drop in two weeks. I'm loving Cali and I've been out here for a month. I don't want to go nowhere."

So being out here's been a positive experience?

"Hell, yeah," he says. "The weather is positive, the women is positive, and the weed is positive." He draws chuckles all around. "That's why I came out here, to kick back and relax. Too much snow at home.

"Am I big enough for the screen?" he asks, watching himself present an award to Toni Braxton. "I need more shine." In the spotlight's glare, Biggie's Jesus pendant glows with impressive iridescence.

"*Haaay!* The Jesus piece," a friend says. "Right now niggaz is, like, 'Son's piece is crazy. Son's piece is off the wall!!'"

On-screen, Big steps up to the mike to open the winner's envelope amid a loud chorus of boos. "What's up Cali?" he says with about as much friendliness as he can muster under the circumstances.

Biggie's still wearing the pendant as we speak. It's an outward demonstration of his newfound faith in God. "I think if more people were into the Lord, there would be a lot less shit going on in the world," he says to me. "I think people need to realize that these are tests and obstacles that everyone has to go through. A lot of niggaz want to give up and do wrong, but they don't even think God is in their corner. What I respect about God is that He always steers you in the right direction."

He rolls up his sleeve to show me the inside of his forearm. Tattooed on his dark skin, in the form of a weathered parchment, are phrases from Psalm 27:

The Lord is my light and my salvation, whom shall I fear?
The Lord is the truth of my life, of whom shall I be afraid?
When the wicked, even my enemies and foes, came upon
me to bite my flesh, they stumbled and fell.

"This is how I feel sometimes," he says. "I want to feel like this all the time. That's why I went and got it, to reassure myself that no matter what goes wrong, no matter how bad shit is looking, God is right here. He's not behind you, He's right here. As long as you believe in Him and in His strength, all these jealous people, all these sharks, and scandalous bitches and haters, He'll stop all of that. He's going to take me where it is I'm going to avoid them.

"What I'm doing right now is right," Big continues with conviction. "I'm taking care of my mother, my kids, and my peers. It's legal, and I'm using a talent that I have to express myself and get paid; so it's only right that I follow the righteous road."

What would he have said a year ago if someone had told him that Tupac would be dead and Suge Knight would be in jail right now?

"I wouldn't have been surprised," he says. "When you start making a whole bunch of money and your lifestyle starts moving too fast, it gotta be up to you to slow that shit down. You can't keep getting pissy drunk, drinking liters of Hennessy, smoking two or three ounces of weed a day. You partyin', you fuckin', and as soon as a nigga is saying something slick, you beating his ass. Something's bound to happen.

"I was kinda getting into that format of living, too, for a second," he says, "but when I got into that car accident, I was in the hospital for two or three months and it kind of made me able to sit down and say, 'Big, you moving too fast. It's time for shit to change.'"

Does he ever get aggravated by his own actions. "Hell, yeah," he says, laughing. "I do a lot of stupid shit. But you have to learn from your mistakes. You never hear about Method Man getting in no kind of problems, or Outkast, because they don't lead the same life that I live. Meth is into his family and his music—that's all he does. Maybe if I chose to live that lifestyle, I wouldn't be involved in a lot of things. But my mother told me if there wasn't no drama, I wouldn't want to be a part of it. There got to be a little spice in it for me. That's my problem."

What's being a father like?

"Cool," he says. "I don't do it the way I want to right now 'cause I'm mad busy; but I want to wake up with my kids, get 'em ready, and take them to school. I want to participate in all of that.

"See, when I first had T'Yanna," he adds, "I was only twenty years old. I was still fuckin' up because I wasn't recognizing that, when honey wakes up, and she's, like, 'I want my daddy,' that there's someone in this world who needs me more than anything. I finally realized it before it was too late. When I see my son and my daughter, it's something to live for. I'm doing it for them.

"Niggas ain't the same young-buck, forty-drinkin' niggas that don't give a fuck if they live or die. I want to see my kids get old. I want to go to my daughter's wedding. I want to go to my son's wedding. I want to go to their son's wedding. And you ain't going to be able to see it wilding."

And then, in his last night on earth, I asked Big a question that still haunts me. How close was he to where he wanted to be in life?

"I think there are a lot more lessons that I need to learn," he says. "There are a lot more things I need to experience, a lot more places I need to go before I can finally say, 'Okay, I had my days.' A lot more shit have to go down, 'cause I want a lot more."

Vibe / May 1997

Haitian Homecoming

SELWYN SEYFU HINDS AND BAKARI KITWANA

wyclef Jean can run His strides are jerky and uneven, yet swift, a maniacal grin plastered on his face as he scampers across the green expanse of lawn that surrounds Haiti's presidential palace. In his wake comes a throng of security personnel, all looking slightly annoyed at the unpredictable antics of this expatriate-turned-cultural-hero.

"We love you, Wyclef!" the subjects of Clef's attention scream out their greeting as he reaches the green wrought-iron fence that separates the masses from the pristine halls of power. Another roar goes up as the crowd catches sight of Lauryn making her own way toward them. Impending motherhood seems to have bestowed an extra level of grace to the divine Ms. Hill. Her careful, measured glide brings a breath of calm to the frenetic excitement of the moment.

"Laureeen, Laureeen, I love you, Laureeen," one little boy cries out, tears streaming from his eyes. Wyclef pauses his mad dash and runs back to grab Lauryn's hand. Together, the two stride toward the people, while the third member of the trio, Pras, angles in from the far right. They all hit the fence at about the same time, breaking into distinct meet-and-greet modes. Wyclef sprints off to the left, shaking hands as fast as they're offered; Lauryn holds down the center, smiling angelically and trying to touch as many people as possible; Pras slides off to the right, slapping hands and nodding at those he cannot reach. The poor masses of Port-au-Prince bask in all the attention. For a people of little material wealth, today must be priceless. Finally, the Fugees have come home.

Haiti's early history goes the way of much of Western imperialism's saga. Columbus landed in 1492, naming the island Hispaniola. Upon the arrival of the Spanish "settlers," the island's native population, the Arawaks, was estimated at eight million. By the 1540s, their numbers had significantly dwindled. A few decades later, they were completely wiped out, due to a combination of disease, slavery, and outright murder.

The African slave trade then provided the colony with its supply of labor. By 1550, at least thirty thousand Africans were forcibly brought to the island. The 1697 Treaty of Ryswick gave the western third of the island to the French, while the Spanish maintained the rest. The French called their colony Saint-Domingue. By the time the United States was being formed in 1776, Saint-Domingue was outproducing all thirteen American colonies. Part of this was due to the harsh, inhumane conditions under which the Africans labored. Some historians say that as many as one in three slaves died in their first three years. Others say that the Africans were being worked to death at such an insane rate that replacements had to be brought in every eight to ten years. Despite this rate of human destruction, by 1791 enslaved Africans in Saint-Domingue numbered nearly five hundred thousand.

These conditions set the stage for the Haitian Revolution. On January 1, 1804, after defeating the French, Jean-Jaques Dessalines declared the former French colony independent and restored the name Haiti, the Arawaks' original name for the island.

One of the first things one notices upon landing at Haiti's airport are the white U.N. observation posts along the side of the runway. The structures are a visible reminder of this country's complicated past and delicate future. Those thoughts can't help but bubble in the mind as our group of weary journalist types emerges from a silver-plated American Airlines jet into Haiti's golden sunshine. With nary a wasted moment, we collect our things and are whisked through the airport with the swiftness accorded American media piggybacking on the fame of an international act like the Fugees.

Haiti is a damnably hot country. That evidence blasts us in the face as we step from the relatively cool confines of the airport, along with the first clear indicator of the economic deprivation that has made this island notorious: a crowd of dark-skinned, poorly tattered, hungrily staring young boys lined up along the wire fence that sets the airport off from the road.

"American?" one asks hopefully, upon catching sight of our party entering a Jeep.

"Fugees!" another says firmly.

"American . . . Fugees!" The words bounce from mouth to mouth, mixed with a smattering of rapidly spoken Creole, as they thrust eager hands in our direction.

"One dollar . . . one dollar." The entire crew takes up that litany as our Jeep tries to navigate through the massed flesh. Finally, we break free as a chorus of despondent howls arises. One brave soul chases our Jeep and leaps up on the passenger side running board, face pressed against the window, mouth uttering the magic words: "One dollar?"

"Yo, hold up," one of our party says irritably as the driver guns the engine. The journalist rolls the window down and hands the kid a dollar bill. A smile splits the child's face and he hops off the running board of a Jeep speeding along at 35 mph.

"Merci . . ."

His thanks comes floating back in the air, settling uneasily on a bunch of shaken, disturbed Americans.

Haiti's bold strike for independence in 1804 was the first successful slave revolt in the New World. But that distinction came with a price. In addition to destroying much of the country's agricultural infrastructure, the war led European countries, along with the United States, to bar Haiti from the international community. The French, for that matter, did not even recognize Haiti as a country until France received reparations for the war ($150 million). In the United States, Congress debated whether or not to refer to Haiti as independent and did not recognize Haitian sovereignty until 1862. Gunboats from the United States, Britain, Germany, and France routinely sailed off its coast.

Although trade continued to go on, Haiti was so ostracized that scholars have come to refer to the hundred years between Haiti's independence and the U.S. invasion in 1915 as the Decade of Isolation. The occupation also set the tone for a history of human rights violations, military-backed governments, and unfair elections. By 1957, François "Papa Doc" Duvalier came to power, declaring himself "President for Life." With a security force, the Tonton Macoutes, responsible only to him, Duvalier was able to secure his own presidency as well as that of his son, Jean-Claude "Baby Doc," creating a dictatorship that lasted until 1986—and through it all maintained U.S. backing.

It was during this time that the off-shore assembly industry jumped off in Haiti, giving U.S. corporations access to cheap labor. The thirty-one-year tenure was marked by killings, beatings, human rights abuses, and corruption, all of which contributed greatly to Haiti's impoverishment and helped shape the country's present international image.

Haiti's more recent international attention was largely inspired by its mass popular movement that gained momentum in the late 1980s and early 1990s. Much like our own civil rights movement, this alliance of peasants, urban poor, student organizations, church workers, and some merchant elite sought power for the people—a turn away from the old way of doing things, which excluded the majority population from the political process. The culmination of these efforts was the 1991 democratic election (with 67 percent of the vote) of Father Jean-Bertrand Aristide. However, Aristide was soon forced to flee the country after a military-backed coup.

The Congressional Black Caucus supported both the return of Aristide as well as U.S. military intervention. But the Caucus was not alone. "We did support multilateral intervention under United Nations supervision. Because the military had the country hostage and wasn't going to let go," says Munthali Mwiza, information specialist at the Library for TransAfrica, a D.C.-based special interest group headed by Randall Robinson. Robinson underwent a hunger strike in 1994, protesting the treatment of Haitian refugees who were fleeing the dire political situation in Haiti. "Mr. Robinson's protest forced the change in that policy. But there had to be a complete change in that regime to avoid further problems in this regard," Mwiza added. On September 19, 1994, the United States launched Operation Uphold Democracy, which set the stage for a U.N.-approved multinational force (MNF) in Haiti. Without this change in the political climate, the Fugees' homecoming would have remained a dream.

"So many beautiful little children, so many beautiful little boys," Lauryn Hill murmurs quietly, as she reaches over to accept a kiss on the cheek from yet another child. The stage is the swanky Le Ritz hotel in Haiti's upper-class suburb of Petionville; the occasion: a reception for the Fugees thrown by the corporate backers of this weekend's benefit concert.

The folks here, particularly the children, stand in marked contrast to the Haitians we encountered at the airport. There are boys dashing around in European sport jackets with ascots around their necks, beautiful young girls who look like they could have stepped from the pages of any high-fashion magazine. Now, one can see the residue of colonialism all throughout the Black diaspora. Even in America we have our own historical dynamic between darker- and lighter-skinned blacks. But I have never seen color and class divisions as rigid as those in Haiti. This is literally two nations in one.

"It's kinda ill, right?" Lauryn comments wryly, catching sight of my bemused expression. "Ill" doesn't even begin to describe it. What's really ill is Wyclef. While Lauryn is African-American and Pras is Brooklyn-born, of Haitian parents, Clef's a child of Haiti's poor—a dark-skinned, unabashed representative of the people. Yet here he stands, holding court with the denizens of Haiti's upper class. A group of about twenty surround him, listening intently as he conducts interviews with the local press. In fact, if you didn't know better you'd swear he was a candidate for office. But don't tell Clef that. "I'm not into politics," he'll insist if pressed, lips curling in disdain. Yet nearly every move he'll make here will be political. Like Haiti, Wyclef reeks of his politics, despite himself. Indeed, the real art of the Fugees may lie in their ability to take their message beyond their music, to show the world that there is still power in Blackness.

The evening passes swiftly. The Fugees smile graciously and chitchat with their admirers. Then the Haitian minister of culture, Raoul Peck, begins the official proceedings, stepping up to a poolside podium to welcome the group to the tune of thunderous applause. Seventeen-year-old Rosalee and eighteen-year-old Anouk squeal with excitement when the Fugees themselves step up to the mic to offer thanks. The two girls are clearly children of privilege. And they are quite proud of the Fugees and what they represent, touting them as representations of Haitian pride. Yet, for them, there's still a degree of class complication in Haitians' appreciation of that representation.

"In Haiti, there are two social classes—higher and lower. We have television, we travel, et cetera, so the lower classes really don't get exposed [to the Fugees] as much," sighs Anouk, eyes fixed on Pras. "The Fugees are more popular with the higher class." But the next few days will give me more than enough evidence to contend that assertion. For now I can only nod and watch two teenage girls struggle with their perception of themselves and the world they occupy.

"It's an important issue [the Haitian poor]," Rosalee continues. "It's very sad that we can't do anything. The differences are so big. The poor dating and mingling with upper class? Not at all . . ."

Wyclef's closing comments suddenly jump out, momentarily breaking our conversation. ". . . and to the kids, you guys are the future to Haiti. I'm getting old right now. You can accomplish anything that you want in the world. God bless you." The attendees break into enthusiastic cheers, yelling out the group members' names and clapping loudly. Anouk, Rosalee, and their friends beam brightly before uttering their final thought: "You just don't have poor people in the U.S. like we have in Haiti."

* * * * * *

Haiti's presidential palace is a grand structure. Built by Americans during the occupation earlier this century, the imposing white building gives off more than a few echoes of Washington, D.C.'s government buildings. The palace is ringed by a green iron fence in some parts, white stone in others. Politically inspired graffiti dots nearly every white portion of the fence. It's an odd sight. After all, one wouldn't expect to see tags coating the outskirts of the White House.

It's Friday morning and all of Port-au-Prince is abuzz. This is the day that the Fugees will receive medals of honor. On the street that borders the palace's side entrance, the local populace is anxious, muttering excitedly and awaiting their heroes' arrival. Grim-faced security men are everywhere, openly touting a variety of arms. A few American personnel are scattered among the security folk, their sweaty red faces clearly setting them apart. "Hurry up, move it," one screams at us, walkie-talkie waving, eyes flashing over the crowd.

A squeal of brakes, a sudden rush of motion, and a throaty roar mark the entrance of the man of the moment. Inexplicably, Wyclef arrives on the back of a motorcycle. Apparently he refused to ride in the Jeep with his bodyguards, preferring to greet his people openly. And they love it. Hands reach out to pound Clef on his back, shake his hand, or just offer a thumbs-up. For a brief moment I'm afraid that he'll be pulled from the bike. But the love is communicated in a respectful manner. No one's trying to snatch a piece of Wyclef's clothing as a keepsake. Maybe it's the multitude of watchful eyes and cocked Uzis. But I doubt that. These people aren't rabid fans; they're celebrating the return of a native son.

The inside of the palace looks equally as grand as its exterior. The central foyer is a huge, open space ringed with busts of Haitian heroes and leaders past. Ornate chandeliers hang from thirty-foot ceilings. On the stage at the head of the room rest six gilded chairs, one of them distinctly thronelike. Haiti is a land large on ceremonial appearance, at least in the case of the elites.

The fifty or so neatly arranged chairs within the foyer area contain a mixed bag of press, Haitian political and business leaders, and other luminaries, all gazing expectantly toward the head of the room. The recipients of the collective eyeballing occupy three of the seats on stage. Wyclef, in black Armani suit and tie, slumps sideways in his chair, a decidedly irreverent expression on his grill. Pras, the very picture of informality in jeans, T-shirt, and Tims, lounges to Clef's left. Lauryn, wearing dark shades and a bright-colored, dashiki-inspired outfit, sits to the right. The other chairs are taken up by Haiti's minister of culture, the prime minister, and in the larger, fancier number, the president, Rene Preval.

Events proceed in a fashion quite similar to last night's reception. The minister of culture sets the proceedings off. He's quickly followed by President Preval himself, then each of the Fugees. The group members look well aware of the gravity and significance of the situation. Nonetheless, Pras doesn't miss an opportunity to keep things real, offering the president a pair of high-fashion sunglasses and suggesting he procure a pair of Tims. Many words are said over the course of the twenty-minute ceremony; but for me, Clef's are the most significant, the most profound:

"I'm the kid that stands behind the palace that cannot come in here today to see the Fugees; that's who I am. It's all good that the media is here and the press, but none of that really matters to the Fugees, because if we didn't sell the millions of records that we did, we wouldn't even be here. I wouldn't be able to get inside the palace to make this speech . . ."

The attendees applaud enthusiastically, and with a flourish of beams from the president and scowls from the security heavies, the stage party is ushered from the foyer. Fifteen minutes finds Lauryn resting on the palace's second-floor balcony, eyes gazing across the lawn at the folk pressed against the fence. Clef's words must still be buzzing in her head. Half tentatively, she raises a hand. A dull cry goes up in response. Lauryn grins.

"That was really heavy," she says very quietly, a slight note of awe in her tone. "My life has not been remotely close to what I might have imagined. If I could've sat down and planned it, then I would've finished college, got a job, and met a man and got married. But it didn't. I don't really try to understand God; I just try to accept His will and performance the best way possible. It's very easy to disassociate your success with God. You think like, 'If I didn't make that beat phat, et cetera.' I recognized that it's not even me, man. It's not even me, 'cause as easy as it could've been me, it could've been someone else. It could've been any one of those kids out there . . ."

Observers of Haiti most often speak of its poverty (poorest in the Western hemisphere and one of the poorest in the world) and unemployment (estimates as high as 80 percent), but they do so without reference. They discuss Haiti by omission. You cannot get a clear sense of the sociopolitical and cultural landscape without considering the resiliency, self-determination, and hard-work ethic of the people. A population of seven million inhabit a country with a land area about the size of Maryland. With 70 percent of the population living in rural areas, the dramatic deforestation and erosion of the land greatly contributes to the country's poverty.

It is difficult to paint a picture of Haiti because its image has so long been distorted. One has to struggle against the stereotypes—boat people, AIDS, poverty, illiteracy, violence—and in doing so, one gets locked into either glorifying the stereotypes or attempting to deny them altogether. You cannot begin to comprehend the making of chaos in any Central American, Caribbean, or South American country without considering the influence of U.S. foreign policy, extending back to even before the Cold War years. (During the Haitian Revolution years, the United States sent troops and military aid to support the French.) And most certainly U.S. influence cannot be minimized in the current global economy. Beneath the surface, between poverty and paradise, Haiti is not much unlike the rest of the world. Even in the grand old U.S. of A., there are pockets of wealth and pockets of poverty, but the distance between the haves and have-nots is shortened by a relatively large middle class. In Haiti, like much of the so-called Third World, this scenario is played out in extremes—an extremely large poor population, an extremely small middle class, and an extremely small elite. A history of dictatorships, corrupt provisional governments, death squads, an often-zealous military, a tiny elite of power brokers, and a majority of disenfranchised poor are all pieces of the puzzle.

Regardless of what the future holds, Haiti gave the black world the reality of independence and self-determination at a time when black enslavement was considered normal. This can never be taken away. While this may be partially responsible for Haiti's fierce independence, it's most certainly a variable in the fierce propaganda that plagues the country and the contempt that many U.S. politicians hold, a contempt that works its way into foreign policy. Whether one is speaking of Foreign Relations chairman Jesse Helms, Bill Clinton, or George W. Bush, it isn't far-fetched to imagine a desire on their part, no matter how subconsious, to punish Haiti for its temerity. The Western imperialist sentiment has never forgiven Haiti for throwing the French out on their ears.

The man called Wyclef is tired. Shit, he has every right to be. Just keeping up with the frenetic pace that he's set since arriving in Haiti has *me* exhausted. Tonight promises to be no exception. We're at Club Med, believe it or not, lounging on an air-conditioned patio surrounded by pampered European tourists and gun-toting guards. It's just another one of those weird dynamics that makes Haiti such a difficult place to pin down. But for now, Clef's just catching a quick moment, preparing for the show the crew came here to perform. Tonight's hundred-dollar-a-head shindig is just a precursor for the real deal tomorrow night. It's also supplying a fair bit of the cash to subsidize Saturday's benefit.

"Ay yo."

Clef turns his red-rimmed eyes toward me.

"How in the hell did you put this together?"

"Just a lot of hard work. You can't do anything in this country of this capacity without getting support from the government. Just like we can't do anything in Jamaica, Cuba, and other islands. Islands have certain conflicts. We felt we had a good chance to make a statement. We wasn't coming here to play, 'cause we could do that. I was just flying back and forth, keeping it real low. Coming in to see the president and being at the cabinet meetings, arguing with them pricks."

Clef offers one of his infectious grins and it suddenly occurs to me how little folks really know about this man. Sure, everyone knows he's the guitar-strumming, occasionally singing dude in the Fugees. But there're layers to Clef—artistically and personally—that have yet to be realized on a large scale.

"Ever since I was three years old, I've been into music," he goes on. "Growing up in Haiti, you can't really grab a guitar or bass; I was the less fortunate. I would beat on bottles and make drum beats, and sing songs just to go with the drums. It's deep, 'cause now I'm like twenty-six, but I play like ten, fifteen different instruments. And I just conducted my first hip-hop symphony, and it tripped them [the New York Philharmonic] out. 'Cause they was like, 'And the conductor is . . .?' And they was reading my music and they knew it was me. So they was like, 'Wow, what a beautiful piece of music. Where's the conductor? Can he conduct it?'"

Flipping expectations on the head. That could be Wyclef Jean's mantra. Sometimes we take the significance of what he's accomplished, of what the Fugees have accomplished, for granted. And it's taken a first-hand visit to the environment that bore Clef for me to realize that. As a kid, Clef didn't live too far from Club Med. And he couldn't even dream of getting within smelling distance. It's an irony that he's all too aware of, leaning over so he can be heard above the din of the tourists.

"I mean, even while I was in the White House, I told them, 'Don't be mistaken. Put the money aside and all that shit aside and I'm the same nigga that's outside the palace. That's what y'all gotta understand, so they're the ones you gotta help. Don't be bringing me here to make things look good when they're not.' So everyone respects that and they respect the Fugees on all levels."

It might be respect back home, but here it's nothing short of love. Aside from reel footage of Chinese girls fainting at the sight of Michael Jackson and vintage Beatle-mania, I've never seen such a heartfelt outpouring of affection toward a musician. Typically enough, Clef downplays his end of the equation, preferring to big up the people.

"The whole thing is that they know I'm really from here. I went to school down here, so it's like you could tell the perpetrator and you can tell the real person, and these people got soul. They can call a bluff, they know who's supposed to be in power and they know who's in power and they know who're the bullshitters. All they do is beg for money, but when they want somebody out of power, they get down. And what they see in me is simplicity. I think what they see in the Fugees is simplicity. The Fugees ain't hiding in a room, under the lights, when we go onstage. Wherever we play at, wherever around the world. So I think that's what makes people respect the Fugees more. You got kids, they're just starstruck and they believe the hype."

"Simplicity? That's the Fugees's key?"

"It's just something we're doing naturally. With this next album, *Carnival,* I'm taking it there. It's thug-related, that's the first thing. It's something we're doing subconsciously. At a carnival, anything could happen. There was a cousin of mine who they assassinated at the carnival here in Haiti. So then I started working on the album while I was on tour. But subconsciously we've been all around the world. So it's bugged, 'cause the album sounds like some thug shit, but it's trippy 'cause it's not the ordinary sampling you're used to listening to. You'll be like, 'Damn, this shit is crazy. Where's he get that loop from?' I think it's just being in different parts of the world, you'll inquire more. And I think for us the way it used to be, the Smokeys, the James Browns, niggas used to travel, son. Niggas went around the world. We just stayin' in this fifty-state thing talkin' about, 'Yeah, yeah, Al Capone!!' You can't see the Mafia. You can't even imagine what a mob is. They think a fifty-state radius is something, but all the music is staying in one place. Hip-hop is the only form of music that can do this to people. I mean, this is all hip-hop, it's what we do. And that's all the kids are listening to and they're convincing the older people who don't have a clue to what's going on."

The carnival has come to Haiti tonight, manifested through the power of the Fugees. In order to grasp what's going on here, you gotta process it with the senses. Smell the dockside air and the wafts of ganja; listen to the crash of music and the ebbs and swells of 75,000 black voices; see the sea of dark skin spreading out from the stage, standing, sitting in treetops, perched on top of buses, on the edge of nearby balconies, rhythmically waving their hands in the air. Even then you'll only have a poor man's approximation of the beauty unfolding tonight.

It's well into the night before the Fugees finally take the stage. The center of attraction: Wyclef Jean. To call him amped would be an understatement. Dressed in a white T-shirt and baggy blue jeans, his dark eyes complement his jet-black skin, locks feeding into his beard, much like he feeds off the energy of the crowd. Tonight he seems to move with a force beyond himself. He is proud of his Haitian heritage. Proud that he can do something for Haiti—and he should be. We should all be. After all, Haiti gave us the Haitian Revolution, kicking the idea of black enslavement in the Western hemisphere into a tailspin.

But this is Wyclef's night, his own chapter in the island's history. "To return to Haiti to perform is his dream," Lauryn confided earlier in the day. Now he's dispersing a sort of libation, pouring bottled water on his dreads and shaking his head Bob Marley–style, saturating those standing closest to the stage. There's simply something magical at work here. When Clef performs his Creole songs, he becomes powerful and commanding in a way most Stateside have never seen.

Part of tonights wonder lies within the Fugees's magnetic appeal to kids on both sides of Haiti's color and class divides. Haiti is often noted for the sharp contrast between its 5 percent mixed-race elite and 95 percent black poor. It took centuries to construct these divisions. A few lyrics from *The Score*, a few from the *Carnival*, and for that moment everyone is unified under one identity—Haitian, and proud of it. From sunset till the early a.m., the audience is eager, energetic, and explosive. The night exudes a spiritual, cleansing force. This is the side of Haiti that those of us limited to sound bites on the six o'clock news never see.

3:30 a.m. The concertgoers are tramping in the streets, blowing away on those unique horns that give rara—a Haitian carnival music—its particular feel. Somewhere in that mass of gliding limbs is Wyclef Jean. Lauryn and Pras have long retired to their respective Jeeps. But Clef can't let this moment go. And I don't think he should, at least not abruptly. The joy that's been created this night has to be lowered slowly into the soul, lest it drops too swiftly and all opportunity to savor it vanishes.

But if sixteen-year-old Stanley Bloy is any indication, that joy will be around for some time. "Wyclef is my life," he says excitedly as the marchers pass by. I look at him curiously, like the jaded New Yorker I am. Your *life?*

"I don't want anything to touch him because he's doing something for my country. I can't explain how much love I've got for this guy. He's a leader. When he plays the music, I'm so happy I cry. It's the first time a Haitian plays music like this in Creole that everybody can understand and appreciate."

Damn.

It occurs to me that we don't give ourselves enough credit. You know, what America fucked up [namely, the Black diaspora] through the export of destabilizing politics, it now has the capacity to connect through its latest cultural export—hip-hop. We just need a little carnival to bring it all together.

I can finally see Clef. Someone's wrapped a flag of sorts around his shoulders. He looks tired, but buoyant on the energy that's been generated tonight. For once, the security dudes are unobtrusive. It's just Clef and his people. Tramping gently off into the night, blowing on them horns.

The Source / July 1997

Allah's on Me

ROBERT MARRIOTT

4. Deliver the poor and needy: rid them out of the hand of the wicked. 5. They know not, neither will they understand; they walk on in darkness: all the foundations of the earth are out of course. 6. I have said, Ye are gods; and all of you are children of the Most High. 7. But ye shall die like men and fall like one of the princes. 8. Arise, O God, judge the earth: for thou shall inherit all nations.   —Psalm 82

Connecticut. Winding past streams and brooks, down a sunlight-freckled road. Surrounded by woods. Looking for the god. Rakim Allah. Been two days. Can't be found. He lives like a corporate fugitive: hard to reach, infamously late, cancels meetings. The cab stops at a sprawling, three-story house. Tall pines stand watch over a Benz 190. White, kitted-out, just wiped down. The rag sits abandoned on the hood. Its eight-cylinder Corvette engine, dormant. Plan was to head to his crib, unannounced. The label rep rings the bell. Wisps of clouds idle above.

The guy from the label shakes his head, vents, "You can't know how difficult this project is. Ra is a hard cat to find. I come out to Connecticut four to five times a week to get him. It's taking a really long time to finish this album. Plus, he's a perfectionist. I'll tell you this story: Once there was this important meeting. He had to give a speech. I told him he had to be there. Absolutely. Well, the thing started, and he wasn't there. So I got on the train. Got to the house, and I saw both his cars were there. I ask Felicia, the mother of his children, if he's there. She's like, no. I'm thinking, the van's right there. No, his boys came and picked him up. But I knew he was there. So I get back on the train. Trying to figure out what I was gonna do. It would look fucked-up if he's not there. I get a call on the cell telling me he's there at the meeting. Mind you, he can drive to New York faster than I can get there by train. He made his speech. It went cool. All I kept sayin' is, 'You a funny nigga.' He's like, 'Wha?' I'm like, 'You a funny nigga.'" He rings again. Ra answers the door, announcing Brooklyn across his chest. He just finished a plate of fish.

Who is God?

That's a deep question. In Psalms it says ye are all children of the Most High. And when you do the knowledge of life itself, man, we all came from one origin. So if we were born from the Most High, the Bible also says we were made in his likeness. On that note, we deal with the science of God. God itself means Gomar Oz Dubar. Gomar means wisdom, Oz means strength, Dubar means beauty. So that right there lets you know that God is physical, visual, something that can be seen. We are mental and physical beings. When I first went on tour, goin' across the state, they were like, "What you mean you God? Can you walk through walls? Can you walk on water?" I'm like, mentally I can do that, but y'all lookin' at the word *God* like it's unhuman. I'm like, yo, this is life, man. Everything in life is real. The word *God*—that's not the Most High. Because the word *God* is not big enough for the Most High. We supposed to start realizin' these things and realize how great we are. First thing they did when they brought us over here was strip us of our knowledge. People say, how could they have stripped you of what you know, what's in your head? No, it's deeper than that. They stripped us of our knowledge of who we are. They stripped us of our title. And what they said is: you not God, God is a mystery. So they took that from us. Then all the wise ones on the boat, you know the story, they killed them off.

So what did you mean when you said you were born to be Sole Controller of the Universe?
We all are. We God by nature, and then when you deal with it, it's nature for us to be God. So you know everybody got a destiny. It was my destiny to drop science on records.

His government name: William Michael Griffin. Three sevens. Born under the sign of Aquarius, the Water Bearer. The man pouring the waters of celestial truth. Was raised in Wyandanch, Long Island. Also known as Crimedance. Was the youngest of five. When his grandmother saw him in the delivery room, she said, "Look at little Poppo." The name stuck. Friends still know him as Pops.

His mother played all types of music in the house: jazz, rock, disco, opera. His older brothers played instruments. He picked up the sax, found hip-hop soon after. Rhymed in the parks and at basement parties. Attained knowledge of self. Realized he was a god. (Eighty-five percent walk through life deaf, dumb, and blind; 10 percent are the bloodsuckers of the poor.) He was among the elect. One of the 5 percent. Learned the Supreme Alphabet. Learned the Supreme Mathematics. Studied his degrees. Righteous name: Ruler, Allah, Kingdom, Eye or Islam, Master. Allah. Became a messenger of Allah. Wrote hip-hop manifestos at seventeen. Recorded with Eric Barrier.

Harry Allen, writer, media assassin: "First time I heard 'My Melody'? It was almost fear-inspiring. It had a very weird rhythm track and that strange whistling. It had a whole different kind of psychological construction. You had the feeling Rakim not only rhymed, but worked out the *curvature* of his rhymes. It was something new. Something else."

* * * * * *

He laid down hip-hop law. There's before *Paid in Full* and after. It was a rare combination of elements. A voice that induced paralysis, lying somewhere between fire and ice. Rhymes crowded with meaning. *I hold the microphone like a grudge.* Or: *I draw a crowd / like an architect.* Or: *Droppin' bombs / but I be peace and calm / any emcee that disagree with me wave your arms.* He personified ghetto majesty. Righteous criminality. Became an icon immediately. Went on tour. Spread Five Percent cosmology like Bob Marley spread Rasta. He changed the music, changed the language, changed the way we see ourselves.

Rolling through Harlem. Mecca. Following Rakim and his boys in a black Expedition. Looking for photo ops. Ride past churches and check-cashing spots, liquor stores and Lotto. Roll past Rastas eating watermelon on the corners. Dice niggas talkin' shit: Jigg niggas cuttin' eyes. Angry children cussin' at grown folk. Big-armed women walking fast, baby powder high up on their necks. Rakim slows his vehicle. "Yo, let's go to this spot, word. Do some real shit."

He leads us to 106th and Park Avenue. A graffiti temple. The Wall of Fame. Rakim stands against a wall, surrounded by lurid color. Letters fold in on themselves around him. Change texture, direction. Implode. A four-armed Puerto Rican Nefertiti rises above us all. A few kids are playing pickup ball nearby. A young kid crosses over, double-clutches, and shoots under three defenders. A small crowd gathers against the fencing. They call Rakim's name, ask him questions. "When the album comin' out?" An elevated train rushes by. Photographer: "You don't even know what cosmic powers y'all are fucking with today." Rakim swaggers toward the camera, eyes silent: an eight-year-old runs into the shot, waving a toy pistol. Ra stops him.

"What's your name?"

"Brian Lopez."

"Take a picture with us, shorty. Make the meanest face you can think of."

Brian Lopez grimaces.

"Yeah, shorty! Tell 'em to back the fuck up. No, don't tell 'em that. Tell 'em back up."

"I know somebody else with guns, that got guns like me. I'm looking for him."

"Yeah?" Ra starin' at the camera.

"Yeah, I'm trying to shoot him."

"Well, look mean for the camera, shorty. Look like you just ate a box of nails."

Brian points his gun, tries to frown but has to smile. Ra crouches over him, holding invisible guns in each hand.

Part God, part gangsta. Played the first hip-hop mafioso in the video for "Follow the Leader," while reciting ethereal verse. Gave us a portrait of the artist as a young badass in the autobiographical "Microphone Fiend." Told the definitive mack tale on "Mahogany." Articulated a worldview as large as the cosmos on "In the Ghetto." But fans were underwhelmed by "Don't Sweat the Technique." Their faith in the god was shaken. Harry Allen: "The video in the mansion with the women in bikinis had a lot to do with it. There was fission between the words and the images. He needed something to visually amplify what he was saying." Wrote and produced the thug masterpiece "Know The Ledge": *Push up like an exercise check the intellect and inspect the thighs.* But things weren't right. Split ways with Eric B. soon after.

What happened exactly?

Wasn't no conflict. It was just best we go our separate ways. It was just about how he was making his moves. At the end of the contract, we did some separate little deals. He was supposed to do his little project. I was supposed to do my little project. He did his project. I signed off so he could get his paper. When my project came up, I had to look all over the world for him, you know. So I just made my move.

Ra was bred on jazz. It courses through his veins. He speaks in its rhythms. *The rhyme is rugged at the same time sharp / I could swing off anything even the string of a harp.* He understands not just the music, but the gesture. The notions of indirection and negative presence come natural. Miles Davis turned his back to the audience; Ra retreated to the lab.

Bill Adler, head of Mouth Almighty Records, director of publicity at Rush, circa 1987: "Eric was looking at the camera and Rakim wasn't. I was nagging him to give something to the camera, something. He turned to me and said, 'I *am* giving something to the camera.' I just shut up, because he was right. I think he cultivated a mystique to a certain extent. But consistent with his writing. The way he wrote just bespoke cool, unruffled, almost icy.

"The thing about him, too, is that he was very self-consciously a writer. I think part of the attraction to Islam was the writing in the Quran. It informs a lot of his writing. There's a certain grandiosity to what he does."

R: I don't like doin' interviews because I'm the type, man: understand me on my records. I've never been one to talk a lot. Same time, I like doing things for a reason. But I haven't been out in a while, so people need to hear me. See, once a word is spoken, there's so many ways people can grasp it and change it. Put prefixes and suffixes on it, and before you know it, it's not even my words. I didn't even say that.

Bill Stepheney, president of Stepson Records: "You can't compare him to Jay-Z or Nas. They exist in the video age. Rakim is the test vestige of the independent-label era. A celebrity for not being present. You don't see him at the parties. Now the medium is almost defined by having this presence. But I think it's coming back [Rakim's way]. He is one of those brothers that remind you of a generation that seems so anonymous, that you don't pay attention to. The ticking time bombs waiting to go off. Not Bigger Thomas per se, but cats waiting to go off. Very quiet but seething."

So who is Rakim? Bigger or the Invisible Man?

"Both. He has Bigger's rage but he is anonymous. Hip-hop is a statement of black male anonymity: I have to yell and scream, because no one's paying any attention to what I'm dealing with. Rakim mirrors that invisibility. No one understands why a Rakim has that seething quality about him, and I hate to say it, but you have to be a black man living in this society to understand why these kids ill the way they do."

Been a long time. Four years since Ra withdrew into the silence. An eternity in hip-hop time. He recorded five songs for an album. Someone leaked them to the street. Was forced to start again from scratch.

He did a sound-track cut every now and again, but people were starting to have doubts: hip-hop is something different now. There's a new generation raised on Mobb Deep and Snoop Dogg. He's up against faster cadences, new rhyme patterns. He has so far to fall, maybe he's burdened by his own greatness. Shit, it happened to Kane.

Do you have any doubts? Any fears?

I fear no man but Allah. I'm just cautious.

You don't feel pressure?

The pressure gonna come. But it's good pressure. With all the fans, it's like I got a million bosses.

What did you intend when you started rhymin'?

I grew up with my family. Musically orientated. My moms used to sing jazz on the radio in Brooklyn. My moms gets down. You know, just comin' up with her, just listenin' to music all day, every day. My brother, my oldest brother played piano. My brother under him played sax. That's what I did. I picked up the sax. Fourth grade. So when hip-hop came out, I'm like a teenager. In fact younger than that, but you know it was there for me. I was like, "Oh, rap? Word? Two turntables? A mic?" So I jumped into that. But I was rhymin' for a while, then I got Knowledge of Self like a year before I started makin' records. I got into that readin' so much, and you know, all that was in me. I had the street life in me, but the knowledge was in me, too. So I was speakin' on what I knew. Just so happened that it came out the way it did. A lot of people tell me it made mad changes in things of that nature.

Do you see that when you look at a song like "The Ghetto" or "My Melody"? When I heard that is when I started taking hip-hop very seriously.

One thing I did notice is a lot of people got more conscious after I came out. And dealing with Islam—when something like that go down, that right there just makes you feel good. 'Cause they say if you can teach one person, then you've done your job.

Do you feel like you were chosen to do that at that certain time?

With myself, B., it's deep. I don't take nothing on face value. I try to figure out a reason for everything. Like my government name is three sevens. My first name got seven letters, my second name got seven letters, and my last name got seven letters, so I put everything together, man. And like I said, I've been rhymin' for a long time before I got on. I've been in music a long time. So sometimes I think maybe I was supposed to set an example.

And it's ill. You're on Universal Records now. On the seventh floor.

Na' mean? Out of all that. Even the fact that I ain't been out in four years. I figure that happened for a reason, too. 'Cause a few years ago, that's when it started gettin' real deep as far as what they called gangsta rap. The majority rules, man, so if I came out in that time, I know I wouldn't have been talkin' 85 percent of that, so brothers would've been like, "Ra still down with his rhymes but"—it's the majority thing, you know? If you doin' what everybody else is doin', then people look at it as different.

Do you have a certain place you write, or do you find yourself inspired in certain places? Like for me, I'm always writing on the train. Every time I'm ridin' the train, shit comes to me.

I'm the same way. I mean wherever I'm livin', gotta have a lab, where I'm most comfortable. But if I gotta write in the studio, then I could do that, too. But what inspires me is life itself. I study it. Like I'll take a ride through New York and just be sittin' there lookin' and it bugs me out a lot 'cause I see things. Like me and my man would be drivin' but he don't see what I see. Nobody sees it, you know? So I take advantage of that. When I'm driving through New York, I don't just see a Hundred-and-such-and-such street or blasé-blah, I see the pain. I see life itself. I see culture.

Sound like an Aquarius.
Exactly so.

See, that's that universal shit. Before the people used the stars as guide-posts. They just looked up in the stars and saw themselves. And now we're blinded from it.
We so far away from the stars now. Take the Egyptians. The pyramids are heaven on earth. The pyramids are in perfect alignment with certain stars. It was like they were in tune with the skies to the point where it's crazy. Nowadays they could take computers and line the stars with the pyramid, and it'll fit perfectly. So in other words, with no machines, how did Egyptians do that? That's another way to show you how powerful we was. And a lot of times over the years, things get weaker, just like our physical form. You never know, a couple of hundred thousands of years from now, there might not be any pinkie toe.

That's why every now and then, the Most High sends out a prophet to show us. Y'all been looking for God? I'ma send y'all one so y'all can be in tune with yourselves. So He sends us one every few years, and we be lookin' at that person like he's so righteous. Like look at Farrakhan and Elijah Muhammad and all them wise brothers. When I was real young, I used to look at them like Martians. But then when you think about it, these are men. I'm a man. All I gotta do is apply myself, and I can speak just like those brothers and know the same things.

And when you look at something like the Million Man March, you can't deny their effect.
And what was love about that was there was no beef out there. You had brothers that were six-six, three hundred pounds and change, crying, son. Cryin' from the love. Seeing what we were capable of.

It kinda changed my whole mentality. I'm sayin' if you can get a million people together, you can do anything. It was like an evolved riot.

We need that, though. It's time. That's an actual fact. We gotta realize how great we are and how great we once was and let the world have it. Show them because they be lookin' at us like we the less.

But like they say, the last shall come first. We are the stone that the builder refused.

And they say the meek shall inherit the earth. *Meek* is just another word for humble.

Wyandanch, Long Island. Looks like a boarded-up Southern town, but with a Brooklyn feel. Muslims in robes and kufis sell incense on the corners. Bootleg Polo. Fila. Tapes of Farrakhan and the Chi-Lites. Rusted up Trans Ams. Several red-eyed men loiter outside one of three liquor stores.

It's Wyandanch Day. There's a big procession of drums and banners. Barbecues in the park. Chicken smothered in sauce. Fish burgers. Cockdiesel Natives beat tom-toms. Old men in straw hats tell lies with Southern intonations. Bare-chested niggas in do-rags and medallions. Barbecue smoke. A brother in a blue Benz blasts the Rakim/Mobb Deep joint: *Quick to say a poem to ricochet in ya dome / My clique told made me leave the nickel plated at home.*

Prodigious asses and thighs parade by in tight camouflage skirts. Flared nostrils. A crowd of young people are dancing around DJ Grandmaster Spark, mixing records in the center of the park. He drops Jay-Z's "Who Ya Wit?" making the crowd frantic. They start to chant. *Where ya at y'all? Sex-money y'all! Where ya at y'all?* High-yellow girls dance with toy guns in their hands, undulating their bodies, then popping to a stop. Two kids start a Bankhead Bounce battle. They vibrate their shoulders, freezing and lunging at each other.

Walk down Straight Path. Stop across the street from the liquor store. James' Barbershop. Been there thirty years. Old men eat spaghetti out of styrofoam cartons. They talk over the drone of clippers. Lameen Self Esteem cuts his sleeping nephew's hair. Ra called him Self. He's one of the firstborn gods of Wyandanch. He was taught by Brooklyn god Raheem U-Allah Son of Allah.

"He would come out to the park and kick it with us." He was one of the only graf artists in Wyandanch. Used to do the handball court every Wyandanch Day. Remembered when Ra was about to blow: "I was out on leave from the service. I went to see my man DJ Maniac. He helped Ra develop his talent. Ra used to be down with the Love Brothers, doing basement parties and such. Maniac gave me a tape, the original version of 'My Melody.' The music was different from later, but it was the same lyrics: shit was banging.

"That day I went over to Ra's crib, 'cause I was hanging with his brother. The place smelled like spray paint. He up there going off. Hookin' up somethin' on his wall. His moms let him do it. It was a picture of Sir Nose from Funkadelic. Pimped-out with a fedora-styled hat and Gazelles. He had a gun, and the barrel was coming right out the wall. It said, 'Kid Wizard.' That's what we called him. Also called him Aldo Chilly Cello, 'cause he was so laid-back.

"Ra was a real down-to-earth brother. But you know, money brings a lot of drama. I seen him go through changes with brothers. A lot of it was jealousy — you always gonna have that. But there was unkept promises, too. I guess even if you intend to, you can't fulfill everybody's dreams."

Framed pictures hang above the barbershop mirrors. Boxers, entertainers. Eric B., L.L., Tyson. One of the pictures is of Rakim, sitting in a burgundy Cherokee at the Nassau Coliseum. Hundred-dollar bills hang from the mirror. Hundreds of people surround the car. Ra gazes forward. Composed as a concerto.

Bill Stepheney: "I remember when we were at Def Jam. It was like an adult black male day camp. You'd have Eric B. and L.L. comparing gold chains. Whodini and Run-D.M.C. were always up there. Slayer would be going upstairs to meet Rick Rubin. Russell Simmons and Lyor Cohen always screaming. Flavor Flav. And Ra would walk through all this madness, unfazed. You know that Spike Lee floating-camera trick? That was Rakim."

Walk farther down the street, across the railroad tracks. Come to a house with violet rhododendrons in the front. Ring the bell. Cynthia Griffin, Rakim's mother, greets me at the door. Several gold records hang in the living room. The couch is a gold velour. There are pictures of Mr. and Mrs. Griffin and the five children. She takes slow pulls off a Virginia Slims. There's laughter in her voice: "Yes, I let him express himself, but it took ten coats of primer to get all the writing off the wall.

"I remember he'd come back from football with bruised ribs and snapback fingers. I was more frightened then than when he went on the road. But he got quite a few trophies in football, basketball. He wore 32.

"I met his father in a nightclub in Newark. Highway Inn. The Orioles and Sarah Vaughan were playing. I told a little fib and snuck over. His father was a very hard worker. Loved his children. His death was very hard on the family. It's been seven years and it's still difficult. Father's Day is particularly hard.

"Rakim became very popular around fifteen, sixteen. I was totally against it. But Eric B. kept asking and asking. We couldn't get too excited about his fame and so forth, because Ra didn't. He's so laid-back about everything. When he was at the Nassau Coliseum nearby, his father and I were ready to explode. The town was going crazy. But it was just another day at work for him. Even when he's troubled, his thing to say is 'Be all right in a minute.' Rakim laughs, but he's not with any foolishness. He's like his father in that way."

Connecticut. Ra points me and the label rep downstairs. The Lab. It's a small, carpeted room. Bare, except for some turntables stacked on crates. A few pictures. There's a drawing of the Master Poet above the turntables. He lays back on a concrete slab as it crushes a dozen MCs in Fila gear and gold chains. Eye of the Storm crackles. Naked records line the wall. Dice are scattered on the carpet. Several books are stacked on the shelf: *Dictionary of Biblical Scripture. Secrets of the I Ching. The African-American in Biblical Symbols. The Theology of Time.* In the corner, there's a large picture of Elijah at the podium. Farrakhan and Malcolm stand at his side completing the trinity. The one small window overlooks a pond.

How can someone claim to be a god and still be humble?
We dealin' with righteousness. That's the key word. Like me, I'm wise enough not to knock nobody for what they believe in. But at the same time, if I can tell them something, then I'll do that. That's what humble is. To be humble is to understand, to know. Like say, I'm right here right now

and a couple of people who buy my records come up to me and speak to me. And I say, "No autographs right now. I'm tired." Or I can say, "Peace. Thank you for buying my joint." That's humbleness. But really it's righteousness. If it wasn't for those who bought my record, I wouldn't be me. You gotta think, "Is this God? Is God evil? Does He deal with evilness? Does He beat people with stipes?" Things of that nature. Look at the black prophet Christ. Humble. When they were about to attack him, he was like, "Nah, let's not get ready to attack them because we'll be the same as them." So we gotta try to abide by righteousness. We gotta walk slow. We not 100 percent righteous, so we gotta take our time.

That's the path to the divine.
No doubt G, 'cause I feel like this, man: everything I do good is gonna come back. Like when I was younger, man, we'd take it straight to you, and it wasn't pretty. But as I get older—say a cat just threw a bottle at me. If I throw a bottle back at him, it's on, and we gonna take it to the fullest. Or I can let that die, I can let that brother slide and go on with my life. And eventually something is gonna happen to that brother. It's like you fall in your own iniquity. You live by the sword, you die by the sword. So I put my sword up. I put my guns up. But hold up. I still got my old ways in me, but I choose not to use them. Don't take my kindness for a weakness because you put anything in a corner, he's gonna find his way out.

Talk a little bit more of when you were playin' the sax. 'Cause it seemed like a lot of that influenced how you rhyme.
No doubt. See, what I did comin' up, I learned music, man. The timin', the different patterns. At the same time, I was listenin' to a lot of different music from jazz to what was happenin' when I was young, disco. I was rhymin' when cats were in the park talkin' 'bout "Stereereo" and "Donald Duck don' give a fuck" and all that shit. So my music background is what got me like deep in the styles of rhymes and deep in the thought. Like when I was real young, I heard how Thelonious Monk went across seas and learned the Asian music skills. In the United States, there's like only

seven notes. He went over there, and it was like, twenty-something. So when he came back home, he started writing songs with different chords. So the other piano cats was like, "Dukes, you playin' the wrong notes," until he come back and play them same notes. Then the cats was like, wait a minute. They started realizin' that this cat was makin' chords. Thelonious Monk was makin' chords! 'Cause he was tired of them eighty-eight keys. John Coltrane was another one. John Coltrane would get two, three notes comin' out at one time, G. It's impossible, damn near. So you know that's lettin' me know there's no limit, man. And I'm just a baby.

You just startin'.
Ain't nothin' I do really impresses me. So if I keep that mental, I'll be all right.

How do you feel about these young cats coming up now?
Like anything new, it keeps brothers in the game on their toes. There's a handful of brothers holdin' rap down—as far as keepin' it grimy, na'mean, street. But they don't have to talk about the same thing every time. Negativity gonna be there. It's gonna be there yesterday, it's gonna be there tomorrow. Can't hide the fact that this crazy shit is going on, but rap is an expression of life. What we gotta do, man, is do a couple of joints explainin' what's goin' on, say how you feel and then do the rest—skills, rhymes like we used to do it. So people will start respecting us as artists. Not just hoodlums, man. Killing ourselves off and everything. It's crazy. Still, I like the progress hip-hop has made as far as styles and music form. I feel brothers learned a lot. They steppin' it up. What they're realizin' is, the more homework you do with music, the better you get. People are startin' to get into the science of being musicians. And that's the only thing that's gonna take us to the next level right now.

So what's the difference between Rakim and Rakim on wax?
On wax, I gotta watch what I say. Otherwise nothin' different. I write what

I feel. I write what I do. But on TV or whatever, I carry myself in a wise manner. 'Cause, you know, all eyes on me.

Ra's driveway. Bill Blass, his manager, and members of Ra's new group, The Last Platoon, roll through. Cats shoot at the hoop in the driveway as Blass talks of extravagant plans for Ra's stage show. We start a pickup game. Tahmel, Rakim's eight-year-old, attempts to steal the ball. Jabar, his younger son, bikes onto the court, oblivious to the game.

Ra's cutting into the lane. He plays ball like he rhymes. Unforced. Relying on indirection. Composed. He crosses over, double-clutches under swinging arms.

A cab honks. Ra's supposed to head to Manhattan. Studio time has been booked. The producer there, too. Ra shakes his head. The lyrics are not ready yet. The studio will have to wait. So will the producer. So will we.

XXL / August 1997

No Respect

A Critic at Large

HILTON ALS

I wouldn't have thought much about any of this had I not caught the Grammy Award–winning pop star Beck presenting the award for Best Rap Video on MTV's 1998 Video Music Awards. Beck can best be described as a soft-rock musician with a conceptual-art pedigree. His branché cool stems not from his doing anything as old-fashioned as playing a musical instrument but from his ability to synthesize computer-generated sounds that play like bright commercial jingles. Some people think Beck has an original image and something to say. His white, male college-student fans try to imitate his flat affect, his stridently ironic, conversational tone, as well as his arresting fashion sense: the slick pimp suits, cowboy hats, and wraparound sunglasses that are the earmarks of his style.

It's a style that has been deeply influenced by that of black American musicians. At the MTV Video Music Awards, though, Beck seemed to be doing his, perhaps ironic, best to trash the culture that inspired his hip persona. He took the stage at the same time as the singer Tori Amos, his copresenter, but upstaged her almost immediately. Parodying the great James Brown's stage moves, he tossed off his light-gray suit jacket and began to dance in a contrived, funky way that seemed calculated to call attention to his appropriated blackness. Then, as Amos prepared to announce the winner, Beck whipped out two cell phones. Holding one to each ear, he mock-talked into them simultaneously, as if he were describing the glam goings-on around him to a couple of brothers stuck back in the hood.

Beck's performance could be considered a send-up of a dopey crossover rap star, Will Smith, say, but to me his assumption that it was okay to parody a certain fraction of black culture because he felt a part of it just didn't seem, as Mammy says in the film version of *Gone With the Wind*, "fittin'." This graceless performance served only to reinforce Beck's obdurate whiteness. It reminded me of a similar story about the all-white hip-hop band the Beastie Boys. In an oral history of their career, the rapper Dr. Dre talks about a concert they gave at the Apollo Theatre, in Harlem. At some point during the show, one of the Boys called out, "All you niggers wave your hands in the air!" ("I've never seen so many blank stares," Dre comments.)

While Beck and many of his musical peers, artists ranging from the Beastie Boys to the Backstreet Boys, have borrowed extensively from black music and style, they don't seem to have much understanding of their position in a tradition that goes beyond ripping off James Brown choreography or sampling his records. And the one aspect of traditional soul music that they haven't tried to reproduce is its surfeit of emotional discipline. In *Why Do Fools Fall in Love*, a biopic about one of the first black crossover stars, the singer Frankie Lymon, Little Richard gives an outstanding performance as himself. "They took my music and made money off it, made it into rock and roll!" he exclaims in one scene. "Now it's my time. I want to get paid!" This culture of not getting paid but being a class act anyway, of smiling through disappointment, which still plays a role in black Americans' real life, has made little mark on the majority of new pop albums, perhaps because today's music industry is unable to market that sort of emotional complexity.

Instead, it supports a kind of reduced soul and artists who are ghostly versions of former stars. It is possible to see in Mariah Carey one of the original Supremes, the difficult Flo Ballard, if Flo had lost a little weight and taken her lessons at the Motown Charm School seriously. And singer Maxwell's nearly inaudible love vibrations come off as a safer, cleaned-up version of Al Green's painful projections of desire. Yet when Carey, Maxwell, Beck, and others take to the stage to perform their idea of blackness, it looks odd on them, almost farcical, like children playing a dangerous game of dress-up.

I grew up in a black community in Brooklyn and went to a predominantly white, progressive high school in Manhattan, in the mid-seventies. Before starting high school, I had had some exposure to white people, but not much. At the parties my new classmates threw in their parents' grand apartments overlooking Central Park West or on the Upper East Side, I discovered that they did not like the kind of dance music that was then popular with blacks, Chic or LaBelle. Instead, they listened to nostalgic funk from the 1960s, presumably because it was more "authentic" or raw. Or perhaps my classmates' choice in music was an illustration of something else: if they could consign blackness to the past by listening only to the black music that had crossed over successfully in the sixties, and which employed the by then unthreatening vocabulary of counterculture ("Psychedelic shack! That's where it's at!"), then they didn't need to know about the expanding new black culture and the world it reflected.

Any Temptations record was guaranteed to fill the dance floor at those parties. So was anything by James Brown. When my classmates danced to Brown's "Say It Loud! I'm Black and I'm Proud," they'd stick out their lower lips and their asses, lock their knees, and strut like Mick Jagger, who had not only legitimated black music for white audiences but also made it acceptable for whites to dance to black music. Though I didn't dare tell them so, I doubted whether James Brown had ever envisioned a circle of towheaded white boys with their arms around each other's shoulders, kicking, Rockettes-style, to "The Ghetto." No amount of observation could make me understand the way they danced. Their bodies didn't seem to connect to the music. It was as if they wanted to control it, to make its rhythm conform to theirs. I don't think I would have minded those parties so much had I not so often been asked at some point during the evening to lead a *Soul Train*–like dance line. The color of my skin made me an "expert" on inner-city dance moves, and for a while I was the Alvin Ailey of those Upper East Side drawing rooms.

Back then, I didn't understand the effect that black music had on white

Americans who responded to its pathos and funk, to its humor and irony, with an attempt to control it, either through parody or dismissal. Black music demands a lot of its audience: it requires direct communication, a kind of call and response. It is also the music of the underclass and therefore politically troublesome. "It was Bessie Smith, through her tone and cadence, who helped . . . reconcile me to being a 'nigger,'" James Baldwin wrote in his essay "The Discovery of What It Means to Be an American." And it is that feeling of not being part of the status quo, of being something as reviled and loaded as a "nigger" and flaunting it, that has been black music's primary narrative since performers like Fats Waller crooned, "What did I do to be so black and blue," more than sixty years ago.

Indeed, it is this drama of disenfranchisement that attracts white suburban kids to black music now more than ever, their need to adopt and hence control the ethnicity that their parents or grandparents fled the cities to avoid. What those kids want is to experience The Real. What placid front-lawned (or even Upper East Side) reality can compete with the fantasy of being a powerful player in a cool black world?

Whenever I danced, at those high-school parties and for a long time afterward, I kept my movements small and close to myself. I tried not to dance black. I couldn't be oblivious or get lost in the music. Instead, I relied on what the Southern Catholic writer Flannery O'Connor described as the black man's "very elaborate manners and great formality which he uses superbly for his own protection and to insure his own privacy." Such "very elaborate manners and great formality" are precisely what's missing from most soul music produced these days. They are what kept it always only almost decipherable, mysterious, a charming but frustratingly fleeting glimpse into a complex culture: trios of girls in chiffon; men with marcelled hair dancing in syncopation. The style that black soul singers promoted had a glamorous, standoffish quality, the pop hauteur of Dionne Warwick's "Don't Make Me Over" or Billie Holiday's near-Brechtian distancing techniques. (In *Sleepless Nights*, Elizabeth Hardwick described Holiday's white audiences: "Infatuated glances saying, Beautiful black star, can you love me? The answer: No!") No black performer who became popular during soul's heyday, in the early 1960s, when Motown Records instigated the new urban sound, would have dreamed of showing his or her true self to a largely white audience. It would have meant selling out, and no self-respecting performer actually wanted to be Sammy Davis, Jr., not even Sammy Davis, Jr. But, in the middle to late sixties, the industry began to change, largely because of the Beatles' sustained success (in those days, any musician got more airplay if he could sing about at least one tangerine dream) and the popularization of youthful rebellion and leftist politics. Soul music was out of sync with this way of being, and its discretion was wiped away in favor of more groovy and accessible pop. Darlene Love's rough-edged, hard-earned style of singing became less popular than Tina Turner's rock-influenced wall of sound.

The complexity of the Crystals' "He Hit Me (It Felt Like a Kiss)" was passé compared with the straightforward fun of songs like Ronnie Spector's "Tandoori Chicken." There was one interesting exception to this shift: Aretha Franklin. Since she started recording, more than forty years ago, Franklin's sound has been linked to gospel. Her hits are not gospel-influenced pop tunes but, rather, gospel songs with pop subject matter, a distinction that Franklin made clear through what the critic Ann Powers calls her celebrated use of melisma (stringing together a series of notes in a single syllable) and "squalling" (bursting unexpectedly into those divine high notes).

Franklin was recognizably church, and she knew how to work the congregation. Her big black sound appealed to whites because it was easy to grasp; she sounded just the way white people imagined a black woman would sound, plaintive but feisty, indomitable but sad. Franklin never really had to cross over, because whites were willing to follow her into her manufactured, impersonal form of blackness, a safe place where no one got cut up after a rowdy fish fry. And, of course, she looked the part. Whether she was sporting marabou feathers and a beehive or, later, a dashiki dress and a turban, she remained a backwoods mama tarted up for big-city doings. While I was growing up, I didn't know one black person who bought Aretha Franklin's records. But, largely through the homogenization of all those who came after her and now stand behind Janet Jackson's *Velvet Rope*, Franklin has managed to survive as soul music's authentic black voice. On VH1's recent special *Divas Live*, a celebration of the singers Mariah Carey, Gloria Estefan, and Shania Twain, among others,

Franklin appeared as the ultimate diva, whom all aspired to emulate. Yet, on-stage, she mostly ignored the girls with big hair who were there to canonize her, and she used her de rigueur performance of "You Make Me Feel Like (A Natural Woman)" as a platform to outvocalize them. Over the years, Franklin has become a lazy singer and an even worse performer. She may scat around "Chain of Fools," but she no longer really sings. Her fans don't seem to mind. What they are most interested in, what they feed on, is her aura of monolithic blackness.

While other black singers' integrity lay in making discreet use of their private tragedies, I never heard Franklin give up anything of herself. She was not nearly as confusing to white audiences as Nina Simone, for example. Un-like Franklin, who was the daughter of a prominent minister, Simone came up on her own, and her voice was the voice of adversity. Born into a family of eight in the South, in 1933, she studied classical piano at Juilliard, then supported herself in the jazz clubs of New York in the fifties. Although she was able to sing songs that related to the counterculture, her crossover success was com-promised by her strange and shocking diction (in the outspoken songs she wrote, like the civil-rights ballad "Mississippi Goddam") and by her tendency to complain about her audiences, about her bad treatment by managers, about white people who ripped her off. "I didn't fit into white ideas of what a black performer should be," she wrote in her autobiography. Where Franklin made her brand of soul music accessible to anyone, Simone told white people a thing or two, then shut them out. As a child, I was introduced to black popular music largely by my older sister. She listened not only to Nina Simone but also to the late, great white soul singer Laura Nyro, to Angela Bofill, and to Joni Mitchell. In short, my sister's take on music was largely integrationist and feminist. For her, soul was not limited by race, even though it grew out of black music. Rather, what she focused on was the singer's voice, and the blues-based guitar or stride piano supporting it. And the way she identified each of those singers as "black" taught me a new definition of the word, one that had little to do with skin color.

One of the reasons my sister and I could call certain white singers black was that they identified themselves as such in their music in their tone and cadence and subject matter. Last year, around the time the songwriter Rickie Lee Jones's gorgeous album *Ghostyhead* came out, I told Jones that she had been one of those singers. Her face took on a look of apprehension and curiosity, but she didn't explain how my confession had affected her until we began discussing Laura Nyro. "I graduated from grade school during the riots in Chicago," Jones told me. "I was the subject of terrible racial brutality, and never for a moment did I consider a Black Panther my brother. When Nyro sang that line 'Black Panther is your brother,' it mended it, and all the people she spoke about were bonded to me." Recently Howie Klein, who records Joni Mitchell on his label, Reprise Records, told me that Mitchell had always felt that her music belonged on black radio. (The first line of Mitchell's proposed autobiography reads, "I was the only black man at the party.") Where Beck uses black music to feed his sense of hipness and adolescent rebellion, Mitchell, Nyro, Jones, and others recognize in it their own identification as emotionally and politically disenfranchised people. The title song of Aretha Franklin's latest album, *A Rose Is Still a Rose*, was written by the twenty-three-year-old black rapper-songwriter Lauryn Hill and is full of the kind of spiritual uplift that Hill publicized as a third of the enormously popular trio the Fugees. Hill released her first solo album, *The Miseducation of Lauryn Hill*, last August, and it has already gone double platinum. Where Franklin was hailed as the Queen of Soul, Hill has been anointed the new Queen of Hip-Hop. *Newsweek* and *Time* have run stories about her, and *Entertainment Weekly* put her on its cover. Like Franklin, Hill is a child of the middle class, who was encouraged in her career by supportive parents. But although she grew up in New Jersey and attended Columbia University, where she majored in history, most reporters present her as a down-home, folksy kind of character, an Aretha for the new millennium. It's a blurring of fact that Hill herself encourages. Some of the tracks on *Miseducation* are introduced by a young male schoolteacher's voice asking a class of presumably inner-city kids such weighty questions as "How many of you have ever been in love?" When the teacher calls out Hill's name, she is absent, presumably because she's out on the streets, learning life's real lessons. The structure of the album reminds me of Toni Morrison's first two books, *The Bluest Eye* and *Sula*, whose evocations of colored people living through everyday dramas have the quiet lyricism of shafts of light seen underwater. Unfortunately, Hill is a less reliable narrator than Morrison. She speaks from a blacker-than-thou stance that feels contrived, and there is something cold and calculated in her expressions of love for her people, which are not unlike Al Sharpton's. (She has a habit of referring to the black race as "we," in the same way that Muslims called the blacks in my neighborhood "brother" and "sister" in the seventies.) And her ideology, which depicts blacks as the chosen people seeking an Israel that is closed to whites—one long-standing false rumor has Hill saying that she'd rather see her children starve than have a white person buy her album— seems shallowly reasoned, as unsatisfying an approach to life's problems as Franklin's Soul-Mama Solution: a little lovin' goes a long way. Hill's "To Zion," a song about her son, is a hymn glorifying the sacrifices of black motherhood. ("Look at your career," they said, "Lauryn, baby, use your head. But instead I chose to use my heart," she sings.) The song is perhaps unintentionally reminiscent of Diana Ross and the Supremes's "Love Child," a ballad about the unhappy life of an illegitimate child in the ghetto. But Hill's version of blackness, at least the version she promotes on *Miseducation*, feels distinctly middle class. It is as if she'd learned the rhetoric of persecution without actually knowing what it is to live it. And, while she slathers *Miseducation* with heavy doses of liberal guilt, it's white kids hoping to brush up against The Real who are buying it, unaware that it's the project of a corporate-minded single mom, geared more toward the airwaves than toward anyone's soul.

Many people believe that Hill represents the future of soul music. But if there's anyone among her contemporaries who can legitimately claim to be the soul-music diva for the new age, it's the white British singer PJ Harvey, whose remarkable fifth album, *Is This Desire?*, delivers on the promise of her less commercially successful previous albums. Polly Jean Harvey is the twenty-nine-year-old daughter of liberal-minded parents, who, she told me recently, "played Howlin' Wolf and Captain Beefheart all the time when I was growing up." By the time she was twenty-one, she had formed a band of her own in Yeovil, her hometown in southwestern England, and had begun to develop her distinctive sound, one that harnesses the power of traditional blues guitar and is as uncompromisingly odd as Nina Simone's. Still, Harvey remained ambivalent about performance, about being seen at all. "I always thought I was hideously ugly, actually," she said. Harvey, whose black hair frames a long, thin, and arresting face, has an almost distorted look: her face is bigger than it needs to be, while her body is barely there at all. Since the early nineties, Harvey has fought off her physical shyness with powerful songs, which rival Nina Simone's in the force of their anger and wit. Harvey is scarily funny and scarily menacing, and her lyrics are a form of revenge for her feelings of undesirability and rage. Her humor has dried blood in it. In "Legs," a song on her second album, *4-Track Demos*, she intones, "I might as well be dead, but I could kill you instead." Harvey's best works on her new album, the dour songs "Catherine" and "The Garden," are extraordinarily evocative. In them, no exchange, whether person to person, or nature to man, is without metaphysical thorniness. And no one, in Harvey's songs, gets away with just being in or out of love: one's emotional life is a real killer. Harvey's desperate contortions of despair identify her as a member of an underclass of one. And her obsession with the heavy carnage of existence says more about the soul than any contemporary music based on imitation. Harvey protects the privacy of soul while wearing its black heart on her sleeve.

The New Yorker / October 26, 1998

What the White Boy Means When He Says Yo

CHARLES AARON

In July of 1998, the future of youth culture was chillin' in the parking lot of a hip-hop concert in suburban New Jersey. Smokin' Grooves, the only annual package tour featuring rap artists, was in town, and as far as the eye could see, in varying shades of pale, were white boys and girls, jocks and nerds, preps and stoners, lounging against family-sized cars, getting their brewski on, or queuing up to be frisked.

All the acts—Wyclef Jean, Busta Rhymes, Cypress Hill, Gang Starr, Canibus, a reunited Public Enemy—were black and Latino, and inside, some black and Latino fans pushed to the front of the stage. But outside, it was a Caucasian invasion. As a security guard waved our car forward, a friend joked, "Are we at the right venue?"

That same week, the country's No. 1 pop band, selling 680,000 copies of their fifth album, was a group of thirtysomething white rappers still called the Beastie Boys. Noreaga, a practically unknown, underground rapper (in the tradition of platinum-come-latelies DMX and Big Punisher), boasted the No. 3 pop album. Barenaked Ladies, a heretofore annoying group of novelty-rock spazzes from Canada, were at No. 6 on the strength of their first rap song, "One Week." Three of MTV's top five videos were from hip-hop artists. The rub is, you could've picked any week in the past year and built a similar case. Like losing your virginity or blaming your parents, hip-hop, for today's average kid, black or white, is just another part of growing up.

In September of 1990, the future of youth culture was a chunky rapper screaming sarcastic obscenities over deafening break beats at Harlem's Apollo Theatre. When Ice Cube ripped up the Apollo stage with his heckler's anthem, "The Nigga Ya Love to Hate," the virtually all-black crowd leapt to its feet, squealing and laughing. Back then, racial and sexual slurs were breaking bones like sticks and stones, and the song's infamous call-and-response chorus—"Fuck you, Ice Cube!"—crushed all that pop-culture name-calling down to its nasty, uncoded essence. Cube wasn't speaking truth to power (nobody bought that shtick anymore). He was talking rebellious trash to the mountain of garbage that passed for truth and power. He was a punk; this was a punk rock show. Hell, this was a Sex Pistols show. And Ice Cube, bless his hatefully charismatic machismo, was Johnny Rotten with a farmer's tan.

So I squealed and laughed like a dutiful audience member. But mostly I wondered, "What am I doing here?" I'd been to lots of hip-hop shows at the Apollo—Doug E. Fresh, Eric B. and Rakim, Juice Crew, EPMD, etc.—but this was the first time I'd felt so badly out of step. For me, hip-hop had always been a two-sided single—sophisticated musical pranks on the A side, and I-am-somebody identity politics on the B side. But this was neither. *This* was a spiteful ego trip. Ice Cube asked us to gob him, then laugh at the absurdity of it all. Big muthaf*&#ing deal.

I'd been in denial about all this, ever since N.W.A's outrageously hyper-real 1989 album *Straight Outta Compton* (penned mostly by Ice Cube and producer Dr. Dre) redefined hip-hop "reality" to emphasize ghettocentric futility. What that meant, in my reality, was that white stereotypes of black people were being blown up, restyled, and thrown back in white people's faces. White America's favorite phantasm—the sexually potent, paranoid, heavily armed, black male outlaw; in N.W.A's words, the "gangsta" was back, bigger and deffer than ever. I tried every justification in the book, even deciding that *Straight Outta*

Compton was the best album of the year because nothing else sounded so pissed off. But ultimately, I couldn't relate. It just didn't fit my notion of hip-hop as a poignant antidote to sickly, smug "white" culture. It did not reflect my experience (or narcissistic expectation) of black people. "Get a clue, fool," I thought I heard Ice Cube taunting as I slouched down 125th Street to the subway.

The next year, N.W.A's *Niggaz4Life* stormed the charts, and then *The Predator*, Ice Cube's '92 solo album, *debuted* at No. 1; forever after, media hand-wringing about rap's corrupting effect on America's youth was cranked into high gear. It became conventional wisdom that record companies designed cartoonish black artists to cater to white consumers (like record companies could ever hope to be that efficient). The black gang member joined the black welfare mom in campaign sound bites. After the Los Angeles Riots stepped off on April 29, 1992, gangsta rappers such as Ice Cube and Ice-T were transformed, overnight, from profitable entertainers into social prophets and ghetto reporters (literalizing Chuck D's metaphor of hip-hop as the "black CNN"). It was during this period that the music shifted from a politicized form of pop art, with multicultural dreams similar to those of rock 'n' roll, into a racial and political *issue*. Blacks and whites were inevitably distanced from each other. Teeth gritted, I wrote piece after piece defending the First Amendment rights of rappers to metaphorically assassinate the establishment. And I don't regret a word of it. At the time, it seemed like the only way left for a white guy to participate in the music.

These days, such issues seem ancient, even quaint. Hip-hop has now loomed over the youth-culture landscape for almost two generations, and though it's still politicized, the music is no longer framed by racial confrontation. Despite being consistently dismissed as a dysfunctional teen phase—especially for white kids—it is commercially stronger than ever. During the early nineties, its preeminence flowed directly from so-called gangsta rap; in the post-riots years, hip-hop's major players have been more than just projections of an angry-white-man's fantasy. Deceased antiheroes Tupac Shakur and the Notorious B.I.G. were far too complex to fit any record-company master plan. The Fugees' 1996 album, *The Score*, a melodic masterpiece of hip-hop populism, has sold 18 million copies worldwide. Fugee Lauryn Hill's solo album is a virtuosic reproach to anyone complaining that the genre lacks songwriting vision; fellow Fugee Wyclef Jean's *The Carnival* wryly mixed one-world manifestos with boyish mea culpas. The quixotic Wu-Tang Clan continue to spin baroque ghetto yarns. Puff Daddy's lavish pop-rap hypnotizes the bubblegum set as well as older R & B fans. Busta Rhymes's dancehall-inflected bugouts boast a Mick Jagger swagger. Missy Elliott and Timbaland socialize over slinkily eccentric syncopation. Lil' Kim gets freaky with every sexist fetish ever conceived. Goodie Mob and Outkast chant down the South's dark spirits. The Roots teach funky seminars on hip-hop semantics. The indie-underground cuts crazy new edges. Is it any surprise that white music fans are flocking to such a multitude of fresh personas and sounds, a multitude that does not exist in rock?

"Why shouldn't [white kids] be exploring us? That's the way it's supposed to be, you know," says Busta Rhymes, aka Trevor Smith, the Grammy-nominated rapper whose second solo album, *When Disaster Strikes* (released in 1997), has sold 1.6 million copies. "If we'd grown up with a different mind-set, then all this shit wouldn't seem so strange. It would be normal and natural for white kids to be idolizing and imitating rap stars. But the powers that be have created all these barriers and segregated us and brought us up not to appreciate each other's cultural significance, so everybody looks at these white kids like they're out of their motherfucking minds."

Though grunge had ties to a rock tradition that many parental units could grasp—Nirvana loved the Beatles, after all—hip-hop has always been another matter entirely. Foregrounding stark rhythm and a declarative, nonsinging voice, it found a way to cut through the usual pop-rock pitty-pat. DJs took technology's instruction manual and phreaked it like cyberpunks before William Gibson regretted coining the term. Ever since Run-D.M.C. matched screeching guitars with minimal, drum-machine beats and turntable scratching (circa "Rock Box," 1984), hip-hop has *sounded* like the rebellious truth for increasing numbers of white youth.

"If you're a white kid, it's hard to get your parents riled up these days playing rock 'n' roll," says Fab 5 Freddy, aka Fred Braithwaite, an original host of *Yo! MTV Raps* when it debuted in 1988. "But if you got some Tupac blasting in your room, your mother's gonna be mad at you, and that's cool. You'll be like, 'Shit, I'm just listening to this black guy talking over some beats and my mom is terrified!'"

Today, Ice Cube is no longer the future; he's the unwitting patron saint of a new generation. He's a featured guest on the chart-topping new album by California rap-metal arrivistes Korn, and his songs have been covered by Korn and Florida rap-metal contenders Limp Bizkit (he shares management with both groups). Thousands of white kids will scream, "Fuck you, Ice Cube," in basketball coliseums nationwide on this year's Family Values tour, which also includes Korn and Limp Bizkit.

White fans no longer listen to hip-hop on the sly or surreptitiously rhyme in front of the mirror; they form bands and rhyme on MTV. Pop's most imaginative artist, Beck, works on the assumption that hip-hop is his generation's folk music. Rock's fiercest guitarist, Rage Against the Machine's Tom Morello, proudly mimicks a stylus wrecking vinyl. Hanson's 1997 sandbox smash "Mmmbop" was livened up by a DJ scratch (courtesy of white hip-hop elders the Dust Brothers). The pervasive slanguage of hip-hop is not just a goofy racist punch line anymore, it's simply how kids communicate. And naïve old hip-hop gringos like yours truly no longer slip up to the Apollo in search of cultural revolution. We cringe in fear that our nieces and nephews will come begging for designer loungewear because they saw Puffy and Mase flashing it on MTV.

Sometime after the death of Nirvana's Kurt Cobain, the hip-hop kid—oversized clothes, syrupy slang, skateboard double-parked outside—emerged as the nineties embodiment of youthful, white alienation. And, as a result, he's become a flash point for politicians and media cynics who insist on pushing the same tired teen "analysis": numbed and perverted by a godless barrage of abusive imagery via music, television, film, Sega, and the Internet, otherwise well-adjusted Billys and Beckys have sunk to new depths of antisocialism. They emulate gang members and shoot up school cafeterias. They wear baggy pants and have unprotected sex. As mindless dupes of the corporate infotainment matrix, our innocent spawn are being debased by dark, unchecked forces, and something *must be done!*

But when you break the racial encryption of this rant, you face an unavoidable reality—millions of white kids are defining themselves through nonwhite culture. Demographically, there's no mystery—the terms *majority* and *minority* are busily playing musical chairs. From 1970 to 1990, the white population in the United States dropped almost 10 percent, while the black population rose slightly, the Hispanic population doubled, and the population of Asians and other nonwhites tripled. The nonwhite middle class is now a substantial suburban presence. Despite pressure to choose "black" or "white," Americans identify themselves more and more as mixed race or biracial. Hip-hop, during this period, has mirrored the country's multicultural shift, becoming a pitched battle of race and identity, often fought over in mind-boggling detail. Emerging as the radical (re)vision of pop-rock that punk never managed, it is *the* crucial cultural influence for Generation X and beyond. It was here years before magazines such as this one anointed grunge the "voice of a generation," and it's been here for years afterward. The music-industry numbers are undeniable. According to a SoundScan study, 71 percent of rap music is purchased by white consumers, and R & B (which includes rap) was the top-selling musical genre overall in 1997, at more than 100 million units. Hip-hop style *is* pop style—Teenage Research Unlimited reported in October '97 that baggy pants were "in" for 78 percent of white teenagers—and fashion designers such as Ralph Lauren and Tommy Hilfiger court hip-hop's imprimatur. From Nike to Sprite, sampling and selling black cool to white consumers is the get-rich-quick scheme of the decade.

For the original black and Latino B-boys who scraped out an urban existence twenty-five years ago in the South Bronx and Manhattan, hip-hop culture was composed of four elements—break dancing, graffiti writing, MCing, and DJing—along with a flashy, seat-of-the-pants fashion sense. Today's white hip-hoppers, with considerably greater resources, attach an endless array of lifestyle statements (tattooing, skateboarding, body piercing) and entrepreneurial projects (fashion, rave promotion, Web design). Their subcultural diversity is bewildering. There's the slam-dancing mooks with their buffed-up chests and testosterone poisoning; the immaculately made-up *chicas* with their go-on-girl strut; the ska-crazed buds with their bong hits and sun-burned tattoos; the rave aesthetes, with their selfless mysticism (the anonymous DJ) and prosaic loathing (the problematic MC); the cooler-than-you indie-underground geeks, with their vinyl Jones and extensive mailing lists; the bored ex-punks and indie-rockers, with their creeping irrelevance; the aging true-believers, with their quiet politics and encyclopedic knowledge. And this is a wildly superficial list.

Then, of course, there's the classic "white homeboy" routine—i.e., acting a fool in daddy's car. Musically inept groups such as the Kottonmouth Kings and Insane Clown Posse, who parade around the suburbs rapping like psychotic pimps, are the most extreme offenders. Sadly, this phenomenon has become the definitive prototype and enduring mass-media cliché. It has also led to the widespread use of the word *wigger*—a nasty slurring of the epithet *white nigger*. *Wigger*, like *nigger lover* during the civil rights era, was first used by whites who objected to other whites embracing black culture. Now, it's also used by whites who embrace black culture to call out other whites who defame black culture. Either way, one timeworn fact remains: with race and class so inter-twined, any white kid (wigger or not) who idolizes an African-American flaunting a fat bankroll will always get under somebody's skin.

While many publications, including *Spin*, have sincerely chronicled and bemoaned the so-called death of alternative rock as a relevant, creative genre (circa 1996, say), what actually faded with alt-rock is a belief in rebel style that exists independently of African-American culture. This was the secret legacy of punk rock (indie rock and grunge) in America—it offered a handbook of cool for whites that basically ignored the existence of black people. What's happening now is that rock 'n' roll is going back to its miscegenated roots. Like suit-and-tied black professionals donning kente cloth and attending the Million Man March, rock's white fans and performers are undergoing an intense redarkening process.

In recent years, a boatload of white scholars have dissected the flimsy foundations of "whiteness" and "blackness" (purely American economic inventions). Two of the more pugnacious palefaces, Harvard's Noel Ignatiev (editor of the journal *Race Traitor*) and the University of Minnesota's David Roediger, have even called for an "abolition" of "white" culture. They argue that such an animal doesn't exist; our bloodlines are too mixed. Even famously cranky hip-hop essayist Stanley Crouch asserts that America is undergoing an unprecedented "cultural miscegenation," a blending of speech, style, and gestures that will result in us being "far and away more comfortable with human commonality and variety." *The New York Times* reported in February that, while adults' television viewing habits split along color lines, their kids watch black and white shows equally. Michael Jordan and Oprah Winfrey are arguably America's two most admired celebrities. Quentin Tarantino, perhaps the nineties' most imitated filmmaker, is a self-proclaimed product of black pop culture whose movies hinge on a volatile racial frisson. *Pulp Fiction* and *Jackie Brown* star Samuel L. Jackson describes Tarantino this way: "He's like my daughters' little white hip-hop friends. They're basically black kids with white skin."

In a cheeky *Baltimore Sun* column, novelist Ishmael Reed wrote that President Bill Clinton seems to be "if not black, a white soul brother," and that so many whites rag on him because he's an "N-word lover." In fact, it often seems as if Clinton's only sincere impulse is his compassion for African-Americans. Then there's the nutty spectacle of White Soul Brother No. 1's Hollywood counterpart, Warren "Super Lover B" Beatty, who released the guilt-ridden political farce *Bulworth* earlier this year, in which a senatorial candidate undergoes a sixties-liberal meltdown and begins telling "the truth." And how does Beatty portray said truth? By romancing black people and "rapping," of course! His reward? The beautiful black female lead (Halle Berry) booty-dances with the senator and reassures him, "Come on, Bulworth, you know you my nigga!"

Not since pre–Civil War blackface minstrelsy has popular culture been such a racial free-for-all. And there's certainly no shortage of opinions on why this is (a) evil; (b) liberating; (c) inevitable; or (d) good for a few laughs and that's about it. Blacks remain suspicious of whites who identify too closely with African-American culture, primarily because those same whites often want to boost the culture wholesale. Traditionally, this suspicion has taken two forms—the Elvis Syndrome and the White Negro Problem. The former has to do with money and fame and goes like this: Elvis Presley, a "white" man, became the biggest pop star of this century by singing and dancing like a "black" man, and from the Rolling Stones to New Kids on the Block, the process has repeated itself as blacks create and whites luxuriate; any white artist who follows such a path is suspect (for the hip-hop era, see the Vanilla Ice Virus, which includes fabricating your past). The second has to do with social status and sex and goes like this: In 1957, as the Beat Generation went pop with the publication of Jack Kerouac's *On the Road*, novelist Norman Mailer wrote a widely cited essay for the political journal *Dissent* called "The White Negro: Superficial Reflections on the Hipster." Ennobling white "urban adventurers" clued into black "existential" dread via the "Negro jazzman," Mailer posited a Sexual Freedom Ride for any white kid with the appropriately cool droop. Foreshadowing *Bulworth's* let's-have-sex-until-we're-all-the-same-color doggerel, Mailer insisted, "I believe it is the absolute human right of the Negro to mate with the white."

Usually when you read an article about white kids who appropriate hip-hop—be it rapping or forming faux-gangs—Elvis and Mailer are invoked. These folks tower over the subject like priapic parents, while smug journalists shrug off the phenomenon as nothing new and rather embarrassing to boot. Of course, it *is* nothing new. In his groundbreaking 1993 work, *Love and Theft: Blackface Minstrelsy and the American Working Class*, Eric Lott could've been nodding at the "wigger" (or the "gangsta") when he wrote, "If . . . we are to understand anything more about popular racial feeling in the United States, we must no longer be satisfied merely to condemn the terrible pleasures of cultural material such as minstrelsy, for their legacy is all around us." The minstrel shows of the nineteenth century (in which both white and black performers wore the cork mask to fulfill audience fantasies), like pop culture of the 1990s (in which both whites and blacks customize their personas to "keep it real"), probably tell us more than we want to hear about our democratic experiment. Blackface was an exorcism of prejudice, self-hatred, forbidden lust, and genuine respect; it threw up feelings onstage that couldn't be expressed anywhere else. These days, on *The Jerry Springer Show* (or *Jenny Jones*), nothing sets off studio-audience alarms like the spectacle of a white hip-hop kid. "Uh-oh!" the racially mixed crowd inevitably hoots. "Before you start talking about anybody, you ought to check yourself in the mirror, 'cause I don't think you know if you're black or white!" Cue to women waving two snaps up. Similar who-do-you-think-you-are? scenarios are now a familiar teen-movie trope—see the moronic rappers-on-a-bus flick *Ride* or the summer-lust vehicle *Can't Hardly Wait*. To suggest that a white kid's immersion in black culture might be a natural, even progressive, step is to risk charges of malicious naïveté. But maybe what's maliciously naïve is to expect American teenagers in 1998 to have any idea who they are.

It's Saturday night in our fair Christian Southland and the white kids are surrendering to the beat. In full sweaty sway, youthful couples at Jacksonville, Florida's Club Five spoon their smoothly tanned bodies to the DJ's studio-gangsta thump. Dateless boys play the wall, eyes hooded beneath Florida Marlins and Jacksonville Jaguars caps, shoulders shifting in rhythm. A weaselly wanna-B-boy with floppy brown bangs wearing a Fuct pentagram T-shirt up-rocks in a break-dance semicircle. As the groove deepens, a kid in a Wu Wear baby-tee and pigtails winks at her neo-rave-nymph partner. Both girls dip their hips and mouth along to the booming lyrics: "Bow down 'cause I ain't a hater like you / Bow down to some niggas that's greater than you."

An hour later, Jacksonville prodigal sons Limp Bizkit—rapper/singer Fred Durst, guitarist Wes Borland, bassist Sam Rivers, drummer John Otto, and ex–House of Pain DJ Lethal—flip the crowd's infant funkiness and give it a loud spank. A mosh pit of signifying monkeys, the Bizkit lurch from sludge metal to funky break beats, grasping for a groove. Durst, sporting a pointy goatee, armfuls of tattoos, baseball cap, baggy shorts, suede Adidas, and an identity crisis as deep as the Atlantic Ocean, howls his version of hip-hop's keeping-it-real incantation: "Wanna change yourself / Because you're sick of yourself." Splashing out of control like a fly plopped in buttermilk, the "kid"—he's twenty-eight, yet seems twenty-one—so badly wants to replace Marilyn Manson as the symbol of suburban America's worst fears that it's almost poignant. Mr. and Mrs. Charlie, latch your screen doors: it's the white B-boy ya love to hate!

The next day is a balmy April afternoon at Durst's modest, ranch-style spread in a rural residential area northeast of town. A crew of about ten friends and hangers-on are stumped together to, as one Bizkit kibitzer puts it, "Chill, dawg." Out back, the front seat of a car, its blue upholstery shredded, rests next to a skateboarding half-pipe. A large wire cage, home to two hulking bullmastiffs, is tucked in the far corner of the yard. Later, we'll drive over to Durst's parents' house for a band barbecue.

"Dude," announces Durst, "you know you're in a boon-ass town when the biggest cheer of the night is for Jerry motherfuckin' Springer." He's referring to the spontaneous "Jer-ry! Jer-ry!" chant that broke out after a reference to Limp Bizkit's appearance on *Springer Break*, the MTV summer fleshfest hosted this year by the talk-show tricknologist. Perched on a vinyl recliner, Durst is watched over by a framed velvet Elvis, while *Springer* blares its version of American reality—black and white transvestites yelling at each other—from a wide-screen TV.

Home to Lynyrd Skynyrd, Molly Hatchet, and a lot of asphalt, Jacksonville, Florida, was once described by a Georgia homeboy as "the official red neck of America." It's one of those New South sinkholes where they plant a bunch of shiny hotels and office buildings downtown and wonder why no culture grows. Soon after Fred Durst's birth there in 1970, the family moved to Orlando, then Cherryville, North Carolina, before settling in Gastonia, North Carolina. It was just down I-85 from Charlotte that black music became his lifeblood.

"The school I went to, Ashley Junior High, was right across the street from our house, and it was, like, eighty percent black. Everybody white was either mad redneck or prep, so I ended up in the 'black' category," says Durst, now sitting by the pool behind his parents' house. To our left, Dad (a retired narcotics officer) grills burgers; Mom sits on a picnic table strumming an acoustic guitar. Durst's seven-year-old daughter (from a failed first marriage) plays badminton with a handful of brats on a patch of grass across the way. "See, I was the type of kid who was into everything—Kiss, Michael Jackson, 'Double Dutch Bus,' fuckin' Willie Nelson. But mostly, I was born with this need for beats. It was weird, a lot of white kids resisted that . . ."

Around 1983, hip-hop flipped Durst's script forever; he threw himself into all of it—music (rapping over Black Sabbath licks he played on guitar, mixing beats on Technics turntables he got for Christmas); breakin' (his dad built a dance studio in the garage, his crew Dynamic 3 performed on a Fresh Fest sidestage during a Run-D.M.C. set); human beat-boxing (after peeping the Fat Boys on *Soul Train*); and graffiti writing (tag name: Whippy Whip). Floored by the '84 film *Beat Street*, he started wearing Puma sweatsuits—maroon, with the gray sleeves—and B-boying at Eastridge Mall. But music was far from a color-less paradise.

"Let's face it, in North Carolina at that time, there was still a heavy racial thing going on. There was a 'black' part of town where white people didn't go. And I was going over to my black friends' houses because they were getting these dope records from New York—Cold Crush Brothers, Fearless Four, Treacherous Three, Soul Sonic Force. And before long I turned into this alien— the 'nigger lover.' I heard that so many times. White girls wouldn't date me be-cause I was hanging out with black people. I was scared to go to white parties. It was the worst, man."

Then, in late 1986, a second bomb dropped. The Beastie Boys, a trio of white boho pranksters from New York City (abetted by suburban rabble-rouser/ producer Rick Rubin), released the punk-rock/rap hybrid *Licensed to Ill*, which immediately became the top-selling hip-hop album of all time, chilling at No. 1 on the pop charts for seven weeks, and making hip-hop forever safe for the suburbs. Suddenly, every hip-hop-hating whitey was fighting for his right to party. And even though Durst respected the Beasties as originals who lovingly goofed on hip-hop (and American pop culture in general), he was unforgiving of the Gastonia bandwagon.

"When I finally got to high school, all the white kids jumped on the rap thing hard, dude. Suddenly everybody's walking around trying to rap like Run-D.M.C. in these stupid little clown voices. Then they're riding around bumpin' [2 Live Crew's] 'We Want Some Pussy' in these big-ass, country-club cars. I was like, 'Great, now the rednecks and preps who wanted to beat me up for listen-ing to hip-hop are making a joke out of it.'"

Though his passion for hip-hop never faltered—he's recently talked with Dr. Dre about recording a solo project—Durst obviously bears the mark of the

Beastie era. "Subconsciously, getting into hip-hop, I think I was probably re-jecting this hateful, white, closed-minded world. I don't know. But I will say this, I felt special. I was like, 'Wow, I get it.' I was so sure that this music was where the world was going." When that same hateful, closed-minded world adopted hip-hop and devalued it, he locked himself in his room.

Purging his rage with skateboarding and punk rock helped, but Durst is still a nervous work in progress. With Limp Bizkit, he says he needs to simplify his raps so mainstream white rock kids can follow along. Actually, it sounds as if he's still trying to convert his butt-headed high school rivals.

"Dude, I got knowledge on hip-hop because I lived it," says Durst, tearing up a hamburger while Styx's "Come Sail Away" blasts from his parents' pool-room. "I'm not a fucking phony, and that's why I sing about phonies. And half the people at my shows, the songs are about them. It's ironic? Of course, it's fucking ironic. I'm, like, you're standing there singing my shit, but this song is about people like you who act like they get it, but they don't get it, and I really *want* them to get it, but they're not going to."

Obviously, hip-hop is no clear window into African-American life; it's just the most popular. Chart-topping rap capitalists such as Master P speak for little but the economic vitality of the Gangsta Entertainment Complex, and white kids kicking Ebonies and wearing Kangols will not end racial discrimination. Real social problems exist that hip-hop will never touch. Our civil rights–era sense of reparation has been squashed; in 1996, the typical black household had a net worth of $4,500, a tenth of the white household figure; poverty among black children is at 40 percent; young black males are murdered at a still star-tling rate—111 per 100,000, according to 1995 figures. All of which puts impas-sioned white hip-hop heads—such as sampling maestro DJ Shadow, aka Josh Davis, from Davis, California; or Eminem, aka Marshall Mathers, a Detroit-based MC whose first album is being produced by Dr. Dre; or Company Flow's El-Producto, aka El-P, aka Jamie Meline, a New York City–based MC/producer—in an odd position. Sure, whites have participated in hip-hop—as fans, pro-moters, writers, breakers, DJs, producers, photographers, label owners, and rappers—for as long as the art form has existed. Still, in 1998, hip-hop Caucasoids of all persuasions are usually lumped together as interlopers or charlatans, self-conscious of both the music's expanding white audience and their role in that expansion.

Says Shadow, "Growing up [in the late eighties], I was very bitter as a fan because I saw how hip-hop was actively suppressed and distorted, and I felt like it was my duty not to misguide anybody about the roots of the culture." El-P adds, "When people ask me about being white in hip-hop, I tell them, 'Look, you can't pretend.' The reason a lot of white people play themselves and just get it wrong is that they have the arrogance to think that they can identify with the experience of the black man or woman in America; not just empathize with it, but *feel* it. And you can't go there. Otherwise, you're sabotaging and belittling the experiences of the people you claim to love." Writing of white 1920s jazzmen such as Bix Beiderbecke, LeRoi Jones (now Amiri Baraka) explained it this way: "The real point [was] not . . . the white American's increased understanding of the Negro, but rather the fact that the Negro had created a music that offered such a profound reflection of America that it could attract white Americans to want to play it or listen to it for exactly that reason."

Fab 5 Freddy has been as responsible as anyone for translating hip-hop culture to mainstream white America. The classic, early-eighties, New York B-boy flick, *Wild Style*, is the story of how Freddy brought white hipsters uptown to black and Latino clubs, and how he then brought black and Latino graffiti writers downtown to white art galleries. He draws a direct line from early be-boppers to rock 'n' rollers to rappers.

"Jazz musicians in the forties were seen in the same light as rappers today: they were the scourge of the earth," says Freddy. "But white kids couldn't see Charlie Parker on cable TV at all times of the day. He didn't have the pulpit . . . Unlike Charlie Parker and Chuck Berry and Howlin' Wolf, Tupac and Biggie were promoted as the baddest stars out there. So part of the rebellion becomes racial; that's America. These kids are rebelling against a society that says they shouldn't have anything to do with black people. So they're like, 'Yo, I'm gonna get down with the illest niggas I can find!'"

Popular culture's racial dynamic is evolving madly, and for folks born before 1970, that is often threatening or downright baffling.

"Hip-hop is the *only* popular culture that takes seriously the relationship between race and democracy in America," says Henry Giroux, a professor at Penn State University and author of *Channel Surfing: Race Talk and the Destruction of Today's Youth*. "This music has had a grip on white kids for fifteen to twenty years, and everybody calls it pathology and that's that. Are all these white kids just idiots who are being duped and manipulated by the record industry? Who is cynical and arrogant and detached enough to believe that? Sure, some kids are just latching onto the moronic gangsta elements, but the vast majority are caught in some middle space where they're trying to figure themselves out."

Corporatized or idealized, hip-hop is the American Dream and African-American Nightmare rolled into one fat-ass blunt. It's not Elvis because black artists remain preeminent; white rappers, aside from the Beastie Boys, and maybe House of Pain or 3rd Bass, haven't won anything. It's not a rerun of jazz or the blues because it represents raw-boned sorrow and opulent success, often bestowed by black executives. Hip-hop rules the world of youth and pop culture for a reason—it's talking about what everybody's thinking. White and black kids know this, even if they can only articulate it by getting stoned to the gills, rejecting proper English, profiling like ghetto supastars, or nodding their heads when Tupac screams on their car stereos that he doesn't "give a fuck."

Danny Hoch may be the most race-conscious man in America. You get the feeling that the twenty-seven-year-old-Queens, New York–born actor really does look in the mirror every morning and remember that he's white (or at least a Jewish New Yorker who's classified as white). But then he starts talking—his B-boy patois flits from street-corner haughty to artsy-insidery to wide-eyed revolutionary—and the confusion flares all over again. As one of Hoch's racially ambiguous characters might inquire, "Who does this crazy-ass motherfucker think he is?"

"When I was twelve years old, I thought I was half-black and half–Puerto

Rican," said Hoch earlier this year, just after his one-man show, *Jails, Hospitals & Hip-Hop*, finished previews at New York City's P.S. 122. "No fucking way I thought I was a Jewish white kid. Then, when I was seventeen or eighteen, I left New York City for the first time—I went away to the North Carolina School of the Arts [in Winston-Salem]—and that's when I met *real* white people. Beer, Domino's pizza, the mall, backyards, guys going, 'Hey, dude, let's score another six-pack!' I was like, 'Is that me? Am I that guy?'"

In *Jails, Hospitals & Hip-Hop*, and his 1994 Obie Award–winning piece, *Some People* (which was produced as a 1996 HBO special), Hoch embodies a head-spinning spectrum of characters who deftly reflect his own childhood in the "middle-class projects" of Lefrak City, Queens, "the geographical center of the most multiethnic county in the world." Dubbed Iraq, Left Back, or Left Crack, it was once home to Boston Celtics guard Kenny Anderson, as well as rappers Capone, Noreaga, and Akinyele. Hoch grew up speaking in all sorts of tongues. His mom was a speech pathologist, his godmother was Cuban, his next-door neighbors were African-American, his best friend was Puerto Rican and Israeli, his running buddies were Pakistani, Filipino, West Indian, and Colombian.

"All these cultures were converging in New York in the late seventies, early eighties, as they are now in the rest of the country," he says. "But among the youth, the prevailing culture was hip-hop. It was the only American culture to really embrace. The parents were trying to assimilate and couldn't, because their accents were too thick or because they couldn't speak English at all. So the kids spoke hip-hop—graffiti, break dancing, MCing, DJing. It was this very powerful, common language of defiance."

Hoch empathizes with his characters to heartrending ends, and the variety of detail, both vocally and physically, can be unnerving (is this guy wearing a wire 24-7?). Some are obviously not white, such as the Havana engineering student who (in flawless Cubano Spanish) asks a white New York tourist to decode a Snoop Doggy Dogg vulgarity (she doesn't speak hip-hop *or* Spanish to his dismay); others are left undefined, such as the light-skinned Harlem street vendor (of O.J. and Bart Simpson T-shirts) who gets a beatdown from a hair-trigger cop when he won't answer the question "What are you?"

Although Hoch obsesses over the essence of his characters, he never tries to "disappear" into them (putting on a baseball cap is his big costume change). At all times, he is fully present—the goofy white boy full of hip-hop chutzpah. In *Jails, Hospitals*'s opening rap, "Message to the Bluntman," he cuttingly boasts, "I know I ain't black to you / But I can take your culture, supe it up, and sell it back to you." When he performed that piece on MTV, rapper MC Lyte, according to Hoch, was so enraged that she threatened to "go to her car and get her gun." Unlike a stand-up comic, Hoch refuses to climb on a pedestal and ridicule stereotypes; he knows he's implicated. His gift is in revealing how America's cherished stereotypes fall apart, comically, tragically, and inevitably. Lost in the briar patch of race, trapped by our thin skins and flawed bodies, we try to talk our way out. And we fight over language—who owns it, who gets to use it.

The program for *Jails, Hospitals & Hip-Hop* quotes KRS-One, first and foremost, then offers up a B-boy testimonial titled "Peace to My Audience!" — it's signed CASEROC, Hoch's graffiti tag. When we met for lunch at a pseudo-Middle Eastern boîte in the racially mixed, boho enclave of Williamsburg, Brooklyn, Hoch wore a black-and-white camouflage cap, PNB Nation T-shirt, African beads and baggy pants, and combat boots; he could've been an assistant director on a Brand Nubian video, circa 1990. The conscious rap of that time, when every bright-eyed kid with a mic adopted a Muslim name and gave shout-outs to Afrocentrism, confirmed Hoch's dream of hip-hop as a "culture of resistance."

Despite lapses into big-city elitism, Hoch has also cultivated a kinship with white hip-hoppers in the suburbs and rural areas. He's currently working on a screenplay, *White Boys*, based on kids like his character Flip Dog, an awkward wannabe gangsta rapper from Montana. "If hip-hop can be a tool for white kids to defy their racial destiny, that's amazing. They may look corny and say some really stupid things, and they may *do* some really stupid things, but I think they're making a genuine effort not to inherit the racism of their forefathers. Their souls tell them it's not right."

* * * * * *

When David Ellis was a kid, his soul told him to spray-paint the letters *S-H-O-C-K* on the side of his daddy's chicken house. Born the son of a Presbyterian minister in the piedmont North Carolina boondocks—"the square mile where we lived wasn't even on the map"—Ellis, aka Skwerm, was one of the "real white people" that Danny Hoch would later meet at art school. But growing up, Ellis was better known for getting jerked on the public school bus.

"I was real quiet and small and skinny and I'd get beat up a lot," he says sheepishly. "Plus, there was definitely some ol' backwoods-redneck-type shit going on out there. I think I was trying to address all that somehow [with graffiti]. It was like, 'Yo, I have a voice, listen to this!'"

On a school trip to Paris, Ellis tried to visit the Louvre, but it was closed for construction. Loitering by the temporary plywood walls outside the museum, he was transfixed by a riot of colorful, spray-painted letters. Asking around, he discovered that New York City graffiti artists Phase II, Futura 2000, and Blade had just passed through town and left their calling cards. "From that moment on, you think I was checking for statues by Michelangelo?" says Ellis. "Naw, no way. I was working on letterforms, B."

Ellis had heard hip-hop on a college radio show from Raleigh, but after his Paris experience he was obsessed. He caught the documentary *Style Wars*, a chronicle of early black, Latino, and white graffiti writers from New York City, on public television. Mix tapes of New York radio shows—Red Alert on Kiss-FM, Mr. Magic and Marley Marl on WBLS—began to appear at school. Hip-hop's birthplace soon became Ellis's mecca. "I fantasized about New York, no doubt. A lot of kids were moving down South from the City, and they were all into hip-hop, so that was real cool. But there were also these horror stories. Crack was real big then [in the mid to late eighties], and brothers and cousins were getting killed on playgrounds and shit, so the parents were sending the kids down to North Carolina to live with their grandparents. The irony was that the parents had fled the South a generation before because of racism."

As Ellis got older, the ironies of being a New York–style B-boy in the South stacked up. "I'd see all these civil rights documentaries of white people from the South and be paralyzed by certain feelings like, 'Man, I'm white, I'm from the South, am I a racist?' I think you're always, subconsciously, trying to separate yourself from things that you think are wrong, and the hip-hop scene seemed like a very deep place that could be an answer to a lot of what was wrong."

Tobacco barns became Ellis's subway trains, his canvas. He'd throw up graffiti pieces for classmates to check out in the morning as they passed by on the bus. With money from picking tobacco, he bought two wack turntables and a Pyramid mixer; he got into break dancing. "I was listening to 'Adventures of Grandmaster Flash on the Wheels of Steel' on my Kmart boom box and the crickets and tree frogs and chickens and woodpeckers were in the background, and I was feeling that shit, man. I was looking down at my fat laces and burgundy pressed Lees and I knew *this was the shit,* creatively, in every way. This was going somewhere."

Now, at twenty-seven, Ellis remains a restless hip-hop product—hates Puffy, loves Mos Def. He lives with his girlfriend in a shambling downtown loft in Manhattan and paints huge, captivating collage pieces, which he regularly shows around town. Like Hoch, he worries critics will downplay the importance of hip-hop on his life and art. "I understood Marcel Duchamp because of hip-hop; he would've been putting crazy *Nude Descending a Staircase* pieces up on the Paris transit system."

Above all, hip-hop helped Ellis come to terms with his own history. "Where you live has a big impact on you," he says. "Our house was, literally, on a long dirt road. The kids I mostly played with, went fishing with, were black and Cherokee and white. That's where I came from, and that's why hip-hop made sense to me. I don't know what it's like to grow up around mostly white folks, and I think it's a shame that other people do. Maybe the white kids who are getting into hip-hop now are feeling like it's a shame, too."

No matter how carefully this article is written or read, it's still likely to be reduced to the "wigger story." So, to beat the rush, I began inventing distinctions between "wiggers" and "wiggas"—e.g., "wiggers" are true-schoolers who are genuinely interested in black culture and have genuinely risked making fools of themselves; "wiggas" are fascinated wannabes who play it safe and get jiggy in the safety of their own cul-de-sac. Wiggers don't try too hard to prove they're down. Wiggas, like Quentin Tarantino, never shut up about it (to the point of allegedly punching a black woman who disagreed with him about the depiction of African-Americans in films). The Beastie Boys are O.W.'s, Original Wiggers, because they were there in the beginning, they're still here, and they wrote the Wigger National Anthem, "Sabotage." Sometimes, though, like at Smokin' Grooves, when thousands of stoned white kids think it's just so cool to fire their little imaginary pistols into the air during Cypress Hill's "How I Could Just Kill a Man," the joke isn't so funny anymore.

Wigga, please!

But how kids act in groups at concerts is much different from how they act individually; and the way they act individually is much different from the way they act around parents, bosses, teachers, or reporters. When I wandered up to sixteen-year-old John Rappa (yes, that's his real name) before a Smokin' Grooves concert at Universal City, the movie theme park just north of Los Angeles, he was sitting alone on a concrete bench smoking—butt pinched between thumb and forefinger, elbow pointed out jauntily. A tiny slip of a boy, he sported an oversized Eddie Bauer T-shirt, low-slung Hilfiger jeans (beeper in the right-side pocket, pack of cigs in the left), and dusty beige skater sneaks. Full of bluster a few minutes ago when he was talking to a black kid he'd just met, his acne-wracked face softened after I identified myself as a *Spin* writer.

"Hip-hop was just what was on the radio when I grew up," he says, squinting, his blond hair a spiky crew cut. A small gold stud sparkles in his left ear. "I remember getting really, really caught up in it when I was, like, nine. It was *my* music, you know? . . . Grunge never really appealed to me; it always felt dirty and depressing, all that holes-in-your-pants shit. I liked the attitude and, I guess, the lifestyle of hip-hop."

What did he think the attitude and lifestyle was about? "You know, hanging out, smoking weed, talking shit about cops, and listening to Cypress Hill. Or riding around in a car with your friends, acting rowdy and listening to Tupac . . . It's like, rappers know what's real, they know how fucked-up things are, but they also know you have to say 'Fuck it' sometimes and have a party, too."

Rappa says he never felt conflicted about being white and listening to hip-hop: "Maybe I thought it might be easier to blend in sometimes if I was black, but I never really *wanted* to be black or nothing like that." Maybe he's a new breed, a kid who sees the Beastie Boys as father figures, unconsciously thinks and talks with hip-hop's knowing edge, yet doesn't understand all the fuss about black and white people not getting along. A teenager who adores the "lifestyle," but can't really buy into it. Or maybe he's just a half-pint who hasn't yet gone through the wringer of the real world.

Molly Hein is only a few years older than Rappa, for instance, but her experience is a world apart. Now a student at Hampshire College in Amherst, Massachusetts, Hein grew up "bilingual in punk rock and hip-hop" in New York City's Washington Heights, a primarily Latino neighborhood north of Harlem. Her world changed color at sixteen when she and her divorced mother moved to the lily-white suburbs of northwest Washington, D.C. "I was going to a private school with all these kids who had grown up in the suburbs, and I got to see how racially isolated they were; it was a wake-up call. That's when I really got into hip-hop. I think I was reacting to the shock."

At Hampshire, she's helped bring Noel Ignatiev to speak and even formed a campus group to discuss white racism and classism. Unfortunately, the group tanked. "Everybody here is so politically correct and self-satisfied and like, 'Hold on, man, I'm not a racist.' Nobody wants to admit that they themselves have ever benefited from racism, especially at a left-wing, alternative hippie college."

Hein—who briefly joined an all-female hip-hop crew and worked with the New York–based Prison Moratorium Project (a nonprofit, hip-hop activist group)—admits to moments of I'm-the-only-white-person-in-the-room conceit, as well as periods of total self-flagellation. "I guess I'm a socially conscious wigger," she says, laughing. "I'm obsessed with the politics of everything I'm doing; I never *just have fun*. And I don't necessarily think that's a bad thing, because I've met my fair share of big-pants-slangin' white kids who are completely unaware of what they're doing . . . I know I'm projecting my own fantasies and cultural baggage. But that's what everybody does, in a way. Hip-hop is great for that; there's no better art form."

Many white hip-hoppers, myself included, still wrestle with an age-old disease, which I call, only somewhat ironically, "double unconsciousness." It's the white flip-side to W.E.B. Du Bois's turn-of-the-century diagnosis "double consciousness," which suggests blacks in America are "always looking at one's self through the eyes of others" and feel a sense of "twoness—an American, a Negro; two souls; two thoughts; two unreconciled strivings . . ." Conversely, double unconsciousness means failing to look at oneself through the eyes of others, and living under a delusion of "oneness," the myth that if you, as an individual, don't behave in an actively racist fashion, then you're not shaped by racism. The doubly unconscious refuse to acknowledge how certain institutions (education, housing) constantly watch their backs. They want extra credit for entertaining different points of view. They love black music, talk to a few black friends, and believe they are developing an understanding of black people (when, in fact, they are only developing an image of themselves). Dead giveaway: if a white guy exclaims "I'm not a racist!" or "But a lot of black people feel the same way I do!" he's doubly unconscious.

Nobody's pondered this Ofay Shuffle more deeply than the hyper, balding graffiti writer from Chicago named William Wimsatt, aka Upski. In fact, he's just about the only person who's bothered. His unjustly overlooked 1994 book, *Bomb the Suburbs*—which followed a fire-starting May '93 article in *The Source* titled "We Use Words Like *Mackadocious* (and Other Progress from the Front Lines of the White Struggle)"—constructs a case, in hilariously explicit detail, for white people (himself included) who desperately love, or think they love, hip-hop and black culture. Then he trashes the joint. The cool fool caught in the middle, Upski's always getting his hands and knees dirty; he doesn't want *anybody* relaxing. In the spirit of Danny Hoch's "Message to the Bluntman," he wrote the following coda to *The Source* article's deft evisceration of wigger hypocrisy: "Let me offer this advice to black artists: next time y'all invent something, you had better find a way to control it financially, because we're going to want that shit." *The Source*—today's most successful hip-hop magazine, which was developed in the late 1980s by white Harvard students David Mays and Jon Schecter—wouldn't print the coda. As Upski wrote in his book, "It was the key to the whole article, the only part that might give a few of us white boys our one precious glimmer of self-doubt."

What's encouraging about Upski, and why he's still ahead of the curve in terms of understanding whiteness and hip-hop, is that he's so proudly *unhip*. He's spastic, vulnerable, and poorly dressed. He doesn't try to impress you with arcane knowledge. He doesn't drop names. He actively campaigns against gratuitous use of slang. And for somebody who's spent so much time actually journeying through the B-boy killing fields, he's almost maddeningly guileless. When I finally reached him by phone—he'd just moved from his parents' house in Chicago to his girlfriend's Manhattan apartment—he said sweetly, "Wow, I didn't know anybody still cared."

The next week, we're walking through the West Village, and he's manically going off about his new book, tentatively titled *Urban Life, Home Schooling, Hip-Hop Leadership, and Why Philanthropy Is the Greatest Art Form of the 20th Century*. I ask if he feels bad for making all those white hip-hop kids look like such bozos. He grins and laughs. "I *have* clowned wiggers over the years, I admit it; but in general, I think it's a great thing for white kids to get into hip-hop. It's had an enormous impact on my life. It caused me to look at the world in a whole new light." But *Bomb the Suburbs*'s sharpest jabs are directed at his own moony, childhood illusions about the power of black style—formed mostly while attending Kenwood Academy, a public magnet school that was about 90 percent black, and the University of Chicago Laboratory School, which was 60 percent white but boasted the sons and daughters of Chicago's African-American elite.

"America is such a racially charged place that white people are afraid to mess up," he says. "Our biggest fear is being embarrassed. We're scared of making a racial faux pas. I want to make it okay to mess up; I sure made my share of messes. I mean, why are we trying to convey to the world that we know what we're doing? We need to start from scratch and mess up a lot!"

There's an old TV-detective-show adage that if you want to find the truth, follow the money. So it made sense to set up a meeting with Jimmy Lovine. The proverbial "Brooklyn street kid" who hustled his way into the music biz, Lovine became a high-profile producer in the seventies and eighties (Bruce Springsteen, Patti Smith, Tom Petty) before founding Interscope Records, which has been home to Nine Inch Nails, Dr. Dre and Snoop Dogg, Marilyn Manson, 2Pac, Limp Bizkit, etc. "Teenagers ten to fifteen years ago, who would've looked to rock 'n' roll as their first choice of music, now listen to rap," says Lovine. "Hip-hop is more reflective of how kids feel today, bottom line. It feels more exciting, more potent, more to the point. Both lyrically and sonically, it's keyed into kids' emotions. Sure, you can put out a pop-rock record and sell a few million copies, but the record that kids have to have the day it comes out is hip-hop."

A slight, wiry guy in wire frames, golf cap, lime-green velour pullover, jeans, and Nike trainers, Lovine is known to many as the white man who did business with Suge Knight (and got out in the nick of time). We're sitting in his intimately cushy, twelfth-floor office on L.A.'s Wilshire Boulevard—fat vinyl sofa, coffee table with an immense bowl of fruit, wide-screen TV, stereo system, and framed family photos on every available surface. An assistant brings in hot tea and announces that Rick Rubin (!) is waiting. Lovine grabs a green apple from the bowl, chomps, and leans over.

"So, what do you need from me?"

Considering there's an ex–Beastie Boy in the bull pen, I cut to the chase. "Aren't white kids who listen to rap, on some level, rejecting their whiteness?"

Lovine fidgets and kicks back on the sofa. "I don't feel that. I think the best hip-hop feels accurate to these kids' emotions, not literally, because most of these white kids haven't had the same experiences as these artists, but emotionally. When I was a teenager in the sixties in Brooklyn listening to [Jimi] Hendrix and Sly Stone, I thought they were singing about my life, even though they weren't."

"But don't you think there's a big difference between, say, Kurt Cobain as a rebel hero and Tupac as a rebel hero?"

"No, I don't. I think it's all about alienation and honesty, and they both expressed that."

"But doesn't hip-hop's success mean a big racial shift?"

"I think it means that a lot of rock music doesn't feel provocative, and I

hope we see more that does. For instance, I'd like to see more rock bands dealing with what's going on in the cities and ghettos."

"But isn't that about race?"

Lovine flashes one of those wincing, why-ya-gotta-bust-my-balls? industry smiles, but he pushes on. "I don't think it has anything to do with color. I
know you do. But I think there's a big difference between why white kids are
listening to hip-hop and why black kids are making it. Those are two entirely
different questions."

The intercom beeps. "Rick Rubin is still here for you," the secretary chirps
impatiently.

"Look," says Lovine, "does racism exist? Sure it does. I grew up in a very
hot period, the sixties, in a heavily ethnic Italian neighborhood that was
squared off by other Italians, you know what I'm saying? But that doesn't reflect who I am today. I don't live my life, you know . . . I can't explain it . . . well,
I can explain it, but . . ."

What Lovine's saying, but not saying, is that music opened his eyes to race
and American society and heightened his sensitivity to people unlike himself.
As a sixties guy, he likes providing a forum for impoverished black kids to express themselves, but he wonders if the materialism, misogyny, and nihilism
that linger in rap music aren't the real white appeal. Though he'd never say it,
I'd bet he believes, deep down, that the thing a white kid gets from listening to
Dr. Dre's *The Chronic* is the cheap buzz of spitting "bitch" or "ho" or "motherfucker" into the pot-hazy night.

Of course, that's just one white man's opinion.

Back in the day, white kids (like me, and Fred Durst, and Elvis, for that matter)
generally had to make a point of crossing over racial lines, especially if we
didn't live in an urban melting pot. Today, the racial lines are crossing over us.
"I work with a lot of artists inside and outside the hip-hop world, and I'm
telling you things are gonna change, you have no idea," enthuses Karyn Racht-
man, an industry player who put together the music for *Bulworth*, as well as
1993's *Judgment Night* sound track, which paired alt rockers with hip-hoppers.

"The hip-hop structure of making music is completely subsuming rock—the beats, the production, the ways of expressing yourself. And the cutting-edge film directors I work with, they all think in terms of hip-hop."

Be that hyperbole, white kids today are being restyled and reoriented by black popular culture, whether they like it or not. The choice they have is whether to resist the process, and what bothers parents and the cultural establishment is how little these kids are resisting. What worries *me* is how white hip-hop kids' familiarity with black pop culture tends to give them a false sense of familiarity with, and knowledge about, black people. Neither black nor white rock fans assume that most white people are like, say, Dave Matthews or Sarah McLachlan. But most white hip-hop fans tend to think DMX or Method Man represent some essential quality about black people. This isn't necessarily their fault—society's arrested racial development is due most of the blame—but it is an assumption that needs to be questioned, regularly. So when I see the autonomous white hip-hop enterprise the Beastie Boys have constructed—which seems to feel more strongly about cool sneakers and Tibetan monks than exploring their relationships with African-Americans—it strikes me as an enormous denial. Then again, the Beasties, like so many of us, aren't that hyped about being racial martyrs. They just want to live.

Black people are quite intimately aware of racial lines crossing over them and martyr complexes and just wanting to live. As Tony Green, a Jacksonville-based music writer who also attended the Limp Bizkit show, told me, "Great numbers of black kids have been crossing over into white society for years. We're like agent provocateurs—we know what white kids are like, but they don't know anything about us. Until a generation of white kids goes through what we've gone through," he says, "things won't start changing. These Limp Bizkit kids need to come home with me and go to church."

As we chase the Illuminati into the next millennium, and as racism evolves as quickly as racial demographics, anything's likely to happen. Discrimination could become less acceptable, the suburbs could become less isolated from cities, concert audiences could become more integrated, radio formats could become more diverse, and Fred Durst might get caught singing "I'll Fly Away" at a Sunday A.M.E. service. Or not. But the so-called hip-hop generation—

white, black, or otherwise—is doing everything in its power to mock our culture's stuttering fear of racial progress. When a kid's identity crisis is ridiculed or blamed for the minstrelsy of the past, racism's foundation is only reinforced. Okay, so much of young white America looks like a bunch of foolish twits playing dress-up. But are they really any less confused than you?

Spin / November 1998

Foxy Brown Is the Illest

DANYEL SMITH

Almost. We've got on paper panties.

We're on top of the Delano hotel in Miami. A spa called Aqua. Sundeck and low walls, pale with white trim. Like sitting on a solid part of sky.

It's hot. Too close to the sun. Just had the salt rub. Getting the custom massage and the Mini Peppermint Twist. They soak Ace bandages in seaweed and hot water and peppermint essential oil. Wrap you tight from the waist down like you've broken all the bones in your lower body. Roll you snug in a Mylar blanket. The kind of material those shiny Happy Birthday balloons are made from. Then you simmer in the hotness. We each end up sitting in a quarter cup of our own minty sweat.

Foxy and I are talking about being female and about just how bananas it is. Foxy, who has been linked to Jay-Z, Rayshawn from Junior M.A.F.I.A., Allen Iverson, Andre Rosen, DMX, Master P, and Nas, but who is in fact engaged to Ricardo "Kurupt" Brown, says that while a lot of times it is all about the hotness, a lot of times it isn't.

Foxy is saying, "I'm talking about love. Love. *Love.* Everybody wanna talk about why Foxy doesn't show up at a video shoot, why I'm late to my show, why

I won't take my sunglasses off in an interview. 'Cause everything ain't always all right with me. Okay? Until you've been in love with a nigga, until you've been standing on the edge of a building ready to give it all up for a nigga—I *ride* for my niggas—until you've done all *that* shit, don't talk to me. I tell a muthafucka, 'Look: Grow titties, get a pussy, get your heart broke before you talk to me about how I'm acting.'" Foxy, sweet brown like the best chocolate, leans back in her lustrous cocoon, face to the heat. "Do *that* before you talk to *me* about *shit*."

On the Delano's veranda. Foxy and I have salty breasts, peppermint butts, ginseng faces. Daisies sit in a tiny vase. Inga Marchand, aka Foxy Brown, says she has more than the blaxploitation princess from whom she took her name for an idol. "Roxanne Shante!" Foxy almost screams. "She's a pioneer for the type of shit I'm doing. I swear by her. She was a *bitch* back in the day—for having skills. She was stepping out of limos with full-length minks. *Diamonds*. She was like, *I'm that bitch, I'm here, and these are my niggas, and this is how we roll.*"

Foxy says *ride* a lot. When she says *I ride for my niggas*, she means she will go with them wherever, whenever, for whatever. She means loyalty.

And she's serious about it. Like she's serious about Jay-Z. "That's my Clyde," she says. "I'm his Bonnie. You ever had a nigga that can't do wrong in your eyes in *any situation*? That's who Jay is to me. Our shit is unconditional." Jay seems to feel pretty strongly about Foxy as well. On "Bonnie & Clyde, Pt. II," from her new album, tentatively titled *Chyna Doll* (Violator/Def Jam), Foxy asks Jay, "Would you die for your nigga?" And he answers chillingly, "I'd hang high from a tree." She says Jay put her on. She met him when she was like thirteen or fourteen through her cousin DJ/producer Clark Kent. "Did I think Jay was cute?" She smiles big. "I wasn't really even looking at him like that. He wasn't even out yet." But then, in 1996, they voiced "Ain't No Nigga" for Def Jam's *The Nutty Professor* sound track: "No one can fuck you better," Jay rapped, however figuratively, to a sixteen-year-old Foxy, who gave as good as she got. "Sleeps around but he gives me a lot" is the way she replied.

So just how much does Jay contribute to Foxy Brown? "What made Jay love me is the verse I wrote for 'Ain't No Nigga,'" she says. "I write my songs and have always written my songs. When my schedule is hectic and I'm too busy to go in the studio, Jay collaborates with me. He catches me when I'm falling. But this is my nine-to-five. This is what I do."

A lot of people don't know that Inga Marchand was signed to Capitol Records as Big Shorty. Soon thereafter she changed her name to AKA and was eventually dropped from the label. Then Red Hot Lover Tone brought her to Puffy Combs, who turned her down. But the Fox was determined.

Chris Lightly, CEO of Violator Records, also manages Noreaga, Cam'Ron, Q-Tip, Busta Rhymes, Missy Elliott, Mobb Deep, and Total. Lightly says he was probably the first, aside from Jay-Z, to give Foxy a shot. "She didn't even have a real demo," he says.

As the story goes, Tone and Steve "the Commisioner" Stoute from Track-masters Entertainment were in Chung King studios in 1995 with L.L. Cool J. Lightly was there, too. He says Foxy "had been bugging me to put her on a record. And Tone had been trying to get me to sign her. We all agreed to put her on [the remix to 'I Shot Ya' (Def Jam, 1995)] without telling L.L."

The night before she recorded her verse, Foxy left the studio "early" because it was three in the morning and she had a big test the next day. "She was caring about school a lot at that time," says Stoute. "Myself, I was just thinking about the money."

"I was the new bitch," says Foxy. "They had me in there with L.L., Keith Murray, Prodigy, and Fat Joe. I was like, 'Y'all got me rhyming against some dope-ass MCs. And you know what? I can *do* his shit.'"

"Foxy wrote her rhyme right then," says Violator's Eric Nicks. It went a little something like this: "Ice rocks / Pussy banging like Versace . . ."

"Everybody ran out of the room screaming like that shit was the *bomb*," she says. "I knew right then it was going to be on for me. I was a female truly rhyming with some real niggas."

Judith Marchand says she didn't know about her daughter's talent until Inga turned sixteen. "Only after every record company head was expressing interest in her did I become aware," says the Ill Mama. "Something that stays with me: I was at a studio. On the other side of the door they were playing a Foxy track. I heard them screaming. A guy ran out and said, 'She is the 50-Foot Woman. She's going to be the Whitney Houston of rap.'" Even if she wasn't doing the remix of "I Will Always Love You," Foxy's a pretty, profane, sexual girl with skills—do the math.

"It was the *craziest* bidding war," Foxy recalls. "Puffy, Russell [Simmons], Sylvia [Rhone], Andre Harrell. I narrowed it down to Bad Boy and Def Jam. Russell had longevity."

"Foxy like to *win*," Eric Nick says. "She spazzes out when something's off. It's got to be the right beat, the right lyric, the right stylist. Everything has to be *win win win*, or she's not doing it."

Back when Foxy was in junior high and Kimberly Jones, aka Lil' Kim, was in high school, they were friends living in Brooklyn. They used to stay on the phone until six in the morning, planning how they were gonna tear shit down. *Who would get on first? Which bitch was baddest?*

"We always had a pact," Foxy says. Each agreed to help the other. Back then, both were under Lance "Un" Rivera's management. "But then Kim went with Big, and I went with Jay. She paid her dues."

"Kim called me one day," says Foxy. "It was like four in the morning, and I had to go to school the next day, and she was like, 'You know AZ?' I was like, 'The rapper? The one that gets with Nas?' She was like, 'Yo, I got him on the other line, he wants you to rap for him.' I was scared. I just started busting for him. He was like, 'Yo, give me your number.'" When she met Nas and AZ, they all just clicked. "It was like, 'This is how we gonna do this. It's gonna be the Firm.'" She says Nas and AZ are her fam. She rides for them. They ended up recording 1997's *The Firm—The Album*.

Lightly says, "If you listen to Foxy's *Ill Na Na* [Def Jam, 1996] and Kim's *Hard Core* [Undeas/Atlantic, 1996], Kim was more underground. We took Foxy straight to the clubs." He slows down for a second. "Kim had Biggie, though. There was a lot of power on that side. Fortunately, we were able to keep up."

Kim and Foxy are not really friends now. "It didn't have to do with Kim and I personally," Foxy says. "It was the people around us." Foxy says they were supposed to cut a song more than a year ago called "Thelma & Louise."

"At the time we were supposed to record, we weren't speaking," says Foxy. "Un came to me and said, 'I know you and Shorty ain't on the best of terms right now, but . . .' And at first I wasn't really with it. The day after, Kim called me. But when you have two women who once were friends, who now have bitter feelings toward each other and are getting fed bull from every angle . . . the conversation was useless."

Foxy says after thirty minutes of going over who said what, "I was talking to a dial tone." She decided to go to the studio and record her verse anyway. Then Foxy, Un, and Lightly waited several hours for Kim. "Shorty never showed," Foxy says. (Kim declined to be interviewed for this piece.)

Rivera, who calls Foxy chipper and energetic, says he's still trying to make "Thelma & Louise" happen. And Foxy says she still has mad love for Kim. When a gunman broke into Foxy's house this past July, it was the scariest moment of her life. "Kim was the first one concerned," Foxy says. "I appreciated that."

Foxy's eating key lime pie and talking about the forthcoming Oliver Stone film, tentatively titled *The League* (Warner Bros.,1999). She's reading for a part, and if she gets it, Foxy'll portray the football hero's girl. "I respect Faith," Foxy says, a little out of nowhere. "When you're the wife, you needn't worry. Anyone can be a girlfriend or a baby's mama. But there's only one wife."

Foxy's engaged to Kurupt, a label-owning West-Coast-by-way-of-Philadelphia all-star who's down with Snoop Dogg. (His double album, *Kuruption*, was released this past October.) Her platinum engagement ring is wide and jammed with diamonds. The couple haven't set a date yet. Foxy says if it were up to Kurupt, she'd already be married. "You know what?" she adds. "We really love each other, but right now, what's really important to me is focusing on my album and getting my career straight."

Her career: Foxy knows that because she sells sex (and she will tell you that, straight out), that when a female is sexual, the impulse to stigmatize her is pretty automatic. "Harlots or Heroines?" was the question posed in a 1997 cover story in *The Source* about Foxy and Kim. "I remember this one article a girl wrote," Foxy says. "She titled it 'Black Girl Lost.'" Foxy hated that. "I'm not lost," she says. "*My* grown ass? I know what the fuck I'm doing."

"Inga has childlike qualities and womanlike qualities," says Judy Marchand. "I've taken heat from a lot of people about her image. I've had to defend her and myself. I'm not going to let anyone take advantage of her. I will fight for her tooth and nail. I have her back. Inga is my little girl."

Joe Sherman, Foxy's bodyguard, is six foot six inches. Three hundred and forty pounds. Very nice guy. He says to me one day in the lobby of Miami's Tides Hotel, like it's a secret, "I've thought about it. If someone ever took a shot at her, would I jump in front of her and take the bullet? I've thought about it, and I would. Because I've lived. She hasn't. She *thinks* she has."

Foxy's got on dark gray Iceberg hot pants, a matching Band-Aid of a top. Gucci slides. Platinum Rolex. "In the beginning," Foxy says, "I was in Chanel, Prada, and Gucci all the time. But now my mom co-manages me, I'm learning to spend wisely. You can be made today and broke tomorrow. I'm not trying to be broke." She owns a house in New Jersey and is about to buy a brownstone in Brooklyn.

"She's supposed to be this extreme bitch," says Lightly. "But we're all rude; we all wake up on the wrong side of the bed. People harp on it because she's female."

On her fierce new album, Foxy remade Howard Johnson's 1982 smash "So Fine" (A&M) with Next singing the hook. "If we skip Prada / You gets nada" is what she says on the song.

I ask if she could ever date a guy with no money. "The brother with no money is gonna spend *time*," she says. "The guy with money is gonna be like, 'I just gave you a thousand dollars to go shopping. What the fuck is you calling me for?' Then I'm sitting around with a bunch of gifts and the nigga's long gone. I don't like that. You ain't got to buy me. I have my own."

Yes, she does. But Foxy's a fast girl. A girl who looks at her lips, her teeth, her waist, her ass, her legs, her breasts, and sees that they are what people, what men, have always responded to. So why not use them, as her old girl-friend Lil' Kim says, to "Get Money"? Foxy was seven years old when Janet Jackson hit with "Control" and "What Have You Done for Me Lately." Five when Madonna broke it down with "Material Girl." No wonder she's so consumed with consuming. Foxy's the kind of girl who believes that financial independ-ence (and the constant display thereof) might just bring about emotional independence—but grown as she is, she hasn't hit the big wall yet. The one that's tagged It Isn't So.

What she does know (and what is true) is attitude is nine-tenths of the law, that shock wins, that profanity is the new norm, that as long as you can pretend to yourself that being a girl with a guy's macho mentality is possible, you can play—and it's fun—but then you fuck around and like a guy. You hear something massive and embracing in his voice, feel all the things you never felt as a baby girl in his arms, and then you are—not lost—but mad at him for being stupid and sexist and human. A victim himself of genes and environment and these wary, changing, sexual times. Mostly you're mad at your life or whatever it is about life in general that makes you need anything from anyone at any time. So you dis dependence. Claim pussy as power. Go all the fly places bad girls go. Do a remake of Gwen Guthrie's 1986 "Ain't Nothin' Going On but the Rent."

I have to ask her, though, since it is a federal law, why she isn't rapping about world peace. "To me, that's normal," she says. "I do things to keep people talking. To bring issues that the average female MC ain't raising. To talk about things average females talk about. Not even so much about niggas. [Females] been fighting for respect; we've been fighting for equality since back in the Bessie Smith days, Millie Jackson, all that. It's like, 'Why can you get mad at me and say, "Fuck you," and I can't say, "Fuck you"?' I want to be the type of rapper that stands up for that. You have rappers that stand up more for African-American culture. You have people that are just into party music, you have rappers who are street. I'm just Foxy."

"Brown-skinned bitches in a Hammer!"

Foxy's talking about her video for the ridiculously catchy first single, "Hot Spot," from *Chyna Doll*. We've limoed over to Bal Harbour Shops, where the people in Gucci know her name, where the people in Prada parade around her with shoes and purses for fall, where the old ladies in Chanel act snobby toward her until Lightly pulls out his gold AmEx, already smoking from all the action. The ladies—foundation cracking, matte lipstick fading—smile and bring Foxy what Foxy wants, which is mostly shoes, size six and a half for herself, seven and a half for Judy Marchand, an elementary-school teacher. Her mom divorced early; raised Inga and her brothers Anton and Gavin mostly by herself.

"My mother wasn't strict," Foxy says. "She would leave notes for me and my two brothers. One day I'd have the dishes . . . we'd rotate days. Everything was organized. Wherever we went, we had to call."

"Right now I'm in awe of my daughter," says Mrs. Marchand. "Inga is very bright. She's been in gifted programs since preschool. She kept you on your toes. She was always reading and talking. We had a special relationship. She's my only daughter. When she got to be a teenager, we went through changes. She was getting to know herself. I call it her creative period."

Between Louis Vuitton and Sergio Rossi, I ask what she would tell a girl who said, "Foxy, my man is tripping." "I can't even tell you 'cause I need all the advice I can get," she says. "But basically, don't chase. Let it go. It'll come back. I got that from my mother. If that person isn't putting in the time and love and effort he should be, you need to back off for a minute. You need to be like, 'Let me step back for a little while. You do *you*. Come back when you're ready to do me.'"

So until he's ready, you toss them titties around. Shake that ass. Make that money. Cultivate that brassy soul-sister shit everybody applauds you for. Yes. Foxy Brown is a star. Be nasty. Be classy. Be extravagant. Be everybody's fantasy. Be Millie, be Pearl, be Whitney, be Diahann, be Janet, be like your girl Kim. Stare down the old rules. Run with the big dogs. Hey, soul sister! Be superstrong, supersexy, supertalented, supersatisfied. Be supergirl. Be like Pam "Original Foxy" Grier. Foxy says Pam and she are buddies. That Pam calls her and tells her when she's fucking up by, like, wearing a wrong dress to some event. Or, says Foxy, when she's, like, not handling business.

The Tides Hotel looks like a wedding cake. White with squares of mauve and pale blue. Umbrella'd tables. You can forget how hot it is when you're sitting in the hotel sipping lemonade made with sparkling water. Ninety-one degrees at 3:15 p.m. Lightly is on the phone again: "Tell them South Beach is on some *art deco* shit. The hotels aren't like the usual hotels we stay at. Everything is small." The Violator crew comes down here to record away from New York and L.A. or Atlanta. Not so many distractions. Foxy says, in L.A., there's a celebrity on every corner. It's time to go to the studio. Foxy's hype about it, but resisting. Besides, we want to talk about guys.

You didn't quite answer me before: Could you date a guy who's not paid?

"I'd rather meet someone who's cool and not in the limelight. But when you do it—and I've tried—it doesn't balance out. It's always like four o'clock in the morning, and I'm getting calls from Russell Simmons, and [the guy'll be] waking up like, 'Niggas is trying to get some *sleep*' . . . you know? We can't go to the movies unless it's 'Ohmigod, it's Foxy!' People want autographs. He'd be feeling left out. My first love, Rayshawn, he's a part of Junior M.A.F.I.A., but he's not in the limelight. And for a while we could keep it together. But then my fame just *went*. And that kinda messed it up. He was reminding me, twenty-four seven, 'I was with you when you didn't have shit.' And I was like, 'I'm trying to be with you and you ain't got shit.' And I'd tell him I'm trying to still get mine. It didn't work out."

Lauryn Hill said that a guy she was with felt like he never had to tell her she was special, because the whole world was telling her that every day.

"I never had that problem. But I have been in a lot of situations where I felt like I was ridin' for niggas, like no matter what, that's *my nigga*, and then they're like, 'Ahh . . . yeah, yeah, she's my [*she shrugs*],' and it's like . . . like shit. That hurts. You have no idea."

I ask Foxy's mom if she'd want a fifteen-year-old girl to grow up and become Foxy Brown, and she says, "Foxy is Foxy. I'd prefer someone to wanna be like Inga. I would tell a fifteen-year-old to be yourself. Foxy Brown's not a bad girl; she really is a good girl. I thought it was fun and games what she does, but she worked hard. She's using the talent she was blessed with. I respect her. I don't always agree with her—what mother agrees with everything her daughter does?"

I've mostly seen Foxy rocking purple eye shadow, skinny superplucked eyebrows, blue mascara. Flowing black hair down to the middle of her back. Fly-ass weave-o-rama. Hazel contact lenses. Deep dark, glossy lipstick. Foxy's a big pop superstar, baby. Don't sleep. In South Beach, where everyone is at least close to cool and good-looking, brothas stare her down, boys beg for a snapshot. Girls nervously approach. Graying men verge on cardiac arrest. They stumble, even, trying to get a look at Foxy Brown. Hot child in the city. Is it bad to be what the brothers call a hoochie mama? Or is the hoochie moment an awesome one? An instant of true equality between man and woman. Power testing on a shaky but level field. Love, for a brief, glittery moment, supreme.

I've seen Foxy, too, though—right before a photo shoot—with no makeup, weave in a lopsided ponytail, old jeans short, and a tan tube top washed too many times. In so many ways, she's total girl. No doubt. The most beautifullest thing in the world.

Vibe / December 1998–January 1999

The Show, the After-Party, the Hotel

KAREN R. GOOD

"Boo, you know how many women we meet with no panties?"
—Mase, "Lookin' at Me" (*Harlem World*, Bad Boy, 1997)

Round a table in the barroom of the Sheraton Hotel over-looking the Elizabeth River to Virginia Beach, Virginia, Jay-Z and his brethren TyTy, Radolfo, Hip Hop, Ja Rule, and Memphis Bleek congregate. Ponies run-neth over with Hennessy VSOP, glasses rise, and then a toast:

"This right here," says Jay-Z soberly, "is for success."

"For success!" his consorts follow.

"Can't have success without . . . loyalty," Jay continues.

"Yeh, yeh!" they respond.

It's Labor Day weekend 1998, the weekend during which thousands of students from surrounding Chesapeake Bay communities and black colleges like Howard and Morgan State (and even more southern campuses like Hampton and Norfolk State) come for one last hurrah before school begins.

Jay-Z, who will perform the next night, Saturday, with DMX at the Hampton Convention Center, lifts another glass. "This one here," he says, quiet now, "this one is for family."

"One love! Roc-A-Fella fa life."

"And this one right here is for the groupies!"

"Long live the groupies! Long live the groupies!"

Tonight, stories flow like Jesus wine. Tales about tours and one-ups on who's slept with the most women—groupies, they call them—while on the road, bragging rites as necessary and orgasmic as the act itself. "I've fucked half the bitches in the USA," one maintains. *"Half."* Grand, mythic, ridiculous accounts are told of women trailing them from state to state like the Feds, of women who dared to do things like stand on their heads, of women lining up in twos and threes to suck the same guy.

"Detroit," Jay-Z promises, "got the best pussy. They just straight 'bout it. I respect that more than somebody who tries to front. I'm in town one night. What the fuck I need with a girl with a value?"

With hip-hop generating billions of dollars a year—edging out rock as the lifestyle of the rich and famous—tales of young-girl groupies who haunt productions like the Hard Knock Life tour and the Puff Daddy and the Family tour have become the stuff of urban legend. *Did you hear about the Italian chicks on Survival of the Illest? Ultimate groupies. In every city they did at least twenty niggas apiece!* A general rule: The fan might accompany an artist to the hotel room to hang out—but the groupie will hit the artist off.

According to Webster's dictionary, the term *groupie* originated in 1967 and is defined as "a fan of a rock group who usually follows the group around on concert tours." Rock fan/girlfriend Pamela Des Barres wrote a book about it called *I'm With the Band: Confessions of a Groupie* (William Morrow, 1987). Des Barres, who stood onstage in the 1970s while the Who played "Tommy" and traveled with Led Zeppelin as Jimmy Page's girl, writes that *groupie* started out as "negative fingerpointing . . . by someone who obviously couldn't get backstage."

Be it rock or hip-hop, the magic of music is that it has always inspired a certain glory and power. Who among us has not been brought to tears, ecstasy, or uprising, by song? But some can't separate the music from the messenger, and to listen is not enough. Like Des Barres, a hip-hop groupie believes in going *behind* the music in search of a real-life fantasy. The artist creates the illusion; the groupie is the true believer.

We must remember, however, that this is a *relationship*, a compromise. An indulgence of egos in need of satiation and acknowledgment. If that were not so, then Joe Rapper, who's well-known and married, wouldn't be standing outside of the Sheraton this warm night, shortly before the football game, passing around a camera showing a videotape of a young girl doing him. She is smiling, has pretty eyes, her expression a bit geisha. All you see of Joe are his knees and toes. See this and you understand that man has needs: voyeurism, bravado, and carnality. Woman has similar needs, but add to that a lust for challenge and a desire to be chosen. Groupies make sure these needs get met.

On Saturday night there are no postconcert parties worth stopping by, so a few hundred people stand loosely on Waterside Avenue, in front of the Sheraton.

Sweetness, Tawana, and Kim (not their real names) are three Virginia high school girls who tell boys they're in college. They are sweet, fast girls, looking to see who's out this balmy evening. Tawana is thin—the kind of thin country girls call po—and wears thick stacked shoes and a micromini. Sweetness, who has dimples and a braided ponytail bun, is thick, sporting secondskins to prove it. Kim, a dark-skinned girl who doesn't seem to know her beauty, is disappointed because she tried to take a picture with Jay-Z and he hurried her along, despite her outfit—again, a micromini and heels—which she thought was perfect. "It's about the women he prefers," she says. As she speaks, a shadow of a guy walks by swiftly and palms Sweetness's ass. She cuts her eyes at his back. "And he ain't no damn body." Her hand rests on her wide hips. *"Nobody."*

What makes a hip-hop groupie different from any other groupie is the difference in the music and culture itself. Something to do with hip-hop's accessibility and the brevity of fame. With being working class and making no way The Way. For girls like Tawana, Kim, and Sweetness, some of this is about closing the degrees of separation, going for the man next to the man next to the man next to The Man. Other times it's less about the man, more about what he manifests: the success and shiny things and, perhaps most important, the suggestion of godliness-God: Rakim, Allah, Nas ("like the Messiah"), Jayhova. The groupie knows that she has limited access to this other world. Her skills of seduction can get her in.

"I know I look like a little slut," Kim says. "Four o'clock in the morning. Little dress, high heels. Trust me, the things I've had said to me tonight . . . you don't even know. The way we're dressed today is nothing [like] how our personalities are. I'm trying to get the attention that will draw the attention to *him*. That's the girl who will fit his image."

Chaka Pilgrim, one of the creators of Fanfamily, a company that answers fan mail for artists such as DMX, Jay-Z, and Foxy Brown, says that sometimes these women have a plan. "You think these women are playing themselves," she says, "but then you'll see them behind the scenes and you'll be like, 'Okay, I was there when we did the concert at the Tunnel. I was there when this bitch came and stuck her tongue in your ear. Okay, here it is three weeks later and she's in the studio.' So there's more than a one-night stand going on.

"Then you get the girls who just want to have sex," Pilgrim continues. "Like, no panties, grab his hand, put between crotch and 'Feel my furry wonder-pouch.' So with that in mind, girls really have their own agenda."

Male groupies are harder to distinguish. Usually they simply linger and try to be cool, but they also cry real tears of regret every time Lauryn Hill gives birth; they offer Lil' Kim money to have sex; they stalk Madonna. Shotgun funk goddess Joi (who's married to Big Gipp of the Goodie Mob) says that male groupies are usually awestruck. "Most times they're respectful of the art and realize, 'This might be bigger than me,'" she says. "Female groupies, on the other hand, are going to test the men. They wanna get up and touch something."

That said, when the girls are asked if they have or would ever have sex with a rapper just because of who he is, Tawana says, "Uh-uh." Sweetness: "Fuck, no." Kim: "Well, Nas," she admits, "Nas Escobar. Yep."

This is Kim's fantasy: "Aiight, boom: I'm at this concert, right? And I'm in the crowd, in the front. And then it be Nas, the whole Firm onstage. I'm in the crowd, right, and Nas pulls me up there. Then I see him backstage and . . ." Kim stops, covers her face. "I don't wanna talk about it."

A guy listening on the sidelines tosses in his two cents. "We know the rest! This is a groupie movie!"

"No! No! No, 'cause we carry on a relationship!" Kim is adamant. "He takes me on tour and everything, and I'm living the lifestyle he rappin' about. Look, I love him. I really do. I'm not tryin' to be funny. I really have a thing for Nas. Unlike anybody else."

As dawn nears, the girls scurry inside the hotel toward the elevators. Their plan is to stop on random floors and knock on random doors until they find Jay-Z. Or Somebody.

"Why are these women in front of the hotel at four in the morning?" Crystal (not her real name) wants to know. The bald desperation is completely lost on her. Crystal is, after all, sophisticated and pretty, exuding the faintest shade of snobbery, focused, and maybe a little neurotic. She flicks a nonexistent ash from her cigarette, then: "Oh! *Riiiight.* Lingering. Oh, I don't do that. Oh, *please.* That's groupie shit. I'm not a groupie. I'm a *neo-groupie.*"

It is a term only she can explain. "The neo-groupie isn't trying to get discarded. That's pathetic. I am the ghetto superstar prize. *Those niggas want me.* And why shouldn't I enjoy being desired?"

Crystal, a tiny woman with soft hair cut low and skin the color of weak tea, pads around her friend Gongo's Lower East Side, New York City, apartment in fuzzy socks, loose blue jeans, and a cozy turtleneck that could swallow her small frame. Gongo and his three friends wander the flat. They pass reefer, flip TV channels, and occasionally interject.

Crystal is the nineties progression of Des Barres in that the attraction to celebrity is still about the power and the glory, claim and sex. But for Crystal, fame isn't the goal. It's about *money*, which she believes grants freedom and certain liberties. No struggling like her parents with two mortgages, grease marks around the light switch, and seventies green velvet everywhere. Maybe, she admits, it's also something to "blackify" her, because she's biracial with a Jewish last name. "A little ghetto dude on my arm with a six-pack and fly Hilfiger latest something or other. I feel like people can't play me if I'm his fly bitch—'cause they don't. You know how nice they are to me?" She laughs. "I love it when people are nice to me that way."

Crystal, who is from a working-class neighborhood in Suffolk County, Long Island, but now lives in Manhattan, does not work but likes nice things. She dates accordingly. "There are definitely fly niggas about," Crystal says, "but power takes it to the next level." She pauses, then, gives estimation:

"Have you ever been to Switzerland?" she asks.

No.

"It's beautiful. It's beautiful this time of year."

So is Morocco, she recalls, and so is Holland, which she visited with a rapper, whom she'd rather not name, while he was touring Europe a few years ago. She says she's no concubine. "I [participate in oral sex], it's true. But I do other things with my day. I ski, read, go horseback riding. I shop."

"You're a dirty whore," Gongo interrupts, and his friends giggle like schoolgirls. Crystal turns from her couch seat to face him, but not immediately. First she blinks.

"So I'm a dirty whore?"

"You're a dirty whore." Not *ho*. *Whore*.

"You know, that's interesting, because I actually like to be called a dirty whore when I'm in bed with men. It gets me hot," she says, and doesn't blink. "So that would make sense. Oh, well." Crystal sits back and crosses her arms. "I'm just saying, keep it real. Sticks and stones may break my bones . . . label, label, label."

Crystal recently completed film studies at New York University, where she wrote psychological shorts about dolls and two others: *Niggas Don't Love You* and *White Men Don't Love You Either*. "Everyone gets hurt in both films," she says. "Everyone gets hurt all the time."

In the relationship between artist and groupie, women offer their bodies and men use status and shiny toys as bait. Nothing personal. As Crystal says, "Love is about love. This is something else." In this arrangement, the question becomes, what, if anything, is compromised? Crystal has some idea. "One time," she says slowly, "I sorta got into this situation," she continues, choosing her words carefully, "where I got really fucked-up and I think a whole bunch of people fucked me. So, you know," she says, lifting an eyebrow, "rape is pretty compromising."

That was two years ago, in New York, in a club she'd rather not name. What she will say is that there were lots of hip-hop artists present. "A lot of mean dick-sucking goes on," she begins, kind of cryptically, "but not all of it is consensual. I try to think that rape is never my fault and move past it." Later she will admit, casually, that "lots of people get raped; it was just a part of my destiny."

Some of this is about the music, as violence and disrespect condoned in one form can only lead to violence and disrespect condoned in another. Some of this, however, is part of the deal. The adoration of celebrity is hero worship. And to worship a hero is to trade part of yourself for something that's not real. A hip-hop groupie sacrifices herself to the heightened emotionalism, eroticism, and rhythm of colored men who think themselves gods. In exchange, the groupie, when picked, gets to feel like the Chosen One. That, to Crystal, is exactly the point.

"When he comes through, I think I'm in a fucking rap video," she says of her current rapper boyfriend. "I've got the fly lingerie. Crazy shit is jumping off." She pauses. "Unless you've been around people who are so powerful, you don't understand why it's such an aphrodisiac. When you're around a man and everybody around him is sweating him [getting with him]. All day long. That's *hot*." A flick of a cigarette, a crossing of arms. "And that's *that*."

Vibe / August 1999

Don't Hate Me Because I'm Ghetto Fabulous

DAVID KAMP

"**Eeeyahhhh,**" says Puffy.

"Go higher," says the doctor. "*Eee, eee . . .*"

"*Ee-yeeahhhh!*"

"But higher now. C'mon—eee, eee . . ."

"Ee—"

"*Higher!*"

"Ee yeeeeüüüaaaaaaagh!"

"Good! Now, let's have a look."

The doctor, Scott Kessler, is wearing a lamp on his head and a surgical glove on his right hand, which has a tight grip on the outstretched tongue of his patient. The patient, Sean "Puffy" Combs, cannot actually produce the sound *eee* in this configuration, but attempting to do so has the effect of tilting his larynx back, so that the doctor can get a better view of his vocal cords. It also has the effect of making the biggest star in hip-hop sound like a wounded cormorant.

Puffy has had difficulty rapping of late. "I don't feel no pain," he tells Dr. Kessler. "But my voice, it feels weak. It sounds hoarse, like . . . like the mike has distortion on it."

Kessler probes and pokes. The left side of Puffy's throat is revealed to be . . . puffy. He is prescribed an anti-inflammatory steroid and a mucus thinner. He is instructed to gargle regularly. He then retreats with the doctor to the privacy of his bathroom, where he is given a shot in the buttocks. He emerges with a temporary Fred Sanford lollop, making his way to the couch before gingerly sitting down and saying, "Damn!"

The salient thing about this scene is not that Puffy Combs is having throat problems, which appear to be unremarkable, but that Puffy Combs is human. It's fascinating (and, one must admit, satisfying) to watch this cocksure, stony monolith of music-video land endure a small awkwardness. The public Puffy, twenty-nine-year-old CEO of Bad Boy Entertainment and all its tentacular profit-making subsidiaries, rolls around town in a silver Bentley, wears Versace furs, romances the awesomely steatopygic beauty Jennifer Lopez, and imbibes copious amounts of Cristal Champagne. The public Puffy is, to use a term of his own invention, ghetto fabulous. "Ghetto fabulous!" he exclaimed to *Interview* magazine. "I'm the nigger who started it: I'm the one driving around in the Rolls-Royce with his hat turned, goin' down Fifth Avenue with the system booming in the back. Walkin' into Gucci, shuttin' it down, buying everything at the motherfuckin' same time! Driving up to Harlem, out to 125th Street, and on my way back downtown goin' and givin' hundred-dollar bills to homeless people. No other nigger out there can say they're ghetto fabulous; I'm ghetto fabulous!"

The private Puffy, by contrast, gargles and has a sore butt. And that's the least of it. How extraordinary it would have been, for example, to have encountered Puffy on that recent spring night when, overcome with emotion from watching *Love Story* on video, he stole away from his Park Avenue town house in tears and headed for Central Park. "I went to the park to cry," he says. "'Cause I know no one's crazy enough to be walking in Central Park at three *a.m.* I could not stop crying. I've never cried so hard in my life on just a movie. It bugged me out! I was, like, embarrassed! I don't know—I guess I had a lot bottled up in me."

Spend some time with Puffy, and he will furnish a litany of his frailties for you. He will describe himself as someone who has "got a lot more maturing to do." He will tell you he's on a diet because he has allowed himself to get too "thick" between tours. You will notice that, despite his celebrated aversion to sleep, he yawns, and that he's "crazy with the itching and sneezing" from allergies and that there's a spot of gray along his hairline. You will hear him say, "There's some hypocritical shit about me. There's some contradictions. There's some mistakes."

Not for nothing does he brood and self-flagellate so. With Puffy, every epochal, fist-pumping moment of triumph seems to be countervailed by some horrific setback. He established himself at the turn of this decade as a hip-hop-party wunderkind, but his reputation was nearly undone in 1991 by the deaths-by-stampede of nine people at a charity basketball game he organized—and oversold—at the City College of New York. He parlayed a college internship at Andre Harrell's Uptown Records into an executive-VP position and his own boutique label, Bad Boy, by the time he was twenty-two—only to wind up fired by Harrell at twenty-three for insubordination. He persuaded the music mogul Clive Davis to take the orphaned Bad Boy into the Arista Records fold and quickly rewarded Davis by creating an unlikely hip-hop megastar in the Notorious B.I.G., aka Biggie Smalls—a corpulent, walleyed ex–crack dealer from Brooklyn, real name Christopher Wallace, with a voice like a wet explosion. But in March 1997, before Puffy's very eyes, Biggie was murdered in a drive-by shooting in Los Angeles—retaliation, many presumed, for the September '96 murder of Tupac Shakur, whose L.A.–based recording label, Death Row, was then embroiled in a rivalry with the New York–based Bad Boy. (Both murders remain unsolved, though in April the Los Angeles Police Department named Death Row's imprisoned head, Marion "Suge" Knight, the chief suspect in Biggie's shooting. Puffy continues to deny that he and Bad Boy had anything to do with Shakur's death: "Not even a not-to-my knowledge thing—straight up, unequivocally.")

And so it goes. Ostensibly, this is another period of joyous fruition for Puffy. He has made himself available to this magazine at this particular moment because he wants to promote his new line of clothing, Sean John, which is just "flying off the shelves," and because *Forever*, his second solo album under his performing name Puff Daddy, will be droppin', as they say, on the twenty-fourth of August. But the overshadowing story, the inescapable bit of bad business to be dealt with this time around, is his April 16 arrest for second-degree assault.

On April 15, he was involved in a confrontation with Steve Stoute, an executive at Interscope Records. Stoute manages the rapper Nas, and Puffy had lent his presence to Nas's latest video, for a song called "Hate Me Now." The video shoot called for Puffy to appear nailed to a cross, a direction he complied with but later regretted, citing his religious beliefs. He pressed Stoute to remove the crucifixion scene; Stoute resisted, arousing Puffy's ire. On April 15, Stoute told the police, Puffy and two minions stormed into his Midtown office, upended his desk, broke his arm and jaw and—an inspired signature touch, if true—bludgeoned him with a champagne bottle.

Puffy disputes these details, arguing that no bones were broken and no bottles of Cristal were brandished, but admits he was guilty of starting the trouble that day. "It's a fuckup. There's really no excuse for it," he says. "It's gotten very sensationalized, but at the end of the day it's a fuckup." Precisely what happened he won't say, though it's clear he resorted to physical intimidation. "I got irrational," he says. "I was moving on my emotions. I wanted to fight."

Puffy says the incident "happened because of my belief in God." He says he made his objections explicit to Stoute well before the video was to be released, with plenty of time for corrections. It was Stoute's unwillingness to budge, he says, that made him act rashly.

I ask him if there wasn't an inherent paradox in his position, which is, in essence, "Respect my religious beliefs or I'll kick your ass."

"Well, you have to go on what I'm saying, not what you're thinking," he says. "I was thinking, whatever I had to do to get that video off the air, I was ready to do. And I was wrong—as a Christian, you have to turn the other cheek."

The concept of the video, says Puffy, was that he and Nas "were supposed to be two people that were getting crucified, like, during the time. We were not supposed to be portraying Jesus. But then, due to the parallels of how big I am and the persecution—when I was looking at it, I could see that people were gonna think that I'm trying to be Jesus. And I'm not at all comfortable with that.

That, to me, is an eternal sin that can't be forgiven . . . I would never, never mock Jesus Christ."

I ask him why he didn't think of this before—when you're nailed to a cross, whom else are you going to invite comparisons to?

"I know!" he says. "I admit it. I made a mistake. I should have thought that out. But believe me, I caught it way in time."

Originally, Stoute vowed to push a criminal case and, according to people on Puffy's side, sought a multimillion-dollar settlement in return for not pressing civil charges. (The lawyer whom Stoute retained in the matter, Thomas Puccio, did not return calls seeking comment.) But in early June, Puffy and Stoute patched things up. The agreement is vague: according to people close to the negotiations, Puffy agreed to pay Stoute $250,000 and send lots of music- and video-production work his way. These same sources suggest that Bertelsmann, the parent company of Arista and Bad Boy, will ultimately have to make some sort of financial accommodation for Interscope. But Puffy flatly denies any of this, saying that he and Stoute reached a strict "man-to-man resolution."

"Straight up, we didn't agree to any money," he says. "It took time, but we got in a room together. I apologized to him. He apologized that the video got messed up. We were laughing and joking two minutes into it. You gotta understand that we were friends before. He [once] gave me a fifty-thousand-dollar Cartier watch."

Despite the laughing and the joking, there is still the matter of criminal prosecution; the Manhattan D.A.'s office is still pursuing the case, even though Stoute agreed not to press charges. "I still have to deal with it someway," says Puffy, "but I won't go to jail."

Puffy will most likely get off lightly—probation, maybe community service—but in the short term the incident occasioned an almost celebratory backlash this spring, a mass unburdening of anti-Puffy sentiment and wishful thinking about his demise as a cultural force. On a more or less daily basis, the New York papers ran belittling items: the invariably unnamed "music exec" saying Puffy "can hang up his career"; multiple citations of Bad Boy Records' plummeting sales figures (a $35 million gross in '98 versus $200 million in '97);

Puffy's "bad-luck streak" further evidenced by the fact that Mariah Carey was given his favorite table at a nightclub one evening (though she did send him over some Cristal). The unifying sentiment being, *He had it coming, the bastard.*

Daddy's House, Puffy's Midtown recording studio, late April. No sense of siege here—the place hums with assistant sound engineers and storyboard-toting video stylists, busy drones in the happy hive of ghetto fabulous. One is greeted in the hallway by Charles, a burly, dreadlocked bodyguard, who asks, in a fluting, exquisite Bobby Short voice, "the nature of your business with Mr. Combs." A satisfactory answer produced, Charles beep-beep-boop-boops the security code into the panel next to an unmarked door, which opens into "the Lounge." The Lounge is a cooling-out place that Arista built for Puffy so that he and his artists would have a civilized place to unwind during recording sessions.

"The whole concept of it," says Puffy, after introductions have been made, "was *Black Sinatra*. Like, if Frank Sinatra was black, and he was my age, and he was me, what kind of hangout would he have for Dean and Sammy and the guys to come see him at the studio."

Puffy's been thinking lately, and he's decided that the Sinatra analogy works. He resisted it when his friends first brought it up—when they, watching A&E's *Biography* special on the Rat Pack earlier this year, detected amazing similarities between his life and the Chairman's. "I went, 'How the hell you gonna compare me with Frank Sinatra?'" he says. "But then I looked at it and was like, 'You know, he had a lot of issues, a lot of things going on—a lot of ups and downs in his life, similar to my life.' A lot of times when you see him going through his downs, you don't really see a lot of people around him. Same thing that I've gone through."

Well, anyway, the Lounge is a successful realization, a large room done up in Palm Springs midcentury modern, in creams and sands, with low-slung furniture and a pair of wet bars. No shoes in the Lounge—the floors will get scuffed. (Though Puffy, being *el jefe*, gets to wear slippers.) Four TV screens line one wall: ESPN, BET, and two overhead surveillance shots of people milling about the adjacent hallways.

Right now Puffy is in the thick of recording *Forever*; it's about 70 percent finished. Puffy describes the new work as "autobiographical for a certain period of my life. It tells a story. The story's just my life and me as a survivor. And I'm not talking about a survivor as anything to do with Biggie—I'm talking about just a survivor in this game of life."

If this sounds a bit cabaret, a bit *Liza* for a rapper, it should be understood that Puffy has never been afraid to reach for the big hankie moment. Tucked between the ritual helpings of hip-hop braggadocio and gunshot sound effects on his last record, the 7-million-selling *No Way Out*, are some astounding spoken interludes, almost therapy-session snippets, in which a dulcet Puffy speaks— as opposed to raps—over choirs, wind chimes, gospel melismata, what have you. "When I think about dying," he says in one such passage, "I think about . . . a sense of release. Just a release from all the pressures . . . and all the negativity . . . I also think about finally getting a chance to see all the loved ones again that left before me—that'd be kinda fly . . . Walk through the gates . . . see my grandmother . . . see Bigg . . . see God . . . [a bemused chuckle]. That shit is crazy."

Puffy says that *Forever* will be "a little bit different and some of the same, but to another level." Wary of explaining further, he decides it's easier to let the music talk for him. We go to the studio down the hall, where today's goal is the album's introduction, an instrumental track over which he will offer some as yet unwritten reflections on his life as a survivor.

Mario Winans, a musician-producer, awaits Puffy in one of the control rooms. Puffy has no musical training, so it falls to people like Winans to execute his vision, which can be as precise as a few hummed bars to be transposed for strings or as vague as "Make it sound real dark and shit." On Puffy's command, Winans begins a playback of the various elements Puffy has ordered up. First come the strings: soft, earnest first-thaw-of-spring strings, followed by a lilting piano figure, very *Young and the Restless* hospital scene, followed by—

No, something's wrong. Playback is stopped. "See, what I want there is for the strings to change, to get . . . *darker*," Puffy tells Winans. "And later on we gotta throw in some effects, backwards shit . . . just . . . just . . . fucking Armageddon!" A sound-effects guy is summoned from the next room, a beanpole white kid with a billy-goat beard and a Bazooka Joe turtleneck.

The intro, once more, from the top. Strings . . . piano . . . and now, with a wave of Puffy's hand, a new element: a church choir singing the Latin Mass.

"I want it to sound like an introduction to the record *and* to me," Puffy explains to Winans and the beanpole guy, shouting over the high-volume playback. "The Catholic choir—that's 'cause I'm Catholic. Well, not a practicing Catholic, but I was an altar boy."

Playback stops. There is some discussion about when, precisely, the Catholic choir should come in. Notes are made. Playback resumes.

Strings . . . piano . . . Catholic choir . . . everything coming in on cue . . . and now . . . cue . . . the . . . *bagpipes!*

Frneeeeee! Frneeeeee! The bagpipes wail on top of the choir, under which the piano still lilts, under which the first-thaw-of-spring strings still sing. It's a pretty thick goulash of sound at this point, but there's still one more ingredient to ladle in. Puffy points, Winans moves a knob, and then, fading in slowly . . . *boom-boom-THWACK, boom-boom-THWACK*—the famous clapped percussion figure from Queen's "We Will Rock You." Everyone loves this. Satisfied smiles all around.

Later Puffy explains that there's nothing free-form about his use of these sounds. "They all have symbolic value," he says. "Like, the church sound was a really happy and quiet type of sound—that's the way I was brought up. The bagpipes are just so dark and strong and warlike. It's more representing the dark side of my life—pains that I felt. And the 'We Will Rock You'—that's just something coming. It's coming at you, building up to the drama . . . the drama of my life."

This is how Puffy works: by *feel*—untutored, but sure of the effect he's after. "Come With Me," Puffy's hit from last summer's *Godzilla* sound track, was basically a bolt from the blue. He never actively sought out the sawing guitar figure from Led Zeppelin's "Kashmir." He simply heard it somewhere—on the radio or in a TV advertisement—and it evoked something. "I hear Zeppelin and it just makes me feel angry," he says. So he persuaded Jimmy Page to reprise the famous riff, rapped some rageful nonsense on top ("You bull me / Ridicule me . . . You want to end me?"), added a new bridge, and voilà!—another Top 10 hit.

For a music person, Puffy is remarkably unscholarly about music. Whereas other hip-hop acts pride themselves on the obscurity of their samples, he has always reached for the obvious: David Bowie's "Let's Dance," the Police's "Every Breath You Take," Grandmaster Flash's "The Message." "I don't even have a record collection," he says. "It's not that much thought that's put into it. It's just organic." As he's happily learned, gut sentiments tethered to familiar music equals hits. Puffy is, in a word, middlebrow. Further along in the *Forever* sessions, I enter the studio to find him behind a microphone in the sound booth, working on a rap in progress: "Livin' in a contradiction / I'm sinnin' and lustin' after all these women . . ." The backing track is a loop of Christopher Cross's "Sailing."

I ask Puffy how he arrived at the idea to use "Sailing," which is as emblematic of late-seventies MOR rock—and therefore as antithetical to hip-hop—as you can get. It's simple, he says. The song is about God. "And the sample, just listening to it, it made me feel free. And God makes me feel free."

This musical choice, and the earnest sentiment underlying it, is very much that of a well-brought-up middle-class kid who attended a suburban Catholic school in the 1980s—which is exactly what Puffy is. He describes his childhood as pleasant and uneventful, with one major exception—the fact that on January 26, 1972, when he was two, his father, Melvin Combs, was shot dead at the age of thirty-three on Central Park West. "I ain't never cried about it or nothing," he says. "I didn't even know him—you know what I'm saying?" All he really knows, at least in terms of what he's been told, is that he's a chip off the old block. "Oh, just like your father," he says, mimicking his relatives. Melvin Combs dealt drugs and ran numbers and was good enough at these jobs to keep his family living well in Harlem, with a Mercedes for Dad and a fur for Mom—ghetto fabulous in its inchoate form. When Melvin died, the victim of a deal gone bad, the Combs family was restructured as a matriarchy, with Puffy and his kid sister, Keisha, being raised with a firm hand by their mother, Janice, and her mother.

Puffy was twelve when the family relocated to the suburb of Mount Vernon, New York— "money-earnin' Mount Vernon," as it's called in *No Way Out's* acknowledgments. "A nice two-family house," he recalls. "A lawn, stand-up pool in the backyard. The block I lived on was, like, eighty percent white."

Puffy attended Mount St. Michael's Academy, a private Catholic school, and the family got by on the money his grandmother earned as a nurse at an old folks' home and on what Janice earned working part-time as a kindergarten teacher and a model. (Janice Combs is spectacular-looking to this day. I meet her briefly one night at Daddy's House, when she stops by en route from Birdland, the Midtown jazz club. You can't miss her, she wears a fine, shimmery honey-blond wig and a beige skirt suit that shows a lot of leg: Mom as Ikette.) It was as a twelve-year-old that Puffy discovered his innate entrepreneurial flair. You needed to be thirteen to get a paper route, so he doctored his birth certificate; there was also a waiting list, so Puffy bought his route off another kid against a promise of his first three weeks' earnings.

By the time Puffy got to Howard University in the late eighties, he was a full-bore huckster, ostensibly majoring in business, but truly majoring in party promotion. He was, by his own admission, something of a loner on campus, the driven, dandified capitalist freak. "I was always moving, always hyper," he says. At the same time, the Bronx-born Andre Harrell was flourishing as a sort of Puffy prototype, having left Def Jam Records in 1986, at the age of twenty-five, to start his own label, Uptown Records. In 1990, Sean Combs, a college sophomore, presented himself at Harrell's office in a white oxford shirt and a polka-dot tie and was taken on as an intern. From there it was the straight Jewboy-in-the-WillMo mailroom trajectory: hustle and ingratiation quickly rewarded with power. "He called me Mr. Harrell, even though I asked him to call me Andre," says Harrell. "The first thing I asked him to do was get me a tape from the studio. He came back with it in five minutes. The studio was ten blocks away." Puffy never went back to Howard. Within a year, Puffy was Uptown's ace A&R man and was chummy enough with Harrell to address him as Dre Boogie. He developed Uptown's best and most sensual acts: the enticingly *difficile* Mary J. Blige, the flagrantly onanistic male quartet Jodeci. But his near instant success imbued Puffy with too much bluster. Though he was Harrell's favorite, his *lemme gimme fuck you* manner rippled unattractively through Uptown's staff. "It was a young company; everyone was around Puffy's age," says Harrell. "And the other young people could not get away with the things he could get away with. They all thought they had to act that way—I had a whole company of potentially disruptive employees."

Puffy was made an example of in 1993. "I deserved to get fired," he says now. He remained on good terms with Harrell, though; last year, after Harrell was ousted from his post-Uptown job as the president of Motown, Puffy invited him to join Bad Boy, where he now works as the label's president.

"The new album is gonna—hullo? Yeah. No. Wait—is gonna—hullo? Yeah, get me Benny, Andre, and David Anthony—is—sorry, hold on—hullo? Yeah, it's Puff. Call up Timbaland and tell him to meet us later in the studio—[singing] *oh, mercy, mercy me*—hullo? Yeah? What! *Daaamn*, let's try to have some better communication 'round here! That shit's corny to me! Corny to me! Hold on—hullo?—yo, pull over at that McDonald's—corny to me!—hullo? Get me Norma—damn, Clint Eastwood don't *show nothin'*!—hullo? Yeah. Send it out! E-mail ev'ry muthafucka!—hullo? No, the Timbaland tracks were unacceptable—hullo? Hullo? *Wassuuup, nigga?* . . . Yeah, we gonna have three summers of madness! I wanna look back and say, 'Damn, I did it!' I'm gonna—hold on—fish sandwich and fries—I'm gonna go to Woodstock this summer. I ain't never been to the south of France. I wanna go to the Cannes Film Festival. I wanna go to *A*frica. I wanna walk *butt-naked* on a beach where there's . . . other *butt-naked people*."

This is the sound of Puffy in his chauffeured Lincoln Navigator SUV, simultaneously watching *The Outlaw—Josey Wales* on the custom-installed DVD screen, listening to *Marvin Gaye Live* on the CD player, and holding down five conversations—with me, with the driver, with the person on the car phone, and with the two people on either side of call-waiting on his headset cellular.

Today he is headed eastward for *GQ*'s photo shoot, to the house on Long Island's East End, the vaunted "East Hampton mansion" of press reports. Last year, on Labor Day weekend, he had a White Party there, a wear-your-spectators-while-you-still-can sort of affair, and it attracted the likes of Martha Stewart, *Rolling Stone* founder Jann Wenner, and Ron Perelman, the billionaire chairman of Revlon. That a black kid born in Harlem could have tossed a party attended by rich white swells in their own summer playground was seen by some as a signal moment in hip-hop's assimilation into the mainstream.

"Not what they make it out to be, right?" says Puffy upon our arrival. "It's a summerhouse—that's all." True enough. The house is neither a mansion nor in the chic Georgia Pond area; it's in an outlying section on the bay side, and it's not a clapboard Stanford White masterpiece out of *Gatsby* but a stuccoed three-bedroom modern with an ordinary rectangular pool and a scrubby back-yard—nice, but bespeaking *prosperous optometrist* more than *entertainment mogul.*

Still, even on a dull off-season spring day, you can see the house's potential as partay central, as it was known last summer, Puffy's first as a Hamptons homeowner. The rooms on the house's upper floor are connected by a nautical-style catwalk, which overlooks the airy, open-plan living room—a natural go-go-cage effect, which would seem to lend itself well to the kind of undulating-buttocks dancing that the ladies do in Puffy's videos. The master bedroom shows no personal touches except for a photograph of Puffy with his one-year-old son, Christian, whose mother is Puffy's current girlfriend, Kim Porter. (He has another son, five-year-old Justin, from a previous relationship.) Off the bedroom is a little Juan Perón balcony that overlooks the pool. Puffy says he jumped off it a few times last year. "Party trick."

Benny Medina, Puffy's forty-one-year-old manager and business partner, does not rise to greet his client, whose arrival at the house he preceded. He is receiving a manicure from a girl in a white lab coat at the dining-room table. As Puffy disappears into makeup and wardrobe, a flute of Cristal in his hand, the jocose, fast-talking Medina, who wears a diamond stud in each ear, holds forth on his and Puffy's shared entrepreneurial spirit. "The only way to figure out a twenty-five-hour day is for you to think that hour is there. You *find* the twenty-fifth hour," he says.

It must be true. Consider, for a moment, the breadth of the Puffy empire: Bad Boy Records; Bad Boy Film and Television (whose first feature project, *King Suckerman*, will be released through Miramax); *Notorious* magazine, a glossy monthly that Puffy recently purchased (his first issue featured the cover line "The Death of Rock and Roll: Why White Boys Don't Rule Anymore"); Sean John clothing (Puffy: "And we're expanding to big and tall; Sean John Shorties, which is for the kids; and Sean John Ladies"); Bad Boy Technologies (Benny: "We're developing e-commerce opportunities"); Bad Boy Management, which has a virtual lock on hip-hop's top producing talent; Justin's, the upscale soul-food restaurant (locations in New York, Atlanta, and soon, Chicago); Justin Combs Publishing, Puffy's music-publishing arm; and Daddy's House, the studio, which is not to be confused with Daddy's House Social Programs Inc., Puffy's not-for-profit charitable organization. In addition, Puffy is trying to get into sports management, hopes to own an NBA franchise, and is looking to form an "urban advertising and marketing company." And, of course, there is the music. Puffy expects 1999 to be a replay of the big year, 1997, during which he enjoyed an unprecedented twenty-five-week streak, spanning from March to September, when the number one spot on the singles chart was held by either a Puff Daddy song or a song he'd produced.

This year Bad Boy is reprising its '97 blockbuster-artist trifecta: Mase, Bad Boy's lovable-imp rapper ("Definitely my Sammy Davis, Jr.," Puffy says), has *Double Up*, which came out on June 15; Puff Daddy's *Forever* is coming out in August; and a posthumous Notorious B.I.G. album, *Born Again*, is due in the fall. "We'll probably have advance orders of fifty million for just those three combined," says Arista's Clive Davis. The Biggie album, Puffy says, is "tracks you haven't heard before. Raw hip-hop. Just real raw." Perhaps too raw: in the studio, I hear Puffy and Harve Pierre, a Bad Boy executive, joking about the extraraunchy material that won't make the cut. Pierre, doing Biggie: "Young girl, fresh and green / No hair between / You know what I *mean*?" Puffy: "It's just *too ill.*"

Puffy's big 1997 inaugurated a prolonged coming-out party for hip-hop that reached its apex this past February, when *Time* magazine ran a celebratory cover story entitled "Hip-Hop Nation." Actually, hip-hop's assimilation into the mainstream had begun years before (to wit: Blondie's 1980 rappish hit "Rapture" and Run-D.M.C.'s collaboration with Aerosmith on 1986's "Walk This

Way"). But it took something greater to jar people into recognizing that hip-hop had become important, the chief engine of American youth culture—and that something was money.

The multimillionaire-mogul status of Puffy and fellow label heads Russell Simmons and Master P, the twenty-eight-year-old founder of the Baton Rouge–based No Limit label, seems to have snuck up on people: *How the hell did these guys get so rich?* The numbers are indeed staggering. The forty-one-year-old Simmons, already a wealthy man, is in the process of selling his shares of Def Jam, the company he founded in 1984, to the Universal Music Group for $100 million. Master P, whose real name is Percy Miller, was tenth on *Forbes*'s 1998 list of the forty top-earning entertainers in America, with a personal income of $56.5 million. Hard behind at number fifteen was Puffy, with an income of $53.5 million.

Among the most visually potent images to come out of popular culture in recent years is a scene from the video for "Mo Money Mo Problems," a Notorious B.I.G. single featuring Puffy and Mase. As the song begins, Puffy and his posse are shown emerging from a car, an imposing group of young black men, advancing in ominous slo-mo . . . except the car is a Bentley, the men are wearing beautiful linens and sweater-vests, and they're off to storm the links—to play golf, the most racially exclusionary of sports. "The message," says Puffy of the video, "is that we've arrived."

Beyond the imagery, much hoo-ha has been made of Puffy's acquaintanceships with such acutely white persons as Donald Trump and Jerry Seinfeld—how weird and unfathomable the juxtaposition! Puffy dismisses such observations as "corny," his all-purpose term for that which he finds disagreeable. "OK, I know I'm young and black," he says, "and these people, they are a little richer and stuff. But they're just people."

This is the long-awaited moment, the realization of the self-determinist template for black American empowerment: black men founding and running successful businesses that generate jobs, opportunities, and hope for black youth. It was telling to hear the father of Isaiah Shoels, the lone black victim of the Columbine High School massacre, speak sadly of his son's unfulfilled dream, to grow up to be an entertainment mogul like Master P. Not a basketball player, not a performer, but an *entrepreneur*.

Puffy says he got goose bumps when he heard about Shoels's dream. "That definitely touched me," he says. "A couple of years ago, there wasn't an outlet. So now we just put another thing into the game."

Still, it's not been a national lovefest for Puffy. No one holds him up in the same saintly light as they do Lauryn Hill, the face of *Time*'s "Hip-Hop Nation" cover. Lauryn Hill you're not allowed *not* to like—she's the embodiment of black strength and beauty; she conforms neatly to the Bill Cosby–Alvin Poussaint Precepts of Noble Blackness. But Puffy? Puffy polarizes. He is forever controversial. The mention of his name elicits a knowing smirk. What is it about him that gets under people's skin?

Puffy's been wondering the same thing. He addresses this very subject in his new single, "Public Enemy 2000." He raps a verse of it for my benefit.

Let me ask you, what you got against me?
Is it my girl, or is it the Bentley?

Is it the house; is it the Bentley? Yes and yes, Puff. There's a sense that you're disgustingly ostentatious.

"My race needs to see that, though," he says. "You know, if you're a white person, you've seen the Kennedys, the Rockefellers, the Rothschilds. You have history pictures of white people living affluently. You go to golf courses. You've been invited to country clubs. We haven't—you know what I'm saying?"

But it's one thing to offer a positive example and another to be a show-off. That birthday party he threw for himself last year! The one at Cipriani's Wall Street restaurant, where the initials PD, for Puff Daddy, were projected onto the ceiling of the beaux arts ballroom while down below a thousand guests, from Trump to Muhammad Ali to Duchess Fergie, awaited his calculatedly late arrival—in a white, three-piece suit, no less. And it was only his *twenty-ninth* birthday! So dangerously extravagant, so suggestive of a man going too far, so redolent of Hammer circa *Too Legit to Quit* . . .

It's suggested to Puffy that his birthday party was the most egomaniacal thing in the world.

Puffy smiles slyly. "Yeah, it wuhzzz," he says. "It was . . . my *birthday* party! When you throw a fuckin' birthday party, you be like, 'It's my party and I'll cry if I want to! I'm not gonna celebrate the way you tell me to celebrate! I'm gonna do it the way I want to do it!' I had a ball."

In this moment, Puffy briefly becomes something you'd never imagine him to be: endearing. That mirthful, singsongy "it wuhzzz" is like nothing he's ever committed to tape: which makes you realize what a curiously joyless public presence he has, especially for someone so famously high-living. In photographs and videos, his face is always the same: blank; lips parted slightly, eyes either unexpressive or hidden behind shades—what behavioral psychologists call flat affect. It's an especially strange sight when he's dancing, since he's a good dancer: the body dips and spins with exuberance, but the face remains impassive. It's like watching the dancing baby on the Internet.

This perceived lack of humor goes a long way toward explaining Puffy's unlovability—it makes him seem like one of those paranoid, armed, gated-community rich people. When I tell Puffy it's a relief to see him smile, that it becomes him, he takes it as a public-relations suggestion: *Must smile more; must be happy.* It's something he's been consciously working on. "I made a decision, as a person, that I was gonna be happy this year," he says half-convincingly.

This is a funny old time for hip-hop, uncharted waters, pointing toward a future where hospital wings and university dorms will be named for philanthropic rappers and label bosses, and masons will etch the benefactors' tags, rather than their real names, into the stone facades: MASTER P CENTER FOR APPLIED MATHEMATICS; SEAN "PUFFY" COMBS BIRTHING PAVILION. (Already there is a Sean "Puffy" Combs and Janice Combs Endowed Scholarship Fund at Howard University.) Like the parallel explosion of Internet wealth among young white and Asian-American men, the mogulization of hip-hop is well past the fad phase and is now a crucial fact of American business life. Down the road, Puffy might be seen as the William K. Vanderbilt of his time, and ticket holders from Fargo and East Moline might queue up a hundred years from now at the corner of Park and Seventy-fifth to see the roped-off suite of rooms where Kim Porter once nursed baby Christian.

In any event, Puffy will be around for the foreseeable future. With the decks apparently cleared of any Steve Stoute–related messiness, he is free to continue his grand happiness experiment. In the coming seasons, he may well succeed in replicating the narrative arc of his friend Donald Trump, the public figure to whom, in the end, he invites closest comparison. ("It was Puffy who told me there are four major rap songs that use the word *Trump* in the sense of 'very Trump,'" says Trump.) Like Puffy, Trump burst upon the scene as an admired, precocious empire builder but through ubiquity, egotism, and sheer ridiculousness soon wore out his welcome. Trump, however, managed to harness his grandiosity and cure it into a selling point, a step toward lovability, and now, somehow, we all feel the world wouldn't be as much fun without him. Puffy, if he manages things correctly, can pull this trick off.

He warns, though, that he won't do the happy thing if he doesn't feel it. "I can't be phony," he says. "I got a lot of different moods and personalities. Like, the next time you see me, I may just be in a totally different mood."

"You may attack me with a champagne bottle," I say.

"I won't hit you with a bottle," Puffy shoots back firmly and seriously. "I might punch you in your eye, though." No smile. "Naw, I'm joking."

GQ / August 1999

The Hip-Hop Nation

Whose Is It? In the End, Black Men Must Lead

TOURÉ

I live in a Country no mapmaker will ever respect. A place with its own language, culture, and history. It is as much a nation as Italy or Zambia. A place my countrymen call the Hip-Hop Nation, purposefully invoking all of the jingoistic pride that nationalists throughout history have leaned on. Our path to nationhood has been paved by a handful of fathers: Muhammad Ali with his ceaseless bravado, Bob Marley with his truth-telling rebel music, Huey Newton with his bodacious political style, James Brown with his obsession with funk.

We are a nation with no precise date of origin, no physical land, no single chief. But if you live in the Hip-Hop Nation, if you are not merely a fan of the music, but a daily imbiber of the culture, if you sprinkle your conversation with phrases like *off the meter* (for something that's great) or *got me open* (for something that gives an explosive positive emotional release), if you know why Dutch Masters make better blunts than Phillies (they're thinner), if you know at a glance why Allen Iverson is hip-hop and Grant Hill is not, if you feel the murders of Tupac Shakur and the Notorious B.I.G. in the 1997–98 civil war were assassinations (no other word fits), if you can say yes to all of the questions (and a yes to some doesn't count), then you know the Hip-Hop Nation is a place as real as America on a pre-Columbus atlas. It's there even though the rest of you ain't been there yet.

The Nation exists in any place where hip-hop music is being played or hip-hop attitude is being exuded. Once I went shopping for a Macintosh. The salesman, a wiry twentysomething white guy rattled on about Macs, then, looking at the rapper, or what we call an MC, on my T-shirt, said, "You like Nas? Did you hear him rhyme last night on the 'Stretch and Bobbito' show?" I felt as if my jaw had dropped. He had invoked a legendary hip-hop radio show broadcast once a week on college radio at two in the morning. It was as if we were secret agents, and he had uttered the code phrase that revealed him to be my contact. We stood for an hour talking MCs and DJs, beats and flows, turning that staid computer store into an outpost of the Hip-Hop Nation.

The Nation's pioneers were a multiracial bunch—whites were among the early elite graffiti artists and Latinos were integral to the shaping of DJing and MCing, B-boying (break dancing) and general hip-hop style. Today's Nation makes brothers of men black, brown, yellow, and white. But this world was built to worship urban black maleness: the way we speak, walk, dance, dress, think. We are revered by others, but our leadership is and will remain black. As it should.

We are a nation with our own Gods and devils, traditions and laws (one of them is to not share them with outsiders), but there never has been and never will be a president of the Hip-Hop Nation. Like black America, we're close-knit, yet still too fractious for one leader. Instead, a powerful senate charts our future. That senate is made up of our leading MCs, their every album and single is a bill or referendum proposing linguistic, musical, and topical directions for the culture. Is Compton a cool spot? Can Edie Brickell, an embodiment of American female whiteness, be the source for a sample? Is a thick, countrified Southern accent something we want to hear? Is police brutality still a rallying point? Like a politician with polls and focus groups, an MC must carefully calibrate his musical message because once his music is released, the people vote with their dollars in the store and their butts in the club, ignoring certain MCs and returning them to private life, while anointing others, granting them more time on our giant national microphone.

Unlike rhythm and blues, hip-hop has a strong memoiristic impulse, meaning our senator MCs speak of themselves, their neighborhoods, the people around them, playing autobiographer, reporter, and oral historian. Telling the stories as they actually happened is what is meant by the catchphrase *keeping it real*. Outsiders laugh that the hallowed phrase is seemingly made hollow by obvious self-mythologizing—materialistic boasts that would be beyond even the Donald or tales of crimes that would be envied by a Gotti. But this bragging is merely people speaking of the people they dream of being, which, of course, is a reflection of the people they are.

How do you get into this senate? The answer is complex, involving both rhyming technique and force of personality. To be a great MC you must have a hypnotizing flow—a cadence and delivery that get inside the drum and bass patterns and create their own rhythm line. You must have a magnetic voice—it can be deliciously nasal like Q-Tip's, or delicate and singsongy like Snoop Doggy Dogg's, or deep-toned like that of Rakim, who sounds as commanding as Moses—but it must be a compelling sound. And you must say rhymes with writerly details, up-to-the-minute slang, bold punch lines, witty metaphors, and original political or sociological insights.

But, again like a politician, to be a great MC you must seem like an extension of the masses and, simultaneously, an extraordinary individual. There must be a certain down-homeness about you, a way of carrying yourself that replicates the way people in your home base feel about life. You must be the embodiment of your audience.

At the same time, you must seem greater than your audience. You must come across as supercool—an attitude based on toughness or sex appeal or intellect or bravado that inspires your listeners to say, "I'd like to be you."

In the first decade and a half since the first hip-hop record was released in 1979, hip-hop was a national conversation—about urban poverty and police brutality, the proliferation of guns and the importance of safe sex, as well as the joy of a good party—in which the only speakers were black men.

In recent years that conversation has opened. Hip-hop has become more democratic, cracking the monopoly that black men from New York and L.A. have long held over the Hip-Hop Nation Senate.

Traditionally, hip-hop has been hypermodern, disdaining the surreal for gritty images of urban life. But Missy Elliott and her producer Timbaland have constructed a postmodern esthetic that manifests, on her latest album, *Da Real World*, in references to the sci-fi film *The Matrix* and videos in which Missy dresses as if she were in a scene from the 1982 movie *Blade Runner*. Her music also has a futuristic feel, from Timbaland's spare, propulsive beats filled with quirky sounds that evoke science fiction to Missy's experiments with singing and rhyming, as well as using onomatopoeias in her rhymes. The duo have become part of the Nation's sonic vanguard, as well as door-openers for a new genre: hip-hop sci-fi.

Groups from the South Coast like Goodie Mob, Eightball and MJG, and Outkast have brought new perspectives. (The Hip-Hop Nation reconfigures American geography with a Saul Steinberg–like eye, maximizing cities where the most important hip-hop has come from, microscoping other places. When we speak of the East Coast, we mean the five boroughs of New York, Long Island, Westchester, New Jersey, and Philadelphia; by West Coast we mean Los Angeles, Compton, Long Beach, Vallejo, and Oakland; and the region made up of Atlanta, New Orleans, Virginia, Miami, and Memphis is called the South Coast.)

Outkast is a pair of Atlanta MCs, Big Boi (Antwan Patton) and Dre (Andre Benjamin), who are not new to many in the Hip-Hop Nation. But with the success of *Aquemini*, their third album, and months of touring as the opening act for Lauryn Hill, they are new to power within hip-hop. Their hip-hop mixes the cerebralness of New York rappers and the George Clinton–drenched funk favored out West with a particularly Southern musicality, soulfulness, twang-drenched rhymes, and Baptist-church-like euphoric joy.

But the most polarizing and revolutionary new entry to the Hip-Hop Senate is Eminem (born Marshall Mathers). There have been white MCs before him, but none have been as complex. Either they were clearly talentless (like Vanilla Ice) or they worshiped blackness (like MC Serch of 3rd Bass). Eminem is different. The fervency of fans black and white marveling at his skill and laughing at his jokes has kept him in office, despite those offended by his whiny white-boy shock-jock shtick.

He is an original voice in the national conversation that is hip-hop because he speaks of the dysfunctionality of his white-trash world—his absentee father, his drugged-out mom, his daughter's hateful mother, his own morally bankrupt conscience. With Eminem the discussion turns to problems in the white community, or at least—because he is from a black neighborhood in Detroit—to the problems of whites in the black community. On a recent song (called "Busa Rhyme" from Missy's new album *Da Real World*) Eminem rhymes darkly: "I'm homicidal / and suicidal / with no friends / holdin' a gun with no handle / just a barrel at both ends." Finally, someone has arrived to represent the Dylan Klebolds and Eric Harrises of America.

A rash of overprotectiveness within our Nation keeps many from enjoying the hip-hop of a sneering white MC, but why shouldn't we welcome a frank discussion of white maladies into our home when millions of white people allow our MCs into their homes to talk about our disorders every day?

The Hip-Hop Nation Senate is swelling to include whites, women, and Southerners, but don't expect that Senate to become a true melting pot anytime soon. As long as upper-class white men stay in charge of the U.S. Senate, urban black men will remain our leading speakers. Hip-hop's history is long enough to grant us the maturity to open our world, but America is still white enough that we know how we need our own oasis.

It all began with a few parties. Jams in New York City parks thrown by DJs like Kool Herc, Grandmaster Flash, and Afrika Bambaataa. To your eyes it would've appeared to be a rapper in a public park, a DJ behind him, his cables plugged into the street lamp, the police not far away, waiting for just the right moment to shut it all down. But to us those parks were the center of a universe. The cops—or rather, five-oh (from the television series *Hawaii Five-O*)—were Satan. The music—James Brown, Sly Stone, Funkadelic, and anything with a stone cold bass and drum rhythm you could rhyme over—breathed meaning and substance and soul into our bodies. It gave life. It was God.

From behind the turntables in his roped-off pulpit in the park, the DJ gave a rousing sermon sonically praising God's glory. Then up stepped the high priest, the conduit between God and you—the MC. How crucial was he? In 1979, in its seminal song, "Rapper's Delight," the Sugarhill Gang explained that even Superman was useless if he couldn't flow: "He may be able to fly all through the night / But can he rock a party til the early light?"

A few years later, in the early eighties, a trickle of cassettes began appearing in urban mom-and-pop record stores like Skippy White's on Blue Hill Avenue in Mattapan Square in Boston. As a twelve-year-old I would walk there from my father's office. Every other month or so a new hip-hop tape would arrive, direct from New York City: Run-D.M.C. . . . MC Shan . . . the Fat Boys. A kid on an allowance could own all the hip-hop albums ever made. For all the force of the music, the culture was so small and precious you held it in your hands as delicately as a wounded bird.

In the mid-eighties hip-hop won the nation's attention and was branded a fad that would soon die like disco. Hip-hoppers closed ranks, constructed a wall and instituted a siege mentality. We became like Jews, a tribe that knew how close extinction was and responded to every attack and affront, no matter how small, as if it were a potential death blow. Where Jews battle anti-Semitic attitudes and actions, we fought fans who are not orthodox and music not purely concerned with art. Where Jews hold holidays that celebrate specific legends, ancestors, and miracles, hip-hoppers spoke of the old school with a holy reverence and urged new jacks to know their history. Our Zionism was the Hip-Hop Nation.

By the late eighties and early nineties mainstreaming had arrived bringing powerful gifts, as the devil always does. Now our music was broadcast on prime-time MTV and our political views, via Chuck D and KRS-One, were heard on CNN and *Nightline*. Hip-hop, like jazz and rock and roll before it, had become the defining force of a generation. It was not going to die. The siege mentality subsided.

The guards at the gate were retired. The fan base grew and the music diversified, which caused the fan base to grow larger still and the music to diversify further. But we continue to live in America, to suffer the daily assaults of racism. And our sanity continues to rely on having a place where the heroes look like us and play by our rules. As long as being a black man is a cross to bear and not a benediction, you can find me and my comrades locked inside one of those mass therapy sessions called a party, inside that tricoastal support group called the Hip-Hop Nation.

The New York Times / August 22, 1999

2000s:

Get Rich
or Die Tryin'

Many of the writers included in this anthology who began their careers writing about hip-hop have become successful authors, on-air personalities, screenwriters, producers, and directors, and some have set out to divorce themselves from the "hip-hop journalist" label altogether. Besides the fact that many of these writers have matured and don't identify with the genre's current incarnation, the term *hip-hop journalist* does not have the irreverent ring it did in the 1980s before the mainstreaming of the culture, or the thrill of documenting its infinite potential in the nineties. In itself, it has become as vague as, say, the term *urban*, which is now used to describe everything that falls under hip-hop's ample umbrella. Not even our own Gatsbys are interested in reinventing the wheel set in motion by hip-hop's founding fathers, evident in the lack of originality plaguing the loudest element of the genre, its music.

Exaggerated images of what white America believes to be authentic depictions of street reality for its ravenous consumers in Middle America—which in all fairness hip-hop's elite are all too happy to hawk—are used to illustrate everything from a rapper's romantic panorama of violence to clothing, fast food, and soft drinks. Because hip-hop journalism is, in general, a reflection of its most reported tenet—rap music—many disenfranchised journalists feel that reporting is now mirroring much of the music in its current state, which has regressed into a redundant and, well, prosaic brand of crude individualism, with relatively few exceptions.

Penning articles about rap music, I was told recently by a frustrated colleague in his early thirties, felt like an exercise in writing insipid advertorials for the Versace brand, jewelry, and guns. Rather than documenting the decade's colorful sonic palette of artists, the music now bumping from your Jeeps sounds, for the most part, like one seamless jingle for Mercedes-Benz Fashion Week.

Hip-hop journalism has taken on a new meaning since the days when editors at *The New York Times* sent Nelson George, pitching an article about Kurtis Blow, a rejection note saying the article was "too specialized for the *Times* audience." Today, coverage has more to do with staying relevant than an inherent zeal to critically document the genre as the alternative press did back in the 1980s. In addition, in an effort to place his or her clientele in magazines with the highest circulation and crossover appeal, the music publicist has played a significant role in controlling the access writers have to the artists they represent. The artists today are savvy, media-trained businessmen and women, more so than hip-hop artists from the past, and are more careful about making any political statements that might incite or upset any potential endorsers. In our lifetime, we have borne witness to a counterculture that has grown, for better and for worse, into a billion-dollar industry that has become as American as apple pie and Osama bin Laden WANTED posters. Hip-hop journalism therefore is as challenging to report today as the music and culture is static.

The articles featured in this young decade take a critical look at the ebb and flow of hip-hop's erratic temperature. While his lyrics take a refreshing break from all that blings in hip-hop, "the promotion of 50 Cent from bootleg king to god of the streets was PR genius . . . [where] crack-era nostalgia [is] taken to the extreme," writes *Village Voice* political reporter Ta-Nehisi Coates. On the cover of *Rolling Stone*, 50 Cent exposed one of his nine bullet holes—reminders of his previous career in the narcotics trade—catapulting him into the persona of a street deity of sorts. But in reality, reports Coates, "the streets that gangsta rappers claim as their source are no longer as angry as they are sad." And while black-on-black crime has been dipping considerably since the midnineties, America is still rushing to buy into a myth of a sinister black man, while gangsta rap "lumbers across the landscape of pop," professing its realness to the masses.

Writer Sacha Jenkins, who cofounded two of the most popular underground magazines in the nineties—*Beat Down* and *ego trip*—began his love affair with hip-hop culture in his youth as a graffiti enthusiast. Considered an expert in graffiti art, he is one of the most popular voices in the genre. In "The Writing on the Wall," he ponders the potential rise of gangs and crack-cocaine violence in hip-hop's prodigal graffiti subculture by chronicling a "modern-day tragedy in Gotham," where young black men kill one another rather than risk the chance of invisibility—their names unknown to fans.

My essay reviewing Lil' Kim's *Notorious K.I.M.* album echoes the misogyny that was rampant in hip-hop culture ten years ago, wherein women today are still objectified in rap's lyrics and are at times willing participants in inflating existing negative stereotypes. There also still exists a turbulent and confusing relationship between men and women, one that seems to break down further each year, while homophobia and (another irony) homoeroticism become more evident in rap lyrics and most visibly in music videos.

But let's be fair; not every aspect of the culture should invoke a hypercritical stance or even merits one. At times, articles are just meant to document the lives and legacies of our icons. Mary J. Blige's profile, written by former chief editor and style maverick Emil Wilbekin, who's been a part of *Vibe* in various capacities since its inception, is an honest, well-balanced look at the roller-coaster rides of our generation's self-professed (and proven) "Queen of Hip-Hop Soul." Jam Master Jay's extended obituary is written by one of hip-hop's most important scribes, the voice on Public Enemy's infamous "Don't Believe the Hype" single, Harry Allen. While Allen, known as the "Media Assassin," has been celebrated as one of hip-hop journalism's pioneering and most respected voices, one of his favorite articles of this new decade was Jay's eulogy because it served as a melancholy reminder of the ever-present violence in hip-hop. The article is structured in a way that aficionados of all ages can bear witness to Jay's healthy contributions to the culture, proving, like many of the articles in this anthology, to be more than a reflection of the consumer-driven undercurrents steering hip-hop to an uncertain artistic future.

Hip-hop is relatively still young—no one can gauge exactly what's going to happen in the future—although Bob Christgau's piece (and Fidel Castro's public "nationalization" of Cuban hip-hop) might very well second my emotion that the international scene is becoming a rather attractive beat to cover. Regardless of what form it may take, the culture will survive its current pimps and reinvent itself before it becomes indistinguishable from other forms of pop music and culture. And, hopefully, it will give a new generation of journalists who were reared in part by hip-hop culture something to write about that will not only rule the world, as it does now, but, as the rap sovereign Rakim said back in the day, "move the crowd."

Fool's Paradise

RAQUEL CEPEDA

It makes me wanna holler every time I hear someone ludicrously tout Lil' Kim as a Generation Now feminist, thus veiling the incredibly low self-esteem neatly tucked away in purple pasties, blue contacts, and blond wigs. On the (very) late *Notorious K.I.M.*, Kim isn't celebrating female sexuality and liberation; she's just gearing her salacious appetite for anal sex and deep-throating your man into hyperdrive (taking a moment to mourn her late lover, Notorious B.I.G.). The kitsch begins with a Puff Daddy–produced courtroom skit-drama, "Lil' Drummer Boy," featuring Redman, Cee-Lo of the Goodie Mob, and Kim hailing herself as the "first female king of rap." And in a sense she might as well be, because Ms. Jones is now the archetype of the so-called gangsta-fabricated goddess Niggas With Attitudes engendered a decade ago: the woman as a holy chitlin and occasional rump. Queen Bee became the vanguard for happy hos everywhere. And still, I'm not mad at her hustle, just deflated at times by one familiar melody after the other forcing me to shake my ass nostalgically. Unlike the merely watered-down samples riddling her *Hard Core* debut, *Notorious* cold-jacks snippets of classic track after track. Not to mention that, since Kim's X-rated coming out, other slap-happy hos like Trina and Strings have made Queen Bee's lyrics sound, uh, prosaic (discuss).

K.I.M.'s first single, "No Matter What They Say," grows on you because of the old-school "interpolations" and Puffy's trademark hypnotic rantings ("yeah, uh, don't stop, come on . . ."). Producer Darren "Limitless" Henson borrows the Latin guitar relish of Jose Feliciano's "Esio Es el Guaguanco"— befittingly enough, an Afro-Cuban type of rumba celebrating the very sexual rivalry between the orishas Chango and Ochun, which theme gives her track a divine swing. And just in case you're not feeling it, Henson jacks the rhythm sections of rap standards that will surely reel you in: Special Ed's "I Got It Made," the Sugarhill Gang's "Rapper's Delight," and Eric B. and Rakim's "I Know You Got Soul." And if you're still not feeling it, the accompanying video features Kim in a see-through body stocking and five-inch stilettos.

bell hooks was right when she wrote that, as with many Americans, the culture of greed validates and legitimizes Lil' Kim; so who cares if she'll ever know love, since the pursuit of money compensates for what she lacks emotionally? She's gone on record attributing her Michael Jackson–esque reinvention (painful breast implants, icy contacts, liposuction, rumored nose job, blond wigs, etc.) to a lifelong self-image problem and scores of manipulating men. And still, we cannot get past the paradox whom *Vogue*'s Andre Leon Talley calls "the black Madonna" long enough to notice. Or give a fuck.

Four years after *Hard Core*, Kim is still less interested in love than in accumulating riches and cultivating a new, unrecognizable persona as a defense mechanism against herself. Unlike Kim's killer verse on Mobb Deep's "Quiet Storm," "Suck My D**k" lyrically contradicts the song's thematic role reversal. Kim rhymes, "Met this dude named Jaleel . . . He said he'd pay me ten grand just to belly dance / Cum all on his pants." Kim turns on Jaleel by placing her burner in his mouth when he doesn't pull out the cash, but not before he and his boy Julio play her out like a ho. Still, you can't help but love the song, mainly because you couldn't help but love B.I.G.'s "Me & My B***h." The lazy, synthesized six-string guitar lick makes it prime for a freestyle session with DJ Cucumber Slice, just like it did back when B.I.G. released it the first time.

But the real ode to Kim's lover, creator, best friend, and pimp (don't front, we've all been there) is "Hold On," beautifully featuring Mary J. Blige mourning in the chorus. Over Willie Hutch's dejecting "Stormy Monday" melody, Kim reveals not the secrets of her affair with B.I.G. but a vulnerable strength by keeping the faith, as Jill Nelson would say. Mary drowns Kim's elegy, though, with the perfect way she agonizes. Mary J. Blige is the Jackie O of hip-hop soul, and we unconditionally love her for it—she wins because, like Sade and Billie Holiday before her, her suffering is sincere and graceful. Kim, on the other hand, has come off as a one-dimensional nymph and sex toy from the very beginning. So again, nobody cares.

There's one catchy yet uncreative moment after another on *Notorious K.I.M.* The lilting title track featuring B.I.G. is unspectacular; the equally coochie-popping "How Many Licks?" predictably features a curiously flamboyant Sisqo on chorus, not to mention Kim showcasing her "designer pussy." And Lil' Louis's house-music moanfest "French Kiss" serves as the almost undoctored foundation for "Custom Made (Give It to You)." Throw in a slew of supa-dupa guests—Grace Jones, Carl Thomas, the Junior M.A.F.I.A.—*Notorious K.I.M.* still wasn't worth the wait or the bootleg.

Debuting at No. 4 in *Billboard*'s 200, Lil' Kim is halfway to her professed goal of being a pop superstar like Michael Jackson. Fine. But there isn't anything womanist or even sisterly going on in *Notorious* . . . just ditties dedicated to the love of ice, c.r.e.a.m., and the glamorous life, with hiccups of humanity. Without self-love, it ain't much. It ain't much.

The Village Voice / August 15, 2000

The Writing on the Wall

Graffiti Culture Crumbles into the Violence It Once Escaped

SACHA JENKINS

They called themselves "writers" because writing is exactly what they did. For the last thirty years, the graffiti culture in New York City has been maintained and elevated by countless teen spirits you know, the kids and big kids (some of them now well into their thirties, forties, fifties even) who, with Magic Markers and spray paint, illegally project their street aliases onto mailboxes, skyscrapers, garbage trucks, and roll-down storefront riot gates, not to mention the interiors and exteriors of subway cars.

Graffiti writing in New York City has not been a profession without honor. I know this to be true because my "tag" made waves on the outsides and insides of subway cars at least ten years before the appearance of my first major byline in print. There was an honor system that guided this subculture of spraying—rules and codes and elders that this society of die-hard aerosolics stood by, for the most part. There was even a system of semi-organized warfare. If you weren't getting along with a fellow writer, if two writers were endlessly crossing out each other's handiwork and there was no cease-fire in sight, a fair, man-to-man fistfight (aka the "fair one") would be arranged. There were no squared rings or boxing gloves involved, but each writer would show up with multiple homeboys, who served as referees and muscle-flexing diplomats, just in case things got ugly in the school yard.

When a nineteen-year-old writer, Timothy "Spek" Falzone, was shot and killed last July, allegedly by a rival writer, twenty-year-old Ricky "Foke" Mouzon, it shook the graffiti world. The headline in the *New York Post* may have read "Deadly 'Tag' Game," but Spek's passing meant so much more to us writers. In the thirty years of baseball-bat-swinging and knuckle-busting that graffiti's brawls have produced, Falzone's murder is a first: never before was a writer killed at the hands of another writer because of a writing-related controversy. The diehards wondered, "Well, whatever happened to the 'fair one'?" Then, the day after September 11, just a few months after Spek's murder, I wondered if the fair one meant anything to anyone anywhere.

In New York's graffiti world, writing "kings" come into power in a few ways: some by way of innovative lettering styles and advanced painting techniques; others through sheer quantity, by "bombing" (stylized signatures and quickly done bubble-letter forms called throw-ups, which they plastered anywhere and everywhere); and still others by way of brute physical force (most writers are like daytime soap-opera gossips who thirst for the dramatic, and a great brawl can amount to even greater publicity for both winner and loser). Your average writer believes that the mightiest king wields the genius strokes of Pablo Picasso and the bloody thrusts of Julius Caesar. In the mid-1990s up through the dawn of the new millennium, the Bronx was Timothy "Spek" Falzone's personal Roman Empire; his graffiti dominated all surfaces, he kicked serious ass (literally), and he was on the verge of artistically evolving far beyond his "mad bomber" status. But thirty years of prearranged jousts could not save the young African-American father of one from the ancient savagery of modern man.

Getting Up

When *The New York Times*, in 1971, wrote about the mysterious name Taki 183 that had begun to appear everywhere in Manhattan, there was already a revolution going on. Street gangs had been a part of New York's makeup for decades, and in the 1970s, gangs with names like the Savage Skulls, the Tomahawks, the Black Spades, and the Savage Nomads owned the streets of Brownsville, Brooklyn, and the South Bronx; these organizations would often use graffiti to mark their territory in order to keep their enemies at bay, as if to say, *This is Savage Skulls turf! Watch your back, Turbans!*

Demetrius was a jobless, gangless Greek lad from Washington Heights who, in the summer of 1970, created work for himself by writing his nickname on local ice cream trucks (*Taki* is a traditional Greek diminutive for Demetrius; *183* represented the street he lived on). Taki wasn't the first writer with a street number to back him up, mind you (Julio 204 had become known for his markings at least two years prior), but it was when Taki scored a gig as a messenger that his celebrity elevated beyond the confines of Mister Softee's route. Lampposts, park benches, elevators in office buildings, subway trains—Taki bombed it all as he quietly weaved through Manhattan making deliveries.

Taki's notoriety opened some sleepy young eyes. His fame helped kids to understand that the masses would hear you if you screamed loud enough. His wide-reaching celebrity meant that you would be recognized in your neighborhood as somebody—as an independent somebody, who had no obligation to no stinking gang. Taki let kids know that it was possible to stand alone and not get hassled, that you could be daring and original. Taki 183 was his own publicly traded corporation, and cats with itchy spraying fingers wanted stock. Skill and artistic ability had nothing to do with the early works of Taki and his pen pals. Their simplistic writings were more about saying, "Hello, I was here," than about making artistic statements or crafting breakthrough painting techniques—that would change within a matter of months. Taki 183 personified the art of *getting up* (writing, in as many places as possible) as a way of getting over.

To be a graffiti writer in the early 1970s was to be different, and the warlords understood this. That's why writers could wander onto Tomahawk land and not get hassled: "foreign" writers were in your stretch of hood to "get up," okay, maybe also to shoplift spray paint from a few hardware stores, or to "borrow" that rich purple ink that most supermarkets use to create window displays. Gang members and writers were two completely different beasts. You were either one or the other, and never both. Spek, on the other hand, was a writer and a member of the notorious Crips street gang; it was this blurring of boundaries that most likely led to his death.

Style Kings

New York City was a fiscal mess back in the mid-1970s, and Mayor John Lindsay knew he was losing his war on subway graffiti. By 1973, the write-your-nickname-on-the-side-of-a-train game was just as popular as shooting playground hoops. Every kid had a Magic Marker, and the city could not afford to scrub or paint over the ever-proliferating streaks of color. The only real obstacles that writers faced were the omnipresent mega-wattage of the third rail (the steel pipeline pumped with electrical current), the Transit Authority's newly formed "sandal squad" (wrist slaps or maybe station cleanup were the punishments juveniles faced), and an increasing shortage of space (because the names were on windows, on doors, where advertisements for Ringling Brothers were supposed to be, even on ceilings). The letterforms had no choice but to get bigger, bolder, more complex. Writers realized that trains were like moving canvases, that the vast system of tunnels and raised platforms were really galleries, museums, roving commercials even: *Everyone takes the train, man! Dig?*

Competition from participants hailing from far-off places like Coney Island, Brooklyn, and Jamaica, Queens, would help push the form from simply "I was here" to "I am here, and I'm leaving this behind to show you that I have style; that I am a style master . . . That I was the first ever to paint a cloud above my 'piece' [shorthand for 'masterpiece'] . . . That I am king, and my style will influence all you 'toys' [shorthand for 'novices']."

And while New York's graffiti may have appeared as nothing more than crude chicken scratches when caught by an untrained eye, the truth wasn't so elementary. Flavorful signatures with squiggles and other elaborations ("tags") would pave the way for block- and bubble-shaped letters; by 1973, these forms would sprout arrows and sharp edges. Soon enough, the goal was to create words that read like abstract puzzles. *Wildstyle* was the term coined by writers—letters hidden behind a color-coated camouflage of funk. Only those in the know could figure it out, but I assure you, if you knew what to look for, you'd find it, plain as day.

One of the golden rules of writing from 1972 on out was, yes, a piece has every right to overtake spaces occupied by tags—it was OK to go over a tag with a multicolored piece, or even a throw-up. But if a writer was to go over another writer's piece with a tag, or cross another writer's piece out deliberately—as opposed to occupational hazards like the odd close nick or an accidental drip that runs onto the next man's masterpiece—then a cross-out war that would eventually lead to a fair one was in order.

In the 1970s, my hands were too small to clutch a can of jungle-green Krylon, so the fair one wasn't even an issue. My parents sported Afros in those days. Africa and pride; culture, freedom, and determination: these are some of the earliest ideas I was presented with. This is how we lived. I was lucky to be raised that way, because in spite of the crazy neighborhood that we called home, Dad the filmmaker and Mom the painter made sure that I understood early on who I was and where I came from. That I was somebody.

Graffiti has been one of the greatest motivating factors in my life. Writing was good to me, especially since I was more court jester than king. It prepared me for the writing I do now. When the time came for me to switch gears and to grow up, I was prepared: instead of trying to get my name up on every train, I aimed to get my name up in as many magazines as possible. Hey, I'm not alone: New York City writers of all ages have often gone on to make their marks on society in more socially accepted ways, from designing motorcycles (Haze) and jeanswear (Futura), to mounting well-received exhibitions of graffiti art throughout Europe (Quik). Writing gave a lot of us direction. It gave us options—hope, if you will.

And hope was something we needed, once crack cocaine was declared president for life in the hood in the mid-1980s. When I was coming up and Spek was but a shorty, crackheads were our real-time zombies; some neighborhoods were dimmer than Transylvania. Fourteen-year-old boys from broken homes were clocking fifteen hundred dollars on a slow day selling crack, and some of the most beautiful black and Puerto Rican girls from your local housing project were willing to perform oral sex in pissy elevators—sans condom—for five dollars and a bag of Wise potato chips.

Crack culture was destructive, selfish. And I suppose as a movement, graffiti, to those who didn't understand it, was also destructive and selfish. But it was my way out: nearly all the kids on my block who were my age or older were either too busy making money or too busy spending money on suicide. Who had time to toss a football? Writing gave me a new identity. A makeover. You could be off in a dark subway tunnel somewhere far from home, hanging out with other like-minded white, Asian, Latino, and whatever kids, being creative. Taxpayers didn't appreciate our art, true, but there was no other game this fun in town. For me, and I imagine for Spek, the adrenaline rush that went along with being where you don't belong, being some Warholian supervillain, was intense.

Bombing the City

Timothy Falzone, born on February 12, 1982, wasn't as lucky as I have been: his father was in and out of jail, which would eventually lead to the breakup of his parents' marriage. Timothy was probably just learning to walk when crack cocaine hit its stride in the inner city. When I heard that it was Falzone's cross-out war with twenty-year-old semigangbanger Ricky "Foke" Mouzon that caused the well-known new-school writer to cross over to the other side, my stomach fell. I'd seen Spek's tags and throw-ups up and about Manhattan for ages, but it was a trip through the Bronx three years ago that made me understand that he was serious about his graf. With Spek, no two throw-ups ever looked the same, which was beyond rare. Because throw-ups were supposed to be cookie-cut, same thing every time, blazing in your face like McDonald's golden arches. So you'd remember and recognize who was who, who was boss. Love him or hate him, you had to respect the kid for that.

The only thing I'd actually heard about Spek was that he was never known to back down from a fight, and that he had superior "knuckle game";

that he was quick to shit-talk because of his incredible gift of jab. He was the Ali of "the fair one," undefeated. He whipped writers twice his size. After his death, I needed to know more. I wondered how this could have happened. I wondered if the fair one had become a dead issue for new-school New York writers.

Falzone began his writing career in 1993—a time when painted subway cars were long gone. The MTA had finally won its war on graffiti through a combination of new trains, improved cleaning methods, and relentless effort to remove any markings. The last painted car rolled off of the J line in May 1989, into the permanent obscurity of a train yard. The new generation of sprayers were forced to make their fame on streets and on the rooftops that hugged the elevated train lines. With the trains gone, writers from generations past moved on: to family life and real-world jobs; to become military men, civilians, lawyers; to land long jail sentences because the crack game was the pro sport with a never-ending draft.

In the nineties, a few die-hard old-schoolers would paint from time to time on "permission" walls scattered throughout the five boroughs, but the connection between accomplished writing pioneers and budding young bucks— the practice of apprenticeship, and the access it offered to history and proto-col—was smashed to bits. Writing was one of the most social antisocial activities around, and early-eighties graf enthusiasts would go to a specific bench on a specific platform in the Bronx (149th Street and Grand Concourse, known as the Writer's Bench) to talk shop with other inkheads and to snap photographs of the trains before and after the doors opened. The photographs were like baseball cards that writers would trade. The trains created an inti-macy that the writing community will never again experience. After all, there are millions of walls in New York to paint, as opposed to the twenty or so stor-age yards that the trains snoozed in at night. The odds of a toy's chance meet-ing with a legend painting a legal wall in 1993 were slim. Besides, some new dudes could care less about what's already been done. Their time to shine is in the present; Spek wasn't about to let anyone stop him from getting get his shines on.

Still, Spek didn't begin his writing career totally uninformed; in fact, he had a main line to writers who did know their history. Maybe he should have known better. Fellow Bronx native Jee, best friends with Spek from age thirteen, happened to be the younger brother of one of the world's most famous active writers, Cope 2. Cope, ten years Jee's senior, was happy to show his little man the ropes. In the Bronx, being Cope's little brother was like being one of the Jacksons, and Jee was looking to score his brother's Michael Jackson–sized majesty.

Writing "crews" developed during the 1970s as the gang movement was fading, pushed out in part by hip-hop culture. Two writers usually came up with a funky name (say, The Death Squad). Those two founders would then dub themselves "prez" and "vice prez," and four like-minded friends would come along for the ride. The six guys would make a name for themselves as prolific bombers, piecers, fighters. By the late 1980s, Cope had made his crew, Kings Destroy, the talk of the Bronx. Jee understood that there is a great crew behind every great writer. BTV—Big Time Vandals—was Jee and Spek's answer to KD.

"At first, Big Time Vandals was just me and some kid from the neighborhood. But I didn't really love the name, so I gave it to Spek," says Jee, now a hulking twenty-year-old Nuyorican with tribal tattoos, from the living room of the Bronx apartment he and Cope share. "So a week or two later, Spek comes up to me like, 'I changed it! I changed it!' So I said, 'All right, what did you change it to?' And he said, 'Bomb the City!' Spek, BTC's de facto commander in chief, was serious about his bombing. And he took no shit. "Ever since junior high school," Jee explains, "if you even looked at Timmy wrong, he would be like, 'Yo, what are you looking at?' And he'd punch you in the face. His father and mother taught him that. His parents were kinda ghetto," he says numbly. Jee, Cope, and other folks who loved Timmy, like Cristina Betancourt, the nineteen-year-old mother of Spek's year-old daughter, Alizaya, swear that the slain writer was a sweet and loving individual who was grossly misunderstood. But they can understand why those who didn't know Timmy, the sensitive animal-lover, would think him a beast.

"At one time, he was crossing a lot of people out," says Cope, who is at least a hundred pounds heavier than Jee, and who sports one of Spek's throw-ups tattooed on his right arm. "See, Spek didn't give a fuck about graffiti rules. He don't care if he had a tag or a throw-up. If you went over his shit with a piece, he's going over you." Cope, a world-class diplomat, found himself catching a lot of flak because of the actions of his protégé. "Practically everybody he went over, I knew, and knew for many years," Cope says. "So people felt that I should try to have some control over this kid."

At one point, Cope says, it seemed like every writer in the Bronx was out to get Spek. But he wasn't just your average writer during the last years of his life: Spek, with the encouragement of his younger brother, Jermell, became a Crip. New York City in general is currently experiencing a gang renaissance, and rogue, loosely organized Crips and Bloods sets—groups with thirty years of history in the greater Los Angeles area but no real strong roots inside of the five boroughs—are running wild.

"These days, you've got guys in certain neighborhoods who are like Spek—they're kinda affiliated with gangs and they write. Whereas in the past, most writers I knew weren't affiliated with gangs," says Wane, an acclaimed veteran Bronx writer. "So when Spek got killed, it shook a lot of people. I think everybody was on standstill for a minute. People thought about it: Is this shit really worth it? Here's a guy who's writing graffiti, and he gets shot? That shit wasn't supposed to happen."

"It started because of a little gossip," Jee says of the behind-the-scenes talk that later sparked the Spek/Foke conflict. "Then Foke started going over Spek." Timothy Falzone wouldn't go out like that; there was no way he was going to let a little-known writer like Foke disrespect him. "Spek seen [Foke] in his neighborhood one day—by chance," Jee says. "He was with a couple of kids from our crew, so they robbed Foke, beat his ass." Foke took his beating like a man; his ego was probably the most bruised after the thrashing.

But there's nothing fair about getting jumped and robbed by a mob. There's no real way to justify Spek's call to pounce on Foke. Spek was dead wrong. Still, even the code of the streets couldn't justify his death. And Spek didn't think twice, because he was regularly beating people up. "Then one day, like four months later," Jee adds, his voice now growing hoarse, "Spek was chillin' in front of his building, and they came out and shot him."

Aftermath

Due to an unspecified violent infraction that occurred during his incarceration, Ricky Mouzon now spends his days locked behind the prison bars of a maximum security unit on Queens' infamous Rikers Island, where he awaits trial. He will be shipped off to one of upstate New York's many stone-faced correctional facilities to serve out his hard time if the murder rap sticks. Although I wrote several letters to Mr. Mouzon, hoping to secure an interview, he did not respond. Some say that Foke didn't actually do the killing himself, that one of his crack-dealing cronies who had little patience or sympathy for bullheaded, weaponless graffiti writers was the culprit. Foke, they say, just wanted to scare Spek—roll up with his strapping buddies to show Spek Falzone that things could go down this way if he didn't rethink his actions. But when Spek turned to walk away after letting his detractors know that he was true to his reputation and ready to fight, somebody wound up shooting him in the back of the head.

Life hasn't been easy for single mom Cristina Betancourt in the months since Spek, her live-in boyfriend, was gunned down on De Kalb Avenue—the street they both grew up on, that Betancourt still calls home. When I visit her on a warm spring day, as preteensters rip up and down the block playing mid-hide-and-go-seek, Betancourt, a comely Latina who beams both the look of innocence and of innocence lost, tries hard to understand the ramifications of grown-up foul play.

"Look at what happened to Timmy," she says, eyes watery. "And they want to keep on doing graffiti? They want to keep on fighting over graffiti?" We're about a hundred feet away from the place where Spek was shot dead; two women with babies and strollers stand in that very spot as we're speaking. "It's not the same. I'm not used to walking around the block without him," she says. "I don't want to live here no more. Every time I walk on De Kalb, I just see that spot where he was laying at." Betancourt says that she's looking forward to getting an associate's degree and then going on to more schooling—to the promise of a better quality of life. "We were supposed to leave—Timmy, me, and the baby," she explains. "We were supposed to go move to Pennsylvania. We were going to raise Alizaya over there."

Just then, Spek's younger brother Jermell happens to walk by. He, too, is reluctant to talk. "Ain't nothin' much to say about it," Jermell says while flexing a thug's half-smile. A fully pledged member of the Crips, he's familiar with the boomerang system of justice that heads on corners subscribe to. "Shit like that happens. But what goes around comes around, you know?" His boss is the streets, and he's currently on the block and on the clock. Meanwhile, the Falzone clan is more scattered than ever: Momma Sarena Falzone fell victim to a brain aneurysm a few months before Spek's murder, and in the days since the passing of his mother and older brother, Jermell says that he doesn't stay in touch with his father, Timmy senior.

"Timmy was a good nigga," he says of his brother, "but I always thought graffiti was bullshit. I used to tell him that. I was like, 'How could you be fighting over writing on the walls?' I can see if he's fighting for money and shit." Fighting for money, and his life, is what Jermell Falzone does every day. "I don't really got nothing to lose, tell you the truth. I've felt that way since my mom died—when both of them left," he says. "There ain't really nothin' to live for. I was trying to get me a record deal. That's the only thing that I'm trying to do right now." With that, Mel, as his friends call him, steps back into the street.

"The day of his funeral, I just broke out in tears," says Noke, a twenty-one-year-old original member of Bomb the City as he rides in the passenger seat of my brown, rusted 1989 Chevy Blazer. "I tried to stop crying. I couldn't believe it. It pissed me off inside. It hurts a lot; makes me want to kill the person, you know? You take my friend's life over something like that. Graffiti? You're supposed to fight the fair one. Or go over their shit. Now, people want to take things to a different level by killing people? People can't be known for graf, so they want to be known for something else—'Oh, I killed that famous person.' Or 'Oh, I cut his face.' It's not about writing anymore. People want to get quick fame."

New York will always be a cutthroat, thirsty place for some and a plentiful oasis for others. The summer of 2002 had its share of particularly hot and sticky runs; weather commentators talked of drought warnings daily. And the fall of 2001 drained us dry in a very different way. Osama bin Laden cut through the face of this city, for sure, and found quick fame. I never used to think that forest fires blazed in concrete jungles, that mass jumbles of black and gray and cold steel could melt down into faceless blobs with such ease. Now I do my best to conserve water because I can see the smoke from the blue flames in the corners of my eyes. I wonder, still: Will Jermell live to be old and free? Will gangs and crack-cocaine violence rise again? Will Cristina and Al-izaya find a better life? Will the World Trade Center's rocket-sized antenna prick the atmosphere once again? Is New York's civilized graffiti culture on the brink of self-destruction? Did the fair one ever exist in anyone's world?

ARTicles / 2002

Planet Rock

ROBERT CHRISTGAU

Paradoxically, or maybe not, hip-hop is at once the fastest spreading and most local pop music in the world. The media-saturated, electronically hooked-up world, anyway. Ethnomusicologists mourn the indigenous idioms that mutate or fall into disuse once their practitioners get a load of Bucharest or Bangui, and in a sense, hip-hop reverses this process, not musicologically but emotionally. From hood to city to coast, what other pop genre makes so much of geography? Early rock and roll lived off a dynamic in which the local went national, usually from a base of local radio; now, local radio barely exists, and even in the Internet-surfing, CD-scarfing indie/college realm, local scenes rarely generate local sounds or more than a smattering of local references. In hip-hop, styles are regionally distinct, although they certainly crossbreed, and representing where you're from is the rule, especially when you're coming up. Hip-hop speaks so loudly to rebellious kids from Greenland to New Zealand not because they identify with young American blacks, although they may, but because it's custom-made to combat the anomie that preys on adolescents wherever nobody knows their name.

The aforementioned antipodes weren't picked out of thin air; I got them from a book and a CD. The book is a recommended anthology from Wesleyan called *Global Noise: Rap and Hip-Hop Outside the USA*, edited by Australian cultural studies lecturer Tony Mitchell, whose own chapters concern Italy and, yes, New Zealand, home to a Maori hip-hop subculture spearheaded by the long-running Upper Hutt Posse. The CD is a recommended compilation on Hip-O called *The Best of International Hip-Hop*, whose single best track originated in, I wouldn't believe it either, Greenland: the even longer-running Nuuk Posse's "Uteqqippugut," aka "Back in Business." Since hearing most of the acts referenced in the book is next to impossible in America, it's good to have the record despite its awful notes ("The land of Aristotle and Socrates found its 21st century hip-hop philosophers in Terror X Crew"). But there's little overlap. France, Japan, and Australia are the only countries that make both, with Canada, the U.K., Germany, Italy, the Netherlands, Bulgaria, Korea, and New Zealand (plus Basque nationalists and Muslims) described in *Global Noise* and Portugal, Switzerland, Austria, Romania, Croatia, Greece, Israel, Greenland, Argentina, Algeria, and South Africa represented on *The Best of International Hip-Hop*.

Assuming the book is accurate (only the Canadian chapter seems inept, but selective reporting is a temptation of such projects), hip-hop is different wherever you find it. In Germany its pop breakthrough dates to 1993, as does a familiar schism: "old school" purists, an Italian-Ghanaian-Haitian immigrant trio rapping "in clear German" about racism, versus white schlagermeisters from the south sprechstimming romantically over "highly polished breakbeat stylings" and insisting that rap doesn't equal hip-hop—which is linked by both sides to not just freestyling but breaking and graffiti. In Japan, having rhymed to the best of their abilities in an unaccented language whose sentences all close on the same handful of verb endings, rappers divide up "underground" (focus of a huge and intense late-night club scene) and "party" (pop in the extreme Japanese Hello Kitty sense); at consecutive outdoor concerts, the audience for the former was 80 percent male, for the latter 80 percent female. Elsewhere the music is far more rudimentary—a techno-flavored symbol of American wealth and worse in Bulgaria, a stylistic trapping in Korea, where the big star is a lower-middle-class surrogate rebel who got large protesting an educational grind more joyless and authoritarian than Japan's. Most telling is the Australian chapter, centered on Def Wish Cast, "westies" from the under-class suburbs thirty miles on the inland side of Sydney, who since the 1980s have given their all to a hip-hop culture open to anyone who gives his or her (usually his, natch) all to it. It opens with headman Ser Reck laying down the hip-hop law to author Ian Maxwell: "They'll tell you it's a black thing, man, but it isn't. It's our thing."

And with the obvious reservations, he's got a right. Ser Reck isn't dissing the African-American originators of the music he's made his life—he reveres them. But he's not them, and good for him for knowing it. Instead he's con-structed the identity and authenticity he craves on a model learned from hip-hop—a model that however arbitrary its specific rituals (graffiti and break dancing again) reconceives community at least as explicitly as the hippies did thirty-five years ago. Ser Reck works, commits, represents. Hip-hop is his. But unless you're Australian—and probably not then unless you're also young, alienated, rebellious, male, etc.—his hip-hop is unlikely to be yours even if you're in the market for rocked-up Public Enemy on a definitive 1992 CD that'll run you thirty-five smackers shipped. That's how I'd put it, anyway. Al-though Maxwell devotes a rapturous paragraph to the fondly remembered funk spell of "White Lines," his only musical description of the local stuff con-trasts Ser Reck's "ragged, guttural, barking" Australian delivery against "the smooth, mellifluous flow of a Nas or a Dr. Dre."

Ah yes, music. Long before rock and roll, the local-goes-national dynamic went global with Italian opera and fake ragtime, but that kind of move is rare. Which is why *The Best of International Hip-Hop* stood quietly on my not-bad shelf for a year before *Global Noise* opened me up. Turns out it's a fun record, and a revealing one, full of catchy beats and local flavors. If you want deep funk, Timbaland or Organized Noize or RZA or Mannie Fresh, listen else-where. What prevails instead is remarkably consistent despite its all-over-the-place provenance, maybe even the real world-beat—a generally uptempo electro groove with universal hooks, insistent bass lines, off-and-on scratch-ing, and such sound effects as oud from Algeria, balalaika from Greece, and whale from Greenland, plus no doubt a few folk melodies. Far from disrupting music that might otherwise go down queasily lite, the language shifts texture it, with the coughed-up consonants of Greenlandic, Croatian, and Hebrew especially welcome.

Apparently some of the rhymes are interesting, too, but when Fijian-Australian Trey comes on, it's not her modest boast that'll perk you up, or even her dulcet female tone—it's her English per se. This isn't chauvinism, it's aesthetics. Although "flow" can mean anything, just like "beats," its relationship to language is always one of its prime pleasures. You don't have to get every word to hear how a rapper's phrasing, intonation, pronunciation, and timbre inflect meaning, reshape sonics, and fuck with the other man's culture. But you have to get some of them. Thus, Nuuk Posse's hip-hop, say, is even less likely to be an English speaker's than Def Wish Cast's. When it comes to African-American music, I scoff at talk of American cultural imperialism. Only a Frenchman could imagine that white capitalists conspired to impose Negroes on the world. But English's status as a lingua franca has always helped African-American music get over. That's why Frenchmen invented *francophonie*.

Skeptical of French pop, and with my personal experience limited to MC Solaar's mellow-to-a-fault, never-quite-released-stateside 1997 *Paradisiaque*, I was intrigued by *Global Noise*'s account of French hip-hop as an oppositional music dominated by Muslim and Muslim-identified immigrants, then surprised to learn from my general nosing around that hip-hop of every sort is a much bigger deal in France than in the U.K. or anywhere else besides America. Perhaps prodded by the Senegalese-born rapper's sometime collaborator Missy Elliott, Elektra has taken a flier on *Cinquième As (Fifth Ace)*, the latest by Solaar, a violence-hating, million-selling girl magnet who's barely described in *Global Noise*. Although the beats continue to go down too easy, they have rather more body than those on *Paradisiaque*, and when I read along or just concentrate, I can appreciate his flow—but still not its verbal components, including what insults it does or doesn't visit on *la belle langue*. Musically, I'm more taken with what little I've heard of Marseille's Sicilian-led, all-Muslim, multiethnic IAM. But even were I to beef up my spoken French, their slang and accents would be beyond me.

So it's no surprise that my favorite non-English rap album to date is the Sahel-generated *Africa Raps* comp. Whatever localism's undeniable validity and just rewards, black people have always been best at taking it worldwide. Be it nurture or nature, rhythm is at the forefront of their musical skills — on *Africa Raps*, the goddamn Ousmane Sembène dialogue sample has some funk — and also at the forefront of hip-hop. So it's striking that African hip-hop is ignored in *Global Noise*. Equally striking is a half-articulated anti-essentialist resentment of the African-American claim on hip-hop. It's as if Jay-Z, to choose our biggest willie, is merely a point man for cultural imperialism — although the perp actually named is that tireless profit-taker and hip-hop ambassador Chuck D, who's criticized for disdaining white fans in Bilbao and white rappers in Sydney.

Maybe that's what Jay-Z gets for rapping over a cushier rhythm bed than Europeans can manage at a five-star hotel. Maybe it's what Chuck D deserves for agitating hearts whose pain he can't comprehend. But what if the dislocation-in-continuity that animates each rapper's deep funk fills a need that upbeat electro cannot? What if it's such a vivid aural metaphor for all attempts to re-create community in this undoing world that no roots rap, however authentic, can replace it? What if it's just better music? What happens to the local then?

The Village Voice / May 14, 2002

Rhythmic Heart of the Kings of Rock

Jam Master Jay, 1965–2002

HARRY ALLEN

As both a technician and craftsman, DJ Jam Master Jay (aka Jason William Mizell), who was murdered last Wednesday night at the age of thirty-seven by an assassin's single bullet, will probably be remembered less for the showy innovations and poly-hyphenated tricks that mark the modern "turntablist" arsenal than he will be for a personal style marked by deference and selflessness.

His was a manner uniquely suited to the era that, as a part of the hip-hop supergroup Run-D.M.C., he dominated culturally. The supporting role he performed—making his vocalists look their absolute best, just as hip-hop, in pursuit of wider audiences, shifted its focus increasingly from the DJ to the MC—also enabled him to act as a global ambassador for the music. He did so in a manner absent of ego, absent of the typical "ugly Americanisms" that frequently mar such contacts. He and rappers Joseph "Run" Simmons and Darryl "D.M.C." McDaniels were the first to perform hip-hop in countless locales across the planet. His was a position that Jam Master Jay served with what many who knew him note as a characteristic form of kindness.

Of course Run-D.M.C. are the most influential crew in hip-hop history, and one of the most influential in the history of popular music. Jay was their instrumental and musical backbone, their melodic voice and rhythmic heart. Like markers dividing time into B.C. and A.D., they literally stand at the nexus of hip-hop's old and new schools: the first artists in the genre to enjoy a career in the style most widely emulated today. Here's the formula: sell African-American music by the multimillions to validating black buyers, but predominantly to relatively empathetic, liquidity-providing white ones—the so-called mainstream. Do so in a manner accentuated by product merchandising, endorsements, radio and music-video marketing, and wide national and international touring. Run-D.M.C.'s progeny, thus, are every hip-hop act that has since partaken in any aspect or effect of the above—and any white musical group that, at the very least, has taken hold of rock and hip-hop's concubinage. Mizell was killed in the lounge of his Queens studio by one shot to the head from a .40-caliber weapon. News reports said that the large, powerful round left both an entry and an exit wound, and that the killer shot him behind his left ear so close that ignited powder from the blast burned Jay's shirt. In other words, he was not just killed, but slaughtered. Brutally.

In the subsequent investigation, NYPD attention has mainly focused on a revenge motive: possibly for unpaid debts, possibly for Jay's association with hip-hop rabble-rouser 50 Cent, aka Curtis Jackson, whose "gangsta rap"–mocking single, "Wanksta," Jay produced, and who has previously been the victim of gun violence. Though newspaper columnists continue to beat the glue out of the notion, and though a federal probe of rumored organized-crime ties within the hip-hop industry is said to be under way, detectives have scoffed at suggestions that the murder is connected to an "East Coast–West Coast rap war." They have also deemed the weekend killing in White Plains of Kenneth Walker, a hip-hop promoter with a criminal record, as having no connection to Jay's murder.

Born in Brooklyn on January 21, 1965, the youngest of three children, to the late Jesse Mizell and Connie Thompson Mizell, Jason was playing drums and singing in the Universal Baptist Church's Young Adult Choir at the age of five. After moving with his family to Hollis in 1975, he discovered DJing at age thirteen and began to practice under the name Jazzy Jase. It was while in Hollis—attending Jackson High School, playing drums and bass in local bands, and learning to disc-jockey—that he would meet future partners Darryl and Joe. The crew officially joined forces in their late teens, then signed with Profile Records, under the management of Joe's older brother, Russell Simmons, who would later have enormous success of his own as head of Def Jam Recordings. Their first single, "It's Like That/Sucker M.C.'s," came out in 1983.

At the peak of their powers, Run-D.M.C. were like the leading technological edge of an advanced missile program. The sound of their beats alone, compared to what had come before—Sugarhill Records' horn-berserk bridges and choruses, for example—were the audio equivalent of low-kiloton-yield bunker busting. The titles of their flinty tracks read like chapter headings for an impending apocalypse: "Hard Times," "30 Days," "It's Like That." Even their own name was odd—in 1983, amid crews with fluorescent, superhero-style monikers like the Funky Four, the Furious Five, and the Treacherous Three, Run-D.M.C. sounded less like the name of a group than that of a metallurgical solvent.

How fitting. Because, with the release of their eponymous debut album in 1984, followed by 1985's *King of Rock*, Run-D.M.C. would more surely dissolve and dispense with the previous musical age than any hip-hop artists before or since. How? Simple: by basically inventing the modern hip-hop music business. It's probably difficult for those born in the age of Run-D.M.C.'s revolution—pretty much anyone under the age of twenty-five—to clearly see its effects, so fundamental are they to what we consider popular music today. They possessed the aura that would make the hip-hop industry's growth spurts possible. Much has been made of their long list of firsts: hip-hop's first gold album (*Run-D.M.C.*); hip-hop's first platinum album (*King of Rock*); first hip-hop artists to be nominated for a Grammy; first rappers to appear on *American Bandstand* and on the cover of *Rolling Stone*.

But these were merely outgrowths of their real innovations:

· Their blending of rock with hip-hop: This hybrid gave Run-D.M.C.'s music a supple, rhythmic density that rock had never enjoyed, and hip-hop a tonic brazenness that perfectly complemented that of the scratch. Their subtle blend attracted fans who might have found this chocolate-in-my-peanut-butter mix anathema, at least initially.

· The breadth of their touring and the depth of their touring lineup: By traveling widely in the early eighties, on the first Fresh Fest tours, then on their own Together Forever tour, and by maintaining a roster of acts that were all distinct from one another, the crew assured wide exposure, both geographically and demographically, for their ideas, and the growth of a relatively broad fan base.

The compactness of their ensemble: Run-D.M.C., compared to earlier crews, were a relatively small combo: two vocalists, one DJ. Basically, they scaled back the workforce, a trend later accelerated as technology and production styles increasingly worked to make the DJ superfluous. Not until the rise of the Wu-Tang Clan on the East Coast and Jurassic 5 on the West would hip-hop see much opposition to the downsizing they initiated.

The extreme dynamism of their live shows: Run-D.M.C. were the first hip-hop artists to yell on their records, to jump from hip-hop's smoothly conspiratorial, R & B–speckled timbres to pounding amplitudes of rage. This enabled them to readily duplicate the volume of their recorded performances in the live setting. (Try to imagine, say, Rakim or Fabolous doing the same thing.) It also helped them make records that a rock audience could embrace. This connected them to an enormous, previously untapped white ethos.

Careful selection and arrangement of graphical elements into a unified whole: The first time I saw the *King of Rock* LP, over at Rock & Soul on Seventh Avenue, I stared at the cover for what seemed like two hours. I remember thinking that it looked "real," as if Run-D.M.C. were real recording artists, as opposed to "just" rappers. They were also probably the first hip-hop act with a logo.

The austerity of their visual aesthetic: They rejected the polychromatic, Rick James–influenced full-body leathers of the Furious Five in favor of a minimalist, all-black, urban hard-rock look that youthful crowds found reasonable and accessible; whether you were a B-boy or a skatepunk, a black T-shirt, black Lee jeans, and Adidas made sense. (And can anyone forget the first time they saw Run-D.M.C. in those big, dookie-rope chains?) The pared-down look extended to their stage set. Jam Master Jay, for instance, was probably the first DJ ever to use Anvil cases—as opposed to crudely cut, makeshift squares of foam—to support turntables during concerts. This gave his instrument a cool, machine-finished look.

Over the course of seven studio album releases with the group and after Run-D.M.C.'s heyday, Jay kept busy and visible with public appearances, live shows, production (his 1993 JMJ Records release by Onyx, *Bacdafucup*, a prime example), and running the studio in the heart of his old neighborhood, about a mile from the home in which he grew up—the studio in which, sadly, his life would violently end.

Aside from the millions of fans, friends, and colleagues he leaves behind, he'll be most dearly remembered by his wife of eleven years, Terri, thirty-two; his sons, Jason, fifteen, Terry, eleven, and Jesse, seven; his mother Connie (Mizell) Perry; his brother, Marvin L. Thompson; and his sister, Bonita Jones.

Jam Master Jay's pivotal role in the history of hip-hop culture is singular, his shoes impossible to fill—a point inevitably made, maybe, by the piles of empty Adidas left at a makeshift memorial outside his murder site. However, this outpouring of love and fond memories, though enough for some, won't be for one.

"I don't want people to just mourn Jay for a month, and then we go back to doing the same things we've been doing," says his longtime friend and recording partner D.M.C., in a voice weary with loss. "We need to add something, in order to make change.

"After we give him his tribute, and bury him with dignity, his legacy's gonna live on. But as long as that legacy lives on, simultaneously, there has to be an idea that goes along with it."

The Village Voice / November 6, 2002

Keepin' It Unreal

$elling the Myth of Bla¢k Male Violen¢e, Long Past Its Expiration Date

TA-NEHISI COATES

from bootleg king to god of the streets was PR genius. His handlers have played the angle magnificently. The attempts on his life come up repeatedly in interviews, and 50 is happy to provide embellishment. Even critics have bought into the mystique—review after review of 50's *Get Rich or Die Tryin'* cites his battle scars as evidence of his true-to-life depiction of the streets. On the cover of *Rolling Stone*, he posed with his back to the camera, exposing one of his wounds. Who knew nine bullet holes could be such a boon?

Now the banners are unfurling: "2003: the year hip-hop returned to the streets." You can thank 50 for that. *Get Rich* has been hyped as the most realistic representation of the ghetto since the heyday of Biggie. To its credit, the album turns down the bling factor considerably. 50 could care less about what whip you're pushing or the cut of your Armani. All that concerns him is your (preferably violent) downfall. Add in 50's work history in the narcotics trade and his random swipes at supposed wanksta Ja Rule and you have the makings of the most legitimate gangsta rapper since Jay-Z.

But not much more. At its core the hubbub around *Get Rich* and the return of gangsta rap is crack-era nostalgia taken to the extreme. Imagine—articulate young black men pining for the heyday of black-on-black crime. Like all nostalgia, neo-gangsta is stuck in history rather than rooted in current reality. The sobering fact is that the streets as 50 presents them, brimming with shoot-outs and crack fiends, do not exist. Of course, drugs are still a plague on America's house, and America's gun violence is a black mark on the developed world. But millennial black America is hardly the Wild West scene it was during gangsta rap's prime. Gangsta could once fairly claim to reflect a brutal present. Now it mythicizes a past that would fade away much faster without it.

In the late eighties, young black men—gangsta rap's creators, and its primary constituency—became their own worst enemies. Drug dealing was becoming a legitimate, if deadly, life option, and with it came an arms race that turned Anyghetto, U.S.A., into Saigon. The Harlem Renaissance drew its power from the optimism of the New Negro, the Black Arts movement pulled from Black Power, gangsta rap tapped the crack age. If Motown and Stax were the joyful noise of us unshackling ourselves into the dream ("Are you ready for a brand-new beat?"), gangsta rap was the sound of us crashing back into the desert of the real ("Life ain't nothin' but bitches and money").

The crash is complete, and in any black community you can find the rubble—uneducated, unemployable young black men. Their narrative no longer rings with the romance of a Nino Brown. Crack is played, and so, apparently, is fratricide—murder rates in the black community have been dropping since the mid-nineties. The way of the gun still takes its toll, but Saigon has been pacified. Mundane afflictions like unpaid child support and industrial flight have once again come to the fore.

The streets that gangsta rappers claim as their source are no longer as angry as they are sad. For that reason alone, gangsta rap should be dead by now. But still it lingers, fueled by America's myth of the menacing black man. Gangsta rap today is about as reflective of reality as, well, a reality show. And yet still it lumbers across the landscape of pop, shouting, "I'm real."

Step away with your fistfight ways / Muthafucka this ain't back in the days.
> —the Notorious B.I.G., "Things Done Changed"

Some seventeen years ago, I was ambling past a local 7-Eleven on my way home from school. There in front of the store where I frequently leafed through copies of *X-Men*, I met gangsta rap in its most tangible form. It was 1986—the year Schoolly D birthed the genre with his single "PSK (What Does It Mean?)"—and the old order of Afro-America was coming apart. Black fathers were going MIA, guns were flooding the streets, and crackheads were multiplying. I was young and too obsessed with *Transformers* and *Galaxy Rangers* to notice the walls caving in around me.

And then at that 7-Eleven I watched a kid unveil the biggest, blackest handgun I'd ever seen. He and his friends had been arguing with another clique when the one kid dropped the trump card. It was like something out of the dollar flicks, scored by my heart pounding like a timpani. No cars pulled into the parking lot. No one ducked or screamed. I did not move. With his point made, the kid returned his tool to his jacket and walked away laughing with his friends, taking my innocence with him.

Whatever I had left was beaten out of me during my first year of middle school. I got jumped so often that I spent that year searching for alternative paths home, some of them integrating bus routes even though I lived around the corner. A new road map might save me from a critical beatdown. But as the gangsta rap era geared up, the bum-rush became the least of my worries.

These were the days when fashion became a health risk. Mothers started shunning Jordans, Lottos, and Diadoras, fearing their sons would come home in their socks, or not at all. Schools ran damage control, implementing uniforms and banning bookbags for fear of what kids might be packing. And still the crazy reports kept filtering through—young boys attacking their mothers or smoking each other over an accidental footprint on someone's suede Pumas.

Then the entire dialogue changed. Nationalists declared black males an officially endangered species and screamed genocide orchestrated by the invisible white hand. I was twelve and understandably short on grand theories, save one—the world had gone crazy. One day I was living for *Jayce and the Wheeled Warriors*, the next my older brother was flashing me a hot .38.

The nationalists were right about one thing. It was a white hand fueling black America's dementia—the white hand of crack cocaine. "When crack arrived in the city, it increased the level of gun violence. You had lots of young people with the money to buy guns and an arms race came with that," says Peter Reuter, professor of criminology at the University of Maryland and coauthor of *Drug War Heresies*. "It was no longer shootings over territory, but over transactions. The amount of money you could steal from someone was a lot larger now, and the drugs themselves made people more violent."

Crack also had the good luck to arrive in cities just as the rust belts were completely eroding employment. Whereas once a man could support his family with a job at the plant, manufacturing was being phased out by automation and the factories' retreat from the cities. Add Reagan's and then Bush's neoconservative attack on social programs, and you have the ingredients of an epidemic.

"This is the Reagan/Bush era, when you have massive social disinvestments in schools, and in urban areas altogether," says Robin Kelley, professor of history and Africana studies at NYU. "Reagan cut back significant amounts of social funding in urban areas and expanded the police force. Playgrounds, community centers, were no longer getting funded and they were disappearing."

While experts opined on the damage wrought on urban communities, gangsta rap laid out the new reality for the young. "PSK" was the foreshadowing. But when KRS-One growled his murderous vocals over a pulsing bass line ("Knew a drug dealer by the name of Peter / Had to buck him down with my 9 millimeter"), and then N.W.A's "Dopeman" hit with its high whistle and crashing drums, a new age in black urban America was ushered in.

Initially, gangsta rap's interpretation of the times was complex. Some acts reveled in the image of boys gone wild, while others deplored the effects of crack on their communities. Most early gangsta rappers, and some of the best (Scarface comes to mind) lived somewhere in between. What was made clear by all gangsta rappers, however, was that the life of crime was becoming a far more appealing career track than flipping burgers.

Harry Holzer, professor of public policy at Georgetown, was involved in a ten-year survey of attitudes among black males toward employment. In 1979, as the manufacturing decline set in, the researchers asked black men whether they had a better chance making a living illegally or legally. Sixty percent preferred to stay straight. When Holzer's team asked the same question again in 1989, the number fell to 40 percent. However hyperbolically, N.W.A's classic *Straight Outta Compton*, released the year before, reflected this trend.

"Think of a world where people make a choice between work in the legal sector and work in the illegal sector, and make it on monetary concerns and whatever risk they might encounter," says Holzer. "What happened was that the labor market for less educated African-American men really disintegrated. The legal sector became less and less attractive, and then with the crack boom, the illegal sector became more attractive. Then there was the glamour. Early on you saw this wholesale shift."

The brilliance of gangsta rap was in how it embodied that shift. *Straight Outta Compton*'s frantic ambience and the sparseness of *Criminal Minded* translated the chaotic and impoverished conditions of black Americans into sound. And their lyrics outlined the changes that were enveloping the community.

The form was most moving when it eschewed shock tactics that haunted it from day one, in favor of bleak, candid shots. Ice Cube's "A Bird in the Hand" was a detailed account of why, for black men, the illegal sector so often trumped the legal one. His "Alive on Arrival," about bleeding to death in the emergency room, presaged the health-care debates of the nineties, while "My Summer Vacation" humorously examined the exportation of gang culture nationwide. Ditto for Biggie. At its best, his seething debut *Ready to Die* bleeds pathos and tragedy. "Things Done Changed" defined the schism between civil rights–movement African-Americans and their cracked-out progeny. Equally astute was Nas's *Illmatic*, which shunned all urges toward didacticism or shock, instead opting for a wide-angle view of the Queensbridge projects. "N.Y. State of Mind," "Memory Lane," and "One Love" constitute a stark and striking black-and-white photo album of Nas's black America.

"Gangsta rap was a critique of ghetto life. So much of it was about turning the cameras on crime and violence and the police," says Kelley. "It wasn't meant to be any kind of uplift narrative. It was a form of reportage—turning the mirror back on the black community."

But as the nineties wore on, and MTV noticed the big dollars generated by gangsta rappers and their associates, the mirror began to crack. Ice Cube faded into Mack 10, Biggie was replaced by the LOX, and Nas gave way to Nastradamus. As the music became more popular, it became more of a cartoon—eventually, the only cartoon in town. Despite an occasional hit by the Roots or Talib Kweli, the popular face of rap has been defined by acts in the mold of Biggie or Tupac, but with less talent and almost no perspective.

Perhaps worse, the music has devolved into a misleading caricature of the world it claims as inspiration—the streets. Crack isn't nearly the force that it was in the late eighties and early nineties. "Very few people have started using crack in the last fifteen years," says Reuter. "Now you have older, sadder crack buyers, less violent, unable to hold a job, and involved with a lot of property crime."

The consequences of crack's rampage still haunt the communities it once infested. But the epidemic is over. "Basically you can think of this like a regular epidemic," says Reuter. "At first people want to try it. Some go and use it regularly and become negative role models. After two or three years it was clear that crack was a very nasty drug, and all you are left with are the people who first started using it."

The decline of crack has brought an attendant decline in the murder rate among the population at large, and African-Americans in particular. In 1991, 50.4 African-Americans per 100,000 were killed. By 2000, that number had halved itself. Actual murders committed by young black males dropped from 244.1 per 100,000 youths in 1993 to 67.3 in 1999.

The sunset looks beautiful over the projects / What a shame, it ain't the same where we stand . . .
                              —Mobb Deep, "Street Raised Me"

None of this means urban black America is experiencing a renaissance. During the nineties the fortunes of almost every segment of society were buoyed by the surging economy. Welfare reform, a frequent and sometimes deserving target of criticism from the left, sent poor women back into the job market in droves. At the same time, Clinton-era programs, such as the expansion of the earned income tax credit, lightened the load of the country's working poor. Only one group seemed to miss the gravy train—young black men, gangsta rap's original constituency.

Over the past two decades, black America made impressive gains in the job and education sector—or anyway, half of black America did. In a study of young, "less educated" African-Americans with only a high school diploma, Holzer and his partner Paul Offner discovered that the employment rate for women rose from 37 percent in 1989 to 52 percent in 2000. The rate actually fell for men, from 62 percent to 52 percent. According to Holzer, in the sixteen-to-twenty-four age range there is actually a higher percentage of black women employed than black men—a stunning statistic, given that many black women in this demographic are also unwed mothers.

Why hasn't gangsta rap morphed to address the new reality of African-American men? In short, because the narrative of today's black man makes a lousy cowboy flick. A central element of gangsta rap was the lionizing of drug dealers as cool, smooth black males fighting their way out of the ghetto. Although the portrayal was highly exaggerated, it definitely wasn't a complete fantasy—the drug trade did produce a few legitimate entrepreneurs. But no amount of hyperbole could salvage the current narrative of the black male—that of the habitual loser.

Gangsta rappers and their advocates argue that they are simply doing what other artists do in emphasizing certain elements of their world. "It's drama, and in drama you take the mundane elements of life and you infuse them at times with hyperbolic meaning," says Todd Boyd, professor of critical studies at the University of Southern California. "When people look at *Scarface*, they don't criticize the film because it overly dramatizes Tony Montana's cocaine use. In reality, if anyone snorted that much cocaine, they would be dead in five minutes, but nobody applies that same standard to hip-hop. That doesn't make it any less authentic. It's not reality, it's a representation of reality from one individual's perspective."

Increasingly, that perspective is skewed. It sounds more like mythology cobbled together from a few shreds of personal experience and a lot of Donald Goines, Biggie Smalls, and *GoodFellas*. For sure, the violence that rappers love to harp on still happens—the murder rate among black men remains several times higher than that of white men. But MCs conveniently ignore less glamorous forms of violence that exert as much, if not greater, influence on their lives.

A true narrative of "the streets" and the black men who inhabit them would depict a deadbeat ex-con, fleeing mounting child support, unable to find work, and disconnected from the lives of his kids. It would chronicle his gradual slide off the American radar even as his mother, daughter, and girlfriend (not wife) make inroads. It's a story that doesn't lend itself to romance. More importantly, it doesn't fit the image of black men in the American imagination.

White America has always had a perverse fascination with the idea of black males as violent and sexually insatiable animals. A prime source of racism's emotional energy was an obsession with protecting white women from black brutes. Since the days of *Birth of a Nation* up through *Native Son* and now with gangsta rap, whites have always been loyal patrons of such imagery, drawn to the visceral fear factor and antisocial fantasies generated by black men. Less appreciated is the extent to which African-Americans have bought into this idea. At least since the era of blaxploitation, the African-American male has taken pride in his depiction as the quintessential man in the black hat. It is a desperate gambit by a group deprived of real power—even on our worst days, we can still scare the shit out of white suburbanites.

"These are corporate-made images," says Kelley. "It's not that the image is new, it's an image that always sold, this idea of a dominant black man—they are violent, they are out of control. But we've established that a lot of these narratives are just made up from Italian gangster movies."

The narrative of the post-crack-era black male—poor, unemployable, and long resigned—is a direct challenge to that mythology. The inglorious plight of the black male is a disturbing reality that might make for compelling art. But for the record industry, that's a nonstarter.

Too bad. Because those few exceptions to this rule offer a glimmer of what postgangsta hip-hop could look like. Outkast began as gangsta rap but evolved with the times and came up gold with—among other gems—"Ms. Jackson," which brilliantly evokes the complexities of black America's skyrocketing rate of out-of-wedlock births. Or think of Andre 3000's verse in the Grammy-winning "Whole World." Instead of clichéd crack dealers, Dre shouts out laid-off airport workers.

Outkast is a platinum act several times over, but rappers pledging loyalty to "the streets" have been uninclined to follow suit and observe the ghetto through an honest lens. What they do instead is live out an overblown stereotype. That such an image has little resemblance to reality is irrelevant. The image of black men that sells to the rest of America wasn't mapped out by Biggie Smalls, but Bigger Thomas.

The Village Voice / June 4, 2003

The Professional

EMIL WILBEKIN

Mary J. Blige is ready to go to work. It's 8:35 a.m. in Chicago. The sky is gray and moody. The air is damp. Outside the Ritz-Carlton, which is down the block from the luxury shopping strip aptly named the Magnificent Mile, there are two hulking security guards, a road manager, two promo guys, an assistant, a videographer, and several bellmen. Waiting. Pacing. Waiting. Suddenly, as if President George W. Bush were about to materialize, everyone starts to scramble, walkie-talkies crackle. "Here she comes," says a radio-modulated voice. Bouncing out of the brass revolving door is a svelte (size 6) Mary.

Ready for action, the thirty-two-year-old singer is wearing a D&G denim, pleated miniskirt and matching jacket, a white bodysuit with holes in the sides, a denim cap, Gucci sunglasses, a Louis Vuitton purse, and caramel gladiator-boot sandals. Without missing a beat, she hops (miniskirt and all) into the black Ford Excursion.

"Good morning," she says flatly to the driver. Right behind her, Kendu Isaacs, her fiancé and producer, who also works with her management team, pops into the SUV. He hands the driver A Tribe Called Quest's *Hits, Rarities & Remixes* disc. "It just keeps bumpin', joint after joint," he says before quickly changing the subject. "Hey, what time is it in L.A.?" he wonders aloud. "We've got to get those songs cleared for the DVD." With that, they're off to work. Another black SUV carrying the support team is following them. Heading east toward Lake Michigan, the minicaravan rolls past a city park. "Look at that," says Kendu, pointing with his chin to a running track. "We should check it out. Let's do it tonight or tomorrow morning." Mary replies, "I think tonight would be better." The conversation goes on like this, from business to the mundane, until the talk switches to another couple, more specifically, Jen and Ben and their *Dateline NBC* exclusive interview. "She look nice," Mary says with a copper bobby pin in her mouth, while twisting her unraveled pigtails into one ponytail. "She's in love and doing her thing. I'm happy for her."

Witnessing Mary and Kendu as they go about their routine is almost like watching a straight-up suburban couple make their morning commute to work. Take away the stodgy, suit-and-sunglasses-sporting driver and Mary's is the face of the American woman. After all, she is one of the 63 percent (8 million, according to the U.S. Census Bureau) of African-American women who are a part of the nation's workforce. But for now, she's not seeing subways, buses, and car pools. This is the Queen of Hip Hop Soul, and she is traveling in urban luxury. Today her job is promoting her sixth studio album, *Love & Life*. And she's revving up for the task.

On this one-month, cross-country tour, today's itinerary looks like this: a live morning-show interview on a pop radio station; another scheduled chat at a different pop station that will be taped to air the following week; lunch; more interviews. Aside from that, the schedule is fluid and could include things like an impromptu CBS TV interview or a quick meeting in the SUV with colorful promo guys—like Kevin "Always Bet On" Black and Troy "the Fire" Marshall— about a listening session scheduled for the next week in New York City for DJs, radio programmers, and press; or a spontaneous trip to Neiman Marcus and Gucci to grab some new gear.

"You have to get a good night's sleep to deal with so many different personalities and people," she says. "There's gotta be a real smile that comes across, because these are die-hard fans. You gotta get on the radio and articulate yourself when you're talking nowadays. You gotta be able to be honest. You have to be able to touch people," Mary continues with the conviction of a Baptist minister. "It takes a lot out of me, because so many people come to me with stories like weird deaths and how *My Life* changed their life. That's a big deal to me. So it's a lot of work."

Mary drinks Double Shot, Starbucks' chilled, minicanned coffee, and a bottle of Fiji water to get it percolating in the morning. "We've been here before," she says, turning to Kendu. "This is where we first heard Michael Jackson's 'You Rock My World.' Remember that!" Mary drinks her Double Shot and then pulls her hat down low. The caravan pulls up in front of the radio station. Security checks out the deserted street in front of the CBS building, spotting three excited fans with gifts and cameras. "Yeah, it's cool. I'll take pictures and sign whatever," Mary tells her crew.

The procession gets in gear, security on both sides of the SUV looking left and right. Doors open. Mary and Kendu jump out, and it's into the entryway of the building. Through the glass doors, down fluorescent-lit hallways, and into a wood-paneled elevator they go. Up. Ding. And out through another badly lit corridor. Past windowed studios and some glad-handing radio execs with ear-to-ear grins. The entourage storms into the studio of WBBM-FM 96.3, Chi-Town's "the New Killer Bee." Mary stops behind the mike, pulls on the earphones, and is ready to get busy.

DISC JOCKEY: "We have Mary J. Blige in the studio with us this morning. Let's just jump into this. Tell me the whole purpose of your CD coming out. With *No More Drama*, we kind of knew that about your life."

MJB: "Well, bottom line is, after you say, 'No more drama,' you really don't have to say it again. You have to work on having no more drama in your life. So *Love & Life* is celebrating the fact that I learned to keep the drama back by loving myself. Really loving myself. I'm talking about Mary. You understand what I'm saying?

"Oh, absolutely, we talked last time. I'm a recovering addict, and I treated myself. But controversy does sell. I love Mary. And by loving Mary, so many great things have been happening. I have a fiancé right now. I have great management. So loving yourself is beautiful, because of all these wonderful things. And that's what this album is about. You know, when you finally fall in love with someone, and then you get a chance to actually sing that love song to someone you love. Well, you can't love if you don't know yourself. If you hate yourself, you can't fall in love."

DISC JOCKEY: "Do you think you're really, really happy with this fiancé?"

MJB: "Yeah, I'm really happy with my fiancé, but it's not just him that puts a smile on my face. If I didn't have any love for myself, or my foundation, which is God, I would be finished. There would be no fiancé, no good management, no Mary loving Mary. I'd be dead right now. That's the real deal."

Mary completes her interview. Shakes hands with the morning-show host. "You're like a breath of fresh air," he says. "You gave me a piece of your soul today." As she steps into the hallway, she's greeted by a line of fans who have also taken a piece of Mary from her heartfelt records. They're waiting to get their pictures taken with—to touch for a moment—the Queen. The line, consisting mostly of women, represents Mary's target audience and followers. They are young and old. Tall and short. Black, white, Asian, and Latin. As they wait their turns, they are all giggling, gasping, and gagging. "We don't usually act like this," offers one petite, bespectacled black woman from the back of the line. "But Mary rocks!"

It's storming in the Windy City. An hour ago, it was a bright and sunny day. Now the sky is black, the rain is falling in sheets, and the digital cable in the world-class Ritz-Carlton has been knocked out. This is the same building that Oprah Winfrey, perhaps the most powerful African-American woman in the world, is rumored to live in, up high in the penthouse. Some thirty floors above the city, in the teeth of the storm, Mary and Kendu are relaxing in their suite.

The hip-hop diva has had a long day. She's curled up on the couch in a white terry-cloth robe and slippers. Her hair is hanging naturally (no beehive, asymmetrical bob, or flip), and her face is totally free of makeup. Mary now has a sensuality and softness to her—in that grown-ass black woman way. Kendu is in the corner of the room at a desk typing on an Apple G4. He's pulling up pictures of Mary from a recent photo shoot by Spicer. There's computer-generated Mary looking sexy, voluptuous, and in control—beautiful.

"I've been working out. We have a trainer," she explains. "I try to go three days out of each week. I do an hour on each body part, but I do abs all the time. I drink a lot of water. And for one whole month, I didn't eat carbs. Now I can eat whatever I want."

In the living room, there are shopping bags from Versace, Yves Saint Laurent, and Gucci, a room service table, an opened case of bottled water. The radio is pumping all of the romantic summer jams: "Crazy in Love," "Beautiful," "Step in the Name of Love," and of course Mary's "Love @ First Sight," *Love & Life*'s first single, featuring her Grammy-winning partner Method Man. The song is about when Mary first met Kendu, and if you hang out with them for more than five minutes, you get the point.

Love is in the air. On Mary's new disc, you hear it on songs like "Ooh!" and "When We." And, while *Love & Life* is reminiscent of *My Life*, there isn't an underlying feeling of torture or turmoil. There is less of a survivor mentality and more of a conqueror's focused conviction. You see that self-love most evident in her work and her three-year relationship with her fiancé. "He was working for Queen Latifah when I met him," she begins, telling the story of their meeting. Kendu was a producer on the rise, tracking songs for Monifah and Divine Styler and anxious to work with Mary. "We were supposed to do a song together. So when I walked into the studio, I just looked at him. I didn't say anything because my mind was on something else. And that night, he came to the concert and then the after-party.

"I started conversing with him, and I just looked at him and his eyes. I saw myself. I just bugged out. That did scare me. So that's how we met." Kendu has a different version of how they came to be. His is a bit more telling: "I had to go to the studio to meet Mary with Dana [aka Queen Latifah]. My head was hurting, I was hungover. So I'm lying on the couch, waiting for [Mary] to come. And she came walking in. She had on these boots with glasses, this really short miniskirt, a Gucci leather jacket. She had blond hair, all this jewelry, nails painted all different colors, and I was just like"—he pauses, searching for the perfect words to describe his first thoughts—"oh, shit!"

After Kendu picked up his jaw, he had to prep Mary for her vocals. He played her the song. Mary just listened. "She went into the booth, and everything that came out the girl's mouth was perfect. She was killing it," he remembers. After the concert in Detroit, Latifah and Kendu went to the afterparty and hung out in VIP with Mary and her sister La Tonya. "So now I'm scheming, to tell you the truth," Kendu continues. "I'm trying to get that. I sat next to where she was dancing. I knew that if she sat down near me, she was interested. Then she sits right next to me. So we hung out that night, all night long. We never did anything sexually, we just continued to be friends."

A month later and a month apart, Kendu called Latifah and asked her to call Mary. One week passed before his phone rang. "I didn't even know what I wanted," Kendu says with a laugh. "And I'm not gaming, this is the truth. I wasn't trying to pitch no lines. Kinda some inner shit going on." When he picked up the receiver, he let his heart do the talking. The conversation went something like this:

Kendu: Yo, what's up?

Mary: Hey, what's up? Dana said you wanted to talk.

I have some things to talk to you about.

About what?

Well, I don't know, but it's gonna hurt.

Well, I don't wanna be hurt no more.

Think of having a wound and it has a scab on it, but it's infected, and it's healing improperly. And the hurting is going to be me pulling that scab off, and then we're going to pour the proper ingredients in there, we're going to fix that infection.

Three years later, and they're living, working, and playing together. There are plans for a wedding, but that, according to Mary, is personal, private, and off-limits to the press. They want to have kids at the right time, but Kendu has two daughters and a son, so they already have a family. "When we are home together, we play a lot," Mary says, smiling. "We're like kids. When we're in the house, he's jumping on me, I'm jumping on him. I'm mad because he's jumping on me. But, I like it. We normally ain't really doing nothing, you know? The computer, working out. We're pretty normal. And then it's time to go to work, and we turn on our engines."

The balance between career and relationship has its challenges for any couple, but even more so when the lovers are also coworkers. "Well, that's something that I need to work on, because she seems to think that when I work, I'm not nice," Kendu says. "It's hard, because it's two different worlds. When we're at home being Mary and Kendu the couple, it's all [he makes baby noises], and all that stupid stuff we do. When I'm at work, people are mean in the business, they want, want, want—so I'm like, 'No, no, no!' I guess sometimes I might be in that mode, and she'll be like, 'Hey, baby,' and I'm like, 'No!'" He pauses to reflect. "And she'll be quick to get mad, and she won't give me time to say I'm sorry—that's hard."

Right now, it's them doing nothing and enjoying it. They have just finished eating room-service chicken fingers, fish, and fries, and drinking soda. They're updating Mary's official Web site, www.mjblige.com, with "Mary TV" clips. "We update it so the fans can see what she's doing," Kendu says, "kind of like a diary." The site also shows video images of Mary being interviewed at radio stations, telling stories, crying, hugging female fans, and grinding across the country.

All of this and the recording process are part of a DVD (Kendu's idea) that will be included in the first five hundred thousand copies of Love & Life. It shows her over a two-month period working with P. Diddy, her old friend and executive producer for What's the 411?, My Life, and Love & Life; in the studio; collaborating; arguing; negotiating mixes, beats, and sounds. It's the new reality TV for the urban music set.

"The album is a throwback to What's the 411? in sound, but it's a positive outlook on what and where I am mentally, physically, and spiritually in my life right now," Mary says, sipping on a soda. "We get to celebrate as lovers now, because we know that when we love ourselves, good things come to us. So old Mary had been searching for real love for a really long time. She's no longer searching for a real love, because she's found love in herself."

It's a family affair for Mary J. Blige on this project. She reunited with her original collaborator and Svengali, Sean "they call me Diddy" Combs. Mary considers him her brother. "She's so motherfuckin' real," says Puffy. "As a friend, as a sister, as a wife, she's just real." And somehow Puffy is able to amplify that realness into something that we can all feel. True Mary fans (the hard-core bunch, and there are many) have been waiting and anticipating this reunion since the release of the now classic hip-hop soul album *My Life* (arguably the most definitive Mary CD to date). "I did *Share My World, Mary,* and *No More Drama,* and they were all very successful," Mary explains. "But it's something about when Puffy and I get together. I guess it's the chemistry we have together." It's the creative tension between Puff and Mary: bling-bling bravado mixed with raw vulnerability; masculine versus feminine; overmodulation or restraint.

But game recognizing game is what makes this partnership work. They make each other shine. "My ears are like Puff's ears," Mary continues. "I'll hear a loop, and I'll just start going crazy over it. He's playing it because he loves it, too. The idea of family is important to me. It doesn't necessarily have to be a blood relative to be family. People who understand and see where you're going and accept it, and one day they'd like to follow—that's family."

Mary is an inspiration to many of us because she represents hope—the American dream come true. Even corporations recognize her round-the-way allure. She's posting up in M.A.C makeup's print ads with Elton John and Shirley Manson and jumping double Dutch in Reebok spots. "We chose her because she's an incredibly strong, willful survivor and role model," says John Demsey, president of M.A.C Cosmetics. "From the first time I met her, I knew she was the real deal."

But this queen has living inspirations that drive her art. "I always wanted to look like Janet Jackson in 'The Pleasure Principle' video," Mary says. "I look to Oprah Winfrey as the epitome of a successful black woman. I respect what Queen Latifah and Halle Berry have done; they opened the door. But no one influenced me like the veterans: the Chakas, the Arethas, the Patti LaBelles, the Anita Bakers, Teena Maries, and Meli'sa Morgans. They do it for me."

Mary's influences are evident, from Aretha's strength to Chaka's soul. "She's like the last breed of the old souls of performers and singers," says

Puffy. "For her, it's like breathing. You feel it from her heart, her conviction. She isn't coming from a scientific point of view. It's more spiritual, the closest thing to going to church. You'll get the same feeling, the same positive impact."

These days, Mary is no longer just the singer, muse, and chanteuse. She is driving the ship: making decisions, taking a hands-on approach to managing her career, and being clear about who she is and what she represents. From writing songs in the studio with Puff and the Hitmen to shopping for clothes (basically, public appearance gear) that symbolize her personal style and taste, Mary is the self-made woman. She's a singer, a writer, a producer, an entertainer, a social activist, a fiancée, a lover, a businesswoman, and a friend. She speaks to everyone through her music and her story. And like the rest of us, her growth has been slow and steady.

"It's not easy. It's like living under a pile of shit," Mary explains, her milky voice now sounding very real. "Like, really think about that. Think about how shit smells and how heavy it would be if someone were to pile it up and you had to dig your way out." Through drama, drugs, and feeling down, she's managed to pull herself up, rise, and keep motivating. And if you're Mary, you never stop climbing. Because loving yourself, you've found, is a full-time job.

Vibe / October 17, 2003

About the Contributors

CHARLES AARON: Charles Aaron is the music editor at *Spin* magazine. He has received the ASCAP Deems-Taylor Award for music writing for his 1998 article titled "The Notorious B.I.G." and has contributed to *The Vibe History of Hip-Hop* and *Da Capo Best Music Writing, 2002*. A National Arts Journalism Fellow at Columbia University, Aaron was born in Rockingham, North Carolina, and currently lives in Brooklyn, New York.

BILL ADLER: Born in Brooklyn and raised in Detroit, Bill Adler returned to New York in 1980 and began writing about music for *People*, *Rolling Stone*, *The Village Voice*, and the *Daily News*. Adler then became the director of publicity at Rush Artist Management/Def Jam Recordings from 1984 to 1990. He wrote *Tougher Than Leather: The Rise of Run-D.M.C.* in 1987, which was republished in 2002. He currently runs Eyejammie Fine Arts, a hip-hop photo gallery, in New York City.

· It was in the course of writing this story that I first connected with Russell Simmons. He took me on a tour of Manhattan's coolest clubs one night when he was promoting Sweet Gee's "Games People Play." We ended up in the Bronx at Disco Fever, which was way cooler than any place we'd been earlier, and it became the focus of my story. A year later, still a desperate freelance writer, I took Russell a song I'd written for Kurtis Blow. He didn't much care for my lyrics, but he liked me well enough to offer me a job. I worked as his director of publicity for the next six years. We've been friends ever since.

HARRY ALLEN: A hip-hop activist and media assassin, Harry Allen writes about race, politics, and culture for *Vibe*, *The Source*, *The Village Voice*, and other publications. Widely hailed as one of hip-hop's most original minds, he has been quoted as an expert in *The Wall Street Journal* and on National Public Radio, MTV, and CNN. Well-known for his association with the seminal band Public Enemy, Allen also founded the world's first not-for-profit Hip-Hop Hall of Fame & Rhythm Cultural Center, Inc., in 1994. Allen is currently developing a book on architecture and building the Hall of Fame. He lives in Harlem.

When I wrote Jam Master Jay's obituary for *The Village Voice*, I wasn't interested in doing one of those tributes where the author talks about hanging out with Jay, or the first time he'd seen Run-D.M.C. perform. I wanted to state, as simply and precisely as I could, who Jason Mizell was, and what he'd contributed to human culture; almost like an inventory or a checklist. I wanted to make sure that, if nobody else cataloged his triumphs, someone would, and somebody would get it right.

HILTON ALS: Hilton Als is a staff writer at *The New Yorker* and author of *The Women*, a meditation on gender and race and their roles in the forging of personal identity (FSG). An award-winning journalist and former staff writer for *The Village Voice* and editor at large at *Vibe* magazine, his work has also appeared in *The Nation*. He has written film scripts for *Swoon* and *Looking for Langston* and edited the catalog for the Whitney Museum of American Art exhibition entitled *Black Male: Representations of Masculinity in Contemporary American Art*. He is also the cowriter (with artist Darryl Turner) of *Don't Explain*, a screenplay being produced by Christine Vachon at Killer Films. Born in Brooklyn, Als attended Manhattan's School for the Performing Arts and Columbia University. He was awarded a Guggenheim in 2000 for Creative Writing, and the George Jean Nathan Award for Dramatic Criticism in 2003. Hilton Als currently resides in New York City.

SALLY BANES: Sally Banes is emerita professor of theater and dance studies at the University of Wisconsin-Madison. Her books include *Terpsichore in Sneakers*, *Greenwich Village 1963*, and *Dancing Women*, among others. In 1981, she published the first article ever about breakdancing in *The Village Voice*. She is also a coauthor of *Fresh: Hip Hop Don't Stop*.

Marty Cooper, photographer for the *New York Post*, contacted me after she was sent to cover an alleged juvenile gang war. Instead, she found the adolescents armed only with graffiti paraphernalia. As best she could tell, they weren't fighting, but involved in the kind of competitive dancing that had something to do with hip-hop culture. She wanted me, as a dance critic, to help her track down this new form. We followed leads for months and we were finally able to document breakdancing in an 8 millimeter film we made of the Rock Steady Crew in the Performing Garage in Soho.

RAQUEL CEPEDA: An award-winning journalist, Raquel Cepeda graduated from Hunter College in New York City, after wasting several years at the University of Pittsburgh, where she was the only Dominicana parlaying in the cut, partying, and working for the city's urban radio station. A lover of words, Cepeda set it off in New York City's underground poetry scene by way of Brooklyn in the early nineties—before it became def—making a transition into journalism by way of *New Word Magazine*, and since has contributed to *Rap Pages*, *Essence*, *The Source*, *Vibe*, *The Village Voice*, *GQ*, and other publications. As editor in chief of Russell Simmons's *Oneworld*, Cepeda fought every day to inject a semblance of social responsibility into the fluffy mix the urban space has regressed into. Cepeda contributed liner notes to Common's *One Day It'll All Make Sense*, and is an avid lover of international hip-hop. She frequents various shows on VH-1 as a talking head, and has been seen on CNN and E!. This is her first anthology.

• The essay I wrote about Lil' Kim's second album was a response to an article written by a wildly popular academic feminist thinker, who touted her as a generation-now feminist. I was shocked at how Kim was glossed over as a role model of sorts because of the salacious way she celebrated sexuality, liberating to this writer, I imagined, who surely bopped her head to Kim's lyrics. I definitely didn't hate on Kim for overcoming her fear of the dick she rapped about on her first album—hip-hop hooray—but the cultural irresponsibility of the aforementioned writer not pointing out the fact that her music and image reeked of self-hatred in a society where young women of color are taught not to love themselves was definitely the conduit for my subsequent piece, featured in this joint.

ROBERT CHRISTGAU: Robert Christgau began writing rock criticism for *Esquire* in 1967, has been a senior editor at *The Village Voice* since 1974, and has been writing about hip-hop since 1981. He has published five books based on his journalism and in 1987 won a Guggenheim Fellowship to study the world history of popular music. He was a Senior Fellow at Columbia University's National Arts Journalism Program in 2002.

• "Planet Rock" was a direct outgrowth of my keynote address at the first Pop Music Conference at the Experience Music Project in Seattle in April 2002. Its title was: "US and Them: Are American Pop (and Semi-Pop) Still Exceptional? And by the Way, Does That Make Them Better?"

TA-NEHISI COATES: Ta-Nehisi Coates is a contributor to *The Village Voice*. He's covered hip-hop and African-Americans for the past seven years. His influences are Ralph Emerson, F. Scott Fitzgerald, Larry Neal, and his parents.

• I'd like to take full credit for this article but I can't. The idea came from the zany brain of Bob Christgau, who sensed that hip-hop was tending to match the realities of black America less and less. His only problem was that, despite his prodigious talents, he felt he wasn't the writer to do it. So he and Chuck Eddy pitched it to me, and I am forever in their debt. Aesthetically, it isn't my personal favorite of the pieces I've written, but it is certainly the nearest and dearest to my heart.

CHEO HODARI COKER: Cheo Hodari Coker has contributed to the *Los Angeles Times*, *Vibe*, *Premiere*, *Essence*, *The Face*, *Details*, *Spin*, *Rolling Stone*, *The Source*, *XXL*, *Rap Pages*, and *The Village Voice*. Coker is frequently featured as a commentator on VH1's popular series "Behind the Music," and is a consultant for the show "Russell Simmons Presents Def Poetry." He is a graduate of Stanford University, where he received a B.A. in English.

Coker cowrote the hip-hop thriller *Flow* with his uncle Richard (*Uptown Saturday Night*) Wesley, and his recent screenplays include *Living in the City: The Marion Barry Story* for HBO, *When I Get Free: The Life and Times of Tupac Amaru Shakur* for MTV, and *Legend: A Bob Marley Story* for Warner Bros. Coker also wrote, executive produced, and created the animated horror Internet series *The Devil's Music* for Urban Entertainment.

His first book, *Unbelievable: The Life, Death, and Afterlife of the Notorious B.I.G.*, was released earlier this year on Vibe/Crown/Three Rivers Press, a subsidiary of Random House.

When I look back on this article, the biggest thing I remember about it was the stress involved. The result, which you're reading right now, is one of the best interviews I've ever done. Big, as usual, made it easy. He was typically funny, candid, and laid-back. However, neither of us had any idea that we were conducting what would be the last full-length interview of his life. Back in the proverbial day, we were fortunate to be writing when hip-hop journalism still meant something. And every time I look at this piece, I remember where I was and what was going on. My hands still hurt when I think about the transcriptions. Unbelievable.

BARRY MICHAEL COOPER: Responsible for coining the term *new jack swing*, Barry Michael Cooper was born in New York City and grew up in Harlem. In 1980, he began to contribute to *The Village Voice* as a freelance music critic, writing the first-ever piece on hip-hop in the paper, titled "Buckaroos of the Bugaloo," in 1981. Cooper also wrote the screenplay for the movie *New Jack City*, along with Thomas Lee Wright, giving rise to the careers of Wesley Snipes, Chris Rock, and Ice T. Cooper went on to write two more movies, *Sugar Hill*, and *Above the Rim*, starring the late Tupac Shakur. He has produced a pilot for UPN, a reality show about two former Philadelphia drug dealers who start a record label, called *Streets, Inc.*, which UPN now has second thoughts about airing.

During that time, I had just finished reading Fitzgerald's *The Great Gatsby* and was struck by the similarities of the jazz age and the age of crack, with the music, the style, and the social abandon that really masked a madness of that epoch in the late eighties. Teddy's music smelled like money, style, and debauchery, the same elements Jay Gatsby surrounded himself with. So *new jack swing* seemed like a perfect fit.

CAROL COOPER: Much to her sainted mother's dismay, Carol Cooper began writing incisive critiques about rap and other popular music for mainstream publications when most current hip-hop critics and editors were still in grammar school. After a celebrated yet admittedly checkered career as a major-label talent scout, Cooper discovered—much to her post-grad-school surprise!—that all this, plus a prepaid MetroCard, merely gets you a ride on the subway.

NELSON GEORGE: Nelson George is the author of numerous books and novels that examine African-Americans through the prism of popular culture. His most recent works include *Hip-Hop America, Post-Soul Nation,* and the novel *Night Work.* He coauthored Russell Simmons's autobiography, *Life and Def.* George was executive producer of the HBO film *Everyday People* and the Trio documentary *The 'N' Word.*

I'd shared an apartment in Queens with a guy named Robert Ford, who went on to produce Kurtis Blow's first records. Through Ford I met Russell, who'd gone to CCNY with Kurtis. So I'd known Russell Simmons since 1979 and seen him go from promoting parties at roller-skating rinks to managing most of the biggest acts in hip-hop. So it is slightly awkward to write about a friend. At the same time, I knew his rise and the rise of rap music was a story that needed to be told. I believe it is the first major profile on Simmons. Who knew?

KAREN R. GOOD: Texas native Karen R. Good graduated from Howard University with a bachelor's in print journalism, landing gigs at *People, Seventeen,* and *Vibe.* In 1997, Good became a writer-at-large for *Vibe,* wrote for *New York, The Village Voice,* and *Interview,* and penned liner notes for Erykah Badu's *Baduizm Live,* subsequently joining *honey* magazine's start-up team. In 1999, Good was one of ten writers chosen for *Mediaweek*'s "Who's Hot in Consumer Magazines" issue. Her *Vibe* feature about hip-hop groupies featured in this anthology was declared a Notable Essay in *Da Capo Best Music Writing, 2000.* At the turn of the century, Good traveled with Mary J. Blige to document her South African tour. Good is currently working on her first book, *The Insurrection,* forthcoming in 2005.

· Groupies is an idea editors throw around every couple of years; the difficulty comes in the nebulous definition of a groupie and finding people willing to claim themselves as such! Usually those who fit the bill are too busy walking toward the light.

STEVEN HAGER: Steven Hager has a master's degree in journalism from the University of Illinois. He began writing about graffiti art while a reporter at the New York *Daily News.*

His interest soon spread to rap music and break dancing. His 1982 article on Afrika Bambaataa, published in *The Village Voice*, was the first article to mention the word *hip-hop*. He later wrote a book titled *Hip-Hop* (St. Martin's Press), which is widely recognized as the most historically accurate investigation into the origins of the movement.

· I submitted the Bambaataa story to *The Village Voice* and they sat on it for over six months before it was finally published. At the time, I queried every major magazine in America requesting an assignment involving graffiti, break dancing, and rap music. No one seemed the least bit interested (I kept all the rejection letters). The only editor who supported my research at the time, I remember, was David Hershkovits of the *SoHo Weekly News*. When gangster rap began dominating the marketplace, I lost interest in the genre because most of the early creators and shapers of hip-hop had been looking for an alternative to gang violence.

DREAM HAMPTON: dream hampton is from Detroit, Michigan. hampton has been writing about music and culture since 1990 and is a proud member of the Malcolm X Grassroots Movement. The short film she directed, *I Am Ali*, opened the 2002 Sundance Film Festival and won *Vanity Fair*'s Newport Film Festival "Best Short" award. She coauthored Jay-Z's autobiography, *The Black Book*, and is writing her first feature film.

· When *The Source* sent me to Los Angeles to do this article, I upgraded the Chevrolet Cavalier they'd reserved for me to a Lexus. A week later I was pulled over and arrested in Marina Del Ray for driving without my rental papers from Alamo. I had to call Pac to get me out. When he got to the jail, the desk sergeant was making thinly veiled threats toward him (he'd just shot two off-duty cops in Atlanta). A couple days after that I hit a minivan full of Samoans, folding their sliding door in completely. I fled the scene for reasons I need not get into here, but before I returned the car, I had to get an accident report to explain the dent. Pac came up with the idea of me driving to Vegas to file a false report, but he never stopped calling me a "fugitive." He said, "*Damn, nigga*, aren't you supposed to be the writer? Your fugitive ass got more cases than *me!*"

CARTER HARRIS: Carter Harris, former executive editor of *Vibe* magazine, has written for *Esquire*, *The New York Times*, *Details*, *Spin*, *The Source*, *Entertainment Weekly*, and *ego trip*. A former Fellow in the National Arts Journalism Program at Columbia University, and a recipient of the ASCAP Deems-Taylor Award, he recently wrote a movie called *Hit Men* that's being executive-produced by Michael Mann. Harris was also a staff writer on the defunct ABC drama *L.A. Dragnet*.

The original hip-hop thugsta Eazy-E paved the way for the likes of Tupac and Biggie, but unlike them he faded from popular memory months after his death. This was due, in part, to his dying on the downslope of his career; but more significantly to his failing to OD or catch a bullet. He was devoured by disease, which made him seem all too human and, unfortunately, all too forgettable.

DAVID HERSHKOVITS: David Hershkovits was born in Israel and moved to Brooklyn in the fifties. He graduated Yeshiva University with a B.A. in literature and received an M.A. from Penn State University. Hershkovits began his journalistic career as associate editor of the *Courier*, a New Orleans weekly. Upon moving back to New York he worked in various editorial positions at the *SoHo Weekly News* and was assistant managing editor when it folded in 1982. In 1984 he founded—along with Kim Hastreiter—*Paper* magazine as a one-sheet poster foldout. Currently copublisher/editor of *Paper*, Hershkovits coedited the book *From Abfab to Zen: Paper's Guide to Pop Culture* and has contributed articles on pop culture and politics to *GQ, Vanity Fair, Max, High Times, New York Post, Daily News,* and *Newsday*. He was a charter member of the Style Council—the VH-1 Fashion Awards nominating committee—and votes on the Council of Fashion Designer of America Awards.

One thing that jumps to mind is the dignity of Afrika Bambaataa—and his openmindedness. Whenever we would arrive at a different city, he would immediately find out where the best record store was and went looking for records to buy. I can't remember any titles but they were of all different types of music. He was not the type of guy you could stereotype.

Watches and Nikes that were available in Europe—but not the U.S.—were like the biggest thing. I remember being in the dressing room one time and seeing Fab 5 Freddy cleaning his sneakers with a toothbrush. In these days of luxe "bling-bling" it's amusing to think back on those days when someone blowing $100 seemed like a big thing.

SELWYN SEYFU HINDS: Journalist and author Selwyn Seyfu Hinds is the award-winning former editor in chief of *The Source* and former executive editor of *Savoy* magazine. Hinds authored the critically acclaimed *Gunshots in My Cook-Up: Bits and Bites from a Hip-Hop Caribbean Life* and coauthored, along with the acclaimed composer and musician Wynton Marsalis, the forthcoming *Letters to a Young Jazz Musician*. Hinds's articles and criticism have appeared in *Vanity Fair, Spin, The Village Voice, Vibe,* and *USA Weekend*, among other periodicals. A graduate of Princeton University, he lives in Brooklyn.

In the spring of 1997 fellow *Source* magazine editor Bakari Kitwana and I trekked to Haiti with the Fugees. From that journey came a story that bore witness to hip-hop's political and populist power.

SACHA JENKINS: Sacha Jenkins is a former graffiti writer turned journalist who was raised by both his Haitian moms and the crack-era streets of Astoria, Queens. In 2000, Jenkins was awarded the National Arts Journalism fellowship at Columbia's Graduate School of

Journalism. A former music editor at *Vibe* and senior contributing writer for *Spin*, Jenkins cofounded the seminal hip-hop zine *ego trip*, known as "the arrogant voice of musical truth." Parlaying the brand into books, Jenkins coauthored *ego trip's Book of Rap Lists* and *ego trip's Big Book of Racism* and subsequently coproduced VH1's *TV's Illest Minority Moments Presented by ego trip*. For fun, Jenkins loves to paint, play guitar, and pet friendly animals. This all takes place where he rests, in the wild kingdom called Brooklyn.

I'd heard for the longest through the graffiti grapevine that Timothy "Spek" Falzone was badass; that if he didn't like you, he'd get on some ol' high school shit and punch you in the face just for living—which turned out to be true. In the graffiti underworld, writers trade photographs of their handiwork like baseball cards. And so there are photos floating around of a young Spek thumping and thumping atop various foes of various height, weight, and age. Spek looks so fresh-faced and innocent as he wails away on faces and chests. Actually, it looks as if he were just horsing around; like a kid messing around. But he wasn't.

DAVID KAMP: David Kamp is a contributing editor at *Vanity Fair* and *GQ* who writes frequently about music.

I wrote this piece at a time when people were just waking up to how huge a business hip-hop had become—when it was still big, shocking news that Master P and Puff Daddy, as he was then known, were enormously wealthy and entrepreneurial. (The ostensible peg for the story, though I barely touched upon it, was that Puffy was launching the Sean John clothing label.) I think Puffy was really pleased that *GQ* was putting him on the cover—yet another phase of his "arrival"—and he gave me a lot of fly-on-the-wall time in the studio and as he went about his business, which the story reflects.

One amusing sidelight: While hanging around in the retro-modern lounge of Daddy's House, Puffy's Midtown studio, I noticed this young kid hunched in a corner, quietly practicing his raps over beats playing from a tiny boom box he held in his lap. I walked over and started talking to the kid, who was sweet, shy, and shaven-headed—he looked like Harold from the children's book *Harold and the Purple Crayon*. He genially told me he was a new protégé of "Mr. Combs" and introduced himself as Shyne. I forgot about him until six months later, when he was arrested for that nightclub shooting that prompted the famous Puffy-and-J.Lo police-car chase, and his eventual incarceration.

BAKARI KITWANA: Bakari Kitwana is the author of *The Hip-Hop Generation: Young Blacks and the Crisis in African-American Culture* (Basic Books, 2002) and the former executive editor of *The Source*. Acknowledged as an expert on hip-hop politics by *The Washington Post*, the *Los Angeles Times*, CNN, *The O'Reilly Factor*, and other leading news outlets, Kitwana has had his writings appear in *The New York Times*, *The Boston Globe*, *Savoy*, *The Village Voice*, *Black Book*, and other publications. Kitwana also writes a column on hip-hop and youth culture called "Do the Knowledge" for *The Plain Dealer* (Cleveland), and is a consultant on hip-hop for the Rock and Roll Hall of Fame. The author of *The Rap on Gangsta Rap* (Third World Press, 1994), he's been a visiting scholar in the political science department at Kent State University, has lectured on hip-hop at colleges and universities across the country, and is the author of the forthcoming *Why White Kids Love Hip-Hop: Wankstas, Wiggers, Wannabes, and the New Reality of Race in America* (Basic Books, 2004).

· One of the highlights of the trip was interviewing President Jean-Bertrand Aristide, surrounded by scores of children at the orphanage where he started his political career. It is easy now to forget that he was the first democratically elected president of Haiti. One of the things he emphasized to me—which haunts me to this day, especially given the recent events in Haiti—was his belief that the U.S. government was setting him up for failure. At the time, although aid had been committed by Congress, it was being held up by the efforts of Senator Jesse Helms, chair of the Senate Foreign Affairs Committee. What was also striking was bearing witness with my own two eyes to heavily armed U.S. military rolling through the strees of Port-au-Prince in broad daylight—even though at that point the U.S. military had supposedly withdrawn. Both were painful reminders that our government's interests are not always on the side of the oppressed and freedom-loving people.

JOHN LELAND: John Leland, an award-winning reporter for *The New York Times*, has written about hip-hop music and culture since 1982. He is the author of *Getting Hip: The Idea That Created America*. During his brief frolic as a hip-hop radio deejay, he lived by the slogan "You can never be too stupid." This wisdom informs his work today.

· In the days when rappers and journalists settled their differences with words, Chuck D took exception with a review I had written in *The Village Voice*. A month or two later he told the English press that he'd gone to a *Spin* party looking for me. This interview, which grew out of those threats, was our first personal encounter; it was confrontational but respectful. I never believed his claim that "Bring the Noise" was about me, but I've dined out on that story ever since.

ROBERT MARRIOTT: Rob Marriott has been writing on urban culture for the last thirteen years. He served as journalist, columnist, and editor for *The Village Voice, Vibe,* and *The Source* magazine and was a founding editor at *XXL*. His work has appeared in *Maxim's Blender, Rolling Stone, Spin, New York, Essence,* and *ego trip*. He has also penned a coffee-table book on pimps entitled *Pimpnosis* and recently completed *Astrology Uncut*, an astrology book for the post-hip-hop generation. He has also produced two top-selling documentaries: *Thug Immortal* and *Gangstresses*. He is currently working on a book on African child soldiers and lives in Lusaka, Zambia.

, The definitive emcee. Writing about Rakim is writing about hip-hop itself. Of course, I failed miserably.

KIERNA MAYO: After over thirteen years of reading and writing about hip-hop (not to mention twenty-five years of dancing to it), Kierna Mayo Dawsey still sees hip-hop's beauty. She still loves the poetry, the wild irreverence, and the potential for shaping revolutionary thought in young people that the music holds. Having said that, she hopes her new baby boy finds another life path besides emceeing. All due respect Tip, Big, Jay, Talib, Chuck, Rakim, Lauryn Hill. Mayo started her career wearing many different hats at *The Source* in the early nineties. She is the cocreator/founding editor in chief of *honey* and is currently senior editor at *CosmoGirl!* in New York. *LikePepper*, a hot-ass magazine project for women, is her affirmation.

Before I met her, I remember having felt anxious about interviewing C. Delores Tucker. Granted, I knew that ideologically speaking we were on different sides of the album (although I, too, had/have problems with many of the lyrics in rap songs). She was a total hip-hop outsider with a critique and plan of action that in my opinion was not born out of any sense of love for the music or culture. She was venomous and cold. I saw myself as everything but that. But the reason I was unsure how to approach Tucker had more to do with my up-bringing—the respect-your-elders thing. I never in my right mind thought I'd battle a woman almost three times my age on anything, let alone hip-hop. I went on to interview her. And it was bizarre. She talked incessantly and condescendingly to me. As I listened to her sermon, I really began to see her crusade as more of an obsession that might've even been providing her with some kind of weird high. She presented such a prude face but would still eagerly re-cite some of the harshest hip-hop lyrics with the gusto of a hype-man. *I didn't even know every single word to every single Snoop song.* Flash forward a few years and Tucker sues Pac's estate for 10 million dollars. Can you say *personal gain*? She claimed his dis of her on *All Eyez on Me* made her husband stop wanting to screw her. So Pac, of all people, is the rea-son you can't get none?! Anyway, the judge threw it out.

JOAN MORGAN: A Wesleyan University graduate born in Jamaica and raised in the South Bronx, Joan Morgan is an award-winning journalist and author and a provocative cultural critic. Her passion and commitment to the accurate documentation of hip-hop, combined with adept cultural criticism, have placed her at the forefront of music journalism. A staff writer at *Vibe* magazine for three years, she has also written extensively about music and gender issues for *The Village Voice, Essence, Interview, Ms., More,* and *Spin* magazine, where she was contributing editor and columnist. She was also the executive editor of *Essence* mag-azine. Frequently reprinted, her work appears in numerous college texts, as well as books on feminism, music, and African-American culture. Morgan's book *When Chickenheads Come*

Home to Roost is used in colleges across the country. She has lectured at high schools and colleges across the country, including Princeton and Yale. She lives in Brooklyn with her son, Sulé.

· The Ice Cube piece is one of my first pieces on hip-hop and one of the first times a woman wrote about her conflict of loving the music but hating the misogyny and trying to come to terms with it. It's the prototype for much of my work to follow and the predecessor for many female hip-hop journalists' discussions on the complicated intersection of aesthetics and gender.

SCOTT POULSON-BRYANT: Scott Poulson-Bryant has been writing about hip-hop culture since he left Brown University in 1989. He was one of the founding editors of *Vibe* magazine in 1992, and his writing has appeared in such publications as *Spin*, *Rolling Stone*, *The New York Times*, and *The Village Voice*. He is the coauthor along with Smokey Fontaine of *What's Your Hi-Fi Q?* His latest book, *Hung*, was published by Doubleday last fall.

· I wrote "The Rebirth of Cool" for *Spin* magazine right before I became the staff writer there. It holds a special place in my heart for a variety of reasons: one, I'd already had a relationship with Todd before I was dispatched to interview him (during which I'd been sorta instrumental in choosing the cover art for *Mama Said Knock You Out*), so that made for a cool dynamic once the tape recorder was running; two, it was my first long profile that took me on the road with an artist; and three, it took place during an interesting time for both Todd and myself: we were both sorta proving ourselves, he that he could 'come back' so to speak, and me that I could produce an article and build a career as a journalist. Many thanks to Steven Daly for showing me the way . . .

KEVIN POWELL: Kevin Powell is a poet, journalist, essayist, editor, cultural curator, hip-hop historian, public speaker, political consultant and fund-raiser, and community activist. A native of Jersey City, New Jersey, Powell is now a resident of Brooklyn, New York. It is from his base in New York City that Powell has published six books and written essays, articles, and reviews for periodicals such as *Essence*, *Newsweek*, *The Washington Post*, *Vibe*, and *Rolling Stone*. Powell's latest book is a collection of essays entitled *Who's Gonna Take the Weight? Manhood, Race, and Power in America.*

The thing I remember about this piece is that I wanted to do it real bad, given that Treach and the Naughty crew were from Jersey like me. But I had one problem: I had a beef with someone down with Treach, someone who had tried to get me jumped just a year before, outside of Roseland in Manhattan. I wrote about that ugly incident in an essay called "Ghetto Bastard," which, of course, came from a Naughty song (Treach was a prophet to me back then). Anyhow, the *Vibe* folks were sweating me about going to Treach's block for some background. There is a scene in the piece where I was on my way to East Orange but could not reach Treach, Vinnie, or Kay Gee. It was on purpose, honestly, and I have never said this before. I was trying to get past all the madness of my life and was not interested in blowing my first big hip-hop article because of my past. Little did I know that this piece would be the cover of *Vibe*'s premier issue, and that it would change my life forever. To this day the Naughty crew have no idea what was going through my mind as I was following them around, interviewing them, how I was hoping that dude would not pop up, causing me to have to throw joints in the middle of this story.

DANYEL SMITH: Danyel Smith is a former editor at large for Time Inc. and the former editor in chief of *Vibe*. She has also written for *The Village Voice, Rolling Stone, Spin, The San Francisco Bay Guardian*, and *The New York Times*. Smith teaches at the New School University and wrote the introduction for the *New York Times* bestseller *Tupac Shakur*. She lives in Brooklyn, but was born and raised in California.

I adore Foxy. That's why I wanted to do the piece in the first place. Our interview, which lasted more than a few days, was one of the best, most "real" times I've spent with an artist, and that's probably why things got so bananas after the article was published. Funny thing is, I still adore her. I see her at the nail salon in Brooklyn occasionally. We speak most times, sometimes we don't. But there's respect between us. Regardless of the drama (and maybe because of it), she's one of the coolest and most talented chicks in hip-hop.

GREG TATE: Greg Tate is a staff writer at *The Village Voice*. His books include *Flyboy in the Buttermilk: Essays on Contemporary America, Midnight Lightning: Jimi Hendrix and the Black Experience*, and *Everything but the Burden: What White People Are Taking from Black Culture*. Tate is also conductor of Burnt Sugar the Arkestra Chamber, whose seventh album, *Black Sex Yall Liberation & Bloody Random Violets*, was just released on their own TruGroid label.

This Tribe review comes from a place of love about one of my all-time favorite hip-hop bands, who by the time they made this album were in the midst of breaking up, and unfortunately the cracks were all too evident in the work.

TOURÉ: Touré is the author of *The Portable Promised Land*, a collection of short stories published by Little, Brown. He's also a contributing editor at *Rolling Stone* and the host of MTV2's *Spoke N' Heard*. He studied at Columbia University's graduate school of creative writing and lives in Fort Greene, Brooklyn. A novel called *Soul City* will arrive in September 2004.

EMIL WILBEKIN: As editorial director/vice president of Brand Development, Emil Wilbekin's role is to "represent, build, and protect" the *Vibe* brand. Wilbekin has been with *Vibe* for eleven years and served as editor in chief from 1999 to 2003. Under his tenure the publication was awarded the National Magazine Award for General Excellence. He has contributed to *The New York Times*, *The Chicago Tribune*, The Associated Press, *Rolling Stone*, and *Essence*, and his writing has been included in books like *Hip-Hop Divas*, *Big Up* by Ben Watts, and *The Last Sunday in June* by Jamel Shabazz. Currently Wilbekin is working on two books and a screenplay. Wilbekin received his B.A. in mass media arts from Hampton University and his M.S. from Columbia University's Graduate School of Journalism. He currently resides in New York City.

I wrote the first cover story on Mary for *Vibe* for the release of *My Life* and then wrote the cover story for her latest, *Love & Life*. Technically that issue was my last as editor in chief of the magazine. So it's a full-circle situation. I've written about Mary four times for *Vibe* and penned a chapter in the *Hip-Hop Divas* book, as well as styling her seven times.

Acknowledgments

I honor the soul of the universe for conspiring with me to make this tangible expression of gratitude I have for hip-hop—for better and worse—a reality. I honor my agent, Mannie Barron, for being in tune with this universal conspiracy. I honor Jonathan Tunick for being the conduit of realization here, and Ayesha Pande, Stacey Barney, Kabir Dandona, Kim Hilario, and the 'heads at FSG for coparenting this labor of love. Right on!

Very special thanks to my assistant on this project, Amber Morgan—yes, black social consciousness is indeed thriving in Cuban hip-hop, just ask Fidel.

I love SHR.

My family, who never really understood how I could invest time and energy in a culture that historically hates women as much as they do the men in the mirror, but alas, supported my madness when all was said and done: Djali, Ervin and Rita Cepeda, Natalie and sisters/brothers, Gail "Mima" Anderson, Marion and Djinji Brown. Roberto Mancebo for buying me my first computer. My godfather, James Alexander Spencer, Jr., Margarita Lizardo and Servilio Mancebo, Ibae.

To my anchors of strength: Anthony Perrone and Carmen Rodriguez, Rosario "Coqui" Dawson and family. Bobbito Garcia, Tracey Levenstein, Gisella Baque, Johnette Stubbs-Vrooman, Bethann Hardison, Danny *"el bachatero"* Hoch, Joan Morgan, Christa Sanders, Andrew, Rio, and Ursula Williams-Kilgore, Lisa Leveque, Jeff Mazzacano, Lorraine West.

Honors go to those whose selves have been sages at one time or another to this self, listed here in no particular order, I swear: Russell Simmons, Rashid Lynn, Q-Tip, Questlove,

BlackThought, Plug I and II, Maceo, Faulu Mtume, Bahamadia and Hurricane G, muMs, Andre Royo, Saul Williams, Fatima Robinson, Special K and Teddy Ted, Mos Def, Talib Kweli, M-1, the late Notorious B.I.G., Zap Mama, Ashaka Givens, Derek Dudley, Rebecca Walker, Maripol, Fab 5 Freddy, Mare, B-Real (*bendicion*), Chuck Eddy, Vincent "Prince Vince" Gallo (for the stories), Henry Chalfant, Susan Taylor, Spencer Ellis, Lumumba Bandele-Akinwole, Archie Dixon, Gizelle Jacobs, Scott Free and little Jr., Sonya Magett, the *crazysexycool* Kim Hastreiter, April Walker, Cree Summer (for the encouraging phone call, my beautiful sister), Nancy Jimenez, Jeff Chang, Lauryn Small, Shirley Petchprapa, Dr. Marta Moreno Vega, Jellybean Benitez, that funky-fresh *ese* by the name of Gabriel Alvarez, Elliot Wilson, Ann Powers and Eric Weisbard, Oliver Wang, John Pasmore, Kovasciar Myvette, Bill Adler, Richard Perez-Ferria, my Gemini brother Maxwell. I can go on.

Honors go to *every* single contributor to this book, many of whom provided me with great stories and wisdom, Nelson George *most of all.*

Index

Ball, Lucille, 148

Ballard, Flo, 203

Ball Busters, xv

Baltimore Sun, The, 218

Bambaataa, Afrika, 3, 12–26, 28, 30–31, 33–
    34, 36, 42, 49, 88, 91, 276, 334, 335

Banes, Sally, 4, 7–11, 330

Bankhead Bounce, 196

Baraka, Amiri, 156, 224

Barenaked Ladies, 211

Barnes, Dee, 127

Basie, Count, 62

Basque hip-hop, 301

Bass, Khadejia, 65

Beastie Boys, 5, 117, 203, 211, 222–23, 225,
    230, 231, 236

beat box, 21

Beat Down magazine, 282

Beatles, 206, 214

Beat Street (film), 3

Beatty, Warren, 218

Beck, 202–204, 208, 215

Bedford-Stuyvesant, 9

Beiderbecke, Bix, 224

Bell, Linda, 150

Bell, Robert "Kool," 59

Belle, Bernard, 65

Bernard, James, 84

Berry, Chuck, 224

Berry, Halle, 208, 326

BET (periodical), 149

Big Al, 57

Big Boi (Antwan Patton), 275

Big Gipp, 251

Big Man (Mark Rucker), 147, 150

Big Pun, 85

Big Shorty, 240

Big Time Vandals (BTV), 295

Billboard, xvi, 24, 45, 52, 162

Bingham, Dinky, 65

Birth of a Nation (film), 317

Black, Kevin, 320

Black History Month, 12

Blackmon, Larry, 57

Black Panthers, 15, 73, 138, 208

Black Phoenix, 94

Black Sabbath, 222

Black Sheep, 5

Black Spades, 15–17, 20, 21, 290

Blackstreet, 159

black teenage music, 49–50

Blass, Bill, 201

Blige, Mary J., 264, 283, 286, 287, 319–27,
    333

Blondie, 267

Bloods, 296

Blow, Kurtis, xi, xii, 3, 36, 39–45, 47–50, 117,
    282, 333

Bloy, Stanley, 186

Blue Magic, 65

Blue Palms Recording Studios, 132–34

Body Rock (film), xv

Bofill, Angela, 207

Bolton, Michael, 100

Bomb the City, 295, 298

Bon Ami label, 117–18

Bone Thugs 'N' Harmony, 149

Boogie Down Productions, 5, 114

Bootee, Duke, 48

Borland, Wes, 220

Boston (Massachusetts), 277

Bowie, David, 263

Boyd, Todd, 316

Boy George, 62

"Boys-N-the Hood," 149

Braithwaite, Fred. *see* Fab 5 Freddy

Brand Nubian, 5, 108, 155, 227

Braxton, Toni, 159, 170

break dancing: clothes style of, 19, 39;
    description of, 7–11; origin of, 8–9, 19,
    273; *see also* hip-hop

Breakin' (film), 3

Breakin' 2 (film), 3

Breakmasters, 9–11

Breakout, 22

Brickell, Edie, 273

Made in the USA
San Bernardino, CA
05 January 2015